D0685897

WITHDRAWN
UTSA Libraries

WITHDRAWN
UTSA Libraries

A TEXTBOOK ON
MONETARY POLICY

A TEXTBOOK ON
MONETARY POLICY

PAUL EINZIG

MACMILLAN
ST. MARTIN'S PRESS

LIBRARY
University of Texas
At San Antonio

© Paul Einzig 1972

All rights reserved. No part of this publication may be
reproduced or transmitted, in any form or by any means,
without permission.

First published, under the title *How Money is Managed*, 1954
Reprinted 1959
Second edition published under the title
Monetary Policy: Ends and Means, 1964
Reprinted with a Postscript 1967
Third edition published under the title
A Textbook on Monetary Policy, 1972

First published 1972 by
THE MACMILLAN PRESS LTD
London and Basingstoke
Associated companies in New York Toronto
Dublin Melbourne Johannesburg and Madras

Library of Congress catalog card no. 72–93031

SBN 333 14379 5

Printed in Great Britain by
R. AND R. CLARK LTD
Edinburgh

LIBRARY
University of Texas
At San Antonio

To the Memory of

SIR DENNIS ROBERTSON

Contents

PART THREE: THE MEANS OF MONETARY POLICY

PART FOUR: CONCLUSION

Preface

WHEN I was preparing the original version of this book in the early fifties, and even when I was revising it for a new edition the last time in the middle sixties, it appeared to be safe to assume that the monetary system and the basic rules of monetary policy had settled down more or less to their permanent form. Although even then there was an ever-present possibility of modifications, there appeared to be no reason to expect revolutionary changes. It is true that there were from time to time major crises, and that practices and devices were subject to fairly frequent changes in consequence. But on the whole it seemed probable that, after the turbulent inter-war period and the gradual return to more or less 'normal' conditions after the war, the Bretton Woods system had become as safely established as the gold standard had been before the First World War.

The situation and the outlook are totally different today. The Bretton Woods system has been suspended and it seems doubtful whether it will ever be restored. The dollar's supremacy, on which the Bretton Woods system had rested, is now a matter of the past. The Sterling Area, which had ensured sterling's prominence as a fairly important rival to the dollar, has virtually ceased to exist. On the other hand, European monetary integration is on its way.

The changes in the fundamental principles of monetary policy were even more far-reaching than the changes in the monetary system. Today stability of the international value of currencies, and even of their domestic purchasing power, no longer enjoys the same priority amongst the ends of monetary policy as it did twenty years ago, or even six or seven years ago. Above all, the basic principles of the monetary system and of monetary policy are no longer as firmly established as they were until recently. It is no longer safe to assume that the existing system will continue for any length of time. Indeed, at the time of writing it is in a state of transition. Money is in the melting-pot and is liable to undergo basic changes.

Nobody who writes about money could honestly claim that he is in a position ever to ascertain eternal truths such as exist in respect of exact sciences. Owing to the possibility of changes in the situation, and in human attitudes towards it, it is impossible to lay down permanent laws. Of course there is nothing new in this. The present historical survey of monetary policy through the ages shows that both the monetary system and the ends and means of its management have often been subject to changes. But I think I am justified in claiming that there has never been such a degree of uncertainty about the prospects of the monetary system as there is at present.

Fashions in economic thinking and in the translation of economic thinking into monetary systems and policies are of course always subject to fundamental changes. It is a mistake to allow ourselves to be misled by these fashions into believing that they can be depended upon to be perpetual. Most of us are inclined to be cocksure about our views of the day. Yet in reality, when and if advocates of new theories or policies should come to know ten times as much about money and about monetary policy as they know now, they might conceivably begin to realise how little they – or for that matter anyone else – can possibly know about them.

Perhaps a historical survey of monetary policy that is not confined to a limited period or to a specific system might conceivably make it more evident how relative the truth is in this sphere, and how today's truth is liable to become to-morrow's absurdity. The recent changes in the monetary system and in monetary policy, and the prospects of further changes, have made it necessary to re-write this book extensively and to cover the changes in additional chapters. The extent of alterations justifies its publication under a different title.

This revised and enlarged version of the book is dedicated to the memory of the late Professor Sir Dennis Robertson. I am indebted to him for having advised me some twenty years ago, when I discussed with him the original plan of my book in which I had intended to deal first with the means of monetary policy before dealing with its ends. Acting on his emphatic advice, I reversed the order. He made me realise that it was a matter of logic to examine the ends of monetary policy before dealing with its means. The change meant much more than a mere formal rearrangement of my material. It reinforced considerably my emphasis on the principal message my book sought to convey – that the future welfare of mankind will depend on our ability to reconcile the conflicting economic and social ends of monetary policy.

I feel I owe Robertson this tribute, inadequate as it is to one who was second only to Keynes amongst the economists of the last generation. While the memory of Keynes is still as much alive as ever – his is still probably the most widely quoted name in contemporary economic literature – Robertson's name no longer receives the acknowledgement it richly deserves. I owe him a debt of gratitude, for I am sure that, had it not been for his wise advice, this book would not have survived to the present day.

120 CLIFFORD'S INN,   P. E.
LONDON, E.C.4.
July 1972

Part One

INTRODUCTION

CHAPTER ONE

Money in the Melting-pot

THE monetary system and the ends and means of monetary policy have never been as firmly established as one is inclined to assume when considering them in retrospect. Money has always been subject to changes from time to time, and barely perceptible adjustment of details was a continuous process. The gradual adoption of monetary systems, the emergence of precious metals as money in the form of coins, the adoption of paper money and credit-money, all involved major changes. The monetary use of gold in modern times was subject to repeated changes, and so was the monetary use of credit-money within each country and between countries. The ends pursued by monetary policies as well as the means adopted were all subject to changes.

But from time to time mankind experienced more or less prolonged periods during which the monetary system and its management settled down to follow certain accepted rules and was subject only to changes in detail. On the other hand there are occasionally major changes of the monetary system and monetary policy. The rules of the system and of its operation, and the principles followed by those responsible for its operation, become from time to time subject to fundamental modifications. The early seventies will go down in monetary history as one of those periods during which the monetary system was in the melting-pot.

There were, of course, major upheavals in the monetary sphere on many previous occasions. Even in the lifetime of the older generation, major changes were caused by the First World War and its consequences, and again by the series of crises in the thirties. A deliberate revision of the rules of the monetary system after the Second World War was brought about by the Bretton Woods Agreement. It appeared as if the Bretton Woods system had come to stay. But in the meantime the situation has undergone far-reaching changes in more than one respect.

(1) The volume of privately held international liquid resources has become multiplied as a result of the emergence and expansion of the Euro-currency markets and of other markets in short-term credits. There is now in existence tens of billions of such credit, all of which is unsecured, and they are not self-liquidating. Its existence makes the inverted pyramid of the monetary system much more precarious than it has ever been.

(2) The dollar, which reigned supreme ever since the beginning of the First World War, no longer enjoys universal confidence. Its gold backing has greatly diminished, while the external short-term liabilities of the United States have greatly increased. The limited convertibility of the dollar under the Bretton Woods rules became largely fictitious during the sixties and was openly suspended in 1971.

(3) The monetary role of gold has become considerably reduced. It is true that its maldistribution resulting from the First World War has become mitigated in recent years. On the other hand, gold now represents a much smaller percentage of the monetary reserves of most countries. Its role as a reserve for domestic monetary purposes has virtually ended, while its role as an international monetary reserve has also greatly diminished.

(4) On the other hand, the role of foreign currencies as monetary reserves has greatly increased. Moreover, the currencies used for reserves are no longer convertible into gold. Central Banks also borrow each other's currencies for the purpose of using them as monetary reserves under reciprocal swap arrangements.

(5) The International Monetary Fund no longer confines itself to granting credits which are repayable on maturity. A

large percentage of the Special Drawing Rights issued to Central Banks are not repayable at all and nobody is responsible for their eventual conversion. Under a new proposal the moderate credit element of Special Drawing Rights is intended to be abolished altogether, so that they will become an entirely fictitious addition to reserves used in international payments.

(6) The maintenance of international stability of currencies no longer enjoys such a high priority among the ends of monetary policy as before. While in the past instability of exchanges was sometimes considered in official, banking and academic quarters a necessary evil, it is now widely considered an advantage and is aimed at as a matter of deliberate monetary policy.

(7) The maintenance of the domestic purchasing power of currencies has come to be considered to be less essential than before. While everybody is still opposed to runaway inflation, a moderate degree of inflation is now widely considered as an acceptable price that a country is willing to pay for the sake of an escalation of its rate of economic growth.

(8) Even though the Bretton Woods Agreement provided for the possibility of occasional uniform all-round changes in gold parities and for more frequent changes of individual parities, the all-round negotiated realignment of parities of 1971, involving both revaluations and devaluations of varying degrees, was a novelty and opened up new possibilities.

(9) The optimistic assumption of the early post-war period that exchange control would be gradually removed, at least as far as non-residents are concerned, has proved to be unwarranted. There were repeated relapses into reinforced restrictions, and the Bretton Woods era of progress towards freedom ended in 1971 with an all-round reversal towards tighter controls.

(10) On the other hand, there was distinct progress towards liberalism in respect of permitted competition between banks. In the United States, Regulation Q fixing the maximum interest rates that banks were permitted to allow on deposits was greatly relaxed. In Britain, the cartel between clearing

banks outlawing competition for clients with the aid of higher deposit rates or lower loan rates was abolished.

(11) There was a considerable increase in the number of money markets, both within the leading financial centres and in other centres which until recently did not possess any money markets. This change has greatly increased arbitrage facilities.

(12) Banking has become increasingly internationalised. The number of foreign banks and affiliates established in financial centres has increased considerably. A number of multinational banks controlled jointly by banks of different countries have been established.

(13) The number and size of multinational industrial and commercial firms has increased. Their operations have become a factor of importance both in the money markets and in the foreign exchange markets.

(14) The importance of the Euro-issue markets has increased very considerably. There is now a variety of currencies in terms of which issues are made. In addition to straight bonds and convertible bonds, Euro-equities are also being issued.

All these changes influence to some extent the requirements of monetary policy. The volume of international operations has greatly increased and this presents new problems to Central Banks. Larger reserves are now needed to meet possible discrepancies between supply of and demand for exchanges. Even the normal commercial requirements have increased, owing to the greater familiarity of commercial firms with foreign exchanges, leading to an increase in the extent of leads and lags – changes in the timing of payments or covering of imports and exports. The increase in the relative importance of foreign trade with capital goods also operates in that direction.

Having regard to all these changes, it is essential to reconsider the ends and means of monetary policy. It is necessary to adopt a more flexible attitude, a higher degree of readiness to change policies in response to changes in the situation. Many of the changes listed above have been unexpected, and the fact that they have occurred out of the blue foreshadows the possibility of other unexpected changes. For this reason it is important to avoid the rigidity of attitude which had created too long time-lags between new developments and the adaptation of policies to the changed requirements.

Requirements are bound to change. There is no means of knowing what system will emerge from the melting-pot. The attempt to restore stability through the conclusion of the Smithsonian Agreement on 18 December 1971 did not bring a lasting solution. It was greatly weakened in six months by the British Government's decision to float sterling temporarily. The dollar was devalued to the extent of $8\frac{1}{2}$ per cent after long resistance to its devaluation and almost everybody assumes that this was only the first instalment, to be followed by other mini-devaluations, or by a relapse into floating.

During 1971–2 practically all currencies floated at one time or another. Some of them are liable to float again. Progress towards the creation of a Common Market system through narrowing the band between the currencies of actual and prospective members of the EEC and through providing for mutual support received a setback when, on 16 June 1972, sterling came to be floated, though it was assumed that it would be restabilised soon after Britain has actually joined the EEC.

Above all, preliminary discussions are being actively pursued for the adoption of the Barber Plan of issuing non-redeemable Special Drawing Rights which are meant eventually to replace gold altogether as the principal reserve currency for inter-governmental transactions. It is to be supplemented by a number of reserve currencies in addition to the dollar. The large non-resident holdings of sterling and dollar balances are to be consolidated through the issue of Special Drawing Rights for that purpose. Other major changes in the monetary system are distinct possibilities.

In such circumstances it would be idle to attempt to lay down rules that must, or are likely to, govern monetary policy. But it is essential to analyse as many alternative rules as possible, in order to enable us to examine critically any new system that is liable to emerge.

CHAPTER TWO

The Monetary System

MONEY is a most remarkable instrument, which can be employed or influenced by a wide variety of devices of monetary policy for many ends and in many ways. Monetary policy is concerned with money in a twofold sense. It is concerned with decisions and measures calculated to affect the monetary situations or the monetary system. And it has to employ the monetary system for the purpose of influencing the non-monetary economic situation, and even the social and political situations. Money may be either the end of monetary policy or its means. It is often both end and means, when monetary devices are used to the end of influencing the monetary situation.

Our task is to define, classify, describe and analyse monetary policy according to its ends and means. Before embarking on this task it is necessary to give a brief outline of the subject-matter with which monetary policy is concerned – the monetary system.

Money, like most other social institutions, has developed gradually over a very long period through trial and error. It appeared in many forms before taking its present form, which, advanced as it may appear to us, cannot be regarded as final. Indeed, it is undergoing major changes even at the time of writing. In the course of its evolution the monetary system seldom remained entirely unchanged for a very long period in any given community. From time to time it was uprooted by some major crisis which brought about some important change. Even during prolonged periods of relative economic and political stability it was liable to change from time to time, if not in its fundamental principles at any rate in some of its essential details. Some monetary changes were spectacular in their circumstances and were accompanied by wide publicity. Other changes came about almost imperceptibly, and their significance was not realised immediately by contemporary observers.

Apart from changes over a period of time there have always been marked differences between the systems in operation at any given moment in different communities. The diversity of monetary systems and their realitvely frequent changes have between them produced an immense variety of systems. It would take many volumes to describe and analyse all, or even a reasonably representative selection of them. For our present purposes it is sufficient to deal with certain features and characteristics of money that are more or less common to most monetary systems. For it is, broadly speaking, true that the similarities between them are more important than their differences. Sir James Frazer, in a much-quoted passage in his *Golden Bough*, remarked : 'Our resemblances to the savage are still far more numerous than our differences from him.' This observation can well be applied to primitive and modern money. Some of the most important elements contained in the highly sophisticated monetary system of our day can be traced back to the rudimentary systems that were in operation during earlier periods' right at the dawn of history.

Generally speaking, we are justified in saying that there is nothing inherently good or inherently bad in any monetary system as such. Its advantages or disadvantages depend largely on its interpretation and application, and even more on the economic, social and political background that conditions the operation of any monetary system. Disorganised monetary systems are usually the result of a war, or a major economic crisis, or some political or social upheaval, or gross mismanagement by Governments. Although the remark addressed by Baron Joseph-Dominique Louis, Finance Minister of Louis XVIII, to his fellow-Ministers, '*Faites-moi de bonne politique, je vous ferai de bonnes finances*', referred to public finance, it is fully valid also in the monetary sphere. During a period of political and economic stability it is easy to operate almost any monetary system satisfactorily, while political or economic unwisdom is liable to discredit almost any currency.

There is, for instance, nothing inherently evil and vicious about inconvertible paper money as such, provided that it is handled sensibly. Writing in the eighteenth century, Goethe, in his *Faust* (Part II, Act 1), represents it as the Devil's own invention. Yet it is only when the printing press is abused that paper money is apt to become a thoroughly bad system. At the other extreme there is nothing fundamentally wrong with the automatic gold standard as such, even though its unduly rigid and dogmatic application is liable to handicap progress and may become from time to time the cause of grave difficulties. The relaxation of the rigidity of that monetary system may be a blessing or a curse, according to the circumstances and the degree to which it is relaxed.

The functions of money may be classified into two broad categories – static and dynamic functions. By its static functions, money serves as a passive technical device ensuring a better operation of the economic system, without actively influencing its trends. By its dynamic functions, money tends to exert a powerful influence on the trends of the price level, on exchange rates, production, trade and consumption, and on the distribution of wealth. It is capable of stimulating or holding up economic and social progress. It may even exert a decisive influence on the course of history and on the progress of civilisation.

Many of the qualities which enable money to fulfil its static functions satisfactorily are substantially the same today as they were many centuries ago. Now as then, money has five main technical functions to fulfil. It is intended to serve as a medium of exchange, a means of non-commerical payments (taxation, fines, gifts, etc.), a standard of value, a standard of deferred payments, and a store of value. In plain English it has to be suitable for use as a means of payment, both commercial and non-commercial; for the measurement of values and their expression in the form of prices; for the determination of future liabilities; and as a medium in which wealth can be accumulated. None of these static functions should normally give rise to any price trends or influence the basic economic trends in other ways, apart from their favourable general influence on progress.

Admittedly, when money was first adopted, or when a more advanced money replaced a less advanced type, such changes necessarily produced a 'once-for-all' dynamic effect. For instance, when trading by barter gave way to trading with the aid of a medium of exchange, this change must have caused a substantial increase in production and trade and a marked acceleration of economic progress. It must have produced also some far-reaching social changes. Once, however, money is established it fulfils its technical functions without producing any such dynamic effects. The normal routine role of those functions is essentially 'neutral' and static. But 'static' is not synonymous with 'stationary' or 'stagnant'. By fulfilling its static role, money makes an important contribution towards a gradual increase of wealth and a progress in the standard of living.

The use of a medium of exchange or of a standard of value does not in itself give rise to dynamic changes in the operation of the economy – at any rate until another major change occurs in the monetary system. Money, by fulfilling the normal functions of a medium of exchange or its other technical functions, does not cause a rise or a fall in the price level, or an expansion or contraction in business activity. Such effects are produced by its dynamic functions. If the role of money were confined to its static functions, monetary policy would be a comparitively simple matter. It would have to pursue the single purpose of maintaining a reasonable degree of stability in the value of money, which is by far the most important among the requirements it has to fulfil in order to be able to perform its technical functions satisfactorily.

The functions of money as a medium of exchange imply its free acceptance in payment for goods and services. It is essential that there should be a sufficient degree of confidence in money and that there should be enough of it to go round. Confidence in a currency and its acceptability as a means of payment is apt to be undermined by its rapid depreciation, or by a possibility that it might cease to become acceptable for some other reason. Its depreciation must reach a very advanced stage, however, before it ceases altogether to be usable as a medium of exchange. Long before that stage is reached its depreciation is apt to cause much inconvenience and grave disadvantages, but a depreciating money may continue to act none the less as a medium of exchange. So long as its recipients spend it within a short time after receiving it they do not stand to suffer any unduly heavy losses through a gradual fall in its value. It is only when its depreciation becomes so rapid that it is apt to lose a large part of its value from one day to another and even from one hour to another that it may cease to be freely acceptable as a medium of exchange and may even cease to be suitable as a means of non-commercial payment. If, in order to maintain confidence in the stability of money, its quantity is kept too low to suit normal requirements, it does not adequately fulfil its role as a medium of exchange. Its value then tends to appreciate, nevertheless, owing to its scarcity.

A rise in the value of money does not interfere with its technical function as a means of payment for goods and services, or as a means of non-commercial payments. On the contrary, an appreciating currency is bound to be much sought after by sellers of goods and services as a medium of exchange and even more as a store of value. An appreciating currency is a good investment even if it bears no interest. On the other hand, any instability in its value tends to make it less suitable for use as a standard of value or as a standard of deferred payments. A measuring-rod the length of which is liable to changes is obviously unsuitable for its purpose. Situations have arisen in the past and also in more recent times in which a depreciating money, while remaining a medium of exchange, ceased to be suitable for other functions. As a result a separation of functions developed by which one object was used for a medium of exchange and a different one for other monetary purposes.

Such a separation of functions characterised some of the primitive monetary systems in the early days of history, and also some recent monetary systems in primitive communities. During troubled periods we are apt to revert to that system, discarded long ago in advanced communities. Many countries in Central and Eastern Europe did in fact revert to it during the chaotic periods that followed the World Wars. While continuing to use paper money extensively as a means of payment, they came to reckon prices and wages in terms of gold or some commodity, or some abstract unit of stable value.

Until recently textbooks on money concentrated on the well-known technical functions – medium of exchange, means of non-commercial payments, standard of value, standard of deferred payments, and store of value – which were regarded as the only essential functions of money. There are, however, other additional static functions which are fully as important as the ones mentioned above. Foremost amongst them is the function of money as the medium through which market mechanism operates and its function of linking national economies with each other.

Under a system of free economy – as distinct from a planned economy under which the volume of production of various categories of goods is determined by the State authority – the quantity of goods that is produced is largely determined by the profit earned on them. This in turn is determined by the prices obtained for them compared with their cost of production. Prices again are determined largely by the relation between supply and demand. Conversely, supply and demand themselves are influenced by cost of production and prices. These tend to adjust themselves according to the quantities available for sale and the number of people who have the desire and the means to buy the goods, but in turn they also tend to effect an increase or reduction of supply of or demand according to the profit margin – if any – they leave to producers. In a free economy movements of individual prices play, therefore, a very important part in determining production, distribution and consumption. And prices are expressed in terms of money. This means that money does much more than merely serve as a convenient technical device to facilitate the exchange of goods and as a unit of account by which the values of various objects can conveniently be compared. It is the medium through which market mechanism in a free economy tends to establish a balance between cost of production and sale price, and between supply and demand.

A market mechanism could, it is true, function in a barter economy, but it would be clumsy and cumbersome. The existence of money makes for a much smoother operation of the mechanism.

It may be a matter of opinion whether ours is an ideal system or whether the system under which production, distribution and consumption are planned by the Government instead of being left to the automatic working of market mechanism is preferable. So long as that mechanism exists, and to the extent to which it continues to operate automatically, money will continue to play a very important part by serving as a medium through which the price mechanism operates. The fundamental character of its role in this respect is recognised by many modern economists who contrast planned totalitarian economy with automatic money economy, in place of the more conventional contradistinction between capitalist and collectivist economies.
The role of money as a medium through which the price mechanism operates is essentially static, in so far as it serves as a passive technical device and does not fundamentally affect the operation of the price system – meaning the functions of individual prices and their relationship with each other, as distinct from those of price levels and of their trends. Admittedly when the prices of certain categories of goods or services rise or fall substantially, the discrepancy in relation to other prices may give rise to major trends which are, in given circumstances, liable to upset the static equilibrium of the economy. But such dynamic influences are not initiated by money in its capacity as a medium through which the price system operates. In that capacity money is an essentially 'neutral' device. It does not determine individual prices: they are merely expressed in terms of money.

In reality, money is something much more than a mere passive technical device to facilitate the exchange of goods and services, to serve as an instrument of their valuation, to provide means for expressing claims and for accumulating wealth, and to act as a medium through which the price system operates. It has several additional roles of fundamental importance in the determination of economic trends. These roles, which may be described as 'dynamic' because they are liable to cause major changes of a fundamental character, are by no means new. Foremost amongst them is the influence of money on the national economy through the effects of its depreciation or appreciation – or, what is the same thing, of a rise or a fall in the general price level. While the individual prices of various goods and services can fluctuate in relation to each other even under a barter economy, there can be no such thing as a change in the general price level except under a monetary economy.

Money plays a very active and highly important dynamic part in the economic system through its function of influencing the general level of prices. The quantity of money, the degree of the liquidity of potential monetary supplies, and the frequency with which it is spent are liable to influence the demand for goods and services. If more money is available for spending or if the available money is spent more freely while the supply of goods and services offered for sale remains the same, the chances are that higher prices will be asked and paid for the same goods and services. If there is not enough money available for spending, or if the amount available is not spent freely enough, sellers of the unchanged volume of goods and services may have to accept lower prices. A general rise or fall in the price level is liable to affect, for better or for worse, the welfare of most sections of the community. It may influence the life of every man, woman and child.

The effect of the trend of the general price level on the economic situation is apt to be very considerable and may have far-reaching social and political consequences. Indeed, it may even affect the course of history. Surely this role goes far beyond that of a convenient device with the aid of which goods and services are exchanged. Nor is the influence of the trend of the price level the only way in which money can influence fundamental economic trends. Money is a powerful factor that is liable to stimulate or hinder economic and cultural progress. Sensible and progressive application of the monetary system tends to result in fuller utilisation of natural resources and of technological inventions leading to a higher standard of living. On the other hand a too narrow and rigid application of the monetary system is apt to handicap progress. And the misuse of facilities provided by the monetary system is apt to lead to grave setbacks through the destructive consequences of a runaway inflation or even of a relatively moderate but persistent 'creeping' inflation.

The system, if it is managed properly, provides for a self-regulating mechanism affecting the trend of trade, encouraging productive activity and commerce when they are in need of stimulus and discouraging them when they appear to be excessive. Monetary conditions are apt to stimulate or discourage consumption as well as production. They are liable to influence even the national character of peoples. Inflation has a demoralising effect on all classes, by providing individuals and groups with opportunity and inducement to secure gains at the expense of the rest of the community, in disregard of the public interest.

According to the 'static' conception money is not supposed to play any such part in the economic system. In normal conditions of equilibrium its quantity is supposed to be just sufficient to meet normal requirements, in which case it could not possibly cause a rise in the price level and in business activity through being in excess of requirements, or a fall in the price level and in business activity through being short of requirements. This conceptions is based on the assumption that in an ideal state the role of money is confined to its 'static' technical functions dealt with above. On the basis of that assumption money is supposed to be 'neutral' and does not play an active part in determining the course of our economy. The possibility that it may cause temporary disturbances is admitted, but according to the static theory money is not amongst the fundamental factors by which our economy is influenced. It is a mere intermediary to ensure a more efficient functioning of the factors that really matter, the factors affecting production, distribution and consumption.

In real life, however, money is seldom completely 'neutral' for any length of time. The laws of nature do not provide the means of ensuring that there should be just enough money, neither too much nor too little, under an 'automatic' operation of the system. Nor has human brain yet devised a foolproof 'managed' system under which it could be ensured that the volume of money should be exactly sufficient, neither excessive nor deficient. It is, therefore, inevitable that money should play an important and active part in influencing economic trends through the inadequacy or excess of its quantity compared with the amount required for maintaining the stability of its value and of the volume of economic activities. These are its normal dynamic functions. But there are others.

With the aid of the modern monetary system Governments are in a position to spend well in excess of the amounts they can raise by taxation. It is possible for them to raise very large amounts by borrowing. Thanks to the modern credit system, Treasuries are now able to create monetary conditions in which they can borrow practically any sums they require. The monetary system enables them therefore, to embark on costly economic, social, political and military policies which would be out of their reach financially were it not for the dynamic functions of money. Such policies are apt to affect fundamentally the economy of the community concerned. These dynamic functions of money enable Governments to create, for better or for worse, a public debt running into astronomic figures.

The monetary system also provides the means by which the burden of such excessive indebtedness, public or private, can be reduced in a relatively unobstrusive manner through a depreciation of the monetary unit. This may obviate in given circumstances the necessity for reducing an intolerable burden of indebtedness through wholesale bankruptcy or repudiation.

The reduction of the burden of indebtedness by means of currency depreciation, though less brutal than an outright default, is liable to have far-reaching effects in the social as well as in the economic sphere. In other respects, too, the monetary system is apt to play an important part in the social sphere as a means for redistribution of wealth as a result of changes in its value or its quantity.

All these dynamic functions of money are fully as important as its static functions on which generations of monetary economists focused their attention. Admittedly, money was not adopted or maintained in use in order to bring about changes in the price level, or to regulate the trend of economic activities, or to enable Governments to finance large expenditure, or to provide a relatively painless means of reducing indebtedness, or to redistribute wealth. Money was adopted and is maintained for meeting the requirements of its technical functions. Indeed, it would not be able to fulfil its dyanmic functions unless it fulfilled its static technical functions. This is no reason, however, for ignoring or underrating the former.

It is true that in everyday life the static functions of money are usually much more in evidence. Its dynamic functions are well in the background during more or less stable and normal periods. Only those engaged in shaping monetary policy, and those who wish to be able to form an opinion about the merits or demerits of that policy, are aware all the time of the dynamic functions of money as well as its static functions. It is in periods of crises or important changes that the dynamic functions force themselves on the attention of the lay public. But from the point of view of monetary policy, considerations relating to these functions must always be present in the minds of the monetary authorities.

Admittedly, the measures taken to ensure that money is able to fulfil its technical functions satisfactorily are often identical with those required in the interests of its dynamic functions. This, however, need not necessarily be the case. From the point of view of its technical functions it is essential to maintain a stable value of money to a reasonable degree. On the other hand, from the point of view of dynamic functions it may appear to be tempting in given circumstances to depart from stability. Situations may arise in which a policy aiming at a rise or a fall in the price level is a necessary evil from the point of view of some dynamic function of money – such as the stimulation of business activity or the discouragement of excessive speculation – however deplorable this may appear from the point of view of its static functions. What matters is that on balance the system as a whole should give the highest possible degree of satisfaction.

Let us now deal briefly with the international role of the monetary system – its function to link national economies with each other. It provides the technical device for financing the international interchange of goods and services and for transferring capital across the borders. In addition to this static role it also plays the static role of equalising discrepancies between national price levels and between national levels of interest rate. In normal conditions of equilibrium, exchange rates tend to preserve or restore the international character of the price level, and forward exchange rates tend to bridge the gap between the levels of interest rates, allowing for factors justifying discrepancies even in such conditions.

The dynamic functions of money in its international aspects tend to change balances of payments, relative changes in domestic supplies of money, relative levels of interest rates, and trends of international movements of capital. Monetary policy – of which foreign exchange policy constitutes a sub-section – may aim at assisting the monetary system in fulfilling its international static functions or its constructive international dynamic functions, or in resisting its disturbing international dynamic functions.

The importance of the dynamic functions of money will be increased very considerably as a result of the adoption of some international monetary reform on the lines suggested by Mr Barber at the annual meeting of the International Fund in September 1971. It would produce two essentially dynamic effects. It would enable Governments, through the International

Monetary Fund controlled by them collectively, to create an immense volume of new money which would create additional credits for both domestic and international purposes, based on Special Drawing Rights. And it would enable deficit countries to settle their deficits with the aid of these Special Drawing Rights, without having to improve their balance of payments or to borrow abroad.

Assuming that these SDRs will be issued in very large amounts, their allocation to the Governments particpating in the scheme would enable the countries concerned to finance a spectacular expansion of their production, public works and social service benefits, far beyond the extent to which they have been able to expand them under the previous monetary systems. At the same time the scheme would relieve them of their balance of payments problem, for, if it should be successful, the claims of surplus countries would automatically be settled by means of SDRs.

Needless to say, it remains to be seen if and to what extent this new scheme would operate satisfactorily. Its excessive use carries grave risks and its collapse would bring about a financial crisis of unprecedented magnitude. Its advantages and disadvantages will be discussed in detail in Chapter 42. Here we confine ourselves to drawing attention to the possibilities of a considerable increase of the dynamic character of the monetary system.

Before concluding this chapter, we must refer very briefly to the evolution of the term 'money'. Originally it meant coins, later it came to include notes and more recently also bank deposits repayable at sight. The modern trend in economic literature is to include also various forms of liquid assets ('potential money' or 'near-money'). Quite recently SDRs have also come to be considered money in transactions between monetary authorities. Monetary policy has to adapt itself to the changing concept of money, implying as it does a changing monetary system.

CHAPTER THREE

The British Monetary System

WE remarked in the last chapter that there have been in operation in the course of monetary history an infinite variety of monetary systems serving broadly the same purposes but differing widely from each other in many material respects. In order to provide at least one detailed instance of a monetary system serving as an object and an instrument of monetary policy, we propose to describe in this chapter the monetary system in operation in Great Britain at the time of writing – in 1972. That system, even though it differs in many respects from the American and other important monetary systems, may be regarded in its broad outlines as a fairly representative example of a modern monetary system.

In its existing form the British monetary system is of very recent origin. It is in an essentially fluid state and is liable to change materially at any moment. Many people of the older generation still remember the totally different system that existed before the First World War, since when a succession of different systems have been adopted and discarded. Sovereigns, which were the principal currency in circulation before 1914, have long been replaced, first by Treasury notes and subsequently by Bank of England notes. Subsidiary coinage, for use as token money, consisting of coins of an inferior metallic value in denominations of ½p to 50p, is now the only metallic money in use.

Bank of England notes, apart from a brief period during and after the Napoleonic Wars, between 1787 and 1821, and again during and after the First World War, had been freely convertible into gold coin or bullion according to the holder's wishes. During the First World War they became inconvertible in practice, even though their convertibility was not legally suspended. Between 1925 and 1931 they were convertible into gold for export but not into coins for domestic circulation. Since 1931 they are no longer convertible into gold. They are taken in payment for goods or services, or in settlement of liabilities, but not on account of their intrinsic value, which is little more than nothing. Nor are they accepted on the ground of any hope that one day they might become convertible into gold. Such hopes have long been abandoned. The reason why the notes are readily accepted is that those who take them have confidence in them, knowing that they in turn are in a position to use them for payments within the United Kingdom. It is largely for the same reason that token money is accepted as small change even though such metallic value as the coins may possess is only a fraction of their face value.

One feature of the British monetary system that has remained substantially the same as it was during the latter part of the nineteenth century is that bank deposits (credit balances on current and deposit account) constitute the major part of the monetary supply. In June 1972 their total was over £43,000 m. while that of the note issue was around £4,600 m. only. The grand total of notes and of bank deposits is generally regarded as the figure of Britain's monetary supply. It is almost as easy to pay with cheques drawn on bank balances as with notes, and in many instances the former are preferred. Deposit accounts, as distinct from current accounts, are somewhat less mobile, but deposits can be converted either into notes or into current-account balances subject to certain formalities and delays, so that they too may be regarded as being part of the supply of money. According to the latest interpretation, Certificates of Deposits, deposits with building societies and finance houses, Savings Certificates etc., may be regarded as money, or at any rate as 'near-money' or 'quasi-money', as they are sometimes called. Holdings of liquid assets, such as Treasury bills or commercial bills, and even short-dated Government loans, are regarded as potential money because they can easily be monetised, even though the cash thus raised can only add to the volume of money if these assets are bought on official account, or if banks buy them from non-banking holders.

Either notes or cheques drawn on current-account balances can be used by the holders in payment for goods, services, and in settlement of liabilities of every kind. The unlimited acceptance of notes in payment within the United Kingdom is ensured not only by the confidence of the public but also by law under which they are 'legal tender'. Subsidiary coins are also legal tender up to limited amounts. There is and can of course be no law to enforce the universal acceptance of cheques, but in practice they are accepted to a very considerable degree. Any reluctance of payees to accept cheques in immediate discharge of current liabilities does not prevent the use of this form of money, because it only means that a few days are allowed for the cheques to be cleared before the payment is recognized as such.

Only a small fraction of the quantity of notes and bank deposits in existence is used in payments on any given day. On the other hand, in the course of a year the volume of turnover settled by means of cash or cheques amounts to many times the amount of the note issue *plus* bank deposits. During 1971 the total amount of cheques cleared was about 23 times the amount of deposits. No corresponding statistics are, of course, available concerning the turnover in notes.

The amount of Bank of England notes and of current-account balances is not the only factor that determines monetary conditions in Britain. A great deal depends on the way in which owners of notes and deposits make use of the purchasing power represented by their monetary resources. The mere existence of these resources does not in itself affect production, prices or consumption. As we shall see later, the Government is in a position to increase or reduce these resources. But their increase does not necessarily mean that the additional amounts are spent in full. Nor does their reduction necessarily mean a corresponding curtailment of purchasing power. The public is in a position to take the initiative for causing an increase or reduction in the volume of money in active circulation. This can be done by freer or more restrained spending of cash holdings or bank balances. It can also be done by reducing or increasing holdings of Savings Certificates or other short-term or maturing Government securities, or by making more extensive or less extensive use of credit facilities available with banks. But in reasonably normal conditions banks and the monetary authorities between them are in a position to ensure the maintenance of the volume of money around a certain level, or its adjustment to a certain level, in accordance with the aims of monetary policy. This will be explained in detail in Chapter 28.

On the other hand, the authorities have little or no control over the velocity of circulation of notes and deposits. Indeed, during much of the post-war period the rise in prices was due as much to the increase in the velocity of circulation of money as to the increase in its volume. Any official action to change the latter is liable to be frustrated by a change of the former in the opposite sense.

The above point is only one of the many that is quoted against the monetarist theory and the policy based on the assumption that the economy of a country can be managed by determining the quantity of money. In the case of the British monetary system the validity of the monetarist school is contested, however, mainly on the ground that since the British Government is committed to a policy of high employment, the supply of money simply cannot be kept short of requirements. This policy encourages high wage demands, and the resulting increase of monetary requirements leads to irresistible pressure for an increase in the supply of money even in circumstances when this is not in accordance with the basic economic interests. That being so, the supply of money is apt to be the effect and not the cause of economic changes.

In the days of the gold standard before 1914, when the pound was convertible, it was widely assumed that the confidence it inspired was due to the fact that holders of notes and of bank balances could always rely on being able to convert their holdings into sovereigns. When after an interval of eleven years the gold standard was resumed in 1925, it was a different gold standard. As we said above, the notes were only convertible into gold bars or into sovereigns for the purpose of shipment abroad. This limited convertibility into gold was suspended in September 1931. Holders of sterling remained entitled, however, up to the outbreak of the Second World War eight years later, to convert their pounds into dollars or other foreign currencies in the foreign exchange market at the prevailing rates of exchange. In September 1939, the convertibility of sterling into currencies of countries other than those of the Sterling Area was also suspended.

Although the watertight war-time exchange control was gradually relaxed after the war, the pre-war freedom of exchanges was never restored in Britain, at any rate as far as UK residents were concerned. From time to time exchange control had to be reinforced for the sake of defending sterling against adverse pressure.

A limited degree of convertibility into certain foreign currencies was gradually resumed after 1945. During the fifties and early sixties sterling became gradually convertible for non-resident holders into foreign currencies, and the extent of its convertibility for UK residents for current requirements was also extended. For capital requirements sterling remains inconvertible for U.K. residents though there are exceptions to this rule, the extent of which varies according to circumstances.

Sterling held privately is not convertible into any definite quantity of gold, as it was before 1914 and again between 1925 and 1931, nor is it freely convertible for British holders into a fluctuating foreign exchange at market rates, as it was between 1931 and 1939. In spite of such cessation of convertibility for UK residents, the pound continues to enjoy a high degree of confidence and is unhesitatingly accepted in payment in the United Kingdom. The fact that it is legal tender would not in itself be sufficient to ensure its acceptability. No law is able to enforce the free acceptance of a rapidly depreciating currency.

In Britain inconvertible paper money is accepted by everybody largely because its quantity is relatively limited, and therefore its value remains relatively steady. Even during the 'cheap money policy' of the early period of the Labour Government between 1945 and 1947, and during the wage inflation which became greatly escalated in the middle sixties and even more in the seventies, there was no runaway inflation. Although sterling was not nearly as scarce as some economists and others would have liked it to be, the increase in the volume of notes and of deposits was not so extensive as to cause a rapid depreciation of money and to inspire acute distrust in it.

It is true that prices in Britain, as in other countries, have been rising almost without a break since 1939. Their rise has not been dramatic, however. The constant decline of the purchasing power of sterling may have discouraged saving because of the likelihood that in ten years' time, or even sooner, the amounts saved would buy half or less than half what they would buy if they were to be spent at once. But the extent of the internal depreciation of sterling form one week to another, or from one month to another, or even from one year to another, was fairly moderate until the seventies. Even now sterling is freely accepted in payment, because it retains its value more or less between the time we receive it and the time we spend it.

Another reason why sterling commanded the confidence of the public during the post war period was that the Government endeavoured to safeguard its international value. Apart from its devaluation in 1949 and in 1967, sterling remained stabilised in terms of gold and dollars throughout the war and during the post-war period till 1971. While in some countries devaluation followed devaluation after 1945, in Britain the Government made a real effort to maintain the gold value of the pound in face of adverse trends and only yielded to sweeping pressure on ten isolated occasions. It is true that during the early post-war period the stability of sterling was maintained largely though preventing unauthorised exchange dealings, cutting down imports in order to improve the balance of payments, and obtaining fina..cial aid from the United States. Again during the late fifties and the sixties sterling was defended largely with the aid of external financial assistance obtained from the IMF and the Federal Reserve and from other Central Banks, instead of restoring its basic strength by adopting sufficiently sound policies to restore equilibrium unaided. Nevertheless, what mattered from the point of view of confidence in sterling was the fact that its international value remained relatively stable, until it was de-stabilised in 1972.

Sterling remained acceptable as a means of payment and continued to be used as a standard of value, standard of deferred payments and store of value. The only substantial change in its use as a unit of account to measure current and future liabilities was in the sphere of collective wages agreements. A large and increasing number of these agreements contain a 'cost-of-living' clause as a result of which the wages of millions of employees are automatically adjusted whenever the cost-of-living index changes to a certain extent. Apart from such arrangements, within the UK liabilities are generally fixed in terms of sterling irrespective of any changes in its purchasing power. Very few contracts contain a gold clause or a dollar clause.

Until the suspension of the gold standard in 1931 the gold value of the pound was fixed by Act of Parliament. During 1946–71 it came to be subjected to the Bretton Woods Agreement under which the IMF had in theory the right to veto any alteration of the gold parity of sterling by more than 10 per cent, in either direction, of its gold and dollar value fixed in 1946. The Government had undertaken to maintain the exchange rate of sterling within 1 per cent of its parity in relation to the dollar. In practice this margin came to be reduced to $\frac{3}{4}$ per cent, making a total spread of $1\frac{1}{2}$ per cent. But in practice the IMF would not have been able to prevent the British Government or any other Government from changing or suspending their parities.

From the outbreak of the Second World War until November 1951 there was no free dealing in foreign currencies in the UK. Importers and others in need of foreign exchanges had to apply to the Bank of England through their banks for the authorisation of the exchanges they needed and were granted licences to buy the exchanges at a fixed rate. They were under obligation to sell to their banks the proceeds of their exports or their other receipts of foreign exchanges at a fixed rate. In November 1951 free dealings in exchanges for commercial requirements were restored, but not for transfers of capital or for speculation.

Any appreciation or depreciation beyond the support points of $2·78 – $2·82 until November 1967, and thereafter $2·38 – $2·42 until 15 August 1971, was prevented by the application of the rules of the IMF. In practice the IMF would not have been able to prevent the British Government, or indeed any other Government, from changing or suspending the parities of their currencies, thereby allowing their exchange rates to depreciate or appreciate beyond support points.

The suspension of the convertibility of the dollar on 15 August 1971 was followed by some six months of floating of exchange rates. Under the Smithsonian Agreement of 18 December 1971, sterling was restabilised at its gold value to which it was devalued in 1967, which meant a $8\frac{1}{2}$ per cent revaluation in relation to the dollar. The authorised spread was widened to $2\frac{1}{4}$ per cent on either side of its parities or 'central rates'. As from 1 May 1972, Britain adhered to the recently implemented agreement between EEC countries, under which the spread between present and prospective EEC currencies was narrowed to $2\frac{1}{4}$ per cent. But within six weeks sterling became subject to a strong selling pressure, and on 16 June 1972 it suspended its parities and came to be allowed to float.

From 1932 until 1972 Britain was the centre of the Sterling Area, a group of countries the currencies of which were closely linked with sterling. The group included the whole Commonwealth with the exception of Canada and Hong Kong. Exchange restrictions for transactions between most members of the Sterling Area were relatively moderate, though various members adopted exchange control measures in relation to each other during difficult periods. Until 1967 practically all

currencies of the Sterling Area maintained a fixed relationship
with sterling. The authorities of the Outer Sterling Area kept
their reserves mostly in sterling, but during the sixties they
gradually diversified their reserves. In 1967 the principle that
Sterling Area currencies were to maintain their fixed parities
with sterling came to be abandoned.

To sum up, the automatic gold standard was abandoned in
1914, the managed gold bullion standard in 1931. the system
of flexible sterling convertible into other currencies but not into
gold gave way at the outbreak of the Second World War to a
system of largely inconvertible, rigidly stabilised and controlled
sterling. The system of 1972 could be described as one of
floating inconvertible sterling. The internal value of the pound
is supported by keeping the quantity of money relatively
scarce, although not sufficiently so to ensure its stability;
'creeping' inflation is allowed to cause a slow but persistent
depreciation. There is a statutory maximum limit to the note
circulation, but this limit is liable to frequent adjustment by
administrative action by the Treasury, subject to subsequent
approval by Parliament if the fiduciary issue is maintained
above its authorised limit over a certain period.

In any case, the amount of the note issue is of secondary
importance compared with that of current-account balances
and deposits with clearing banks. The volume of money
represented by such bank deposits is kept down by a ratio of
$12\frac{1}{4}$ per cent between liquid assets and short-term liabilities.
It is not kept down as effectively as it was under the gold
standard, when an expansion of the volume of currency and
credit was liable to correct itself automatically by causing an
outflow of gold leading in turn to a contraction of credit. Under
post-war conditions it has come to depend to a very large
degree on the volume of Treasury bills. Its dependence on the
increased post-war liquidity of the entire economy reduced its
dependence on official policy.

Under the existing system there is no built-in technical
arrangement that would prevent a runaway inflation such as we
have witnessed in other countries. In spite of this, inflation has

been relatively slow because those responsible for the management of our monetary policy have practised a certain degree of restraint. As Robertson rightly put it in an article appearing in *Lloyds Bank Review*, sterling is maintained sound not through any qualities inherent in the system but through the wisdom and ability of those in charge of its management. It is of course a matter of opinion whether the degree of their wisdom and their ability could and should have been higher, so as to prevent the gradual but none the less inexorable erosion of the currency.

Thanks to the relatively moderate extent and gradual character of its depreciation, sterling was able to fulfil satisfactorily its role as a standard of value. But owing to the persistence of its internal depreciation, post-war sterling has not been ideal as a standard of deferred payments or as a store of value. Although debtors have benefited by the decline in the real burden of their liabilities, their gain has been the loss of creditors, investors in fixed-interest-bearing securities, and other recipients of deferred fixed payments, such as pensioners, holders of life policies, etc.

Sterling has fulfilled its role as an international means of payment tolerably well, in spite of the devaluations of 1949 and 1967, and of the frequently recurrent waves of distrust in its stability. It is no longer the currency in which the bulk of international trade is transacted. In this respect its relative importance declined during the late fifties and even more during the sixties as a result of the increasing use of Eurodollars for that purpose.

On the whole sterling fulfilled its technical 'static' functions reasonably well. Its 'dynamic' functions as a major factor in influencing economic trends included the stimulus given by rising prices and the expanding volume of money to war-time production, to post-war reconstruction and to the development of the Welfare State. They facilitated the earning of excessive wages and excessive profits. The reduction in the real value of fixed incomes caused by the depreciation of the monetary unit, was in sharp contrast with the increase of other incomes and of capital values.

At the time of writing, in 1972, the British monetary system is far from being stable. The pound is a floating exchange and its value is therefore at the mercy of the caprices of speculators and of foreign holders of excessive sterling balances. Its basic strength is threatened by excessive wage demands and by other manifestations of the 'English disease'. That disease is not confined to the so-called working classes. British banking has departed from the sound fundamental principles which had earned sterling its unique reputation. Today in Britain, as in every other country, much less attention is paid to those principles. Bank credits are no longer nearly as well secured and as self-liquidating as they were before 1914 and between the wars. The inherently sound principles that safeguarded London from bank crises between 1919 and 1965 have been greatly relaxed. It is true that British banks help British and foreign industry much more effectively than they did in the past, but only at the cost of being incomparably less liquid. Admittedly, banks in other countries pursue the same policies. But this only means that British banks are no longer as superior to them as they had been. For this reason among others sterling is no longer the same symbol of security and integrity as it was in the past.

CHAPTER FOUR

What is Monetary Policy?

THE term 'monetary policy' is of comparatively recent origin. It did not appear in economic literature, political debates and in the Press until the nineteenth century. Yet monetary policy has been pursued since time immemorial. Early writers on money from Plato, Aristotle and Xenophon onward dealt with questions of monetary policy without referring to them as such. Long before their writings practical administrators had taken decisions relating to the monetary system without being aware that they were pursuing monetary policies. They had done so probably with little or no theoretical background. They may have experimented with money, learning through trial and error at the expense of their community. Or they may have followed monetary developments elsewhere, learning from the lessons of the past, or at the expense of other communities. As a rule there were, however, no easily accessible records of the results of past monetary experiments, or of those of contemporary distant communities, so that statesmen and administrators had to rediscover the same elementary truths after making the same mistakes again and again.

It would be interesting to speculate how monetary history would have been affected if the ancient Greeks had devoted as much attention to monetary theory and policy as they did to philosophy and the arts, or if the best brains af ancient Rome had brought monetary knowledge to the same high standard as they brought legal knowledge. Conceivably the Roman Empire, the stability of which became undermined partly as a result of the confused monetary situation prevailing during and after the third century A.D., might have prolonged its existence by centuries if its rulers had known more about monetary policy. It is also possible that the late medieval period might have been a period of progress instead of virtual stagnation if Europe had borrowed the idea of paper money from China in the eleventh century. It might then have been possible to mitigate the handicap of inadequate metallic supplies, which held up production and commerce until after the discovery of the gold and silver resources of the New World. On the other hand, it might simply have meant earlier experience in runaway inflation.

Although in the medieval period there were isolated instances of attempts by writers to teach Governments how to run their monetary systems it was not until the beginning of the modern period that we encounter an extensive literature on the subject of monetary policy. It is worth noting that it was always during troubled or unsettled periods that writers on monetary policy became active. During the sixteenth century the inflation caused by the heavy influx of precious metals from the New World gave rise to extensive literature on the subject, especially in Spain and in France. In Britain there was a crop of contributions to problems of monetary policy towards the end of the seventeenth century, inspired by the economic and financial troubles of the 1690s. During the same period the difficulties caused by commodity-currencies and paper money in the North American colonies gave rise to some interesting writings on the subject. In the eighteenth century John Law's experiment with paper money gave a strong stimulus to the study of monetary problems and so did the inflation that accompanied the American War of Independence and the French Revolution.

It was not until the nineteenth century that questions of monetary policy came to be investigated systematically. They were taken up by theoretical and practical experts in connection with the problems arising from the Napoleonic Wars and their aftermaths, and later in connection with the periodically recurrent business cycles. By the end of that century the original trickle of literature on monetary policy developed into a vast flood. It continued to grow throughout the twentieth century, and it may be claimed that in our days few specialised subjects have a more extensive literature than monetary policy.

Notwithstanding this, relatively little thought has so far been given to finding a definition for the meaning of monetary policy. Although the term is used with increasing frequency by experts and laymen, it has occurred to very few of those who write or talk about monetary policy to define what precisely they mean by it. Most of them assume that the actual scope of the discussions on the subject implies its definition. While it would be too much to expect those concerned with some current problem of monetary policy to embark on an attempt at defining the scope of the whole subject, clearly it is the duty of the monetary economist dealing with the principles of monetary policy to state precisely what he means by it.

In my *Primitive Money* I define monetary policy as 'the attitude of the political authority towards the monetary system of the community under its control'. A monetary policy may be either active, when it involves decisions to apply measures, or passive, when it involves decisions to abstain from applying measures. A passive attitude towards monetary developments, in order to constitute monetary policy, must be deliberate.

The above definition is admittedly too vague to be of sufficient practical use. Monetary policy may also be defined as the effort to reduce to a minimum the disadvantages, and increase the advantages, resulting from the existence and operation of a monetary system. Even this definition only applies to an ideal monetary policy. We might say that in theory the object of monetary policy *should be* as indicated above. In reality throughout monetary history we often encounter instances of the disadvantages derived from the monetary system rather than their reduction, and a reduction of advantages rather than their increase. When politicians or administrators decide to plunge their country into inflation with inadequate justification they abuse the monetary system. Their decision is undoubtedly an act of monetary policy, even through it does not aim at minimising the disadvantages or increasing the advantages derived from the monetary system.

It is, of course, possible to try to interpret 'advantages' and 'disadvantages' in a sense that would come within the terms of our definition. It is arguable, for instance, that the frequent debasements of the French coinage during the Middle Ages were justified from a national point of view as the only means by which the French kings were able to finance their defensive wars against English invasions. Likewise, although the inflation of paper currency that accompanied many major wars from the American War of Independence onwards inflicted grave economic and social hardships on the nations concerned, it may be claimed to have been justified as the means for financing fights for national survival.

In this sense it may be argued that the inflationary monetary policies adopted by many Governments during the Napoleonic Wars and the two World Wars had for their object to secure advantages from the working of the monetary system, even though those advantages were outside the monetary, economic or social sphere. To be able to finance a war with the aid of inflation may be claimed to have political and military advantages. Even inflationary policy pursued to prepare and wage an aggressive imperialist war – as during Hitler's rearmament of 1933–9 and his war of 1939–45 – may be said to aim at advantages, at any rate if viewed from the one-sided point of view of the regime that pursues it.

There were many instances in which decisions on monetary policy could not possibly be claimed to have served the public advantage in any sense. The coinage was debased on various occasions for the sake of meeting the excessive requirements of extravagant royal courts. For instance, Cleopatra devalued the drachma by 75 per cent to finance her life of luxury, and Charles the Bad, king of Navarre, debased his country's coinage by one-third in 1383, with the object of securing funds to celebrate the release of the heir to the throne from French captivity.

In such instances, as in the case of debasements or inflation for the sake of financing aggressive wars, a bad monetary policy did not even have the excuse of trying to serve the advantages of the community as a whole. Both its method and its object were bad, so that the end could not be claimed to have justified the means. In spite of this fact such debasements, and more recently Hitler's inflation, must be regarded as coming within the scope of monetary policy. A bad monetary policy is none the less a monetary policy for being bad.

A different approach may be attempted by defining monetary policy in such a way as to include all monetary decisions and measures irrespective of whether their aims are monetary or non-monetary, and all non-monetary decisions and measures that aim at affecting the monetary system. Under this definition we could include within the scope of monetary policy not only measures of every kind which are taken for the purpose of influencing the value, volume, etc., of money, but also monetary measures which pursue non-monetary economic, social or political aims. From this point of view debasement or inflation undertaken for no matter what purpose would come within our definition. Likewise, non-monetary measures such as control of prices or wages, physical controls, Budgetary measures, export drives or import cuts, incomes policy, measures to deal with pockets of unemployment, etc., would be included within the scope of monetary policy in so far as their primary aim is to influence the monetary situation. One of the earliest forms of highly developed deliberate monetary policy was Mercantilism, which aimed largely at monetary ends partly with the aid of non-monetary means.

In order to circumscribe the scope of monetary policy it is necessary to draw a distinction between monetary policy on the one hand and fiscal policy, banking policy and economic policy on the other. These various policies overlap with monetary policy to a very considerable extent and it is not easy to draw a borderline between them. It all depends on whether a measure is aimed at producing mainly monetary or non-monetary effects and whether it employs monetary means.

Fiscal policy – which under my definition includes Budgetary policy, debt-management policy and taxation policy – covers the ground of Government finance, that is public revenue public expenditure, public borrowing, public debt repayment and other public debt operations. It is almost impossible to

envisage any major measure affecting the Budgetary positions
or any major decision concerning the public debt which would
not produce some effect in the monetary sphere even if no such
effects were intended or desired. Keynesian monetary policy
aims at counter-cyclical Budgetary surpluses and deficits – that
is, at the mopping up of excessive purchasing power with the
aid of Budgetary surpluses and replenishing deficient purchasing power with the aid of deliberately incurred Budgetary deficits. It aims at regulating the volume of money with the aid of
fiscal instead of monetary means. Accordingly fiscal measures
have come to be regarded in our days as constituting measures
of monetary policy.

In reality this view is too sweeping. Important measures of
taxation may fall outside the scope of monetary policy if they
consist of the replacement of one source of revenue by some other
source, so long as they are not liable to affect materially the
level of prices, the volume of purchasing power or some other
major factor in the monetary situation, Likewise, a decision
determining the terms of a conversion scheme, as a result of
which a maturing Government loan is replaced by another
Government loan, does not come within the scope of monetary
policy unless its aim is to affect the liquidity of the banking
system, that is, the proportion between the banks' holdings of
long-term and short-term securities on which the banks' ability
to grant credits largely depends.

According to the Radcliffe Committee, the management of
the public debt should be influenced largely by considerations of
monetary policy, also from the point of view of an appropriate
'grading' of the maturities of the medium- and long-terms loans,
as we propose to show in Chapter 33. An increase or reduction of specific classes of expenditure does not as a rule come
within the scope of monetary policy unless the grand total of
expenditure is materially affected or unless the change from one
type of expenditure to another affects materially some major
factor in the monetary situation.

On the other hand, any change in the Budgetary surplus or
deficit inevitably affects the monetary situation, even if it comes

about as a result of decisions aiming at results outside the monetary sphere. In pre-Keynesian days, when little or no attention was paid to the monetary effects of fiscal changes, such decisions were not monetary policy decisions. In our days, however, Governments often take even decisions relating to individual taxes in full knowledge of their monetary effects, so that they come within the sphere of monetary policy, at any rate in the sense that the Government concerned is prepared to put up with the monetary effects for the sake of the non-monetary effects. In the same sense, since the Radcliffe Report any major funding or de-funding decision taken for non-monetary reasons is regarded as a monetary policy decision, for the Treasuries are now supposed to be aware of its monetary effects even though it was made in spite of, or independently of, such monetary effects.

It goes without saying that monetary policy and banking policy are closely interrelated. The volume of credit and the level of interest rates constitute most important elements in the monetary situation in a modern community. It is arguable therefore that any banking measures affecting them comes within the scope of monetary policy even if it is not initiated by the authorities but by the banks themselves, provided that they act on what they know or assume to be the official policy. There are, on the other hand, many kinds of decisions and measures within the sphere of banking policy which are outside the scope of monetary policy.

The credit policy of the banks, in so far as it affects not the total volume of loans but their distributions among categories of borrowers, not the general level of interest rates but interest charges on particular types of credits, may or may not affect the monetary situation to the nature of the categories affected and the extent of the effect. An expansion of consumer credits, for instance, or of credits for capital investment, is liable to become a factor in the monetary situation, An increase in the volume of credits in one branch of industry, and a simultaneous and corresponding reduction of credits in some other branches, is liable to produce monetary effects in given circumstances. Selective

credit control, to stimulate exports for instance, is a devi
monetary policy. On the other hand changes in the cha.ges
made by banks to their customers – apart from changes made in
interest rates – remain within the scope of banking policy unless
their nature and extent is such as to influence the monetary
situation. This may be the case if banking charges are reduced
in order to encourage the banking habit, and thereby to reduce
requirements for notes, or if they are increased in order to
discourage borrowing to finance personal consumption.

The policy relating to new public issues of securities, or to
limitations on the construction of factories, may pursue monetary ends if it aims at influencing the total volume of capital
investment. If it merely aims at discouraging certain types of
issues – whether in order to safeguard the investing public or to
prevent unwanted expansion in certain industries and encourage expansion in other industries – it does not come within
the scope of monetary policy, unless it serves ends such as
encouraging exports.

Monetary policy is part of the broader sphere of economic
policy. It is possible and necessary to distinguish between monetary policy and non-monetary aspects of economic policy as they
affect industry, commerce, agriculture, labour, etc. Economic
policy aiming at expansion or contraction in the volume of
production is liable to produce monetary effects even if its aim
is not primarily within the monetary sphere. Although the level
of wages is a matter of first-rate importance from the point of
view of monetary policy, a wages policy may concern itself with
matters other than the total of wages. It may aim at encouraging coal-mining by means of raising miners' wages above the
general level, or at encouraging the training of skilled labour,
or at some other non-monetary end. It is often a matter of
degree whether some economic policy measure comes within
the sphere of monetary policy. Any measure resulting in a more
equal distribution of income concerns the monetary situation
if the change is substantial, even though it pursues primarily
a social objective. Any wages policy aimed at preventing a
'leapfrogging' of wage demands by seeking to co-ordinate wage

claim pursues an essentially monetary aim.

There is bound to be an immense variety of borderline cases. Whether or not they come within the sphere of monetary policy depends partly on the nature of the action and its actual result and partly on the Governments' intention. 'Policy' implies deliberate decisions. This does not mean, however, that if a Government embarks on large-scale spending on rearmament or social services, without taking into consideration the inflationary effects of its action, it can disclaim the pursuit of a deliberate inflationary monetary policy. Even if inflation is merely an unwanted incidental result of the policy pursued, the decision to risk such an effect, and even an ostrich-like attitude of ignoring it, constitutes a monetary policy decision.

The scope of monetary policy has widened immensely within the brief span of our lifetime, and even within the last ten years or so. The extent to which Budgetary and other non-monetary measures are often adopted largely if not entirely with an eye on the monetary situation has increased. Indeed, as we shall see later, a school of thought developed during the thirties among economists and practical experts, especially in the United States but inspired largely by Keynes, which advocated that monetary measures in the narrower sense of the term should be replaced largely by fiscal measures aiming at monetary ends. Another revolutionary extension of the scoop of monetary policy occurred in recent years, largely as a result of the recommendations made by the Radcliffe Committee, to place the management of the public debt in the service of monetary policy. Although the idea of regulating the liquidity of the economy by means of funding or de-funding is not new, its scientific application in the form of official intervention to influence the entire range of maturities is an innovation which is still in its experimental stage.

In Britain and other countries physical controls were advocated in many quarters as permanent substitutes for conventional measures of monetary policy. In so far as rationing, price controls, import and export controls, etc., affected the monetary situation, their deliberate application to serve partly that purpose come within the scope of monetary policy.

As we saw above, policies aiming at influencing wage levels may constitute monetary policies; likewise, measures aiming at influencing production, distribution, consumption, foreign trade etc., may be taken for ends of monetary policy.

Monetary policy stands somewhere half-way between monetary theory and monetary practice. The former is concerned with broad principles which should form the background to monetary policy and which are liable to affect it. The latter is concerned with practical monetary measures which translate monetary policy decisions into action involving a mass of technical detail. It is difficult to determine the borderline between monetary policy and monetary theory. Many theoretical principles imply or suggest decisions of policy. On frequent occasions policy decisions arise logically from the acceptance of certain theoretical principles, even though those reponsible for the actual decision may not neccessarily be aware of this. Very often monetary theories are elaborated in order to give theoretical justification for a preconceived monetary policy decision or proposal. Only too often, however, monetary theories – especially static monetary theories – are too far divorced from reality to be of practical use for guidance to monetary policy. They apply to hypothetical conditions elaborated for purely theoretical purposes. Moreover, the same theory is liable to lend itself for serving as a basis for different policies. Nevertheless, a thorough knowledge of monetary theory and its latest developments is essential as a background to monetary policy decisions.

The actual excution of details of a monetary policy is necessarily in the hands of Government officials or Central Bank officials whose concern lies entirely within the practical sphere, and who are not always able to appreciate the broad principles of the monetary policy they apply, let alone the theoretical principles serving as its background. Those responsible for decisions of monetary policy, on the other hand, may not necessarily be acquainted with all practical details the knowledge of which is indispensable not only for the execution of their policy but also for its planning. Such details may concern the money market, the foreign exchange market, practical banking, price control, etc. There must obviously be co-operation with practical men to bridge the gap. It is at times impossible to ascertain the point where policy begins and technique ends. There are, however, subjects which quite evidently come within the definition of technical details. For instance, official tactics in the foreign exchange market or money market are clearly distinguishable from strategy in those spheres. Nevertheless, the systematic application of certain tactics is often a matter for policy decision.

Within the broad category of monetary policy it is possible to distinguish subdivisions such as currency policy, credit policy, discount-rate to interest-rate policy, debt management policy, fiscal policy, open-market policy, reserve policy, foreign exchange policy, gold policy, price policy, foreign trade policy, incomes policy, etc. All these policies are subdivisions of monetary policy just as monetary policy itself is a subdivision of economic policy, and economic policy may be said to be a subdivision of public administration or social policy. Nevertheless, some of the policies enumerated above have aspects which fall outside the sphere of monetary policy. For instance, price policy may pursue the end of changing the level of certain groups of prices in relation to each other with some non-monetary object in view, Generally speaking, it is only if price policy aims at affecting the average price level, or those elements in the price level which determine the cost of living of the wage-earning classes, or which affect exports or imports, that it may be considered to be within the sphere of monetary policy.

According to a fairly widespread conception, decisions concerning fundamental changes in the monetary system are beyond the scope of monetary policy, which is supposed to be confined to the working of the system of the day. Under that conception a change in the Bank Rate or of the exchange parity of the currency is an act of monetary policy, but the adoption or abandonment of stable exchange parities or of exchange control is a change of the whole system and amounts therefore to a measure of monetary reform. There seems to be no justification for such discrimination. Often a fundamental change of the monetary system is brought about by decisions which at the time they are made are considered merely tactical decisions. Moreover, fundamental changes are usually undertaken with the object of influencing the immediate monetary situation. For instance, rigid parities may be abandoned in order to be able to expand credit more freely, or to be able to intervene in the foreign exchange market more effectively. In any event it is difficult to see into what category, other than that of monetary policy, decisions relating to changes in the system could be classed.

There is also some tendency in many quarters to discriminate between short-term and long-term monetary measures. But it is arguable that long-term tendencies are made up of short-term fluctuations, and that long-term trends can only be influenced through the medium of short-term fluctuations. It is only when official action is directed against some purely technical aspect of the monetary situation that the scope of this action can be claimed to be too narrow to come within our definition of monetary policy.

The monetary situation is liable to be influenced by private as well as by official action. An outstanding example of the former was the effort made by McKenna, Chairman of the Midland Bank, during the twenties, to bring about an expansion of credit by importing gold when such transactions could hardly be profitable. Banks in the United Kingdom are in a position to influence monetary policy by deciding to alter their conventional liquidity ratios, subject to a lower limit of $12\frac{1}{2}$ per cent. Hire-purchase finance companies may influence the monetary trend by attracting more deposits with the aid of higher desposit rates, thereby converting dorment deposits into active deposits and increasing the velocity of circulation of deposits, or by changing their terms of lending. Trade unions may influence the monetary trend materially by deciding whether or not to resist an official aiming at wages restraint.

Although these and similar decisions unquestionably affect

the monetary situation, they cannot be considered to come within the scope of monetary policy – which to our mind implies official decision or action - unless they are inspired by official policy. If we were to accept the principle that private decision or action may also constitute monetary policy, it would be impossible to draw a borderline. After all, the attitude of each firm or individual in deciding whether to spend or save, whether to borrow or lend, whether to cut prices or hold for higher prices, whether or not to resist paying high prices or wages, etc., is liable to affect the monetary situation. Decisions taken by large firms or wealthy individuals are, of course, liable to produce a more pronounced effect than those of the average businessman, consumer or wage-earner. The effect of the decisions of any one of us many be infinitesimal, but the combined effect of action by millions of individuals or thousands of firms, or the attitude of certain categories of producers or consumers, may well be so strong as to defeat the object of the official policy, or, alternatively, to support it effectively. Indeed, the effectiveness of official policies very often largely depends on the willingness of private firms and individuals or groups of individuals to allow themselves to be influenced by their desire to act in accordance with the public interest instead of following rigidly what they consider, rightly or wrongly, to be in accordance with their selfish private interest. Nevertheless, it would be absurd to regard as a decision of monetary policy an individual's decision whether to buy Savings Certificates or a television set. On the other hand, official decisions to exhort firms and individuals to take their decisions in accordance with public interest come within that category.

We are apt to think of monetary policy as something essentially national. There is, however, such a thing as an international monetary policy. To some extent, at any rate, that is not a Utopian dream but is already practical reality. In recent years it has greatly increased in importance. Within limits a large number of Governments have relinquished part of their power in the sphere of monetary policy, either through agreements with other Governments limiting that power, or by submitting to the authority of some international body. About this more will be said in Chapter 45. The aim which is regarded by many people as ideal is to give some international authority full powers to determine the world's monetary policy. It seems inconceivable, however, that such an ambitious object could be attained unless and until the nations are prepared to relinquish their sovereignty and submit to the will of some international Parliament and Government. As things are at present and as they are likely to remain for a long time, monetary policy is essentially national, Even the implementation of the Barber Plan would not make a fundamental difference in this respect, for once the additional tranches of SDRs. are allotted to the Central Banks of the participating countries their use would be decided by the Governments and Central Banks of the countries concerned.

The Werner Plan, aiming at the complete integration of the monetary systems of the European Economic Community, appears at the time of writing to be bordering on the Utopian.

There is, however, much co-operation in the international monetary sphere, incomparably more that at any other time in monetary history. But even to the extent to which major monetary policy decisions are at present subject to international consultations, negotiations or approvals, the Governments concerned always reserve the right to contract out of any arrangement which prevents them from exercising their full sovereignty in the monetary sphere. This means that their willingness to abstain from exercising freely the right to take monetary decisions may be treated as part of their national monetary policies.

International monetary policy in the form of mutual support, whether directly or through institutions such as the IMF, has made considerable progress since the end of the Second World War, and more especially since 1961 when a group of leading Central Banks came to an understanding to support each other's currencies systematically in given circumstances. Regional arrangements such as the Sterling Area, the Franc Area, the European Payments Union or the European Common

Market, have played an important part in the international-isation of monetary policy, even if countries participating in them have retained much of the independence of their monetary policies. More will be said about this subject in Chapter 45.

As the Radcliffe Report rightly states, monetary policy is necessarily moulded by the world in which it takes shape. 'The scope for its excercise is not invariable, and the aims which it is intended to serve, . . . and the technique which gives it effect are all conditioned by the facts of the economic situation and the ideas of the time.'

The present generation has witnessed many important changes of monetary policy, and is likely to witness many more, due partly to changes in the situation and partly to change in the attitude of official opinion, expert opinion, political opinion and public opinion towards the ends that monetary policy should pursue and towards the means with which it should pursue them.

Part Two

THE ENDS OF MONETARY POLICY

CHAPTER FIVE

Alternative Ends

IN Chapter 4 ideal monetary policy was defined as official effort to increase the advantages the community can derive from the operation of the monetary system or to reduce the disadvantages it is liable to suffer through it in the absence of such effort. It is simpler, however, to lay down such a broad rule than to determine the meaning of 'advantages' and 'disadvantages'. What may be regarded as an advantage or a disadvantage is largely a matter of opinion. If often depends on our point of view or on our interests. Admittedly, certain developments are on balance inherently advantageous or disadvantageous. Even so there remains the question of priorities. As we shall see in subsequent chapters, monetary policy may choose between many different ends. It can aim at achieving various advantages or preventing various disadvantages.

Very often the monetary authorities are confronted with the choice between alternative ends. No dilemma arises when several ends can be achieved by the same means. For instance, credit expansion can serve the ends of stimulating trade, raising prices or preventing them from falling, and lowering interest rates. Assuming that those in charge of monetary policy are in favour of all these ends, or at any rate are not against any of them, their task is simple. Their difficulties begin when they are in favour of some ends and opposed to others. They may be in favour of stimulating trade and of lowering interest rates, but they may be opposed to a rise in prices. In such a situation they have to decide whether it is more important to forgo the advantages of a trade expansion and cheap money for the sake of avoiding a rise in prices, or whether they are prepared to sacrifice stability of prices for the sake of stimulating trade and lowering interest rates.

The question of priorities among the ends of monetary policy assumes considerable importance when the alternative ends to be pursued are incompatible with each other or conflict with each other. As we saw from the above example, certain ends can be pursued only at the expense of other ends. Very often certain advantages can be achieved by monetary policy only at the cost of sacrificing other advantages or submitting to disadvantages in some other direction.

The first step by those responsible for the shaping of monetary policy, and by those who wish to take an intelligent interest in it, is to form a clear idea about the range of choice between its various ends. It is impossible for anyone who has not studied the subject systematically to realise the wide variety of uses to which monetary policy can be put. Even amongst those who have spent their lives in the theoretical study of monetary policy or in its practical application, there may be many who have never deemed it necessary to elaborate a comprehensive list of its possible ends. They may not be unaware of the manifold uses of monetary policy. But they do not consciously weigh the arguments for and against any monetary decision according to the way in which it is liable to affect all the diverse ends. Only too often they are only concerned with the particular end that is supreme in their minds. Yet it is of the utmost importance that the effects of their monetary policy from the point of view of all the alternative ends should be borne in mind.

There is no universally accepted or acceptable set of rules about the point of view from which the conflicting requirements of various ends of monetary policy should be weighed against each other. Economists may well lay down the law about the ideal solution in what they regard as an ideal world. Statesmen and administrators, however, must allow for practical consider-ations, having regard to the changing and often conflicting needs of our imperfect world. Their emphasis has to shift between various monetary, fiscal, economic, social, political and other objectives. Monetary 'purists' may attach the utmost importance to the maintenance of the stable value of money irrespective of the disadvantages such a policy entails in the economic, social or political sphere. Monetary policy, however, does not exist in a vacuum, but forms part of the much broader system of public administration. Those in charge of monetary policy are not theoretical purists but practical men. While they may listen to economists about the ideal ends that their monetary policy should pursue, they usually allow their decisions to be influenced, rightly or wrongly, by considerations of practical expediency.

Only too frequently the choice does not even rest with the monetary authorities, that is, Central Banks and Treasuries. Their hand is forced by policy decisions on the highest level, to sacrifice the end of monetary stability for the sake of meeting the requirements of national defence or for some other consideration that rightly or wrongly takes precedence over monetary considerations. In time of war military ends must prevail over any others, though even then the Government must bear in mind economic, social and political considerations in shaping its monetary policy. Failure to do so is liable to react unfavourably on the military situation, by causing a decline of resources available for vital imports, or a fall in the output, or by generating widespread discontent as a result of a sharp rise in prices.

In time of peace, too, politicians upon whom major monetary policy decisions rest often allow themselves to be influenced in their choice between priorities, by their desire to ensure adequate support in Parliament or in the country. To that end they may be tempted to reject the advice given by experts and pursue ends which are not necessarily in accordance with the best interests of the community. They may be tempted to sacrifice long-range benefits for the sake of immediate improvements, only too often out of sheer political opportunism.

Emphasis on alternative ends of monetary policy is liable to change in the course of time. The priority of certain ends may give way to the priority of other ends as a result of the development of the economy or of the development of economic science, or even of a change in the fashion of thinking. The emphasis may be shifted through a change in social policy or in the political balance of power. Monetary policy is subject to the influence of passing fashions as well as to fundamental trends, not only in the choice of its means but also in the pursuit of its ends. In the thirties revival of trade was the principal end; in the post-war period full employment, economic growth and monetary stability were waging an incessant battle for the priority. In 1963 the ends of full employment and of economic growth came to be given top priority in Britain, at the expense of the ends of preventing inflation and balancing international payments.

No monetary policy, however well conceived, however skilfully executed, can reasonably be expected to serve all the conflicting ends adequately. Those who determine the ends of monetary policy are constantly faced by dilemmas. They may sacrifice some ends for the sake of others. Or they may seek to strike a compromise between their conflicting requirements. Or they may try to serve the various ends in turn.

There can be no rigid line of distinction between the ends of monetary policy and its means. For one thing, whether or not the achievement of certain ends in certain circumstances is practicable depends on the means the monetary authorities are able and willing to employ to achieve those ends. There is bound to be a great deal of overlapping between ends and means. Many ends are at the same time means towards other ends. In a way, all monetary, economic, social or political ends are, or ought to be, merely means towards the supreme end of human happiness. Nevertheless, it is possible to avoid confusion between ends and means by distinguishing between them according to the main emphasis in the minds of those in charge of monetary policy. A reduction in the price level may be aimed at for its own sake or it may be aimed at for the sake of increasing exports. In given circumstances it may seem reasonable to class it among the ends rather than the means of monetary policy. Such classification may be arbitrary, but this need not give any cause for difficulties provided that we adhere to it consistently.

It is tempting to compare the distinction between the ends and the means of monetary policy with the distinction between military strategy and tactics. Even in the military sphere the borderline between the two is most indistinct. If we were to attempt to adapt the terms 'strategy' and 'tactics' to the sphere of monetary policy, we should inevitably encounter difficulties. We could not use 'strategy' as being synonymous with the pursuit of ends and 'tactics' as being synonmous with the application of means. The choice of the means for the execution of monetary policy would very often come under the heading of strategy. Only the technical details of its application would always come within the meaning of tactics. Thus a decision to expand credit would be regarded as a decision of strategy. It is the decision whether it should be expanded by means of lowering interest rates or through open-market operations or through debt de-funding that could be regarded as a matter of tactics. Indeed, it is open to question whether many technical details which would come under tactics could be regarded as belonging to the sphere of monetary policy at all.

The best way of determining the range of the ends of monetary policy is to enumerate and describe the types of policy that may be regarded as concerning wholly or mainly ends and not means. We propose to do this in the ensuing chapters.

CHAPTER SIX

Adoption of Money

THE adoption of a monetary system by the tribal or State authority, or the recognition – expressly or by implication – of one that had developed spontaneously on private initiative, constituted the earliest end of monetary policy. All acts of active monetary policy originated from this end. The provision of a technical device which greatly facilitated all economic activities and which became a necessity after a community had reached a certain stage in its progress constituted an act of incalculable importance. Very often the primitive State authority adopted a purely passive attitude: it confined itself to allowing money to develop for some time unaided by official action. Even in such instances, sooner or later a stage was bound to be reached at which the State authority had to come to a deliberate decision whether to allow the monetary system to develop, and, if so, whether it should intervene to encourage its development and to confirm, regulate, safeguard or adjust the system.

To appreciate the significance of this decision we must cast our minds back to distant periods of pre-history or early history, before a monetary system had developed. It has often been suggested – not only by economists and economic historians but even by some anthropologists who ought to know better – that communities without some rudimentary form of money have never yet been found. This assertion is in striking conflict with factual evidence about the early periods of some historical races, and even more with what we know about primitive communities in recent periods. There are, in fact, many known instances of communities in which it has so far been impossible to find any evidence of the use of any kind of money up to a certain stage in their evolution. Admittedly this does not conclusively prove that they did not possess a monetary system. Possibly a more thorough investigation might produce evidence indicating the existence of some primitive form of money that has so far escaped our attention. But on the basis of evidence at present available those communities must be regarded as having been moneyless at one time. Those who deny that there have never been moneyless communities are entitled to insist that final judgment should be reserved pending closer investigation. They are not justified, however, in stating categorically that moneyless communities have never been found. The onus of proving the existence of money in communities which are at present claimed to have been moneyless rests upon them.

Everything depends, of course, on what we mean by money. If we apply a narrow and rigid definition it is, of course, possible to quote a very large number of historical and ethnological instances of moneyless communities. Many authors are inclined to define money in accordance with modern usage. On the basis of such a definition it inevitably follows that many primitive communities in recent times and civilised communities during early historical periods, should be described as moneyless. They had no money in the modern sense of the term any more than they had government, or religion, or legislation, in the modern sense of these terms. The other extreme is represented by the school of thought which applies an unduly elastic and loose definition of money, as a result of which any object which is used in barter transactions more frequently than other objects is claimed to be the currency of the community concerned. On such a basis there is bound to be found a 'currency' in practically every community in the same way as there is bound to be an oldest inhabitant in every village. However, in some instances at any rate the absence of money has been sufficiently firmly established to satisfy all but the most extreme school favouring an elastic definition.

For the purpose of this book money may be defined as an object or unit conforming in a reasonable degree to some standard of uniformity, used for reckoning and making payments and accepted with the ultimate intentions of using it for making payments. Many readers would probably prefer different definitions, but it does not really matter so long as they know that the term is employed in the above sense in this book. A moneyless community, for our purposes, is one where there is no money in this sense of the term.

The absence of money in a community may be due to a wide variety of reasons. The following are some of these:

(1) Low standard of intelligence.
(2) Absence of an adequate sense of values.
(3) Low stage of economic development.
(4) Absence of a system of private property.
(5) Existence of a more or less totalitarian planned economy.
(6) Religious objection to the use of money.
(7) Existence of closed self-sufficient economic units.
(8) Extreme distrust of the monetary system.

We need not concern ourselves with instances in which the absence of money was due to the prevalence of a low standard of intelligence or low stage of development. There were, however, a number of instances in which the communities concerned were sufficiently developed for the use of money but abstained from using it as a matter of deliberate policy. The earliest known instance of this kind was that of ancient Egypt. Until a comparatively advanced phase of its history it was moneyless in the sense that it possessed no medium of exchange, even though it had an abstract unit of account on the basis of which barter was transacted. The value of goods and services exchanged against each other was reckoned on the basis of a unit of weight of copper. But copper was merely an abstract standard of value and was not used regularly in payment for goods and services. Since ancient Egypt had reached a very advanced stage of civilisation and of statecraft, it seems reasonable to assume that the absence of a monetary system was due not to ignorance or to indifference of the State authority towards the existence or non-existence of money, but to deliberate policy preventing its adoption. Indeed, the Egyptian

State authority was firmly opposed to the introduction of coinage for a long time after its adoption by other Mediterranean countries. Its attitude comes within our definition of a passive monetary policy.

A more recent and more circumstantial historical instance of deliberate exclusion of money from the economic system was provided by evidence concerning the Inca Empire before the Spanish conquest of Peru. Prior to the arrival of Pizarro's army, no money had been in use in the country. Although it possessed exceptionally rich gold and silver resources, those metals were not used for monetary purposes. The Inca Empire was a perfect example of a collectivist totalitarian State where every phase of the economic activities of the population was strictly regulated by the State authority. The central administration at Cuzco determined in minute detail what everybody had to produce and how the output should be allocated. There was no need for money in connection with the production or distribution of goods. Producers of goods had to surrender a fixed proportion of their output to the authorities and the latter provided for the requirements of those who did not take a direct part in production or those engaged in public works which were executed with conscript labour. There was no profit motive and no individual initiative. Wages and salaries as such were unknown. Accumulated possessions were redistributed from time to time. In the circumstances there could be no scope for the use of a medium or exchange or a standardised store of value. There was a limited amount of barter, but there was no evidence of the use of any unit of account, let alone means of payment. The country's large supply of precious metals was used solely for ornamental or industrial purposes. The whole economic system was planned on the basis of elaborate statistics collected by the central administration. Even more than in the case of ancient Egypt the absence of money was due to deliberate policy.

Another instance in which the State authority deliberately abstained from adopting money was the Jesuit Republic of Paraguay during the sixteenth and seventeenth centuries. The

Jesuits established a benevolent dictatorship in Paraguay in order to safeguard the population against the cruelty and rapacity of the *conquistadores* and of the adventurers who usually followed in their wake. They transacted a certain amount of foreign trade with the aid of money but organised the internal economy of the country on a planned moneyless basis. The system continued to a large degree even after the Jesuits had lost their administrative authority. Barter continued to prevail right to the end of the eighteenth century, and all salaries and taxes were payable in kind. There was not even a unit of account to facilitate barter, which was based on fixed lists of the exchange values of goods in terms of other goods.

The system of the Jesuit Republic of Paraguay, under which money was used for foreign trade but not for domestic requirements, had many precedents in medieval Europe. The history of that period abounded in instances of closed economies which were for all internal purposes moneyless. Many large monsteries and baronial estates were such economic units. They were practically self-sufficient and under an authoritarian regime their production and distribution was planned without the use of money. Everybody had definite functions to perform, not in return for payment in money but as a duty to the community, which in return provided them with what they needed. There were similar closed economies in more recent periods in Latin America, where certain large estates – the *pueblo* and the *hacienda* – achieved almost complete self-sufficiency and no money was used in their internal economies.

More recently certain religious communities, especially in North America, operated moneyless systems. Some such communities are still in existence. They are closed economies the members of which regard themselves and each other as members of a large family within which everyone contributes his share of the work and everyone gets his share of the result.

After the Communist Revolution of 1917 in Russia it was expected for some time that the Soviet regime would adopt a moneyless economy. This at any rate was inferred from the way in which the existing monetary system was reduced to absurdity through extreme inflation. That was done, however, out of sheer necessity, rather than out of deliberate policy, owing to the impossibility of balancing the Budget amidst the prevailing chaotic conditions. During the period when paper money became utterly depreciated and discredited Russia was practically moneyless, though in various localities some limited primitive media of exchange or standards of value came to be adopted spontaneously without State approval. After the end of the Civil War, and with the consolidation of political and economic conditions, a monetary system was established which, in outward form at any rate, conformed to a high degree to the systems in operation in capitalist countries.

The extreme depreciation of the currency after the Second World War under the Communist-controlled regime in Hungary is said to have been a matter of deliberate policy the object of which was to wipe out all 'bourgeois' wealth and incomes. The aim of the alleged official policy could not have been, however, the elimination of the monetary system as such, but merely the elimination of the existing currency and its replacement by a newly created currency. It must also be remembered that inflation in anti-Communist Greece or Nationalist China was not very much more restrained than in Communist Hungary.

While some Socialist writers flirt from time to time with the idea of a moneyless community, the achievement of that aim cannot be regarded as forming an integral part of Socialist or Communist policy. Karl Marx himself regarded the idea as Utopian. Indeed, it has always been one of the favourite ideas of those who have elaborated Utopian systems. Sir Thomas More himself envisaged his Utopia as a moneyless community. In order to discredit gold and make it unsuitable for monetary use he suggested that it should be used as a material for the production of degrading objects. such as fetters or certain humble household utensils. On the other hand, Robert Owen's system, which was put into operation to a very limited extent during the early part of the nineteenth century, cannot be classed among the planned moneyless economies, since it merely aimed at the substitution of labour tickets for the conventional form of money. For all practical purposes these labour tickets were money under a different name.

Decisions of the authorities in any of the moneyless communities to adopt money or to abstain from opposing its spontaneous development constituted an act of monetary policy. As we said above, sooner or later in the course of economic evolution the State authority of each community must have taken some such decision. This does not necessarily mean that in each instance the chief of the tribe, or the king and his advisers, decided after careful deliberation in favour of adopting money or allowing it to develop. Such a conception would be as unrealistic as that of Rousseau's *Contrat Social*, which assumed that early communities decided by general agreement the form of their respective social systems. Things did not happen that way either in the social or in the monetary sphere. The evolution of money was largely a gradual and unconscious process, the significance of which was probably not grasped for a long time by those witnessing it.

It seems reasonable to assume that in the overwhelming majority of instances there was originally no deliberate decision by the State authority to establish a monetary system or to sanction in so many words a monetary system that had developed on private initiative. What must have happened in the very large majority of instances was that at a given stage the State authority came to assist in the adoption or development of a monetary unit by decreeing that certain payments, such as taxation, tribute, fines, blood money, etc., must be made in the form of standardised objects, or that, if made in other forms, they should be reckoned on the basis of some standardised unit of account. Presumably long before the authorities deliberately adopted such media of payment or units of account, the objects or units in question had already been in widespread use on private initiative for the purpose of religious sacrifices or tribute, blood money, the payment of bride price, or in other non-commercial transactions. The earliest monetary policy – if it could be described as such – consisted probably of the official supervision of the quantity and quality of objects adopted on private initiative. There is evidence of such intervention in respect of metallic money from a very early period in Asia Minor and Greece.

According to the classical conception of economic history, money is supposed to have developed through the progress of division of labour and the resulting complexity of trade, which made barter increasingly cumbersome and inconvenient. In my *Primitive Money* I sought to refute this theory on the ground that during early phases of economic evolution non-commercial payments such as those mentioned above were incomparably more important than the limited amount of barter that was transacted. I took the view that long before the progress of commerce and specialisation in production through advanced division of labour had reduced barter to absurdity, some standardised monetary objects or units must have been in use for non-commercial payments, and that owing to the regular demand for such objects for those purposes they had become eminently suitable for eventual adoption as a medium of exchange.

It seems probable that in many instances long before that stage was reached the tribal or State authority deemed it necessary to intervene in some form. In all probability there was no question of deliberately decreeing that the objects in question should be used as money. They were presumably recognised officially as such by implication, through some measure under which it was made compulsory for members of the community to make or accept certain payments in the form of those objects, or to reckon them in terms of the units employed in transactions with the State authority or with one another. It was probably only at a relatively advanced stage that legislation was enacted giving the means of payment in question a formal status as money. The monetary use of barley and silver in Babylonia, for instance, was regulated legally by the Code of Hammurabi towards the end of the twenty-first century B.C., but there is documentary evidence of their much earlier joint monetary use under the Dynasty of Akkad towards the beginning of the twenty-eighth century B.C.

It seems reasonable to assume that in most instances when we encounter evidence in the form of legislation regulating the use of money, whether in Babylonia, the Hittite Empire or ancient China, the laws adopted did not actually establish the monetary system but merely confirmed substantially an existing state of affairs. They regulated and legalised some actual practices which must have been in force for a considerable time before the State authority came to consider it necessary to intervene. Its intervention constituted, nevertheless, a most important act of monetary policy, a landmark in the monetary history of the country concerned. Indeed, it is possible to argue – as many authors do – that it was not until this stage had been reached that money came into existence. It is in this question-begging sense that Knapp's *State Theory of Money* is entitled to claim that 'money is the creature of law'.

The adoption of coinage in Lydia by King Gyges in the early part of the seventh century B.C. was by far the most important act of monetary policy in the ancient period, and indeed one of the most important events in the history of monetary policy. There had probably been some primitive forms of money in existence in Lydia before that decision. Nor were the sealed electrum dumps of Gyges the first instances of the monetary use of sealed ingots. The sealing of ingots to guarantee their weight or fineness is believed to have originated in Cappadocia, a dependency of Assyria, towards the end of the third millennium B.C. Such ingots, bearing the seal of a magistrate, were regularly employed in commercial transactions. There were also sealed ingots circulating in Babylonia during the same period, but there is no evidence that the guarantee implied by the seals was that of the Central Government. It seems more probable that it was given by cities, temples or merchants of standing.

Notwithstanding these precedents, the adoption of coinage in Lydia, and its almost simultaneous adoption in the Greek city-state of Argos and also in ancient China, constitutes a most important landmark in the evolution of monetary policy. It is the first clear instance of a policy which has remained in force right up to our day, under which the State authority does not confine itself to the approval of some existing currency or even to decreeing its creation, but takes it on itself actually to provide the community with a standardised medium of exchange. Henceforth this came to be considered as forming part of the functions of the State, although in many communities during the medieval period the right to mint coins was often ceded to private interests, and during the modern period the issue of paper money was ceded to banks of issue.

It must be borne in mind, however, that the power of the State to adopt a monetary system or to maintain it is not unlimited. It is impossible to force a monetary system on a community which is not ready for its adoption or which does not trust the money chosen by the State authority. In many instances throughout history communities relapesd into natural economy as a result of an extreme depreciation of the currency, notwithstanding the effort of the State authority to maintain it in monetary use. This is but one of the innumerable instances to show that monetary policy is far from being all-powerful.

Modern colonising powers which tried to force primitive communities to adopt a monetary system encountered at times considerable difficulties. It was not until the economic and cultural development of these communities had reached a relatively advanced stage that they began to respond to these efforts. The monetary system, in order to be acceptable and in order that it should work satisfactorily, must bear some relation to the economic and cultural background, and this must be borne in mind by the State authority in its decision to adopt a monetary system.

In itself a decision by the State authority to adopt a monetary system was not necessarily sufficient to ensure the achievement of that end. It was necessary to enact some form of law and to enforce it. The practical use of the monetary object by the State authority for making and accepting payments in itself went a long way towards ensuring the adoption of money. Various ways in which money was made more suitable to fulfil its functions – the adoption of coinage was one of these ways – also reinforced the decision to adopt money. It was not, however, enough to ensure the adoption of money. On many occasions throughout history the Governments had to pursue a policy to ensure that the money of their choice remained in monetary use, in face of a strong inclination on the part of the community to reject it and either to revert to natural economy or to adopt spontaneously some unauthorised form of money. Measures to force the community to retain the legal money in monetary use, or decisions to replace the discredited money by some new money, were adopted on many occasions by the State authorities in pursuing the end of imposing on the community a money of their choice.

CHAPTER SEVEN

Choice of Monetary System

THE choice of a monetary system is a monetary policy decision of the utmost importance. To a very large extent it predetermines the ends of the monetary policy which have to be pursued once the system chosen by the State authority has become operative. The decision whether to choose a scarce or a plentiful object to serve as currency is bound to influence the basic monetary trend. In primitive communities the monetary object chosen was in a large number of instances something which could not be produced within the community and which was bound to have therefore a scarcity value. For instance, in many African communities salt was for a long time the favourite medium of exchange because the demand for it usually exceeded the available supply. In various Pacific islands the shell currency in monetary use consisted of shells which had to be imported from some remote island in preference to those which could be picked up on the local beaches.

It would be a mistake, however, to conclude from such instances that primitive monetary policy always aimed at choosing a monetary system that tended to keep money scarce – that, in the jargon of economists, it was necessarily 'deflationary'. For in a very large number of instances monetary policy pursued exactly the opposite end. It was the staple product of the country which was selected for monetary use. By such means an adequate and even plentiful supply of the monetary object was ensured, and a steady and substantial additional demand was created for the staple product of the community.

In many ethnological and historical instances the same

communities adopted systems that combined the use of some relatively scarce object with that of some relatively plentiful one. Thus in the monetary system of Babylonia the inadequate monetary supply of silver was supplemented by the monetary use of barley, which was the staple product of the fertile plains between the Tigris and the Euphrates. One of the reasons why during most of the course of history more than one object was used for monetary purposes was precisely the inadequacy of the quantity of the object which was considered the most suitable for that purpose.

In my *Primitive Money* I give a detailed account of the very large number of objects or units chosen for monetary use. The use of more than one object in the same community resulted in an almost infinite variety of combinations. In addition the use of the same object or unit gave rise to several different systems according to the way it was applied for monetary purposes. In a large number of instances the choice was made spontaneously and largely unconsciously by the community itself. Nevertheless, as we saw in the last chapter, the tribal or State authority sooner or later played a decisive role, if not in choosing the system at any rate in officially recognising, confirming and regulating it. At a more advanced phase the choice and the change of the monetary system had become increasingly a matter of monetary policy decision, although in many instances the hands of the State authority were forced by spontaneous monetary developments that preceded it decision.

Generally speaking, it is true to say that soon after the stage was reached at which metals came to be used as money the State authority had come to play a decisive role in the choice of the monetary system. Monetary policy in countries of the ancient Mediterranean civilisation aimed, whenever possible, at the monetary use of a metal which happened to be produced in the country concerned. It was not by accident that lead was the original currency of Assyria. The reason why silver was preferred to gold by the Semitic races in Western Asia – to such an extent that in Semitic languages the same word was used for 'money' as for 'silver' – was that these countries did not possess any gold resources. The coinage adopted in Lydia during the first half of the seventh century B.C. consisted of punch-marked dumps of electrum because in Lydia the gold ore had a silver content and metallurgy did not until later reach a sufficiently advanced stage to separate the two metals. On the other hand silver was adopted as the principal currency of Athens because of the rich silver deposits at Laurium. Both Persia and Macedonia chose gold for their coinage because they happened to be rich in that metal.

There is at least a possibility that the reason why Sparta selected iron for her clumsy currency was not really the pursuit of a deliberate policy of austerity but the fact that the Peloponnesus contained the most important iron mines in ancient Greece. The choice of copper in Sicily and in early Rome was again connected with the nature of the metal resources available locally. Nor would the ancient Britons have used sword-shaped iron bars as their currency at the time of Julius Caesar if they had had to import the metal for that purpose.

At a later stage of monetary history gold and silver became universally adopted as monetary metals in most civilised countries, irrespective of whether they were able to mine the metals at home or whether they had to depend on imports for their monetary supplies. Both gold and silver were used simultaneously for monetary purposes in many countries from the seventh century B.C. to the nineteenth century A.D. There remained, however, wide scope for monetary policy decisions to determine which of the two metals should be the main currency and which should act as a secondary currency. This did not always depend on the authorities, but in thory at any rate they had the initiative in influencing the relative monetary roles of the two metals according to the figure at which they fixed the gold-silver ratio. Decisions to alter that ratio, to debase the coinage or to fix the terms of re-coinage went beyond mere changes in the monetary units. They very often resulted in fundamental if temporary changes of the monetary system, because silver was replaced by gold as the main monetary metal or vice versa. The highly involved bimetallist system provided a wide scope for such fundamental changes.

The advent of paper money introduced yet another element of complication and further widened the scope of monetary policy in respect of the choice of the system. During the course of the eighteenth century most Governments decided to adopt paper money to supplement their coinage. The question whether it should be issued by the Government or by privileged banks, which was an important policy decision, had to be settled, just as in earlier centuries the State authority had to decide whether minting should remain in its own hands or whether this right should be ceded to private interests.

The authorities had also to choose between the systems of convertible and inconvertible paper money. Originally most note issues were intended to be convertible, and their purpose was to serve not as a non-interest-bearing Government loan but merely as a convenient device to facilitate monetary circulation. In most instances, from the medieval experiences of China onward, suspension of convertibility was not the result of any preconceived deliberate policy. There were instances, however, in which the suspension of specie payments was decided upon as a matter of expediency in preference to other measures which might have arrested the decline of the metallic reserve. In particular, Russia and the Austro-Hungarian Monarchy in the nineteenth century provided instances of such policy decisions as a result of which the system of convertible paper money was replaced by one of inconvertible paper money. Restoration of convertibility is yet another policy decision changing the whole monetary system in operation in the community concerned.

Decisions to abandon the bimetallic standard, under which both gold and silver served as a basis for the currencies with a fixed ratio between them, and to replace it by the gold standard, were made by most Governments of the Western civilisation during the latter part of the nineteenth century. This was an important policy decision and was accompanied in many countries by bitter political controversy. In the United

States a Presidential election was fought over it in the nineties, and the slogan of Bryan, the candidate favouring bimetallism: 'You shall not crucify mankind upon a cross of gold' will long be remembered.

Many important countries had adopted some form of gold standard by the end of the nineteenth century, though relatively few countries had a fully effective gold standard in actual operation, in the sense in which the system was defined before 1914. In many instances before the First World War a system was chosen under which the notes remained inconvertible but the exchange value of the currency was maintained stable in relation to gold. This system is loosely called the gold exchange standard, though properly speaking that term should be reserved for the system in which the monetary authorities have to convert their currency at a fixed rate into another currency which itself is on the gold standard. The Indian rupee before 1914 provided the classic example of that system. Many countries were on a gold exchange standard in fact if not in law, because, although their Central Bank was under no legal obligation to convert its notes into some currency that was convertible into gold, in practice it intervened in the foreign exchange market whenever this was necessary in order to maintain the national exchange stable in relation to the convertible currencies. In a number of countries before 1914 a 'limping standard' was in force under which silver was allowed to retain a certain limited role. For instance, in France the Central Bank reserved the right to pay out silver instead of gold in certain circumstances when the French authorities were anxious to moderate the drain on the Bank of France's gold reserve. The choice of one or other type of the gold standard and its effective adoption constituted one of the major ends of monetary policy.

After the First World War various types of gold standard were adopted in various countries. Indeed, when in the early thirties the League of Nations published a volume containing the details of the gold legislation of all member countries, it was found that there were very few in which the rules were absolutely identical. The reconstruction of the currencies in a number of countries under the auspices of the League's Finance Committee introduced a certain degree of uniformity, because the adoption of certain rules regarding the form of gold standard to be applied was made one of the conditions for the grant of financial assistance by the League. Even so there were minor discrepancies.

Britain decided in 1925 to adopt the 'gold bullion standard' as distinct from the full gold standard with gold coins circulating freely as before 1914. This meant that the notes were not convertible into coins, but holders of sterling were entitled to buy gold from the Bank of England for shipment overseas, or for keeping on deposit with the Bank on account of foreign holders. A number of countries adopted either the same system or the gold exchange standard. The Central Banks of the latter, instead of aiming at building up large gold reserves of their own, endeavoured to accumulate large foreign exchange reserves consisting mainly of currencies on a gold basis such as sterling and dollars. The Central Banks were buyers of dollars or sterling whenever an excessive demand tended to cause an unwanted appreciation of the national currency, and they were sellers whenever an excessive supply threatened to depreciate it.

The pre-1914 ideal was the adoption and maintenance of the automatic gold standard under which equilibrium was maintained as a result of the effect produced by any deviation of a currency from its equilibrium level, whether as a result of an appreciation or depreciation of the currency or as a result of a change of the differential between the price levels of the countries concerned. If a Government allowed economic expansion in its country to proceed too far, the effect on its balance of payments caused a depreciation of its exchange and a decline of its gold reserve. That again entailed a contraction in the volume of its currency and credit, checking and reversing the expansionary trend. A restrictive policy produced the opposite effect on the price level, the balance of payments, the exchange rate and the gold reserve, the increase of which automatically reversed the basic trend towards contraction.

After the First World War this automatic system came to be abandoned, however, and came to be replaced to a varying degree by a managed gold standard. Under it Central Banks aimed at modifying or resisting the natural effects that gold movements had tended to produce. The contraction of expansion of credit which an outflow or an inflow of gold tended to cause was neutralised with the aid of a variety of policy devices.

The adoption of some form of gold standard by most countries constituted an important policy decision, replacing as it did silver currencies, or bimetallist currencies, or inconvertible paper currencies by more or less convertible and stable currencies. Decisions in the opposite sense were taken during the thirties when, following on the suspension of the gold standard by Britain in 1931, most countries adopted fluctuating paper currencies during subsequent years. Many currencies were made inconvertible in the full sense of the term. Not only did the monetary authorities cease to convert them into gold and foreign exchanges either at a fixed rate or at a fluctuating rate, but residents of the countries were forbidden by law to acquire gold or foreign currencies.

This brings us to another important set of monetary policy decisions aiming at a fundamental change in the monetary system in force, namely, the adoption and removal of exchange restrictions interfering with the freedom to transfer money abroad. There is nothing new in that system. In my *History of Foreign Exchange* I gave a detailed account of how it had operated in various instances already during the Ancient period and the Middle Ages, when on many occasions restrictions were imposed on international movements of gold or silver and on exchange operations between national and foreign coins. Later these rules came to be supplemented by restrictions on transactions in foreign bills.

During the First World War and the period of inflation that followed it, many Governments adopted exchange restrictions. It was not until the thirties, however, that the system reached its full development. In this respect the choice of the Governments between the various systems of restricted currencies was even wider than in respect of their choice of the exact type of gold standard. Having decided in favour of the principle of exchange restrictions, the Governments had to decide on the nature and extent of those restrictions. They had to decide whether to forbid capital movements only, or whether to place under official control also exchange transactions arising from current foreign commerce. They had to decide if and to what extent free dealing in the open market in foreign exchange should be allowed to continue.

Again the authorities in many countries had to decide whether, having suspended free dealing in foreign exchanges, they should allocate the foreign exchanges required by importers and others for approved purposes, or whether they should adopt the 'exchange clearing' system invented in 1931. During the thirties a very large number of Governments in Central and Eastern Europe and also some Governments in Western Europe concluded such clearing agreements, the nature and operation of which will be explained briefly in Chapter 39. There was an endless variety in the terms of such agreements. The international aspects of the monetary system of some countries came to be based almost entirely on them. They were not always confined to relations between two countries. In addition to bilateral clearing systems some countries adopted triangular and multilateral systems under which three or more countries participated in the arrangement.

An almost infinite variety of multiple currency systems developed during the thirties and it continued in many countries after the Second World War. As a result of the limitation of the use of foreign exchanges for various purposes and in relation to various countries, different exchange rates came to be quoted for the same currency at any given moment The restrictions affecting this system were subject to frequent changes.

The thirties witnessed the development of currency areas under which a number of countries established closer monetary relations with each other than they had with the rest of the world. This system was not new. Currency unions had already existed in ancient Greece. They had existed before the First World War in the form of arrangements such as the Latin Monetary Union, the Scandinavian Monetary Union, etc. Those arrangements, however, amounted to little more than adopting identical official gold parities and in some cases identical names for the monetary units.

In 1932 the foundations were laid for the Sterling Area, which was quite a different system of currency union. In fact the system actually came into operation in September 1931, when, following on the suspension of the gold standard in Britain, practically all countries of the British Commonwealth decided to allow their currencies to fluctuate in terms of gold in sympathy with sterling in order to maintain rigidly stable relations with sterling. The Ottawa Conference of 1932 led to the formal establishment of the Sterling Area. In addition to stability in relation to sterling it created a certain uniformity of monetary policy in other respects. Subsequently, when after the outbreak of the Second World War Britain and other countries adopted exchange restrictions, the freedom of the exchange operations within countries of the Sterling Area was maintained and assumed considerable significance. Decisions to form such international monetary unions, to join existing unions or to relinquish membership of them constitute very important monetary policy decisions affecting the monetary system.

Another way in which Governments have to take monetary policy decisions is in respect to the extent to which actually operating systems are provided with legal foundations. Writers in the thirties learnt to discriminate between *de jure* stabilisation and *de facto* stabilisation, according to whether the exchange rate of the national currency is maintained stable by the Government with or without legal obligation to do so. Changes in the extent to which various types of currency are legal tender are also decisions resulting in changes in the monetary system. Decisions admitting or preventing the monetary use of foreign coins or notes formed yet another category of monetary policy decisions affecting the monetary system. In my *History of*

Foreign Exchange I give details of such decisions in the Middle Ages and during the sixteenth century, and also of more recent instances. After the Second World War sovereigns became a most important currency in Greece through the initiative of the public, but their monetary use was officially confirmed and regulated to a large degree by the Greek monetary authorities.

There are innumerable changes of detail decided upon by the monetary authorities, which are liable to modify the monetary system to some degree. These will be dealt with in later chapters covering the various aspects of monetary policy.

Adherence to the Bretton Woods system after the Second World War by submitting to the rules of the IMF constituted another monetary policy decision to choose a new monetary system. In theory it meant the acceptance of a more or less uniform system, though in practice the rules were not enforced equally rigorously. Even though the basic principle was the maintenance of stable parities – subject to changes in case of fundamental disequilibrium – some countries resorted to floating exchanges for prolonged periods. In principle, exchange control and multiple currency practices were outlawed, but in many instances the IMF raised no objections if weak countries failed to implement their undertakings or relapsed into their former unsound practices.

While under the Bretton Woods system member countries were supposed to adhere to the same system, and a number of them did adhere to it for prolonged periods, the difficulties arising from the resulting rigidity made many economists, politicians and bankers forget the much graver difficulties suffered during the inter-war period of currency chaos. They found themselves confronted with the choice between various degrees of rigidity and various degrees of elasticity.

To what extent is the selection of a particular monetary system an end in itself, and to what extent is it a means with the aid of which the Government intends to pursue some monetary policy? Beyond doubt, certain systems are at times selected because they are liable to make the pursuit of certain policies possible or even inevitable. Nevertheless, the importance of choosing a system which, in the Government's opinion, is best suited to the requirements of the country in prevailing circumstances is so overwhelming that the decision may rightly be claimed to pursue primarily that end, even if the adoption of the new system is liable to predetermine the subsequent pursuit of certain other ends. The restoration of the gold standard in Britain in 1925 was an end of monetary policies pursued ever since 1918 by Governments of all political parties. It compelled all Governments holding office between 1918 and 1931 to follow restrictionist monetary policies in order to be able to maintain the gold standard. All these policies were means to the end of maintaining the gold standard and restoring the pound to its pre-war parity and maintaining it there. On the other hand, it is conceivable that in other instances the gold standard was adopted as a means to the end of imposing a vigorous discipline on the economy of the country concerned, making the pursuit of a deflationary or at any rate anti-inflationary policy inevitable.

Likewise, it is conceivable that decisions in favour of choosing a system of flexible exchange were the result of a desire for an all-round loosening of economic discipline in a permissive society. Those taking the decision may have been inspired by the desire to be in a position to pursue anti-deflationary or inflationary policies. They retained their freedom to safeguard the stability of their currencies, but the choice of a much less rigid system provided much more temptation and opportunity for yielding to expansionist pressure for the sake of the popularity of accelerated growth.

CHAPTER EIGHT

Determining the Value of Money

THE determination of the value of the monetary unit has always been regarded by most people as one of the most important – if not *the* most important – ends of monetary policy. Beyond doubt the State authorities have considerable power in this sphere, though not nearly as much as was attributed to them by a school of thought that gained prominence during the early part of this century. The conception that the State is in a position to determine the value of money is not new. It appears in the writings of medieval authors who regarded the prince as all-powerful in this respect, as in so many others. In its modern form it originated G. F. Knapp's famous work *The State Theory of Money*. This much-quoted work emphasises the powers which the State possesses of ensuring the monetary use of the object of its choice and of determining the nominal value of the monetary unit irrespective of its intrinsic value. In all fairness to Knapp it must be admitted that it was not he but the interpreters of this theory who put forward the view that the State is in a position to determine not merely the choice of money and it nominal value, but also its purchasing power. This view misrepresented Knapp's basic theory, which does not go beyond claiming that the State was in a position to ensure the *validity* of some object chosen for monetary use. To claim this is something quite different from suggesting that the State has unlimited powers in determining the *value* of money.

Opponents of Knapp's theory, provoked by its exaggerated interpretation by its supporters, are inclined to fall into the opposite extreme. They flatly deny that the State has any powers at all to impose its will in face of economic trends which alone determine the value of money. They hold the State theory responsible for the German inflation during and after the First World War. According to them it was the belief in the omnipotence of the State in the monetary sphere, generated by Knapp's theory, that encouraged the German Government to embark upon an unlimited issue of paper money on the assumption that it would be in a position to maintain the value of the mark notes notwithstanding the increase in their quantity.

Critics of Knapp triumphantly pointed out that the disastrous collapse of the mark after the First World War conclusively proved the worthlessness of the State theory by showing how utterly helpless the State was in the face of major economic forces.

The truth lies between the two extreme views. Even though the capacity of the State to determine the value of money is far from absolute, it is in given circumstances very considerable. Its powers are not confined to choosing the money and ensuring that it is accepted in payment. The State is in a position to determine or influence the value of money to a large extent in more than one sense.

(1) *Choice of monetary unit.* The power to choose the currency gives the State a considerable power to determine the value of money. The State authority is in a position to decide whether objects or units of high or low value should serve as money. By this decision alone it can decide whether prices should be high or low in terms of the monetary unit. On the face of it this is merely a matter-of simple arithmetic. Whether the unit is, say, an ounce of silver or a pound of silver does not affect the value of silver coins, even though prices in the former case are sixteen times as high as in the latter. In reality, the magnitude of the unit does tend to affect the cost of living to some extent. This fact was discovered in West Africa when coins took the place of cowries as currency. Even the smallest coin was equivalent to a very large number of cowries, and prices of the cheapest goods and services rose to the minimum level which could be expressed in the lowest denomination of the new unit and which could be paid in the smallest coin in circulation.

In a much less flagrant instance, but much nearer home, the decimalisation of the currency in Britain did bring about some increase in prices as a result of the increase of the penny from 1/240th to 1/100th of a pound, and of the disappearance of the shilling as a monetary unit.

The State is, of course, in a position to issue moneys representing subdivisions or multiples of units for various requirements. During the Ancient period the most generally known unit was the talent, which was, however, a very large unit, so that only princes and the wealthiest members of the community were in a position to transact business in it. For the requirements of the less wealthy classes the State authority in various Eastern countries fixed the unit of the mina, and smaller units such as the drachma and the obol in Greece.

The need for the State authority to choose currencies of various values to circulate concurrently was realised at an early stage. In primitive communities we encounter many instances of the use of different moneys by different classes. In some of these instances there was practically no connecting link between these currencies, and price levels expressed in them were largely independent of one another. Certain goods could only be purchased against one or the other of the currencies. In other instances, however, the State authority determined the ratios between the various officially chosen or officially recognised currencies, and these ratios were often largely artificial and independent of economic considerations.

Indeed, such is the power of State authority in determining the value of monetary units that at times it could defy not only economic laws but even the laws of simple arithmetic. The Chinese Emperor Wang Mang, who ruled from A.D. 8 to 23, introduced a new copper coinage in which the smallest unit contained proportionately the largest amount of metal and each higher denomination contained proportionately less metal. The largest coin contained only one quarter per cent as much metal per unit as the smallest coin. Such abnormal ratios could of course, only be maintained with the aid of drastic penalties against those who refused to comply with the law. Even so, the system did not work very smoothly, and in A.D. 14 a new system was introduced in which the disproportion was considerably less pronounced, though the laws of arithmetic continued to be defied.

A more recent instance of the power of State authority to interfere with the arithmetic of the monetary system was found in the French Sudan by the German traveller Lenz during the 1880s. In Timbuktu eight times ten cowries had to be reckoned as 100, ten times eighty (nominally 100) was reckoned as 1,000, and so forth, so that what was called 100,000 was really only 64,000.

(2) *Choice of monetary material.* The power of the State authority to choose the monetary material and to determine the extent of its monetary use is bound to influence considerably the value of the material chosen. The monetary use of any object necessarily creates a very considerable additional demand for it. Unless it is accompanied by a corresponding increase in the output of the monetary object, its value in terms of goods and services is bound to rise considerably. What usually happens is that its monetary use tends to increase its value and its increase in value in turn tends to stimulate an increase in its production whenever that is possible. When the supply of the monetary material is limited, however, as in the case of the precious metals, the increase of its monetary use through State decisions necessarily entails an increase in its value. It is not generally realised that, although gold has a by no means inconsiderable value as a metal for industrial or ornamental purposes, it owes a very large part of its value to its widespread monetary use. But for the withdrawal of very large quantities of gold from the market for monetary requirements, its price would be considerably under its present level, in spite of the unquestionably high intrinsic value of the metal.

The claim is justified, therefore, that even gold owes a very large proportion of its value to monetary policy decisions by a large number of Governments. This fact was brought home very clearly by the heavy slump in the value of silver during the lifetime of the present generation. The slump was brought about during the inter-war period by monetary policy decisions in China and elsewhere to discontinue the use of silver as money. The extent to which its demonetisation during the late nineteenth and early twentieth centuries affected its value may be appreciated from the fact that while the proportion of the value of gold to that of silver from the Ancient period to the late nineteenth century varied within the approximate range from 1 to 8 to 1 to 15, its present proportion is about 1 to 38, having been even higher before the rise in silver during the sixties. Although the preceding slump was due in part to the increase in the output of silver through mining and metallurgical developments which lowered its cost and increased its quantity, to a large extent it was the consequence of monetary policy decisions. There can be no doubt that gold would suffer a slump in the event of monetary policy decisions curtailing or eliminating its present limited monetary use as reserves for international payments.

(3) *Maintenance of the value of the monetary unit.* Monetary policy plays a highly important part in defending the value of the monetary unit against adverse pressure. It is one of the principal duties of the State authority to try to safeguard the value of the national currency. The earliest steps taken to that end were measures against counterfeiting currency. Indeed, the main object of the adoption of coinage through affixing an official seal to pieces of monetary metal was to make debasement of that metal more difficult. It was not as if the State itself had insurmountable objections to debasement. That practice soon came to be regarded, however, as a profitable State monopoly. Polycrates of Samos brought it to a fine art in the sixth century B.C., and his example was followed by innumerable rulers during the Ancient and medieval periods and even in more recent centuries. Nevertheless, the State authority employed all its might to prevent debasement by private enterprise. It continued to do so after the adoption of paper money, the counterfeiting of which it has sought to prevent by the imposition of drastic penalties and by concluding international conventions ensuring co-operation between States. Of course

some Governments themselves are not averse to printing large quantities of paper money, or creating large quantities of paper credit, as an easy way of covering their Budgetary deficits, even though they are aware that in doing so they cause a fall in the value of that unit.

Some State authorities also endeavoured to uphold the value of their coinage by a relatively frequent replacement of worn coins and coins debased as a result of deliberate clipping. In many instances, however, it was considered profitable or expedient to lower the value of the new coins to the depreciated value of the coins in circulation. In other instances the State authorities decided in favour of restoring the old value of the coinage by bearing the loss on the exchange of good coin for bad. This was done by the British Government on Sir Isaac Newton's advice on the occasion of the re-coinage of 1693.

Monetary policy plays a very important part in defending the exchange value and the internal purchasing power of the national currency by a wide variety of means which will be discussed in detail in later chapters. Policy decisions to that end cover measures aiming at preventing an undue increase in the quantity of money and in the volume of purchasing power, moderating the effect of any inevitable increase of it on prices, safeguarding the exchange rates at an approved level, etc. To the extent to which these devices are practised successfully the State authority does indeed influence the value of money. The State has means at its disposal for defying, at least in part and temporarily, the economic forces making for a currency depreciation. Such measures include credit squeeze, Bank Rate change, fiscal devices, incomes policy, price control, rationing, exchange control, subsidies, official operations on the money markets, foreign exchange markets and commodity markets, borrowing abroad, or selling national assets abroad for the sake of bolstering up the exchange, etc. The frequent examples of prolonged suppressed inflation bear witness to the power of the state to influence the value of money.

As for the power of the State to bring about a deliberate depreciation in the value of the national currency, or to prevent an appreciation which would take place if natural tendencies were allowed to produce their effects, it is almost unlimited. There have been many instances in monetary history of debasements and devaluations, undertaken by the State authority not under irresistible pressure of economic forces nor as a legal confirmation of actual depreciations which had already taken place, but as a matter of deliberate monetary policy for the sake of financial or other advantages. In many other instances the official monetary policy successfully resisted tendencies which, if allowed to take their course, would have raised the purchasing power or the exchange rates of the national currency above the level approved by the authorities. Even on occasions on which Governments yield to economic pressure in favour of an unwanted appreciation of their currencies – the revaluation of the D.mark in 1961, 1969 and 1971 provided recent instances of this – it only means that they deemed it to be a smaller evil on balance than alternative solutions would have been. Both Germany and Japan revalued after prolonged resistance.

(4) *Changes in the value of monetary units.* One of the unquestionable merits of Knapp's theory is that it draws attention to the power of the State to fix the ratio between a new monetary unit and the monetary unit it replaces. When Britain, for instance, adopted the decimal system, under which the pound is equated to 100 pennies instead of 240, the Government enacted legislation adjusting outstanding liabilities of old pence in new pennies. The price level was determined immediately after the change by the ration between the old and the new unit. The nominal amounts in which prices are expressed was in the above instance 2·4 times higher than they had been immediately before the change. Needless to say, the State authority could not prevent an immediate rise or fall in prices following on the change if, as a result of the operation of economic forces, such rise or fall would have taken place in the absence of a change of the monetary unit. Indeed, a change in the unit itself did actually set into motion additional trends which affected the value of the new unit after the change. All

the Government could do was to define a new unit in terms of the old unit at the moment of the change, and to ensure that the payment of old liabilities contracted in terms of the old unit became dischargeable in terms of the new unit on the basis of the official ratio. When in France the metallic content of the franc was raised in 1960 from 2 to 200 milligrams of gold, prices, wages, debts, etc., in terms of new francs were reduced to 1:100 of those in terms of old francs. Almost immediately after the change, prices and wages, having been reduced to 1 per cent of their nominal amount, resumed their moderate rise.

During the period of metallic currencies the State authority was in a position to reduce the value of the unit by debasement or devaluation. This could assume various forms. The Government was in a position to issue coins with the same nominal value but containing less metal. This was done repeatedly in Rome during the Punic Wars and very frequently during the third and fourth centuries A.D. Or it could maintain the metallic content of the coins unchanged while decreeing that they be acceptable in debt settlement for larger amounts than before. The first known instance of such a measure was that of Solon in Athens in the sixth century B.C. Yet another method of changing the value of money through State action is the changing of the price at which the Mint accepts metals for coinage. The nominal value of coins in circulation was frequently 'called up' or 'cried up' during the Middle Ages and after; it was (less frequently) 'called down' or 'cried down'. Increasing and (less frequently) reducing the seignorage – that is, the profit charged by Governments for the coinage of the metals – was a favourite device throughout the Middle Ages and the two centuries that followed. England was one of the first countries to do away with seignorage and pay the full value of the monetary metals to those who delivered them to the Mint.

Changes in the value of the monetary units could be brought about by changing the gold–silver parity (the value of gold expressed in silver, or vice versa) in countries where both metals played a monetary role. The possibility of influencing the flow of bullion by changing the gold–silver ratio provided ample scope for monetary policy. If an ounce of gold in the Low Countries was equivalent to, say, thirteen ounces of silver, and the English authorities wanted to attract more gold, all they had to do was to raise the gold–silver ratio in England to, say, fourteen, to make it profitable to ship gold from Antwerp for sale to the Royal Mint in London. Such changes were of very frequent occurrence.

Although history produced many instances of drastic debasements of coinage, the extent of most of them was insignificant compared with the devaluations of paper currencies – except possibly those of the Roman denarius and the Egyptian drachma during the fourth century A.D. Paper money was first invented in China in the eleventh century. Its history is the history of a long succession of devaluations. Each one of them is evidence to show the power of the State to determine the value of money by changes in a downward direction.

John Law's experiment in France between 1718 and 1720 provided an unusual instance of changing the value of currency as a matter of monetary policy. His idea was to strengthen confidence in his paper money by trying to discredit gold and silver coins. He sought to achieve this end by frequent changes in the value of the coins in terms of paper money, as a contrast with the 'stability' of the nominal value of his notes. Between September 1719 and December 1720 he changed the value of gold coins on twenty-eight occasions and that of silver coins on thirty-five occasions in an effort to induce holders to rid themselves of such 'unstable' currency and seek safety in converting their coins into 'stable' notes. The disastrous failure of the experiment shows that monetary policy is helpless in face of economic forces brought about by large-scale inflation.

One of the most interesting instances of devaluation was provided by Austria during and after the Napoleonic Wars. In 1811 the florin notes were devalued to one-fifth of their original value, and in 1817 they were further devalued to two-fifths of their reduced value, so that twenty-five florins became reduced to two florins. Simultaneously with this devaluation a detailed schedule was issued indicating the rates at which debts contracted in the old currency at various times during the period of depreciation were to be repaid in the new currency. Allowance was made in this schedule for the degree of the actual depreciation of the flroin at the time when the debt was contracted. The object of this measure was to safeguard creditors against being victimised through the repayment of their claims in devalued currency. It tried to achieve a kind of rough justice – which is more than could be said about most other devaluations in monetary history.

The periods that followed both World Wars provided a large number of instances of the fixing of the value of currencies as a matter of policy. In Czechoslovakia, Yugoslavia, Romania and Poland, several different currencies were in circulation in the various territories taken over after the Armistice of 1918. It was one of the tasks of the monetary policies of the Governments concerned to unify the monetary system and to that end to fix a ratio between the various currencies. As a general rule that ratio was fixed not on the basis of the prevailing market exchange rates but in such a way as to secure an advantage to the peoples of the territories taken over by the countries concerned, by exchanging their notes at rates higher than the prevailing market rates. This is another instance of the power of the State authority to determine the value of a currency independently of the natural economic forces.

Changes decreed by Governments in the value of their national currencies have not always been in a downward direction. As we already pointed out above, there were many instances in monetary history of upward revaluations in connection with coinage reforms following a bad period of debasement. Both Sweden and Canada revalued their currencies after the Second World War, and in 1961 and 1969 Germany and Holland revalued their currencies. In 1971 a number of currencies were revalued. Instances of revaluations are, however, incomparably less frequent than those of devaluations, and the secular trend of the value of money over a period of centuries is distinctly downward. This is recognised and accepted by most Governments. They are, on the whole, inclined to abandon resistance to any persistent downward trend, and do not attempt to reverse it. One of the abortive attempts at swimming against the tide was that of Great Britain after the First World War, when the official monetary policy aimed at raising the value of sterling to its pre-war level of $4·86. This end was achieved in 1925, but within six years the Government felt impelled to abandon its efforts to maintain sterling at its pre-war level, and allowed it to depreciate in 1931.

Instances of monetary policy decisions resulting in changes in the value of currency could be multiplied almost indefinitely. Admittedly, in a large proportion of such instances the hands of the authorities were forced by powerful trends. Their action in devaluing or revaluing was the consequence of fundamental changes which could not be prevented or reversed without efforts involving major sacrifices. Even so there are a sufficient number of instances to show that to a very large extent Governments are the masters of the monetary destinies of their countries. Their decisions to change the value of their currencies often became inevitable as a result of the deliberate pursuit of economic, social or political policies, the importance of which, in their opinion, overshadowed purely monetary considerations. Very often Governments must have failed to foresee the consequences of such policies in the monetary sphere. In the majority of instances, however, a stage must have been reached some time or another when the Governments were confronted with the dilemma whether to pursue their various policies at the cost of monetary instability or to abandon them in order to save their currency. For this reason it seems justifiable to take the view that even though subsequently their hands may have been forced by trends which they could not foresee in good time, the depreciation or appreciation of their currencies was strictly speaking the outcome of monetary policy decisions taken at some stage.

Admittedly, in many instances monetary trends were not the result of policies pursued by the Governments concerned, but of 'imported' international trends. Even in such instances the

Governments would have been in a position to pursue policies neutralising the 'imported' trends. They were, to a large degree, masters of their monetary destinies, provided that they were willing and politically able to apply the necessary unpopular measures.

The realisation of this should go a long way towards disposing of much one-sided criticism of Knapp's theory concerning the power of the State to determine the value of money. What the critics really mean is that the State has no power to eat its cake and keep it. Given the adoption of various inflationary economic, social and political policies the Government is, of course, powerless in the long run to prevent these policies from producing their natural, logical and inevitable effects on the value of money. That effect may be delayed with the aid of various measures of control and intervention, but in the long run it cannot be prevented except through a timely reversal or abandonment of the policies responsible for the trend they generate. To do so may be considered politically inexpedient or economically costly. What matters from the point of view with which we are concerned in this chapter is that the decision rests with Governments and their Parliamentary majorities.

We are, therefore, entitled to claim that the State authority has immense power in determining the value of money. It has not the power, however, in the sense in which supporters of Knapp claim it to have. They are right in claiming that the State has the power to bring about changes in the value of money by a stroke of the pen. They are wrong in assuming that the passing of laws is in itself sufficient to ensure the maintenace of that value. A great deal more is required to achieve that end, in the form of monetary policy decisions and their application. Even those decisions are far from being able to produce the full effect aimed at. Nevertheless, as we shall see in the following chapters, they are apt to produce far reaching effects. And if Governments are prepared, rightly or wrongly, to sacrifice every other consideration for the sake of pursuing a policy aimed at maintaining the value of money, that policy is often able to achieve that end.

CHAPTER NINE

Maintaining Internal and External Stability

THE last chapter dealt with the power of the State to determine the value of its money. In the present and the two following chapters we shall examine the ends for which that power can be used. From this point of view there are, broadly speaking, two schools of thought, according to whether money is regarded as a technical device or as a major instrument of economic policy. The first conception is a static one and favours a monetary policy aiming at stability. The second conception is essentially dynamic and favours a policy aiming at changes, whether in the direction of a rise or a fall in the value of money. Those who regard money as a mere technical device, the object of which is to facilitate the smooth functioning of the economy, do not expect monetary policy to influence fundamental economic trends. They expect money to remain 'neutral', which means that it is not supposed to cause a general rise or fall in prices, nor to stimulate or handicap production, distribution or consumption. Under this conception the main task of monetary policy should be to prevent any departure of money from 'neutrality'. A well-behaved money is one which does not cause any movements of the general price level. This was the predominant view during the first two decades of the twentieth century. The monetary system and the monetary policies responsible for its management were subject to much criticism during that period mainly on the ground of the instability of the value of money.

On the other hand, those who consider money a major

dynamic factor, and a major instrument of economic and social policy, take the view that monetary policy must aim at intervening actively to influence economic trends. An important school of thought – fashionable during the twenty years between 1931 and 1951 and again during the sixties – advocates the use of money as a means of stimulating production with the aid of an expansionary monetary policy. It favours an increase in the quantity of money in order to finance the production of more goods and to enable consumers to buy more. A rising trend of prices usually accompanies the successful application of an expansionary monetary policy. In the view of some of the supporters of such an 'inflationary' policy this is a necessary evil, but they deem it to be worth while for the community to put up with it for the sake of the beneficial effects of monetary expansion on the rate of growth.

The opposite extreme is represented by the school which holds the view that monetary policy must aim at ensuring a steady fall of prices in accordance with the downward trend in the cost of production, in order to be on the safe side against the ever-present forces of evil that would make for inflation in the absence of such safeguards. According to this 'deflationary' school – which has now very few supporters – to that end money must always be kept in short supply.

Although it is easy to quote early instances of inflationary and deflationary monetary policies, it seems probable that in the majority of instances throughout history the aim of monetary policy was the achievement of stability. When other aims were pursued it was not because a rise or a fall in the price level was preferred to stability. Inflationary policies were usually adopted during periods of war, though very often the extravagance of princes – or, for that matter, of Parliamentary Governments – or their unwillingness to adopt unpopular measures, forced their countries into inflation in time of peace. In so far as deflation was a result of deliberate policy and not of circumstances over which the authorities had no control, it occurred on many occasions as a result of excessive measures taken to ensure that money remained sufficiently scarce to maintain its stability.

The adoption of precious metals for monetary purposes was in itself, consciously or otherwise, an act in accordance with the requirements of monetary stability, owing to the relative scarcity of these metals. It is true, from a very early stage metallic moneys were frequently debased; their quantity was thus increased and their value reduced. Many rulers, though trying hard to avoid this, were unable to resist the temptation to debase their coinage. Others, however, went out of their way to restore monetary stability through re-coinage operations or through calling down the nominal value of coins, as a result of which the excessive quantity of debased coins was replaced by a smaller quantity of full-valued coins.

The adoption of paper currency provided additional temptation and opportunity for departures from the policy of stability on a hitherto unkown scale. The early history of paper money abounds in such instances. After the Napoleonic Wars, however, most European Governments endeavoured to maintain the stability of their currency by maintaining a metallic standard, and thereby putting an automatic brake on monetary expansion. Viewed from the perspective of history the century that followed the Battle of Waterloo may appear to us a very stable century. In reality, even during that period monetary trends showed noteworthy ups and downs which, moderate as they may seem to us after the experience of the First and Second World Wars and their aftermaths, were considered very unsettling in their days. To a large degree they were connected with changes in the output of monetary gold in relation to expanding commercial requirements, and with the abandonment of the monetary use of silver. Moreover, even during that stable period, paper-money inflation and currency depreciation occurred at some time or other in most countries.

The discovery of the Californian and Australian gold fields towards the middle of the nineteenth century, and again the South African and Alaskan gold rush towards the end of that century, resulted in rising trends in the volume of money and in prices, not as a matter of monetary policy but through the automatic working of the gold standard, under which system an increase of the gold reserves meant a monetary expansion. In between those two gold rushes the additions of new gold to the world's monetary gold supplies failed to keep pace with the needs of expanding trade. There were in consequence shortages of money, all the more so as expansion of population, technical progress and the rising standard of living made for larger monetary requirements. The result was a deflationary trend accentuated by the demonetisation of silver in many countries.

It is, therefore, incorrect to claim that during the nineteenth century stabilisationist monetary policy fully achieved its end. The intention had been, however, to maintain relative stability by adhering to a system which ensured relative scarcity. The maintenance of a metallic standard set a limit to the increase in the quantity of notes, and also in the volume of credit which came to play an increasingly important part in the monetary system. The view was held widely if not generally that the working of the automatic gold standard with the minimum of official interference was the best – indeed the only – way of ensuring relative monetary stability in the long run.

It was not until the period between the two World Wars that an alternative means to the same end began to emerge in the form of scientific monetary management. From the late twenties onwards the view was gaining ground that monetary trends should not be left to the caprices of nature but should be made independent of the ebb and flow of newly mined gold supplies. The idea originated with the opponents of monetary stability who had hoped that through an abandonment of the gold standard it would be possible to embark on a degree of monetary expansion which had been impossible so long as the restraining influence of the gold standard had continued to prevail. It was taken up, however, also by many monetary economists and monetary authorities who favoured the maintenance of the gold standard but realised the need for its more elastic application.

The 'managed' gold standard which developed during the twenties aimed at maintaining monetary stability by neutralising the effects on price levels of an unwanted increase or decrease of the gold reserves. This was done primarily not on account of any disturbing effects of fluctuations in the gold output but in order to minimise the inconvenience caused by fluctuations in the gold reserves of individual countries. During the late twenties when Britain was losing gold the decline of her reserve was not allowed to produce its full effect on the volume of credit. On other occasions a credit expansion through an unwanted gold influx was prevented by official action in the opposite sense. This policy of 'neutralisation' was practised more systematically in the United States.

One of the reasons why even some highly orthodox quarters were inclined to favour the replacement of the automatic gold standard by the managed gold standard was the realisation that the world's supply of monetary gold was not longer sufficient to ensure the smooth working of the automatic system, which made for a decline of prices through monetary scarcity. This was partly because of the maldistribution of gold that developed during and after the First World War. A disproportionately large percentage of the monetary gold supplies found its way to the United States, and, owing to the persistently favourable American balance of payments, there was no possibility of securing a more even distribution. The rest of the world had to be content with an inadequate stock of the monetary metal. Its inadequacy became accentuated because, while the price of gold remained at its pre-1914 figure, the monetary requirements of most countries rose quite substantially above their pre-war level. A smaller amount of gold in the world outside the United States had to finance a much higher turnover of trade. And since the current output of newly mined gold was not sufficient to make up for the deficiency, monetary policy experts all over the world elaborated devices for economising in the use of gold. These devices – which will be examined in the chapter dealing with the means of monetary policy – aimed at maintaining the stability of the value of money. It was rightly feared that a world-wide scarcity of gold might result in a heavy decline in prices. This was in fact what happened eventually in spite of efforts to economise in the use of gold. Stabilisationist policy was even less successful during this period than it had been in the nineteenth century. But it seems reasonable to suggest that in the absence of that policy the fall in prices would have been even sharper, or that it would have culminated long before 1931 in a slump and the abandonment of the gold standard.

The managed gold standard during the twenties provided a useful transition from stabilisation policy under the gold standard to the stabilisation policy under inconvertible paper currency. During the thirties the gold standard came to be suspended everywhere, but the methods of managing the gold standard in the interests of stability were largely retained and adapted to the requirements of managing inconvertible currencies after their restabilisation.

At the same time, however, while the technique for maintaining stability was improved, the objective of a stable monetary system to be pursued by monetary policy was largely replaced by one of monetary expansion. This was because the downward trend in world prices during the early thirties caused grave disturbances in world economy. The idea that it was the object of monetary policy to arrest and reverse this process and to prevent its recurrence at all costs, even at the cost of producing some inflation (or, as it came to be called, 'reflation'), became increasingly popular.

By 1937, however, the United States Government adopted the view that the rise in prices had gone far enough. Once more the monetary authorities in Washington reverted to the pursuit of stability. In Britain by the late thirties the problem which the Government had to face was not one of choosing between deflation and reflation but one of preventing rearmament from producing an inflationary effect. Even though the extent of rearmament was negligible until the outbreak of the Second World War, from 1937 onwards the Government was preoccupied with fiscal and other measures aiming at preventing a rise in prices.

With the outbreak of the war in 1939 monetary policy in all well-organised countries came to concentrate on an effort to keep war-time inflation under control. On the basis of the experience of the First World War, and also on the basis of the experience of Nazi Germany during the rearmament drive of the late thirties, various devices were adopted to neutralise inflation or to suppress its effect on prices. As the war was proceeding these devices became increasingly effective. Every belligerent Government realised that in war-time conditions it would be useless to try to prevent inflation altogether. Indeed, they went so far as to admit to themselves the need for a certain degree of inflation to stimulate the economic war effort. Their monetary policies aimed at keeping down the extent of inflation as far as possible, and in so far as inflation had to take place they aimed at preventing it from producing its full effect on prices. In face of the practical arguments in favour of minimising the inevitable rise in prices for the duration of the emergency, theoretical arguments against price controls and against physical controls pursuing the same end were brushed aside. Never before in modern history had the pursuit of stability assumed the form of such far-reaching and effective Government action interfering with economic trends. Considering the extent of war-time inflation, the extent of the rise in prices was in most countries remarkably moderate.

The comparative success of the stabilisationist policies pursued during the war encouraged their continuation after the war, at first in the interest of reconstruction and then in that of raising the standard of living. As during the war, the object of monetary policy was to combine the advantages of an expanding monetary system with those of an outward stability. In most countries the Governments aimed not at the elimination of inflation but at the suppression or mitigation of its effects on prices. The difference between monetary policies in the thirties and those in the late forties and early fifties was that for some years before the war a rise in prices was the declared object of the authorities, while after the war they sought to disclaim responsibility for it. The pursuit of stability was not openly discarded as the end of monetary policy. Governments paid lip service to it but were not prepared to adopt measures which would have checked the rise in prices, because it would have checked or at any rate materially mitigated and also delayed the rise in the standard of living. That rise was achieved largely through monetary expansion at the cost of a gradual depreciation of the purchasing power of money. For a long time most post-war Governments were in favour of stability only in so far as its achievement did not call for measures that would have been detrimental to social security, expansion of productive capacity or rearmament. By the middle fifties, however, the disadvantages of the progressive 'creeping inflation' came to be increasingly realised. Many Governments came to recognise the need for an effort to keep prices down even at the cost of a slowing down of the increase in production. In theory, expansion and full employment had an equal priority with stability among the declared aims of monetary policy both in Britain and in the United States. But from time to time the desire to check inflation came to overshadow the other ends for a while. In due course this policy came to be reversed.

Hitherto we have been dealing with the pursuit of stability without trying to discriminate between internal and international stability of currencies. Under the classical conception the same policies are calculated to further both the end of a stable domestic price level and that of stable exchange rates. This view was powerfully reinforced during and after the First World War by Cassel's Purchasing Power Parity Theory, according to which exchange rates were determined by the relative changes in the domestic price levels of the countries concerned, and a rise in prices at home is accompanied by a depreciating trend of the exchange rate. On this assumption the only effective defence against exchange depreciation in the long run would be a prevention of inflation at home.

Other economists of the same period argued in the opposite sense, claiming that the domestic price levels of countries with inconvertible paper currencies were determined by the movements of their exchange rates. Beyond doubt a sharp depreciation of an exchange through speculative causes tended to bring about a sharp rise in the domestic price level of the country concerned, unless the movement was reversed before it had produced its effect. For this reason it was urged that internal monetary policies could not be pursued effectively unless and until the disturbing influences affecting exchange rates – adverse trade balance, speculation, international movements of funds, etc. – were eliminated.

Both theories contain a great deal of truth. Instead of being rival theories, in reality they complete each other. What matters from our point of view is that under their joint influence the concept that the interests of internal and external stability are identical became firmly established in the twenties. This in spite of Irving Fisher's proposal that domestic prices in the United States should be kept stable by means of adjustments of the gold value of the dollar, which would of course mean fluctuating exchange rates.

During the thirties the possibility of a conflict between the requirements of internal stability and those of external stability came to be widely realised. Deflation was proceeding rapidly all over the world, though in some countries faster than in others. This meant that, given stability of exchanges, the price levels in some countries became higher than in others even in the absence of any inflationary policy that would tend to produce that result. The country which was unable or unwilling to swim with the deflationary tide fast enough had to suffer grave disadvantages because its prices became relatively high and non-competitive. It was losing markets abroad and even at home. Confronted with such situations the monetary authorities had to decide whether to restore equilibrium by enforcing a sufficiently drastic deflationary policy or whether to take the line of least resistance by reducing the external value of their currency. By means of a devaluation or depreciation it was possible to restore equilibrium between the higher domestic price level and the lower world price level with a stroke of the pen, instead of undergoing a painful process of deflation.

The same problem presented itself in the opposite sense from the late fifties and subsequent years. Inflation was proceeding at a different rate in various industrial countries; it was slower in Western Germany and Holland than elsewhere. As a result the D.mark and the guilder became undervalued. Both countries had large export surpluses and there was a heavy influx of foreign funds. This became the source of international embarrassment and in many ways it became embarrassing even to the two countries concerned. They could have brought about a readjustment by allowing the resulting increase of their reserves to produce its natural inflationary effect on their price levels. But they preferred to revalue their exchanges in order to obviate an unwanted rise in domestic prices.

Concern about the stability of the external value of money is presumably as old as the monetary system itself. It is only in modern times, however, that the close association between monetary policies and domestic prices has come to be fully realised. This is partly because the statistical measurement of changes in the average price level is a comparatively recent invention, and partly because until recent centuries the response of price levels to monetary changes was relatively slow and incomplete. On the other hand changes in the international value of money had always been evident – at any rate to those directly concerned with commercial and financial transactions between countries. Opposition to debasements during the Middle Ages was mainly due to their effect on the value of the national coins abroad, and probably to a much less extent to fears of a rise in the domestic price level.

A century of uninterrupted stability in the exchange value of sterling was accompanied by fairly wide fluctuations in its domestic purchasing power. Nevertheless, when in 1931 the gold standard was suspended the depreciation of the international value of sterling was viewed with indifference by the British public. 'A pound is a pound, no matter at what rate it is quoted in the foreign exchange markets', sums up the reaction of the man in the street. In many other countries, with experience in more advanced inflation, the general public became much more exchange-rate conscious. Indeed, a stage was reached in some countries when domestic prices came to be adjusted daily, and even hourly, to the changes in the quotations of foreign exchanges. In such countries internal stability was of course inconceivable without external stability. On the other hand in countries such as Britain it was possible for monetary policies aiming respectively at internal and external stability to come into conflict with each other.

One of the reasons why in Britain there was a possibility of internal stability even in the absence of external stability was that she was part of the Sterling Area which supplied a large proportion of her food and raw material requirements. Since currencies of the Sterling Area usually appreciated or depreciated in sympathy with the pound, the sterling price of imports from the Sterling Area was not affected directly and immediately by a change in the external value of sterling. This circumstance tended to reduce the extent to which the domestic price level was liable to be affected by exchange fluctuations. Thus the policy of sacrificing external stability for the sake of maintaining internal stability, which was pursued in Britain during the thirties, stood a better chance of succeeding than it would have done in some isolated country.

The alternative policy aimed at upholding external stability at the cost of submitting to unwanted changes in the domestic price level. For instance, in 1931 Britain might have saved the external stability of sterling if the Government had taken timely and drastic deflationary measures leading to a sharp fall in the domestic price level. Instead, sterling exchange was allowed to depreciate in order to avoid the need for bringing about such a fall, even though deflationary measures were taken eventually to minimise the depreciation of sterling.

Between 1931 and the outbreak of the Second World War British monetary policy aimed at the internal stability of sterling at the cost of external instability. From time to time the sterling exchange was allowed to depreciate in order to avoid 'importing' deflation. It was allowed to appreciate when exchange stability would have meant a rise in the domestic price level. In 1933 the United States adopted a similar policy. One of the aims of the deliberate depreciation of the dollar was to check and reverse the deflationary trend that was causing immense economic and social hardship. There was for some time during the thirties a period of competitive currency depreciation during which the Governments aimed at safeguarding themselves against 'importing' deflation by outbidding each other in the depreciation of their exchanges. This policy came to an end as a result of the Tripartite Currency Agreement of 1936, between the United States, Great Britain and France. During the Second World War most exchanges were maintained rigidly stable regardless of the relative degree of domestic depreciations.

The main object of the Bretton Woods Agreement was to prevent the resumption of competitive currency depreciation after the war. Nevertheless, the Bretton Woods system admitted the principle that if the price level of a country finds itself to be out of equilibrium with the world price level, that country is entitled to restore equilibrium through a devaluation or revaluation of its exchange, in order to obviate the necessity for lowering or raising its domestic price level. The fact that many countries were actually authorised by the International Monetary Fund, which controls the application of the principle, to alter their exchange parities, has proved that the principle established at Bretton Woods can operate in practice. Neither the International Monetary Fund nor indeed the Governments of the member countries were keen on resorting too frequently to such adjustments. They were prepared to put up with considerable inconvenience to avoid a change in their exchange parities. For instance, although it became increasingly obvious in the early fifties that prices in France were too high, the French Governments which followed each other in office in close succession were for a long time unwilling to adjust the situation by means of devaluation. They were prepared to put up with grave economic and political difficulties in pursuing the end of the international stability of the franc. In this respect they merely reverted to the policy pursued during the thirties when France kept aloof for a long time from the policy of competitive currency depreciation and preferred to put up with an endless succession of crises rather than devalue the franc. The same policy was followed during the middle twenties by Mussolini, who declared in 1926 that he would defend the lira with the last drop of his blood. It was pursued by Germany after the depreciation of sterling, and the resulting internal difficulties were largely responsible for the advent of Hitler in 1933.

In reality the conflict between the requirements of internal stability and those of international stability is in many instances not so sharp as it might appear from the foregoing. The reason why the French Governments in the thirties were unwilling to devalue the franc was not that they attached undue importance to its external stability but that they realised that another devaluation would only set into motion a fresh vicious spiral leading to a further rise in the domestic price level. This was the experience of France also after the Second World War. Each successive devaluation secured only a temporary respite; prices soon caught up with the depreciation of the international value of the franc, and even went beyond it, so that after a year or two the price level in France was once more too high compared with the world level. In the case of France the pursuit of stability called for internal disinflationary measures which, if effective, would have safeguarded the external as well as the internal stability of the franc.

On the other hand, post-war monetary policy in Britain and other countries which did not have as extensive experience in devaluations as France attached more importance to external stability than to internal stability. All post-war Governments in Britain abstained from resorting to drastic disinflationary measures so long as inflation did not endanger the external stability of sterling. While they submitted to the rise in domestic prices without attempting to resist it very firmly, they took action whenever the resulting adverse balance of payments and the speculative or quasi-speculative pressure on sterling that accompanied it began to threaten the gold reserve. Mr Douglas Dillon, Secretary to the United States Treasury, pointed out in his evidence before the Subcommittee on International

Exchanges and Payments in 1961, 'In the final analysis, there is no substitute for balance-of-payments discipline in this or any economy.'

Amidst post-war conditions of full employment, prices were apt to react promptly to exchange depreciation, but not to exchange appreciation. For this reason, floating exchanges are liable to result in a chronic depreciating trend operating in stages instead of domestic stability. More will be said about this in Chapter 39 on Foreign Exchange Policy.

A stabilisationist monetary policy is concerned only with the stability of the average price level. There may be wide movements in individual prices or groups of prices without calling for official action to safeguard stability so long as the changes in the prices more or less offset each other. According to one school of thought, the function of a monetary policy should confine itself to neutralising any monetary trends that threaten to upset stability. If price movements are caused by *non-monetary* factors, such as, for instance, failure or superabundance of a crop, there is no cause for official intervention. This view is not held generally, however. It has been gradually realised that a movement of prices initiated by non-monetary causes might easily assume a monetary character by setting into motion a vicious spiral. For this reason among others, some monetary economists believe that a stabilisationist monetary policy must endeavour to prevent or correct any price movements even if they are due to non-monetary causes.

For instance, should the failure of crops cause a rise in the prices of land products, in the absence of official action this tends to bring about a rise in the average price level. To counteract the resulting increase in monetary requirements, the authorities would have to adopt deflationary measures, or at any rate they would have to prevent the rise in prices from bringing about a credit espansion due to the larger monetary requirements. Conversely, an exceptionally large crop may cause a fall in the average price level through the fall in prices of land products. A suggested remedy is expansionary devices which tend to restore the average level of prices.

According to a static theory, in the absence of a change in the volume of credit, a rise in a group of prices is offset by a fall in other prices. Under a dynamic theory, however, if an economy has an inflationary bias a rise in one group is liable to trigger off an all-round rise. That being so, the authorities can ill afford to ignore price changes on the ground that, since they are due to non-monetary causes, they do not call for monetary policy measures. In any case, it is not always easy to discriminate between monetary and non-monetary causes of a change in the price level.

CHAPTER TEN

Raising the Price Level

As in the previous chapter, so in the present one we are concerned solely with price tendencies brought about as a matter of deliberate policy. We are not concerned here with price increases that occur spontaneously, or with those that come about because official efforts to prevent them have failed or with those which are incidental and unwanted results of monetary policies pursuing some other purpose. We are concerned, however, with price increases that take place not as a consequence of deliberate official action, but as a result of deliberate decisions to abstain from taking action in order to prevent them.

Official policy favouring a rise in the price level may be decided upon for the following reasons :

(1) Pursuit of a stabilisation policy with an inflationary bias. In an effort to safeguard against the risk of deflation the authorities may take deliberately excessive anti-deflationary measures, thereby causing a rise in prices.

(2) Reflationary efforts aiming at a restoration of prices to their previous higher level, or to an even higher level.

(3) Deliberate reduction of the burden of public or private indebtedness through raising the price level.

(4) Efforts to improve the 'terms of trade' by raising the prices of exports so that their proceeds should buy a larger quantity of imports.

(5) A policy of stimulating production by means of a deliberate increase of prices in order to achieve a high degree of employment, or in order to make fuller use of the community's productive capacity.

(6) A policy of stimulating consumption by inducing consumers to make their purchases in anticipation of further rises in prices.

(7) A policy of correcting and undervaluation of the exchange, as an alternative to its revaluation, in order to relieve pressure on other exchanges.

Since the dawn of history the progress of mankind in the monetary sphere has been accompanied, temporary intervals apart, by a rising trend in prices. Throughout the centuries prices have been rising to new high levels. Admittedly, the progress has not been uninterrupted. In the long run, however, after each period of decline the price level reached new high records.

To what extent has the depreciation of money during the last five thousand years been due to deliberate inflationary policy? Although there are many instances of such a policy, generally speaking it is correct to say that more often than not currency depreciations throughout the ages were largely due to circumstances over which the monetary authorities had no control. As a result of the improvement of mining and metallurgical methods and of the discoveries of unexplored mineral deposits, there had been a natural increase in the volume of precious metals. From time to time this increase had caused a spontaneous rise in prices. Further, even in the absence of an increase in the volume of monetary metals, price increases were caused by debasements of the coinage. Debasements were often necessitated by wars or by the policy of defending the specie supply against a drain caused by the export of good coins, and were not undertaken for the purpose of raising prices.

The same is true about more recent instances of paper-money inflation and credit inflation. In the majority of instances there was no question of any deliberate policy aiming at raising the price level. The State authority was merely prepared to put up with such a rise as the inevitable consequence of monetary expansion undertaken to finance wars, or for other purposes. Indeed, it seems reasonable to believe that very often the State authority drifted into inflation without knowing in advance the consequences of its actions. Inflation was usually due to decisions taken outside the realms of monetary policy, such as a declaration of war or measures of defence against enemy invasion. Monetary policy had to adapt itself willy-nilly to the consequences of such non-monetary decisions. Or it was due to decisions to spend more, or to decisions to encourage expansion of production or at any rate to refrain from discouraging it. In many instances the decisions were taken on the assumption, or in the hope, that they would not lead to a rise in prices.

The experience of the thirties provides instances of deliberate reflationary efforts to restore prices to their pre-slump levels. This was the declared aim of President Roosevelt's monetary policy. The United States and other countries, having suffered gravely through the slump, were anxious to restore prices to their 1929 level.

Monetary experience after the Second World War provides several instances of stabilisation policies with a bias in favour of inflation. It was certainly not the aim of the United States authorities, for instance, to raise prices. They wanted to maintain stable prices. On the other hand, they were even more anxious to avoid a slump than to avoid inflation. For this reason, each time there was a minor recession, they preferred to err on the safe side by following a policy which resulted in a relatively moderate rise in prices, as an insurance against a much-dreaded fall in prices.

Need for reduction of the excessive burden of debts figured prominently from very early times among the considerations determining monetary policy. The devaluation of the drachma by Solon in the sixth century B.C. served that purpose. Some economists are in favour of the secular trend of rising prices as the only possible way in which the otherwise intolerable increase in the burden of public debt can be offset. A policy aiming at a decline in the purchasing power of money is sometimes also advocated as a means for reducing the burden of private indebtedness. Consciously or otherwise, monetary policy may be influenced by such pressure which tends to weaken the will to resist the rising trend of prices.

Desire to undersell exporters of other countries is apt to be tempered by unwillingness to sell the national products at unduly low prices. If the prices of exports are unnecessarily low, it means that larger quantities have to be exported in order to secure the same quantity of imports. In other words, the 'terms of trade' are unfavourable to the country concerned. One way of correcting this is by allowing domestic prices to rise for the sake of improving the terms of trade. This is done when there is full employment, because in such a situation there is no possibility of increasing employment through selling larger quantities abroad. It is advantageous when there is predominantly a 'sellers' market' – that is, a state of affairs in which sellers can virtually dictate their terms – so that it is comparatively easy to export in spite of the higher prices. The post-war period provides instances of non-resistance to rising trends of prices for considerations of improving the terms of trade.

By far the most important motive of the policy of higher prices is the desire to stimulate production. Indeed, moderate inflation has come to be widely regarded as being inseparable from economic progress both as a cause and as an effect. More and more money is undoubtedly needed to finance an expanding volume of output and an increasingly complex production, and also to meet higher consumers' requirements due to the higher standard of living of a growing population. Admittedly, in theory there is no cause for a rise in prices if the volume of goods increases to the same extent as the volume of money. In practice, however, it is necessary first to increase the volume of money in order to be able to produce more, and the monetary expansion is apt to affect prices before the additional goods become available. This is true to a particularly high degree concerning the production of capital goods.

One way in which an increase of the output tends to raise wages is through the time-lag between the increase in the expenditure on wages, materials, etc., and the emergence of the additional goods from the pipeline. During that time-lag the additional purchasing power thus created is not matched by an additional volume of goods, so that there is a tendency for demand to exceed supply.

Prosperous periods are usually accompanied by rising prices, while depressions are accompanied by falling prices. It is difficult to achieve prosperity through an expanding economy unless the monetary authorities are prepared to put up with some rise in prices. Prosperity is achieved partly through monetary expansion and the expansion of the wages bill, and partly through the stimulating effect of the rise in prices. Some inflationists regard the rise as a necessary evil which has to be accepted in order to reap the benefits of expansion. Others go further by maintaining that a moderate rise in prices is worth having for its own sake, because of its stimulating effect on production and consumption. Indeed, they feel that a credit expansion could not be effective unless there were a rising trend of prices without which producers would be reluctant to avail themselves of the larger credit facilities offered to them. Rising prices are favoured because they mean the prospects of higher turnovers, higher profits and lower risks. They mean a sellers' market in which almost anything that is produced can be unloaded, thanks to the ability and eagerness of consumers to buy.

It is true that higher profits earned as a result of rising prices are apt to be largely fictitious. For by the time the producers are able to dispose of their goods their cost of production may have risen to such an extent that the replacement cost of the goods sold is much higher than their cost of production had been a few months earlier. Many producers discovered after a few years of rise in prices that, although they had made handsome book-keeping profits, on balance they were worse off than before because they had to contract large bank debts in order to finance their production at a higher cost and because their equipment had to be renewed at a higher cost. Notwithstanding this, producers are apt to be hypnotised by the prospects of higher nominal profits. They are eager to produce to the limit of their capacity when prices are rising and to spend freely on capital investment in order to expand their productive capacity. If the Government wishes to encourage such expansion, that end can be achieved through causing prices to rise, or at any rate allowing them to rise. A rising price level is indeed a very powerful stimulus to trade, and it is tempting for Governments to take the line that a moderate depreciation of money is a small price to pay for the advantages of higher output.

During 1945–51 rising prices in Britain largely contributed towards the increase of industrial output. This explains why industrialists, in spite of their dissatisfaction with high taxation, interference with business by controls, and the Government's anti-capitalist attitude, continued to increase their output and their capacity. Although the Labour Government did not deliberately aim at raising prices for the sake of inducing private enterprise to function satisfactorily under a Socialist regime, this was how it worked out in practice. Some Socialist spokesmen candidly favoured the moderate non-stop rise in prices as a stimulus to production. Similar views were expressed during the long depression of the thirties by many non-Socialist economists. Although few Governments would ever admit that they favoured a policy of deliberately raising the price level for the sake of stimulating production, there can be no doubt that this consideration is apt to weaken resistance to an upward trend of prices.

The Conservative Governments that followed each other after 1951 continued the same policy of tolerating the rise in prices for the sake of raising the standard of living, in pursuit of the slogan 'You've never had it so good', though they had to intervene from time to time to check inflation because of its effect on the balance of payments.

Rising prices stimulate not only production but also consumption. While high prices may in given circumstances discourage buying, increasing prices tend to induce producers, wholesalers, retailers and consumers to buy before a further rise occurs. The pursuit of a policy of higher prices is therefore apt to kill two birds with one stone. It not only ensures an increase of the output, but secures a market for the larger output, without which over-production is liable to occur.

Temptation to stimulate production and consumption with the aid of a policy of 'creeping inflation' is tempered by the many obvious disadvantages of a depreciation of money. Those capable of seeing beyond the immediate future are bound to be concerned by the dangers that lie ahead. In the past rising trends of prices were interrupted sooner or later, and more often than not it was followed not by stability but by a decline. The longer the rise continues the graver the dangers of a sharp reaction are apt to become. It is true, that a policy of rising prices may have for its aim the perpetuation of a moderate rising trend - with the accent on 'moderate' - precisely in order to avoid a slump. The difficulty is that once it is widely realised that the rise is perpetual, it is not likely to remain moderate. More and more people will be inclined to 'live with inflation' - that is, to anticipate further rises by making purchases before things become more expensive, and to 'hedge' against inflation. The pressure of their demand for goods is liable to accentuate the upward movement.

Needless to say, once inflation has reached an advanced stage its constructive aspects disappear and its destructive aspects become prominent. One of the reasons why a policy of moderate inflation finds favour in many quarters in the Anglo-Saxon world is that neither the United States nor Britain nor the Commonwealth has experienced runaway inflation, at any rate in the lifeteime of the present generation. The United States had her dose of advanced inflation during the War of Independence in the eighteenth century, but the memory of that experience is too remote to be an effective deterrent. In countries such as Germany which have experienced advanced inflation, a policy of inflation, however moderate, is seldom advocated from responsible quarters.

Even on the assumption that a moderate rise in prices need not be followed either by a slump or by galloping inflation, the policy has many weighty disadvantages. One of them is that it tends to discourage saving and encourage extravagance on the part of both consumers and producers. There is no inducement for the latter to keep down their costs of production, since in a sellers' market they are able to pass on to the consumer any increase of their costs. What is perhaps even worse, there is little inducement for producers to exercise their judgment, since in a period of a non-stop rise in prices they can sell almost anything they produce. For this reason quality may become a secondary consideration. Producers are liable to make mistakes in misjudging their market, but amidst rising prices such mistakes may only mean a slower turnover and smaller profits. In one word, a policy of rising prices is apt to create not only a fool's paradise where producers work for fictitious book-keeping profits, but also a more or less foolproof system where mistakes escape their penalty. Even incompetent managements may be able to 'pinpoint the winner' by a lucky choice of the goods to be produced or purchased.

Under creeping inflation trade unions get into the habit of regarding an annual round of wage increases as their birthright, regardless of whether there is an increase of productivity to justify them. Employers, finding it too easy to pass on the increase of cost to the consumer, concede unjustified wage demands and encourage the greed of the trade unions at the expense of the long-suffering consumer.

It would be easy to multiply the arguments for and against a policy of rising prices. Practical administrators cannot afford to be dogmatic about it. But they must be, at any rate, aware of the sacrifices and the risks involved and decide the extent of currency depreciation which may be regarded as justifiable in given circumstances notwithstanding those risks and sacrifices. It has become all a matter of degree rather than one of rigid principle.

CHAPTER ELEVEN

Raising the Value of Money

THROUGHOUT monetary history the upward trend in prices was often interrupted by periods of decline. Documentary evidence shows that the purchasing power of silver had its ups as well as its downs in the chequered monetary history of Babylonia and Assyria. The inflation that resulted from the dispersal of the Persian gold hoard by Alexander the Great was followed, twenty years after the conqueror's death, by half a century of decline in prices throughout the area of the Eastern Mediterranean civilisation. The period of decline of the Roman Empire has been quoted – among others by Keynes – as an early instance of prolonged deflation, but actually prices in terms of the debased denarius were rising almost without interruption during the third and fourth centuries A.D. On the other hand, there are instances of declining prices during the medieval period, owing to scarcity of gold and silver, even though frequent debasements maintained the broad secular trend of rising prices. In modern times too, price trends have shown some long periods of decline. Nevertheless, Feavearyear was right in saying in the concluding section of his standard work, *The Pound Sterling*: 'There is no doubt that the world's history can afford no example of a monetary unit which has been allowed for any very long period to appreciate.'

From time to time, however, Governments did pursue monetary policies which not only allowed the monetary unit to appreciate, but even deliberately caused it to appreciate. In this chapter we are concerned solely with falls in prices deliberately aimed at by monetary policy. We are not concerned here with price declines which take place spontaneously or incidentally as a result of monetary actions pursuing other aims, or with declines which monetary authorities were unable to prevent. Official action to lower the price level is liable to be taken as a matter of deliberate policy for the following reasons:

(1) Pursuit of a stabilisation policy with a deflationary bias, in order to safeguard the community gainst the risk of inflation by means of excessive anti-inflationary measures.

(2) Resistance to the adjustment of the volume of money to a previous increase in prices caused by non-monetary factors.

(3) Compliance with consumers' clamour for returning to the 'good old days' of low prices.

(4) Allowing lower cost of production caused by technological progress to produce its effect on prices.

(5) Restoration of confidence in a depreciated and discredited currency through deliberately raising its purchasing power.

(6) Efforts to check a speculative boom and to enforce the liquidation of unsound ventures that had developed under the influence of prolonged inflation.

(7) The favouring of creditors and encouragement of saving.

(8) The lowering of the cost of production in order to stimulate exports and discourage imports.

(9) Reduction of the cost of living in order to avoid wages demands and industrial disputes.

(10) Enabling of the Treasury to borrow on more satisfactory terms.

It is impracticable to strike a happy medium exactly halfway between inflation and deflation. Monetary trends cannot be regulated with absolute accuracy for any length of time. We saw in the last chapter that even though the official policy may aim at stability, it is sometimes inclined to have an anti-deflationary bias and is prepared to cause a moderate rise in prices rather than risk a fall. Conversely, monetary policy may have an anti-inflationary bias, which means that for the sake of making sure that inflation is avoided it aims at a slight reduction in prices. If a Government is more afraid of inflation than of deflation it may consider it expedient to adopt disinflationary measures as soon as there is the slightest indication of inflation. It may be inclined to apply deliberately excessive doses of that remedy in order to prevent the development of the disease. A Government with a strong anti-inflationary bias may even consider it expedient to adopt preventive anti-inflationary measures in anticipation of the appearance of the first symptoms of inflation.

A fall in prices may be caused as a matter of deliberate policy through preventing the volume of money from adjusting itself to a previous rise in prices. Such a rise may have occurred for a very wide variety of reasons other than a previous increase in the volume of money. It may have been caused, for instance, by an increase of prices abroad, or by a devaluation of the national currency, or by excessive wage demands not warranted by a previous rise in the cost of living. It may even have been caused by an anticipation of a further rise in prices by buyers anxious to cover their requirements. Whatever may be the cause, the effect is an increase of the requirements for money in order to finance the same volume of production and consumption on the basis of the higher level of prices.

More often than not the monetary authorities yield to the pressure and allow the volume of currency and credit to adjust itself to the higher level of prices. This was what happened to a very large degree in Britain during the post-war period. From time to time prices rose, not in consequence of any previous monetary expansion, but owing to the devaluation of sterling, or an all-round increase of wages, or a boom in commodities abroad, or excessive public expenditure, or an excess of capital expenditure over saving. The rise could have been reversed if the Government had firmly prevented the adjustment of the volume of money to the higher requirements caused by the rise in prices. This was not done, however, and the rise in prices became confirmed and consolidated through a corresponding monetary expansion which was regarded in these cases as the effect and not the cause of the rise in prices. It was not until 1952 that an attempt was made to reverse the movement by preventing the adjustment of the volume of money to the higher price level. Although the rising trend in prices was arrested, the policy of preventing a monetary expansion was not carried sufficiently far to reverse it even temporarily. On some later occasions half-hearted efforts to prevent an upward adjustment of the volume of credit were not even able to check the rise in prices.

A policy aiming at a reduction of prices may be adopted in order to satisfy popular clamour for lowering the cost of living. There is reason to believe that, subconsciously at any rate, the restoration of sterling to its pre-war parity in 1925 was largely inspired by a desire to restore the pre-war price level. By 1931, however, the Macmillan Committee arrived at the conclusion that if any downward adjustment of the price level must exceed 10 per cent 'the game in not worth the candle'.

Seen from the consumers' point of view, it is tempting to regard the lowering of prices as the ideal end of a monetary policy. It has always been a habit of the older generation to feel nostalgic about the good old days when things were so much cheaper. The fact that in those days many people were unable to buy much more than bare necessities in spite of the low prices is apt to be overlooked by those to whom a low cost of living has come to be regarded as synonymous with universal happiness. During and after the First World War, when prices were rising, it was a widespread conception that this was bound to be a temporary abnormal phenomenon and that it was the Government's duty to aim at restoring the 'normal' pre-1914 price level. After a while such wishful thinking was abandoned and the higher prices were accepted as permanent. The depression in the thirties tended to restore the pre-war level, but this was not the result of any deliberate policy. Nor had many people cause for being happy about it. Having learnt from this experience, in the Second World War most people knew better than to expect a return to the 1939 price level. Tempting as it was for Governments to aim at assisting consumers by a policy favouring a decline of prices, they had to bear in mind the effect of such a policy on producers, merchants and debtors. They remembered that when in 1933 prices in the

United States declined to their pre-1914, level the result was a crisis without precedent. The return to pre-war prices brought happiness to very few people.

A downward trend of prices should be a normal consequence of technological progress. New inventions, the application of labour-saving automatic devices and a more efficient organisation of production and distribution tend to reduce costs. In a competitive economic system producers tend to pass on to the customer at least a great part of the benefit of their economies in the form of lower prices. In a world of monopolies producers may be inclined to keep for themselves all or most of such benefit. When the balance of power is in favour of employees under conditions of over-full employment, employers may have to cede most of the economies to the employees in the form of higher wages and salaries, or shorter working hours, in which case prices cannot decline in proportion to the cuts in costs. In the absence of monetary expansion, however, technological progress tends to lower the price to some extent, because employers are not in a position to concede demands for high wages.

The question is, what aim monetary policy should pursue if automation or other methods of reducing costs should tend to cause a fall in prices. The authorities are in a position, should they wish to do so, to maintain a stable price level by means of an expansionary monetary policy, in spite of a decline in the cost of production of a large number of goods. The alternative would be to allow a decline in prices to take place. This would necessarily mean great hardship to a large proportion of producers who are unable to lower their costs sufficiently.

Any substantial lowering of prices through the reduction of costs would set in operation the ruthless principle of 'the survival of the fittest'. Only the efficient producers would be able to make an adequate profit on the basis of the lower prices, and the less efficient units would have to go out of business. In the opinion of many people this is an argument in favour of the policy of allowing lower costs to produce their full effect on prices. The elimination of less efficient units would tend to

increase production, especially during periods of full employment when the more efficient units are unable to expand
sufficiently for lack of manpower. It is, however, a cruel doctrine that condemns to extinction smaller units which have not
the advantage of being able to achieve economies through
mass production.

During periods of rising price levels, cuts in individual prices
would be relatively moderate, if indeed there would be any
cuts at all, because in a sellers' market there is no need for the
producers to pass on to the consumers the whole benefit of their
economies. They tend to take the line of least resistance in face
of excessive wage demands, so that employees secure for
themselves the lion's share of the benefits, leaving nothing for
the consumer. The less efficient firms earn enough profits to
ensure their survival, while under a policy aiming at ensuring
that the consumer should benefit by technological progress in
the form of price cuts during periods of declining prices they are
doomed to extinction. This may be in accordance with the
requirements of efficiency. Efficiency, however, is not an end
itself, but merely a means to the supreme end of human
happiness. Many people feel that the extermination of small
firms would be a matter for regret. Production would become
less individual and more stereotyped. On the other hand, the
disappearance of larger firms which are unable or unwilling
to adopt modern methods might be a price worth paying for
the sake of progress.

The inconvenience for employees to have to change jobs
as a result of the elimination of inefficient firms through
declining prices – during periods of full employment no real
hardship is involved in such changes – is offset by the need for
releasing manpower to cover the requirements of efficient and
expanding industries.

It is arguable that if the process of elimination through a
decline in prices continued long enough, even efficient big
units might eventually become its victims, because there is
always a possibility that some other unit will become even
more efficient and produce at even lower costs. For one thing,

it is impossible for established firms to scrap their costly capital equipment each time a new labour-saving device is invented, so that the latest arrivals in the trade are at an advantage because they can equip their plant with the very latest machinery. The elimination of units, big or small, producing at a higher cost is necessarily a painful process involving heavy losses of invested capital and inflicting hardship on employees who may find it difficult to secure equally suitable new employment. The answer is adequate compensation of redundant workers, with adequate safeguards against an abuse of their bargaining power which is bound to be strengthened greatly by the adoption of a redundancy scheme.

If the monetary authorities are opposed to the full application of the doctrine of the survival of the fittest, they can pursue a moderate expansionary policy to counteract the declining trend of prices brought about by lower costs of production. If those responsible for monetary policy are in favour of a decline of prices, they have to resist rigidly any monetary expansion that would enable employers to concede wage demands.

On the one hand, the monetary authorities must bear in mind that price cuts resulting from automation and other methods of progress are the only way in which consumers can share in the benefit derived from progress, unless they happen to belong to some trade union in a strong bargaining position. On the other hand, they must bear in mind that a declining price level is liable to be detrimental to expansion of production. Even though the reduced profits may represent a higher real purchasing power, a contraction of profit margins always tends to discourage capital expenditure by industry.

In our days this dilemma seldom arises. Throughout modern history there has been uninterrupted technological progress. It is reasonable to assume that ever since the beginning of the industrial revolution in the middle of the eighteenth century the cost of goods in terms of human effort has been declining. Nevertheless, temporary intervals apart, prices have been increasing. This is due in part to the rise in real wages that has been going on in modern times. In the long run the wages bill of the smaller number of workmen required for the production of certain goods tends to be higher than that of the larger number of workmen had been prior to the adoption of labour-saving devices. The standard of living of employees and their wages requirements tend to rise simultaneously with techno-logical progress and to absorb a large part of the savings in costs achieved as a result of that progress. Working hours tend to be shorter, and restrictive practices are apt to limit the output.

Moreover, one of the obvious effects of progress is the increase in the proportion of 'white-collared' workers to factory workers. Their salaries have to be added to the wages bill. In addition, the proportion of those engaged in providing services tends to increase, and their pay, too, contributes in one form or another towards increasing the cost of living and the cost of production.

Another reason why technological progress has failed to reduce prices is that, relatively brief intervals apart, the monetary trend has been basically inflationary. It is reasonable to assume that, but for the decline in the cost of production through technical progress, the rise in prices would have been even more pronounced since the end of the war. The decline in costs has been unable to cause a fall in prices, but has to some extent moderated their rise. From time to time it has actually led to provisional setbacks in prices. For instance, during the inter-war period the mechanisation of agriculture through the widespread use of tractors, combine harvesters, etc., brought about a declining trend in the price level. The monetary authorities sought to counteract this and aimed at maintaining a stable price level. The result was over-production which played a decisive part in the series of crises and the long de-pression of the thirties. Owing to the change in the balance of power between employers and employees since the Second World War, it seems probable that in future the effect of technological progress on prices will always be more than offset by higher wages and social benefits and by more favourable working conditions and other 'fringe benefits'.

After a period of prolonged currency depreciation the Governments may favour a policy of deliberate fall of prices in order to restore confidence in a currency discredited by prolonged inflation. The choice is between trying to stabilise the value of money at the level to which it has declined or bringing about a partial recovery before stabilising it. There are many instances of both policies in the monetary experience of the periods that followed the First and Second World Wars. In cases of runaway inflation it may be necessary to reverse the trend instead of merely halting it, before stabilisation of the value of money can be attempted with a fair chance of success.

A policy aiming at lower prices may be decided upon in an attempt to check a speculative boom. During the course of a prolonged boom a number of unsound ventures are bound to come into existence, and it may be deemed expedient to force them into liquidation before they have a chance to grow too big. A policy aiming at a lower price level tends to eliminate mushroom growths which have no *raison d'être* except during periods of boom.

An important argument in favour of a reversal of price increases is that it is an effective antidote to the demoralising effect of prolonged inflation, which tends to generate greed, short-sighted selfishness and disregard of public interest, in employers and employees alike.

The deliberate lowering of the price level is often suspected, rightly or wrongly, of being due to a desire to favour creditors at the expense of debtors. Beyond doubt such a consideration played an important part in many primitive communities. They chose their monetary objects with a view to ensuring a perpetual scarcity of money for the benefit of the ruling classes, which were the principal holders of money and the principal creditors. In modern times, however, there can be little ground for such suspicion. Advantages derived by creditors from a decline in prices are liable to be offset by wholesale defaults or repudiations on the part of debtors affected by the increase in the real burden of their debts caused by the decline of prices. It may become necessary to consent to a moratorium or to legislation involving a reduction of the interest and capital of the claims. Creditors may have to pay a high price for the advantage of an increase in the commodity value of their claims. While their influence may be effective in inducing Governments to resist an inflationary rise in prices, they are hardly likely to persuade any Government to pursue a policy of lowering prices for their special benefit.

A much more realistic reason for which a policy of lower prices may be favoured is that it tends to improve the balance of payments. If the price level is higher than that of other countries, then this disequilibrium may be corrected either by causing a decline in the price level or by reducing the exchange value of the currency. If the discrepancy is not very pronounced, the former alternative is likely to be found preferable, as it is hardly worth while to upset well-established parities by a devaluation of, say, 5 per cent.

Situations may arise in which the Government may resort to a policy aiming at a lowering of the price level in order to avoid an epidemic of wage disputes or a wave of wage increases leading to a rise in the price level. Wage claims may be disarmed through evidence being produced of a fall in the cost of living. It was with this object in view that the French Government in 1948 enforced a uniform cut in prices.

One of the main arguments against a policy of deliberately lowering the price level is that once a deflationary spiral is initiated, the Government may find it very difficult to check it. The fall is apt to proceed well beyond the extent to which it is considered expedient for the purpose that inspired the adoption of the policy. Since falling prices are usually accompanied by an increase of unemployment, the pursuit of a policy of falling prices has become politically and socially more difficult since the Second World War. Such a policy is liable to encounter much political opposition not only on the part of workers fearing unemployment but also from industrial and commercial firms which stand to lose as a result of a business depression. In the fifties, and again in the seventies, there was much discontent with the British Government's disinflationary policies even among businessmen who supported the Conservative Party politically. The United States had a similar experience when at various times since the war Republican Administrations attempted to pursue policies aimed at resisting the rise in prices. The case for such a policy has to be very strong indeed before any Government would dare to expose itself to unpopularity by its adoption.

In 1972, being election year in the United States, President Nixon, who was courageous enough to escalate the air offensive against North Vietnam, deemed it politically expedient to reverse his earlier disinflationary measures of credit restraint, so as to improve business conditions and reduce unemployment during the months preceding election day.

There is now little likelihood of adopting in any country effective measures to bring down prices. The most a Government that feels strongly about inflation is likely to do would be to adopt measures to mitigate or halt the rise in prices, without actually reversing it.

CHAPTER TWELVE

Accumulating and Safeguarding
Monetary Reserves

ACCUMULATION of stocks of monetary metals has always been an important end of monetary policy. During the days of the gold standard the main object was the provision of adequate backing for the monetary system of the country. Since the volume of money depended on the amount of the gold reserve, it was necessary to accumulate enough gold to be able to satisfy essential demands for currency and credit. In our days the object of building up and safeguarding gold stocks is to provide the country with a substantial liquid reserve to meet any adverse trade balances and other international requirements.

In earlier centuries the kings and their advisers aimed at building up gold or silver reserves largely from the point of view of sound public finance. The extent to which they were able to raise money through borrowing was limited. It was necessary to accumulate a cash reserve in the Treasury to meet future deficiencies in receipts as compared with expenditure. In countries which had gold or silver mines, of which ruled over colonies possessing such resources, the need to accumulate reserves called for measures of mining policy rather than of monetary policy, though even such countries had to resort to devices of monetary policy in order retain a sufficient amount of the precious metals. Medieval England being almost entirely devoid of gold or silver deposits, had to depend on devices of monetary policy for attracting and retaining a metallic reserve.

The significance of being able to accumulate and retain a large gold and silver stock in the Treasury was political as well as financial and economic. It was a most important means of establishing and maintaing the supremacy of the monarch's power within the country. A king with a considerable reserve in coin and bullion was in a strong position to assert his authority against the fedual lords, or against any pretender coveting his throne. Externally too, he was in a much better position to wage defensive or aggressive wars, to secure allies, or to equip expeditions for securing colonies, He was in a strong negotiating position in the frequent disagreements between Church and State. He was not so dependent on supplies voted by Parliament and did not have to pledge valuable domains as securities for loans. That the advantages of possessing large cash reserves were duly realised is indicated by the fact that contemporary historians, and even more recent authorities, judged rulers according to whether they were able to keep their Treasury well filled. History speaks of Henry VII in terms of the highest praise because he was able to leave a substantial monetary reserve to his successor.

Even in our days the possession of a large monetary reserve makes for political prestige at home and abroad. The inadequacy of her gold and foreign exchange reserve during the entire post-war period materially weakened Britain's power to pull her full weight in international affairs, dependent as she was on external support form time to time. The reason why West Germany's voice came to carry weight in the council of nations even while the country was disarmed was that during the late fifties she succeeded in accumulating a large gold and dollar reserve.

Early writers on monetary policy were strongly influenced by the realisation of the need for a large and increasing metallic reserve. During the late medieval period and the two centuries that followed, the school of thought, according to which it was the principle task of Governments to secure an influx and prevent an efflux of money and monetary metals, reigned supreme. Administrators resorted to a variety of devices to attract precious metals. The object of these policies was not only to procure monetary reserves for the Treasuries but also to secure an expanding circulation of coins to meet expanding commercial needs. Even so, the desire to fill the Treasuries played an important part, especially in England, where all imported foreign coins had to be sold to the Royal Exchanger who had a monopoly of dealing in foreign gold and silver coins. To achieve the desired end the kings adopted measures which gravely handicapped foreign trade. They engaged in competitive currency debasement in order to attract gold or silver to the country. A fair proportion of it was bound to find its way to their Treasuries.

As a reaction to the mercantilist policies, a school of thought developed in the eighteenth century advocating a diametrically opposite policy. It favoured the removal of all obstacles to foreign trade. Under the influence of Adam Smith this school of thought gained growing ascendancy during the eighteenth century and succeeded in determining the policy of Britain and other countries. British economists during the nineteenth century ridiculed their forerunners' desire to safeguard monetary reserves by means of restricting trade. They held the view that all a country had to do was to import freely and lend abroad freely, and the rest would take care of itself. They were indeed right – amidst the unusual conditions of prosperity prevailing in nineteenth-century Britain. There was no need for British statesmen of that period to worry about the gold reserve. As the British industrial revolution was well ahead of that of other countries Britain certainly held most of the trumps and could afford to be liberal. In the case of countries as in that of individuals the rich always stand a better chance of earning more. 'To him that hath shall be given and from him that hath not shall be taken away.' Other countries which were less favourably placed had to make an effort to safeguard and increase their gold reserves with the aid of import duties and other devices at their disposal. Britain on the other hand managed with a relatively small gold reserve, relying on her ability to attract more gold, when needed, with the aid of an increase of the Bank Rate. She did not have to pursue a policy of accumulating a large permanent gold reserve but left it to the operation of the automatic gold standard to secure additional gold when required.

As a result of the First World War this situation underwent a fundamental change. Britain no longer held all the trumps in the sphere of international trade and finance. She could no longer rely on the automatic working of the system. However, British monetary policy refused to recognise the change and continued to work on the assumption that Britain could afford to uphold free trade with the aid of a gold reserve that was a fraction of the American and even of the French gold reserve. It was not until the run on the pound in 1931 that the need for a substantial gold reserve came to be realised in Britain.

The experience of 1931 taught Britain and other countries yet another lesson – that a monetary reserve, in order to be usable, must be liquid. At the time of the gold standard crisis, when the Bank of England's gold reserve was practically exhausted, Britain held overseas investments to a value of some £3,500 million In normal times the realisation of a fraction of these holdings – in addition to the recalling of the short-term credits of some £150 million – would have been sufficent to restore stability and confidence. Amidst a world-wide crisis, however, these investments became utterly immobilised and were quite useless for immediate requirements. Even the greater part of short term claims on foreign countries became frozen owing to the insolvency of the debtor countries if not of the individual debtors. A 'standstill' was imposed on all short-term claims on Germany, Austria and Hungry. Many other debtor foreign countries stopped the transfer of credit repayments aboard.

Evidently the aims of monetary policy in respect of the building-up of monetary reserves had to be reconsidered. Up to the outbreak of the Second World War it was one of the main objectives of the activities of the Exchange Equalisation Fund and of British monetary policy in general to build up a gold reserve commensurate with the country's importance in world trade and world finance. It was realised that, amidst the prevailing instability, the policy of keeping barely enough gold for immediate requirements was no longer satisfactory. In particular it was realised that a gold reserve representing a fraction of the foreign short-term claims on Britain was inadequate. The experience of 1931 showed that foreign balances were liable to be withdrawn on a large scale at short notice. It brought home the necessity for building up a sufficiently large reserve to meet such withdrawals in addition to meeting adverse trade balances and any temporary losses due to persistent speculative pressure.

Amidst the unstable conditions that both preceded and succeeded the Second World War, monetary policy had to aim at maintaining a large and liquid monetary reserve. Hence the conclusion of a large dollar loan in 1945. But the ease with which the proceeds of that loan became depleted in a matter of months shows that in the prevailing world conditions even an exceptionally large and absolutely liquid monetary reserve is liable to fail to achieve its end. Evidently no reserve is inexhaustible. As a result of the heavy outflow of gold from the United States between the late fifties and early seventies, it had become possible to visualise conditions in which even the gigantic American gold reserve might become inadequate to meet prolonged and persistent adverse pressure. Each time it declined to a new post-war low there was concern in American opinion, and even more in World opinion. Amidst the prevailing instability even the United States could no longer afford to abstain from conducting her monetary policy with an eye in the monetary reserve. Indeed, when in August 1971 the gold reserve declined below $10 billion, The Government decided to suspend the convertibility of the dollar and to devalue it.

In his book *The Dollar*, written in 1952, when the American gold stock was high and rising, Harrod urged the United Srates to double the dollar price of gold, in order to be able to write up the *value* of her gold reserve, and thus to ensure that it was adequate in case of another major war. Meanwhile, the sharp decline of the American gold reserve has induced many experts to advocate that remedy. Devaluations may be undertaken not only for the purpose of increasing the book-keeping value of gold and foreign exchange reserves, but also for raising their amount through an improvement of the balance of payments and a reversal of the outflow of 'hot money'.

The fact that no monetary reserve is inexhaustible is an additional reason for concentrating much thought and effort on its reinforcement. Monetary policies pursuing directly that end have to be supplemented by monetary and economic policies making for sound internal conditions Even the biggest gold reserve is liable to disappear if pressure on it is justified by a persistently adverse trade balance due to inflated cost of production; by inadequate production and excessive consumption; by inadequate saving and excessive spending; by maladjustment of production, overambitious capital investment, etc. It would be a mistake to imagine that once the monetary policy aimed at building up a large gold reserve has achieved its end we can afford to over-spend or over-lend or relax our productive effort, trusting, as we did before 1914, that the automatic working of natural tendencies would correct the situation when correction was needed. A big gold reserve must be regarded as the means to the end of safeguarding the stability and the prosperity of the national economy against the ups and downs of the trade balance and other uncontrollable international factors. Behind the shielding wall of an adequate gold reserve the nation fortunate enough to possess it is in a position to expand safely. But its Government should be wise enough to know how to safeguard its strength by maintaining a well-balanced production and resisting the temptation of excessive consumption or of investment beyond its means.

Monetary policy aiming at a large gold reserve is complementary to monetary policy aiming at expanding production for the purpose of increasing exports or reducing import requirements. Situations may arise, however, in which the two aims may come into conflict with each other. Such situations are apt to come about when full employment is reached and any further monetary expansion is liable to produce inflationary effects. The aim of maintaining full employment may demand the continuation of the expansionary monetary policy. On the othe hand, the aim of safeguarding the monetary reserve may call for disinflation. Under the gold standard this prevailed over everything else – if for no other reason than because a loss of gold would automatically have caused a contraction of credit, resulting in an increase of unemployment. Now that there is no direct and obvious connection between the volume of monetary reserve and that of currency and credit, it is tempting to adopt the view that considerations of full employment must in all circumstances prevail over safeguarding the monetary reserve. It is widely believed that a high level of employment can now be maintained irrespective of a decline of the monetary reserve, the gold content of which has in any case declined considerably.

This belief is based partly on the increased extent of international financial co-operation through the IMF and other channels, co-operation which has greatly weakened the balance of payments discipline, even though the IMF and Central Banks often attach strings to their financial assistance. The revival of private international lending – largely through Euro-currency and Euro-issue operations – has also assisted deficit countries to pursue a policy aimed at accelerating economic growth irrespective of the resulting drain on their monetary reserves which can now be offset through borrowing instead of adopting sound policies. In addition two major innovations in the sphere of international finance pursue the same end and are likely to pursue it even more in years to come – flexible exchange rates and SDRs.

Any restrictionist monetary measure undertaken for the sake of safeguarding the monetary reserve is always widely condemned on account of its adverse effect on employment. Beyond doubt the supreme end of avoiding large-scale unemployment must always be borne in mind. It was accepted as the basic principle of monetary policy in various official pronouncements and it was emphatically reaffirmed in the Radcliffe Report. When there is a run on the monetary reserve, however, the question is not whether employment should be sacrificed for the sake of saving the reserve, but whether employment can be better maintained through safeguarding the monetary reserve by means of credit restrictions at the cost of causing thereby some relatively moderate temporary unemployment, or whether an increase in unemployment should be deferred until the reserve is exhausted, in which case when it does come, as a result of a scarcity of imported raw materials, it is liable to be extensive and lasting. It is dangerous to dogmatise about this question as indeed about any subject relating to monetary policy.

The requirements of external monetary stability may, in given situations, conflict with those of safeguarding or increasing the gold reserve. In 1931 the gold standard was abandoned and sterling was allowed to depreciate in order to replenish the depleted gold reserve. The devaluation of 1949 pursued the same end. The agitation in favour of a "floating" pound that developed during the fifties was largely based on the assumption that, by allowing sterling 'to find its own level' instead of supporting it against an adverse pressure, it would be possible to avoid heavy losses of monetary reserve. In 1963 the British Government actually declared its policy to allow the reserve to decline, and to accept a "negative reserve" in the form of foreign short-term credits, for the sake of being able to reduce unemployment and to increase the annual rate of growth to 4 per cent.

Hitherto we have been dealing with the international aspects of monetary policy aiming at the accumulation and maintenance of monetary reserves. It had, however, also domestic aspects in the past. Monetary reserves were liable to changes not only through imports and exports of monetary metals but also through increases or decreases of private holdings of such metals. For many centuries privately held silver plate was regarded as an important secondary monetary reserve of England. Demand for bullion for the manufacture of plate absorbed a large proportion of the available monetary metals, to the detriment of the Mint. On the other hand, from time to time it provided an important domestic source out of which the Mint was able to secure monetary metals. In more recent times private holdings of gold coins were regarded as a kind of secondary gold reserve. Indeed, de-hoarded sovereigns came in very useful to the Government after 1931 and again at the beginning of the

Second World War. In other countries too hoarded gold or silver coins provide a useful secondary reserve, especially in India where de-hoarding became an important factor after 1931.

The disadvantage of the dispersal of gold by the hoarding of coins among private individuals is that the gold cannot necessarily be made available in sufficient quantites when needed. Monetary policy has only a limited influence over movements of gold between private hoards and public reserves. The authorities are usually in a position to increase private holdings at the expense of public holdings through the issue of coins. Movements in the opposite sense depend, however. largely on the willingness of private holders to surrender their holdings. Nevertheless, the authorities have various means at their disposal with the aid of which they can pursue the end of concentrating a large proportion of privately held gold in their own hands. Even so, in view of the drain on the world's monetary stocks of gold caused by private hoarding, the advantages of possessing a second line of defence are offset by the disadvantages of weakening the first line of defence.

The modern trend of monetary policy is decidedly in favour of ensuring the concentration of gold hoards in the hands of the authorities. The issue of gold coins has practically ceased and coins issued in the past gradually find their way into monetary reserves. During the World Wars the need for safeguarding the largest possible proportion of gold supplies for monetary purposes was already generally realised. Monetary policy in various countries aimed at attracting gold both from abroad and from internal holdings. Unfortunately from the point of view of the adequacy of monetary reserves, a large part of the gold output after the Second World War found its way to hoards, in spite of the efforts of the International Monetary Fund to discourage such dispersal of the monetary metal.

Between the two wars an influential school of thought developed under the leadership of Keynes, according to which it was a mistake for monetary policy to aim at the accumulation and maintenance of a gold reserve. Although Keynes influenced the

trend of monetary policy in many other ways, he entirely failed
to influence it in the respect. In spite of the radical changes in
the monetary system that have taken place during the last two
decades the accumulation and maintenance of a gold reserve
has remained one of the most important ends of monetary
policy.

Even the inter-war trend of employing foreign exchange
reserves in addition to, or instead of, gold reserves had become
reversed to some extent as a result of losses suffered by Central
Banks and Treasuries through devaluations. The practice was
revived, however, on an unprecedented scale after the Second
World War. Anyhow, from the point of view of monetary policy
it is a matter of detail whether the reserve it aims at increasing
consists of gold or foreign exchange.

The Radcliffe Report stressed the need for strengthening the
reserves, not only in order to adapt them to the high level of
Britain's external short-term liabilities but also in order to cope
with the wide post-war fluctuations of the balance of payments
and of the amount of foreign sterling balances to meet requirements of the Sterling Area, and to enable sterling to serve as an
international currency.

Two important factors have emerged since the Radcliffe
Report's findings concerning the British reserves – the weakening of the ties of the Sterling Area and the emergence of SDRs
as a new form of reserve asset, with the possibility of a considerable increase in its importance through the adoption of the
Barber Plan. During the sixties Central Banks of the Outer
Sterling Area made considerable progress towards a diversification of their reserves, but under the Basle Agreement of 1968
they agreed to abstain from continuing withdrawals of their
reserves from London in return for a dollar guarantee. Although
the improvement of sterling's position in 1969–71 induced many
of them to increase their sterling reserves, they changed their
policy after the relapse of sterling in 1972. The weakening of
Sterling Area ties by the British authorities through the adoption of exchange restrictions in relation to Sterling Area countries is also likely to induce Sterling Area Central Banks to make

further progress towards the diversification of their reserves, especially after Britain's entry into the EEC.

The adoption of SDRs resulted in a noteworthy addition to the British reserves. Further additions are expected either through the issue of an additional tranche of the orginal SDRs or through the adoption of the Barber Plan. But to a large degree the new SDRs to be allocated to Britain and to the United States will not be used for the reinforcement of the reserves but for the repayment of external short-term liabilities.

The officially declared policy of Britain and the United States is to eliminate gold from the monetary system. Nevertheless the authorities of both countries endeavour to maintain a gold reserve.

CHAPTER THIRTEEN

Influencing Foreign Trade

WE saw in the last chapter that the aim of monetary policy to accumulate and maintain a substantial monetary reserve is attained largely through measures in the sphere of foreign trade. Accumulation and maintenance of metallic or foreign exchange reserves or SDRs is not, however, the only object of influencing exports and imports by monetary policy devices. From an early period the State authority also endeavoured to encourage exports and to discourage imports for the purpose of attracting money from abroad to meet the financial requirements of domestic production and trade. A third purpose for which exports are stimulated is to provide the means with which to pay for essential imports. A fourth object of monetary policy aiming at influencing foreign trade is to create foreign demand for domestic products as a means of increasing the prosperity of producers and of creating employment.

Already in early mercantilist literature there was a distinct tendency towards favouring exports as an exceptionally worthwhile type of trade. Various authors throughout the sixteenth and seventeenth centuries emphasised that export trade was more important than domestic trade. They said that the latter merely amounted to taking in each other's washing – a process by which one individual may profit at the expense of another, but the nation as a whole does not stand to gain. On the other hand they claimed that in foreign trade there was a possibility of their nation making a profit at the expense of other nations. This view was the beginning of the policy of priority to foreign trade that still prevails. Exaltation of foreign trade over home trade was not confined to the mercantilists. Their opponents, the Free Traders, adopted the same cult, even though they arrived at it on totally different grounds.

Whatever may have been the reason for this preference for foreign trade, it was bound to influence monetary policy. The encouragement of foreign trade was one of the objectives of mercantilist policy and remained one of the objectives of nineteenth-century liberal policy. The liberal view favoured exports not for the sake of any influx of money it might produce but for the sake of furthering international division of labour under which everything is produced in the country where it can be produced in the most favourable conditions and at the lowest cost. This aspect of it was not appreciated until Adam Smith and his successors of the liberal school.

The original reason for favouring export trade, apart from increasing the monetary reserve of Treasuries and the monetary circulation of the country, was that its proceeds provided the means for buying much-sought-after imports. Even though the prevailing policy was to discourage imports, especially luxuries, the need for certain imports had always been realised. Exports were favoured in order to be able to pay for essential raw materials, for food, or for certain much-coveted manufactures which could not be produced within the country.

It was not until a later stage that the need for encouraging export trade and reducing import trade for the sake of stimulating home production came to be realised. It was the consequence of the development of mass production calling for extensive foreign markets. Technical progress and the increase of the population enabled both industrial and agricultural countries to produce large surpluses available for export. This increased productive capacity could not be fully utilised without the danger of over-production unless foreign markets could be secured. Once this stage was reached, the motive for assisting export trade through devices of monetary policy became considerably stronger. In particular, during periods of large-scale industrial unemployment the possibility of 'exporting unemployment' with the aid of monetary devices came to be realised.

The aim of stimulating export trade can, of course, be approached through various non-monetary means which are outside the scope of this book. Monetary policy can be, however, very helpful to an export drive. The manipulation of exchange rates to stimulate exports had been a device that was frequently resorted to in earlier centuries and again since the First World War. Devices of domestic monetary policy, too, can be placed at the service of an export drive. That end can be pursued by curtailing domestic consumption and reducing the cost of production with the aid of deflation, but also by stimulating the expansion of exporting or import-saving industries by means of subsidies or, if necessary, even by means of a certain degree of inflation. To that end discriminatory credit facilities can be applied in order to divert productive resources to capital investment in industries producing largely for export or to those capable of replacing imports.

The same devices of monetary policy may serve all the objectives of expanding exports. An export surplus achieved with their aid can increase the monetary reserve and the monetary circulation at the same time as providing means for increasing imports and stimulating the development of home production. This does not mean, however, that these various considerations never come into conflict with each other. In medieval times the State authority was primarily concerned with filling the Treasury through attracting bullion and coin by imposing customs duties on exports as well as on imports. Obviously export duties tended to discourage export trade to the same extent as import duties tended to handicap import trade. Nevertheless, the kings of that period were satisfied that they stood to gain both on the swings and on the roundabouts by levying and collecting substantial duties on goods entering and leaving the country. By foregoing their claim on export duties they could have assisted export trade and could have improved the trade balance, which would have meant a larger amount of coins for the requirements of their subjects. Since, however, they were primarily concerned with their own Treasury, they resorted to a policy which they expected would help to accumulate treasure even though this was to be to the detriment of export trade and of the domestic monetary circulation. They did not, however, ignore the latter consideration. They imposed export duties mainly on goods badly needed abroad, which were bought in spite of the export duty. Moreover, by means of bans on the export of precious metals, and Statutes of Employment under which the proceeds of imports from abroad had to be spent in England, they endeavoured to maintain a balance between exports and imports and avoid a drain on the monetary circulation. This, however, was a secondary objective.

This medieval policy gradually gave way during the sixteenth and seventeenth centuries to a policy which aimed at securing an export surplus not so much for the sake of the benefit of the Treasury as in order to provide trade with an adequate money supply. This attitude gained ground with the progress of the merchant and manufacturer classes and the decline of the absolute power of the rulers. For some time, however, it was deemed to be of relatively small importance whether the much-desired export surplus was achieved through a curtailment of imports or an expansion of exports. In this respect again the development of industrial production with its growing requirements of imported raw materials played a decisive part in influencing the ends of monetary policy. Once the need for large imports came to be realised, import restrictions had to be relaxed. In order to be able to pay for growing imports the volume of exports had to be increased.

An outstanding example of a conflict between the ends of monetary policy in the sphere of foreign trade was provided in Britain soon after the Second World War. The execution of many extensive domestic capital investment schemes entailed inflation. Yet is was necessary in the interest of Britain's future exporting capacity, for the sake of which plants had to be modernised and expanded, new industries had to be created, and additional electric power supplies had to be provided. On the other hand, the urgent claims of export trade called for a curtailment of domestic demand for capital equipment, so as to enable and induce heavy industries to produce largely for export. When there was chronic large-scale unemployment in Britain before the Second World War this conflict did not arise in an acute form. There was ample productive capacity for satisfying the requirements of capital investment and also those of domestic consumption, and there was an ample capacity for producing larger exportable surpluses. Even then an ambitious capital investment programme meant a rising trend in prices which was liable to discourage exports. The difficulty of overcoming this handicap, however, was not insuperable.

On the other hand, after the Second World War, with the virtual disappearance of unemployment, the British authorities were often faced by a choice between reducing their capital investment programme and accepting an adverse trade balance. At first the solution was found in the financing of the adverse trade balance out of American aid. But from time to time it was found necessary to make drastic cuts in the investment programme because of the decline of the gold reserve owing to an adverse balance of payments in excess of the proceeds of dollar aid. Inflation had to be curtailed from time to time, and this was done largely by cutting investment expenditure. Even though this was detrimental to Britain's future capacity to export, it was considered inevitable in order to cope with the immediate problem of the adverse balance of payments. That problem presented itself in a more acute form after dollar aid came to an end.

During the sixties and early seventies the increase of unemployment made it appear once more necessary to pursue policies aiming at increasing exports. This was done to a large extent by means of Government-guaranteed long-term credits. By such means it was possible to create employment, but only at the cost of prolonged delays in receiving the proceeds of a large proportion of exports, which were detrimental to leads and lags.

Stimulating exports is not the only foreign trade objective pursued with the aid of monetary policy devices for monetary ends. In given circumstances monetary policy devices are also apt to be applied for stimulating imports. Immediately after the Second World War, when there was a world-wide scarcity of many essential commodities, the mercantilist principle came to be reversed. Instead of competing for each other's gold and silver, the Governments were competing for the scarce supplies of essential goods – raw materials, food, capital equipment, etc. In order to be able to pay high prices for these goods without unduly raising their prices in terms of domestic currency, the monetary policy of several countries aimed at raising the exchange value of the national currency, or at any rate at maintaining it at a high level.

While before the war there was competitive currency depreciation to stimulate exports, after the war the volume of exportable surpluses was limited. Countries posssesing essential goods endeavoured to obtain the maximum of foreign exchange for them and to that end a high exchange value of the national currency was called for. There were indications of a competitive currency *appreciation*, though it did not proceed very far in spite of the prolonged existence of a sellers' market. With the advent of a buyers' market the inducement to overvalue the exchanges ceased.

Another instance of a monetary policy aiming at the encouragement of imports rather than exports was provided by Germany under the Nazi regime. One of the best-known 'Schachtian' devices was to compel countries under German occupation or under German influence to accept the reichsmark at an abnormally high exchange value in payment for their exports to Germany. By such means Germany secured the necessary imports at a low price in terms of Reichsmarks or indeed in terms of German goods exported to the countries concerned. The same practice was pursued by the USSR after the Second World War in the satellite States, which had to accept the rouble at an excessively high value in payment for their exports to Soviet Russia.

Monetary policy may also pursue the end of stimulating re-export trade and various international commercial and financial activities. In order that a country should be able to fulfil the functions of an international commercial, banking, insurance, etc., centre, it has to possess a stable and convertible currency. Its monetary policy is liable to be influenced considerably by the desire to serve the requirements of these activities. It was one of the major considerations which induced the British Governments in the early twenties to adopt a monetary policy aiming at the restoration of the gold standard. This was achieved in 1925, but the appreciation of sterling to $4·86 imposed a grave handicap on both home trade and export trade. Although the restoration and maintenance of London's international position was not the sole end of that policy, it undoubtedly played a very important part. Likewise, after the Second World War premature attempts at convertibility were largely inspired by the desire to secure the benefits of invisible exports represented by earnings from the international financial and commercial activities of London. This subject is discussed in detail in Chapter 17.

Monetary policies aimed at securing the role of international currency came to be reversed in the late sixties and early seventies. The series of sterling and dollar crises created a strong public opinion, first in Britain and then in the United States, in favour of divesting the national currency of its onerous role of international currency. Governments with strong currencies were determined to avoid playing that role. Political opinion, academic opinion and official opinion were swimming as usual with the prevailing tide. The view came to be widely adopted that to play the role of an international financial centre was, from the point of view of national interests, more trouble than it was worth. This attitude came to receive strong support from inflationists, for measures adopted to defend the currency for the sake of upholding its international role often necessitated a slowing down of expansion. Few people were aware that, since it is in accordance with long-term national interests to resist inflation, the defence of currencies serves national as well as international interests.

Beyond doubt monetary policy can play an important part in encouraging international trade by aiming at facilitating international payments. Free trade is inconceivable without free transfers. During the nineteenth century, when exchange restrictions were virtually unknown, high tariffs were considered to be the main obstacles to a really free international interchange of goods. In more recent times free traders have discovered that the most formidable enemy is not the tariff wall but import quotas, embargoes on imports and exchange restrictions. Under the experience of the thirties and forties trade came to be regarded as being relatively free if it had to cope with nothing worse than high tariffs. By making the allocation of foreign exchanges to importers subject to licence, the authorities had in fact imposed a watertight control over imports, far more effective than any tariff wall. A monetary policy aiming at free trade had to remove exchange restrictions, at any rate as far as current commercial payments were concerned. This principle may sound very simple; in reality its application gives rise to difficult dilemmas. In time of peace it is usually possible for a well-governed country to do without exchange restrictions in the interests of free trading. Indeed, the adoption and maintenance of a stable and convertible currency is a very effective contribution of monetary policy towards an expansion of international trade. But very often this end can only be achieved by sacrificing other monetary ends.

Monetary policy may aim at overcoming transfer difficulties that would otherwise hamper free international trade, by means of international arrangements. This subject will be dealt with in Chapter 45.

CHAPTER FOURTEEN

Flexible Exchange Rates

ONE of the major ends of monetary policy is to ensure that economic growth is not handicapped by setbacks caused by foreign exchange crises. There was a widespread feeling that the main cause of the frequently recurrent currency crises which lead to deflationary measures and other restrictions was the undue rigidity of the parities under the gold standard and again under the Bretton Woods system. Accordingly, the remedy that was widely advocated was an increased flexibility of exchange rates. Although this subject will be dealt with briefly in Chapter 39 on Foreign Exchange Policy, in view of the controversy that is raging over it, and even more in view of the recent experiments in flexibility, it deserves more attention. The subject was covered in great detail in my book *The Case against Floating Exchanges*.

There can be little doubt that undue rigidity of parities during the inter-war period and also since the war was the source of much trouble. In a number of instances Governments were unable or unwilling to take the necessary measures to lower or raise the price levels of their respective countries in order to correct the overvaluation or undervaluation of their exchanges. Yet they refused to concede defeat and devalue or revalue their currencies as an alternative to the adjustment of their domestic purchasing power. Prolonged defence of the wrong parities caused an immense amount of difficulties both to the countries directly concerned and to other countries. The resulting foreign exchange crises created a feeling of uncertainty which was damaging to national economies and to world economy.

To avoid such crises it has been suggested that parities should be done away with altogether and that exchange rates should be allowed to float freely. This was actually done in a number of instances not under irresistible pressure but as a matter of deliberate policy. Thus the Canadian dollar was allowed to float between 1956 and 1962, and again since 1971. During various periods the Deutsche Mark, the Dutch guilder and other currencies were allowed to float, and following on the suspension of the convertibility of the dollar on 15 August 1971, practically all currencies were allowed to float until the conclusion of the Smithsonian Agreement on 18 December 1971. Again on 16 June 1972 sterling was allowed to float and several other currencies followed the lead.

The assumption on which this policy is based is that if exchange rates are allowed to find their level they will float to a level at which imports and exports would balance. This assumption is, however, entirely fallacious. It rests on the false belief that there are only commercial transactions in the foreign exchange market, and it ignores any possibility that capital movements, speculative transactions and arbitrage transactions might divert the exchange rates from the level at which imports and exports would balance. In any case, even if only commercial transactions existed there are always time-lags between changes in exchange rates and their effects on imports and exports, and the timing of payments for imports and exports is subject to variable degrees of leads and lags. The chances that a floating exchange would float to its commercial equilibrium rate are extremely remote. The equilibrium levels for speculative transactions, arbitrage and short-term capital movements are quite different from the equilibrium level for commercial transactions, and there is no equilibrium level for long-term capital movements, especially those resulting from direct investment abroad.

It was found in almost every instance that exchanges which were allowed to float could not be allowed to float freely, and Governments had to intervene to step up or resist their rise or fall. This experience disposes of one of the main arguments in

favour of floating – that it obviates the necessity for maintaining big reserves or borrowing abroad in order to be able to
support the national currency. It becomes very often necessary
to support a floating exchange, especially if its depreciation
assumes a self-aggravating character.

Most practical bankers and businessmen are opposed to
floating exchanges because the resulting uncertainty increases
the requirements for forward exchange facilities, at the same
time as reducing the volume of facilities available. As a result
the cost of forward covering is liable to become prohibitive,
expecially when trading in goods on which the profit margin
is narrow. This obvious practical point is usually ignored by
academic economists and is casually dismissed if their attention
is drawn to it.

The untenable case for floating exchanges is supported by a
large number of economists with a fanaticism worthy of a much
better cause. Many of those who realise its utter absurdity, but
who feel none the less that something must be done to mitigate
the undue rigidity of parities, are in favour of some different
form of flexibility of a less extreme degree. One of the systems
advocated by many Central Banks and Treasuries is a widening
of the spread between the maximum and minimum support
points of the exchanges. Some supporters of this system would
like to widen the spread to something like 10 per cent on either
side of parities, which would virtually amount to the adoption
of floating exchanges with limits fixed for their fluctuations.

This system is based on the assumption that if the spread is
wide enough speculators will not have the advantage of considerable profit possibilities and only limited risks. Wider
spreads admittedly increase the risks to speculators and increase
the chances of the authorities to inflict penalties on them.
Advocates of a broader band overlook, however, while that,
under systems of narrow bands only those speculators take a
hand who expect a change of parities, under systems of broader,
bands it is likely to appear worth while to speculate even if no
changes of parities are expected.

The Smithsonian Agreement provided for a widening of the

band from $1\frac{1}{2}$ per cent to $4\frac{1}{2}$ per cent. Judging by the volume of speculative operations even before the crisis of June and July 1972, the reduction of the spread failed to reduce perceptibly the volume of speculative activity. However, it is beyond doubt that the narrowing of the band is preferable to the adoption of floating rates. It is also preferable to the system of crawling pegs under which the equilibrium of an overvalued or undervalued exchange is sought to be restored by slow gradual adjustments spread over a prolonged period, so that each adjustment would be fractional. What advocates of this system overlook is that, once the Government's intention to adjust the parities becomes obvious, speculators would not await the completion of the crawl but would anticipate it, thereby forcing the Government's hand to make the full adjustment without the projected delay. It is difficult to understand why it should be assumed that anyone who distrusts the British Government's ability or willingness to defend sterling at, say, $2·38 would trust its ability and willingness to defend it at, say, $2·37\frac{3}{4}$ in spite of its intention to lower the rate to, say, $2·20 in the course of the next twelve months.

The flexible system which is much more in accordance with common sense is negotiated realignments of parities on the formula of the Smithsonian Agreement. The leading Governments should meet from time to time and negotiate an agreed pattern of parities which appears to be more easy to defend than the existing parities. Admittedly, this system is far from being foolproof, for there is always likely to be hard bargaining, and Governments are far from being infallible. Thus the Smithsonian Agreement provided for an excessive devaluation of the dollar against sterling, with the result that in less than six months there was a landslide-like selling pressure on sterling, leading to its depreciation which again triggered off a wave of selling of dollars and a flight into Swiss francs and Deutsche Marks. But the principle of periodic revisions of parities is sound, always provided that its too frequent application will not convey the impression that the Government does not intend to defend the existing parities.

This unfortunate impression was what doomed sterling in June 1972. In his Budget speech in March 1972 Mr Barber made it plain that his Government did not intend to defend sterling if doing so would entail a slowing down of economic growth. As a result, on the first occasion on which sterling became subject to selling pressure, overseas holders of sterling balances, speculators and firms engaged in foreign trade came to assume that sterling would not be defended and made their arrangements accordingly. When after the beginning of the wave of selling it was found that the Government had really no intention of adopting effective defensive measures, the selling pressure assumed a landslide-like character.

Another practice which should be avoided is too frequent devaluations or revaluations. If parities are changed as frequently as they have been in Brazil, for instance, during most of the post-war period, it almost amounts to the adoption of floating exchanges. There must surely be a happy medium between the stubborn defence of parities at an impossible level and light-hearted yielding to pressures whenever they arise.

Up to now we have been dealing mostly with devaluation-prone currencies. But revaluation-prone currencies too are liable to cause much trouble. Their frequent mini-revaluations or their upward floating is liable to encourage the flight of funds into those currencies, and this is liable to undermine confidence in currencies out of which the funds seek flight into revaluation-prone currencies. The influx of large amounts of hot money is a dubious blessing, because it increases the amount that is liable to be withdrawn when the tide turns. This was what happened with sterling. Its strength in 1971 caused by the export surplus attracted very large amounts of hot money, so that when the tide did turn amounts of unprecedented magnitude came to be withdrawn in a matter of days. The false feeling of security generated by the increase of the British reserve as a result of the influx of hot money must have contributed towards the stepping-up of wage demands, and it was the satisfaction of many of these demands that turned the tide against sterling.

It seems evident that, no matter what system is adopted, a currency cannot be defended unless the authorities are prepared to give its stability a high priority over other ends of monetary policy. While a high degree of fundamental disequilibrium may have to be dealt with through changes of parities, a more moderate degree of overvaluation or undervaluation could and should be dealt with by adjustments of the domestic purchasing power of the currency concerned. Speculators and others dealing in exchanges should be left in no doubt about the Government's ability and willingness to make sacrifices if necessary in order to avoid unduly frequent and too light-hearted changes of parities.

CHAPTER FIFTEEN

Fiscal Objectives

ONE of the earliest ends of monetary policy must have been to serve the financial interests of the State authority. Indeed, it seems reasonable to assume that in many instances money owed its origin to the desire of primitive rulers to further the aims of their treasuries. At an early stage of economic evolution the subjects of these rulers contributed their dues in kind, surrendering a proportion of their products. The accumulation of an odd assortment of objects in the primitive treasuries, however, presented grave problems. Ancient Egyptian history provides much evidence about such treasuries which had to store a wide range of industrial and agricultural products, including such incongruous objects as furniture, grain, wine, cattle, etc. For some reason which is difficult to understand, the Egyptians were prepared to put up with the clumsiness and costliness of the system even after having reached an advanced stage of civilisation and statecraft. Other communities must have felt at a much earlier stage of their development the need for standardising the contributions to tribal or national treasuries.

Even before the means in which compulsory gifts to the tribal authority, tributes, fines or taxes had to be discharged became standardised, there was bound to be some unit of account on the basis of which the relative value of the various contributions in kind could be reckoned. The primitive State authority, having realised the inconvenience of accumulating and distributing its treasure in kind, sooner or later imposed on its subjects its rules about the standardised form in which payments must be made, leaving it to the subjects to convert their sundry possessions into that form before making payments.

It is, of course, impossible to form an opinion about the relative part played by this factor in the adoption of monetary systems and the gradual improvement that was achieved largely in order that they should serve better the convenience of the Treasuries. It seems probable, however, that this consideration played an important part in influencing early decisions of monetary policy. Sooner or later the State authority came to regulate and operate its monetary system largely from the point of view of fiscal advantages. Monetary policy was placed at the service of public finance many centuries before public finance came to be placed at the service of monetary policy.

The fiscal ends monetary policy can pursue can be manifold. Kings or their treasurers in the past and their modern equivalents in more recent times found many ingenious ways in which they could use their power over the monetary system for the benefit of their Treasuries.

The royal prerogative to issue money and to determine the metallic content and face value of the coinage has been for many centuries an important direct source of revenue. Indeed, from the early origins of the monetary system the issue of coins was apt to be regarded as being largely, if not exclusively, a revenue-producing device. The State often secured for itself the monopoly of producing or importing the monetary material. Thus in many countries the mining of precious metals was made a State monopoly. The mints, whether run by the State or farmed out to private enterprise against substantial payment, charged a seignorage for the benefit of the Treasury, varying during the Middle Ages between 2 and 12 per cent. For this reason alone the Treasury had a vested interest in ensuring that the mints were kept busy. This consideration influenced medieval monetary policy to no slight degree and was responsible for many debasement decisions. Whenever the mint stood idle because the market value of gold or silver at home or abroad was higher than the mint price, the kings always felt tempted to ensure an increased activity through raising the mint price of the metals. In such instances – and they were many – the fiscal ends of monetary policy often outweighed other ends.

Debasement served fiscal interests also through securing a profit for the kings on the re-coinage of the coins in circulation on the basis of a lower metallic content of the monetary unit. Contemporary writers frequently argued that even from a purely fiscal point of view this was a very short-sighted policy. It is true that the kings collected on each occasion a handsome immediate profit. But they were also obliged to collect their revenue thereafter in a currency of an inferior value. Admittedly, during the medieval period prices were rather inelastic, so that it took some time before the princes came to feel the full disadvantages of debasement in the form of higher prices and the resulting higher expenditure. Rising prices worked out, however, in the long run to their disadvantage, because feudal dues had been rigidly fixed and revenue from the royal domains was also inclined to lag far behind the rise in prices. Nevertheless, many monarchs found it difficult to resist the temptation of an immediate profit on debasement or re-coinage.

The adoption of paper currency opened new possibilities for treasuries to secure large financial resources with the aid of monetary policy devices. This was done on a gigantic scale during various major wars in modern times. It was also resorted to by many Governments to a more moderate but substantial extent even between wars. In countries where the paper currency was issued by State banks the Treasuries had a direct and unlimited control over the printing press. In countries where Central Banks were in charge of the note issue it was necessary for the Treasuries to induce these institutions to grant them advances. This was usually done in return for granting or renewing their charter. Though in many instances Central Banks resisted such inflationary borrowing, they usually yielded eventually. Their loans to the Treasuries were in many cases never repaid.

Another way in which paper money was used to serve fiscal ends was through its devaluation, as a result of which the book-keeping value of the gold reserves of Central Banks was written up and the profit surrendered to the Treasuries. What is even more important, public debts running into astronomical figures were reduced to more bearable proportions in real terms. In the majority of instances this result was incidental, however, and the currency was devalued for other reasons.

As a result of the nationalisation of many Central Banks after the Second World War, the extent of the control of Treasuries over the printing press increased. There is, therefore, more temptation and more opportunity to use the note issue for fiscal ends. Nevertheless, thanks to the broadening of the responsibilities of the Treasury in Britain and other countries – it has now come to be regarded as being responsible not only for public finance but for the entire national economy – Finance Ministers are now liable to think twice before embarking on crude monetary inflation unless it is under pressure of extreme emergency. In any event, in advanced countries inflation through the operation of the printing press has now been replaced by more sophisticated versions of monetary policy pursuing fiscal ends.

We saw above that the adoption of a standardised means of payment and the improvement of its form were in themselves calculated to help the State authority in the collection of taxation revenue. The power of the State authority to influence the quantity of money was also often used in the interests of revenue. In his *Essay on the Nature of Trade*, published more than two centuries ago, Cantillon remarked: 'The revenues of the State are raised more easily and in comparatively much larger amounts where money abounds.' It was to the interests of rulers, however despotic and selfish, to endeavour to ensure plentiful monetary supplies in their countries, if only in order to be able to take away a great part of it in high taxation. Beyond a certain limit the increase in the volume of currency is apt, however, to react unfavourably on public revenue. One of the causes of the weakening of royal authority in England during the seventeenth century was that the rise in prices resulting from the influx of precious metals from the New World reduced the purchasing power of the largely inflexible royal revenues from Crown domains. Kings were no longer able even in times of peace to live on the proceeds of their domains, and became increasingly dependent on the voting of supplies by Parliaments. In earlier periods, however, their capacity to collect taxation was often reduced not through an inflationary depreciation of the coinage but through the inadequate volume of coins in circulation. In such situations it was to their interest to do everything possible to attract precious metals to the country, not only for the sake of their revenue derived from the Mint or from the collection of customs duties, but also because the increase in the circulation of coins made it easier to collect revenue.

In modern times too, a moderate degree of inflation may assist Treasuries in solving their Budgetary problems by automatically raising the yield of taxes. Advanced inflation, however, is liable to operate in the opposite direction because the increase of expenditure may well outdistance that of revenue. Much depends, of course, on the system of taxation in force and on the relative extent of tax evasion. While in Britain after the Second World War the rise in prices produced a series of unexpectedly large revenue surpluses, in France it resulted in a perennial Budgetary deficit owing to the high degree of resistance of the French public to taxation. This is an instance to illustrate that the same rule does not necessarily meet the requirements of monetary policy in different countries even though the ends of their monetary policies may be identical. Moderate inflation may serve the purpose of augmenting revenue in countries where the yield of taxation is elastic while the expenditure is relatively inelastic. The existence of a large public debt is also said to increase the advantages of currency depreciation from a fiscal point of view, because the burden of interest charges does not rise in proportion to other items of public expenditure. On the other hand, in countries where the public is inflation-conscious, wages and salaries become adapted quickly to the rise in prices, especially if they are linked with the cost-of-living index. Consequently, public expenditure is apt to rise in sympathy with the price level.

Because of the uncertainty of the relative effect of higher

prices on revenue and expenditure, it is always risky to pursue fiscal ends by means of a deliberate policy of inflation. Likewise, it would be a leap in the dark to embark on deflation for the sake of securing Budgetary advantages. It is impossible to foresee how a fall in prices would affect revenue and expenditure respectively. Its disadvantages from a fiscal point of view are obvious when there is a large public debt, the burden of which will increase through a fall in prices. If the national income is reduced as a result of deflation, while the cost of the debt service remains unchanged, a higher proportion of the revenue has to be devoted to it.

Hitherto we have been dealing mainly with Budgetary ends of monetary policy. Another equally important fiscal end which monetary policy has to pursue is that of facilitating Government borrowing and the management of public debt. It is the duty of Treasuries to prepare the financial markets for the issue of new Government loans in order to ensure favourable terms and a satisfactory response by subscribers. To that end, the creation of easy money conditions is naturally helpful. On the other hand, in this respect as in respect of facilitating the collection of revenue, monetary expansionism is a double-edged weapon. If it leads to a persistent rising trend of prices it might discourage demand for fixed-interest securities unless interest rates are raised sufficiently to compensate investors for the prospective decline in the purchasing power of their investment income. It is, of course, possible for some time to ensure a satisfactory response to Government issues on terms favourable to the Treasury by means of further monetary expansion causing an increase in the volume of funds seeking investment. This is, however, a vicious circle which cannot be operated with impunity beyond a certain point. When it is eventually brought to an end the prices of Government securities are bound to fall heavily. This is what happened in Britain each time after the policy of bolstering up the Gilt-edged market came to an end.

Taking a long view, monetary policy can assist Treasuries very effectively in their task of financing Government deficits on favourable terms by ensuring monetary stability and strengthening confidence in the national currency instead of 'rigging the market' for Government loans. The benefits of such a policy, though less spectacular than those of stimulating investment demand artificially by monetary expansion, are apt to be more valuable in the long run. Even so, in special circumstances such as a war or a rearmament drive it may be found expedient to resort temporarily to the system of creating easy money conditions in order to ensure favourable terms during periods of heavy borrowing. A policy of cheap and plentiful money may also help Treasuries in their conversion operations. It tends to reduce or keep down the cost of the existing public debt. This consideration is of particular importance when a large proportion of the public debt is floating debt or is due to mature in the near future.

Under the modern currency and credit system the Treasuries are placed in the enviable position of being able to determine to a large degree the rate of interest at which they borrow. This was done systematically in Britain during the Second World War, and also during the early post-war years. In more recent times, however, the idea of 'rigging' the market in order to be able to carry out a necessary operation on favourable terms came to be looked upon critically. In their evidence before the Radcliffe Committee, official spokesmen said that their policy nowadays was to abstain from Bank Rate reductions on the eve of Treasury operations, so as to avoid giving rise to suspicions that the market was being rigged.

The end of economising in public debt charges is, moreover, apt to conflict with various other ends of monetary policy. Very often it may appear advisable to raise money rates in order to discourage inflation or an attack on the currency or a speculative boom. Until recently it was generally assumed that this could only be done at the expense of increasing the burden of interest charges on the public debt. After the Second World War attempts were made, however, in several countries to insulate interest charges on Government debt from those payable by the private sector of the economy. The methods employed to that end will be described in detail in chapters dealing with the means of monetary policy. It will be seen that to some extent at any rate some of these experiments were successful. It has proved to be possible in this respect to eat our cake and keep it. Several Treasuries resorted to credit restrictions in the private sector in order to resist inflation. In spite of this they were able to avoid corresponding increases of interest rates on the public debt.

Such successes as this policy was able to achieve were, however, limited and temporary. Generally speaking, the public sector had to share the cost of resisting inflation. In particular, cuts in spending for the sake of dealing with an overheated economy had to affect the public sector as well as the private sector. The Plowden Report – the Report of the Committee of Enquiry into Treasury Control of Public Expenditure – published in 1961, suggested that capital spending planned by Government Departments should not be interfered with by 'stop–go' policies, the burden of which should fall entirely on the private sector. This thoroughly unsound principle was actually applied on a number of occasions in the sixties.

CHAPTER SIXTEEN

Monetary Isolation

MONETARY policy has served isolationist ends in a large number of instances from the early thirties. It is our task to examine the monetary policies pursuing the end of economic isolationism and to take into account arguments both for and against. Of course, the pursuit of sound economic policies would obviate the need for monetary isolationism. This is, however, an imperfect world in which the pursuit of sound economic policies is often politically inexpedient. Situations are apt to arise in which various controls are resorted to in monetary isolation in preference to drastic deflation or devaluation.

Governments may resort to monetary isolationism because of the inadequacy of their foreign exchange reserves with which to maintain a system of free exchanges. In other instances they adopted or maintained a policy of isolationism in order to be able to expand their production or consumption with comparative impunity behind the shelter of an isolated monetary system.

Under an internationalist system any increase in domestic price level resulting from an expansionist policy, or any increase in domestic consumption that takes place as a result of artificially preventing an expansion of purchasing power from causing an increase of prices, is liable to bring its retribution in the form of an adverse balance of payments. Beyond doubt, the perpetuation of disequilibrium, by preventing an increase of demand from causing an increase of the price level, has proved to be feasible up to a point, as a result of the application of rationing and other control devices. If carried too far, the system is liable to break down sooner or later, apart altogether from its effect on the balance of payments. Even Stalin in his much-quoted article that appeared in the *Bolshevik*, just before the Communinst Party Congress of 1952, admitted with considerable emphasis that in the USSR economic laws could not be ignored indefinitely and to an unlimited extent. Nevertheless, even in countries which have not isolated themselves economically to such an extent as the USSR, it is possible to defy economic laws for a while so far as the internal economy is concerned.

The penalty for ignoring economic laws is apt to come much more swiftly in the sphere of the balance of payments than in internal economy. Monetary expansion in an already fully employed domestic economy necessarily means that too large a proportion of the products is used up for domestic capital investment or consumption, and that import requirements for both purposes tend to increase, while the volume of exportable supplies declines and their prices increase. In the absence of watertight and comprehensive price control there is a rise in the domestic price level which tends to handicap exports and stimulate imports. Given freedom of trade and of international payments, the adverse balance thus created is liable to deplete the reserve, especially in the conditions since the Second World War, as the monetary reserve of many countries is now very small relative to their foreign trade turnover. Foreign aid, or an influx of private capital from abroad, may bolster up the situation for some time, but it cannot be depended upon to continue indefinitely. Nor is the devaluation or depreciation of the national currency liable to provide more than temporary relief. If it is resorted to too frequently the extent of relief it provides is likely to be diminishing, because domestic prices will tend to catch up with the depreciating exchange more quickly. A non-stop depreciation or a too frequent repetition of devaluations tends to produce an all-round demoralising effect.

Under conditions of free trade, it is impracticable in the long run to defend the balance of payments against the effects of inflation by means of price controls and physical controls. It is true that the domestic price level may be kept artificially low, and this would maintain or even increase the competitive capacity of exporters. On the other hand, the surplus purchasing power which is not spent on necessities owing to their low prices and their rationing is likely to be spent on imported goods or on goods which might otherwise be exported; or the inflated domestic demand might induce industries to produce for the home market in preference to producing for export. Nothing short of a completely watertight control on the domestic economy – something on the lines practised in the Inca Empire – would provide a solution under free international trading. Such a degree of control is impracticable in times of peace in democratic countries.

Nevertheless, it has been found that whenever a Government is reluctant to maintain or improve the balance of payments in the hard way by means of painful deflationary devices and does not dare to face the responsibility for a decision to devalue the currency, it is inclined to try to reduce the effect of inflationary domestic disequilibrium on the balance of payments by means of an isolationist policy. With the aid of isolationist measures it is possible to defy economic laws with comparative impunity for a much longer time.

There are many historical instances of more or less advanced economic isolation. The medieval baronial estates constituted independent economic units. Until the second half of the nineteenth century Japan isolated herself completely from the rest of the world and carried on no foreign trade whatsoever. In these and other instances of economic isolationism, however, considerations of monetary policy did not arise. On the other hand, in the case of the Soviet Union economic isolation from non-Communist countries, achieved by drastic political and economic measures, is accompanied by a watertight system of exchange control. No payment to and from abroad can take place except through the authorities. This system completes the political control on contact with the outside world and the foreign trade monopoly with which isolation was enforced. Even in the absence of exchange control the State authority would be in a position to control import and export prices independently of the exchange rates. Under the Communist system it is possible to reserve for export trade any goods selected for that purpose and it would be possible to sell them even at a permanent loss if necessary in order to secure markets for them. Likewise, goods are imported not because they are cheaper abroad or because consumers demand it, but because the State authority deems it necessary to import them irrespective of considerations of price. A Communist State is like a big business firm which may deliberately incur losses in one of its departments for the sake of the overall profits of the whole firm. Nevertheless, as is indicated by Stalin's article, there are limits to the extent to which even a Communist State is prepared and able to disregard economic laws.

Many non-Communist States too have resorted to a high degree of economic isolation in recent decades. During the Second World War relative prices played a very subordinate part in determining the international flow of goods. As in the USSR, it was the Governments of belligerent countries that decided what to export and import, and to or from which countries. In the absence of free interchange of goods and of free foreign exchange markets, the price levels of various countries lost touch with each other. Thanks to the adoption of a policy of economic isolation, there was no need for the Governments to worry about the growing discrepancies between price levels at home and abroad or to take inopportune measures of deflation – which might have interfered with the economic war effort – for the sake of restoring equilibrium. This state of disequilibrium between price levels continued for some time after the war, though to a diminishing extent. The price levels remained out of touch with each other and in most instances the Governments were reluctant to adjust the exchange rates to offset the discrepancies between the price levels. They were even more reluctant to adopt drastic deflationary measures in order to lower their price levels to those of other countries. Indeed, they were even reluctant to resist pressure in favour of extending social services and increasing capital investment, although by yielding to such pressure they tended to accentuate the rise in their price level and to widen the disequilibrium with the price levels of other countries. Fortunately for them, most other countries also pursued expansionary monetary policies, so that the world level of prices was rising, even if the extent of the rise varied from country to country. In order to be able to avoid, minimise or delay unpopular measures for the sake of adjusting their price levels to those of other countries, many countries maintained their war-time isolationist policies to a large extent throughout the forties, and to a large if diminishing extent throughout the fifties.

Economic isolation can be attained through physical control over imports and exports, or through controls over financial transfers in payment for imports and exports. On the face of it it would seem that effective control over foreign trade would in itself suffice, since the extent of the circumvention of such control by means of smuggling must be negligible. In reality, it is essential to supplement physical trade controls by monetary devices, not only in order to make circumvention of trade controls more difficult but also to prevent unwanted transfers of funds for purposes unconnected with current trade.

This brings us to the other main object of isolation. Gold reserves can be exhausted, not only through adverse balances of payment, but also through a large-scale or persistent capital outflow. From time to time under the gold standard the domestic trade of a country found itself penalised through no fault of its own, as a result of a crisis or a boom in some other part of the world, which caused heavy transfers of funds. To check such transfers the country concerned had to raise its Bank Rate even though domestic trade conditions did not necessitate or justify such a change. Such experience provided a strong argument in favour of isolationism by means of monetary policy devices.

During the late twenties Poincaré's success in stabilising the franc resulted in a large-scale repatriation of French capital from London. This caused acute embarrassment to Britain, especially as it coincided with a large-scale drain of capital attracted to the United States by the Wall Street boom. Many similar instances could be quoted to show how embarrassing international movements of capital are liable to be. Throughout the thirties large funds were being shifted from one country to another in order to avoid anticipated devaluations or depreciations. Similar movements, only on a much larger scale, occurred since the restoration of foreign exchange markets in the fifties. Such movements of funds were a source of trouble, not only to the country which was loosing them, but also for the country which was receiving them. It was justly remarked that such funds were like teeth – they were a nuisance when they were coming, they were apt to be a nuisance when they were there, and they were the worst nuisance of all when they were going.

Although after 1931 many of the financially weaker countries resorted to exchange restrictions in order to check such unwanted capital movements, the financially stronger countries allowed them to proceed unhampered. British monetary policy in the thirties aimed at discouraging an unwanted outflow of foreign balances by allowing sterling to depreciate, and at discouraging an unwanted inflow of foreign balances by allowing sterling to appreciate. It was not until the outbreak of the Second World War that international capital movements came to be checked by isolationist monetary measures.

In Germany, on the other hand, advanced exchange control and trade control was adopted in 1931 and was greatly reinforced in 1933 after the advent of the Hitler regime. The country became economically isolated from the outside world. This, together with effective measures of control over internal economic activities, made it possible for Germany to follow a policy of fairly advanced monetary expansion in connection with the rearmament drive of 1933–9, without having to pay the full price in the form of deterioration of the balance of payments and an enforced curtailment of essential imports. Isolation went a long way towards enabling Nazi Germany to have guns *and* butter – or at any rate margarine.

From 1945 monetary isolationism in Britain enabled the

Socialist Government to establish the Welfare State. A more limited degree of monetary isolation enabled the Conservative Government to pursue its expansionary policy. This would have been difficult if exchanges had been entirely free, even for UK residents. The policy came to produce its natural effects on the balance of payments after exchange control and import restrictions were relaxed for non-residents. On the occasion of every crisis, monetary isolationism became reinforced.

Monetary isolationism is liable to be applied whenever a Government is engaged in economic experiments such as the adoption of a semi-Socialistic system in a capitalist country. If the basic system is changed into Communism, then the problem of monetary isolationism against capital movements does not arise in a particularly acute form. Most liquid capital is confiscated by a stroke of the pen and cannot therefore be exported. In any case, as we saw above, a Communist State has other means of preventing a capital outflow. On the other hand, if the basic characteristics of the capitalist system are retained but the Government adopts an anti-capitalist policy by means of the nationalisation of certain industries, very high taxation of profits and advanced control of business activities, then monetary isolation is likely to be resorted to in order to prevent a large-scale flight of capital. But for the operation of exchange control in Britain during 1945–51 the outflow of capital trying to escape from Socialism and high taxation would have wiped out the monetary reserves in a very short time and would have transferred the ownership of a very large proportion of British assets to holders resident overseas.

Large-scale flight of national capital may be caused also by fears of external aggression or internal upheavals. Many of those who can afford it would like to play for safety by accumulating nest-eggs in safer countries. The extent of such movements might well prove to be disastrous to the country menaced by aggression or civil disturbances. Considerations of national survival may justify measures of monetary isolation to prevent such flights of capital. But if the flight of capital is due to irresponsible policies pursued by the Government or to malevolent anti-capitalist measures which are damaging to national interests for the sake of party or class interests, it is very much a matter of opinion whether there is moral justification for salvaging part of the national patrimony by moving it out of the reach of a greedy or incompetent Government. The large number of Frenchmen who transferred their money abroad in the twenties and in the fifties returned it to France when Poincaré and de Gaulle came to adopt sensible policies, so that in the long run the flight of their capital from France benefited France.

Beyond doubt isolationist monetary policy is liable to entail grave disadvantages. It enables Governments to prolong a state of disequilibrium instead of resorting to unpopular methods of correcting it. Nevertheless, without overlooking its disadvantages, it is necessary to bear in mind that in given circumstances it is the smaller evil to put up with them. This is apt to be overlooked by those who are dogmatically opposed to isolationist measures regardless of circumstances.

It is arguable that monetary isolationism is fundamentally unsound and harmful, precisely because it enables Governments to prolong the pursuit of unsound economic policies and to defer the inevitable day when realities have to be faced and unpopular measures resorted to in order to correct an artificial situation. Even so, there are situations in which there is much to be said for deferring the evil day. In such situations, such as wars or threats of wars, isolation can serve useful national ends. Like many other policies, it is of course liable to be misused. But its use in moderation in the right circumstances may obviate worse evils and it may even secure substantial benefits. Whether or not those who consider it a thousand pities that it has ever been invented are right or wrong, the policy is there for better or for worse, to be used or to be abused.

During the thirties monetary isolationism actually prevented a further contraction of foreign trade as a result of the prolonged depression and the series of crises. It enabled financially weak Governments to husband their dwindling gold and foreign exchange resources for essential requirements. Exchange clearing made it possible in many instances to increase imports beyond the limits imposed on them by the inadequacy of the reserves.

In more recent times restrictions confined to transactions arising from international capital movements were one of the favourite forms of monetary isolationism, while current transactions were relatively free from restrictions.

Monetary isolationism can serve not only the purpose of protecting weak countries but also the end of mitigating the *embarras de richesse* of strong countries. During the sixties and seventies Germany, Switzerland, Japan and other surplus countries resorted to elaborate monetary measures to safeguard themselves against the consequences of an unwanted influx of hot money.

In a sense, adjustments of parities and the adoption of floating exchanges also constitute measures of monetary isolationism, in that they seek to safeguard the domestic economies against unwanted internal changes and trends. If exchange rates are adjusted, or are allowed to adjust themselves, in order to offset discrepancies between national price levels, it obviates the necessity for major adjustments of price levels that would have been necessary otherwise in order to restore equilibrium.

CHAPTER SEVENTEEN

The Role of Reserve Currency

MONETARY policy may aim at achieving or maintaining the role of the national currency as an international reserve currency. Or it may pursue the opposite aim – to discard the role of a reserve currency or to avoid assuming that role. It depends on whether the country concerned can afford to let its currency play that part without having to pay too dearly for it, and whether the Government of that country gives to the achievement of that ambition a high priority.

It must always be borne in mind that the role of a currency as a reserve currency does not depend altogether on decisions of monetary policy. If a currency enjoys universal or widespread confidence abroad, it will assume the role of reserve currency even if the Government of the country concerned does not go out of its way to ensure the achievement of that role. During the nineteenth century sterling played the role of reserve currency not because it was in accordance with the official policy but because it was trusted all over the world as the strongest and most dependable currency. At that time gold was the principal reserve asset, but Central Banks which preferred to hold some of their monetary reserve in the form of foreign exchange used sterling for that purpose.

Of course the fact that the Bank of England pursued a sound policy was largely responsible for the confidence enjoyed by sterling. But the Bank of England did not pursue a sound policy for the sake of ensuring that role for sterling. It was a purely incidental consequence of the Bank of England's policy aimed at maintaining sound currency and sound banking. Because sterling could be depended upon remaining within its gold points, it was considered a safe currency in which to hold official reserves or private liquid assets. It came to be used as a vehicle currency with which to transact international trade, not only between Britain and other countries but also between foreign countries. This extensive international use of sterling made its use as official monetary reserve more attractive, because banks, merchants and Central Banks had to hold balances in London.

It was not until the inter-war period that deliberate monetary policies aimed at securing and maintaining the role of a currency as a reserve currency came to be adopted. When sterling lost its lead for the benefit of the dollar during and after the First World War, it came to be realised that its loss was a matter for regret. For a century while sterling was the leading international currency its role as a reserve currency was taken too much for granted. But in the early twenties it became one of the main objects of British monetary policy that sterling should recover its lost lead – 'to make the pound look the dollar in the face'. To that end, the British authorities deemed it worth their while to pursue a deflationary policy involving considerable sacrifices, so as to restore sterling to its pre-war parity, on the assumption that it was an essential condition of the resumption of sterling's pre-war role.

After the return to the gold standard and to the pre-war parity of sterling, one of the principal aims of the British monetary policy was the maintenance of sterling's role as an international reserve currency. Although it was at a disadvantage compared with the dollar, it put up a strong fight to retain its position. The United States authorities did not go out of their way to maintain the dollar's supremacy over sterling. Quite on the contrary, they were willing to assist Britain in her effort to overcome the difficulties arising from the overvaluation of sterling and the resulting perennial adverse pressure.

Sterling became the subject of attacks from another direction. Having restored the stability and strength of the franc, the French authorities aimed at securing for it a lead for the sake of the political prestige and power it entailed. During the late twenties and after the turn of the decade French monetary policy aimed at ensuring supremacy for the franc. To that end they endeavoured to weaken sterling and even the dollar. It was the declared object of French monetary policy to make Paris the leading international monetary centre, not so much for the sake of the financial benefits it would have brought for France as for the sake of the political power she had hoped to gain by it.

This fight for financial supremacy ended in the crisis of 1931 culminating in the suspension of the gold standard by Britain. The chain reactions to this act and to the ensuing depreciation of sterling, and to the moratorium in Germany and other countries, created conditions in which no country was able or willing to pursue a policy aimed at securing the role of reserve currency for its currency. Within a limited sphere Britain achieved that role for sterling, however, through the creation of the Sterling Area, consisting mostly of the British Commonwealth and Empire.

During 1932–3 the dollar came under pressure, and after the suspension of the gold standard by the United States in was the turn of the French franc and the other currencies of the Gold Bloc – France, Holland, Switzerland and Belgium – to become the subject of speculative attacks. so that sterling remained in a relatively strong position. But with the growing threat to peace in Europe the dollar assumed once more a supremacy which it retained unchallenged for the next three decades. By that time the economic and political advantages of the dollar's role as reserve currency came to be realised in Washington and New York, and it became the object of American monetary policy to retain that role for the dollar.

The Bretton Woods Agreement created an international monetary system which was based on the dollar, even though sterling recovered much of its pre-war role as an international currency. Until the late sixties it was the official British policy to retain for sterling that role, at any rate as far as the Sterling Area was concerned.

As during the twenties, the American authorities tolerated the limited international role of sterling and were quite agreeable that it should share with the dollar the role of reserve currency. It was not until the series of currency crises between 1964 and 1969 that pressure came to develop in favour of divesting sterling of its role as a reserve currency. Although Britain received ample assistance from abroad to enable her to maintain sterling at the parity to which it was devalued in 1949, there was a growing demand, especially from France, that Britain should relinquish the burdens attached to the role of an international banking centre. Similar demands were also put forward from various British quarters, and there was a lively controversy over the relative extent of advantages and disadvantages derived by Britain from the international role of sterling.

During recent years a committee set up by London bankers produced much hitherto unobtainable statistical information about the amounts of Britain's invisible earnings, the total of which was found to be much larger than it had been estimated. It was assumed that a considerable part of these earnings would be lost if London ceased to be a leading international banking centre. Against this case in favour of retaining sterling's international role it was argued – not only in Leftish political circles but also in many industrial quarters and by all shades of inflationists – that the cost of maintaining sterling's role as a reserve currency was far too high in terms of the loss of production caused by the deflationary measures it necessitated from time to time. The series of sterling crises during the sixties greatly strengthened this opinion, and the Labour Government was in any case not enthusiastic about London's role as an international banking community.

There was, however, very little that the Government could do towards achieving the end of reducing the volume of foreign sterling balances so long as Britain's balance of payments remained adverse, and in 1968 agreement was reached in Basle granting a dollar guarantee for a high proportion of the official Sterling Area balances, so as to avoid their withdrawal. This precaution was made necessary by the ill-advised effort made by the Labour Government to dissuade the Governments of the Outer Sterling Area to devalue their currencies in 1967 in sympathy with sterling. Since in the past it was an established rule that all Sterling Area currencies moved in sympathy with sterling, so that Sterling Area holders of sterling balances did not stand to suffer any losses in terms of their own currencies in case of a devaluation of sterling, this new policy greatly increased the risk attached to holding sterling balances. To avoid large-scale withdrawals of such balances they were guaranteed up to a certain limit. But this move reduced sterling's prestige as an international currency.

Nevertheless, with the return of confidence in sterling as a result of the improvement of the balance of payments in 1969–1971, the amount of foreign sterling balances increased very considerably in spite of the repayment of the billions of dollars borrowed by the Labour Government. Official Sterling Area balances increased well in excess of the limits of the Basle guarantees. Although the Government did not go out of its way to restore sterling's international role, it increased nevertheless because of the return of confidence.

By that time the official view was that, so long as London played an important part as an international banking centre, it did not matter very much whether business was transacted in sterling or in other currencies. For this reason the development of the Euro-dollar market and of the Euro-issue market was officially encouraged, even though it meant a reduction of sterling's importance as an international currency.

In 1972 there was another turn of the trend, this time against sterling, owing to the wage inflation which affected the balance of payments unfavourably. It came to be realised that the revaluation of sterling by $8\frac{1}{2}$ per cent against the dollar under the Smithsonian realignment was excessive in the circumstances, having regard to the aggravation of the 'English disease' and the anticipation of the heavy costs of joining the Common Market in 1973. Accordingly, a sweeping flight from sterling developed during June 1972, and on 16 June the Government announced its decision to allow sterling to float.

This decision was not the inevitable act of God it had been

claimed to be. The Government could have resorted to a variety of devices with which to defend sterling. Indeed, the main cause of the crisis was Mr Barber's statement of policy in his Budget Speech on 21 March to the effect that the Government would not uphold the stability of sterling if it could only do so at the cost of a lower rate of growth. This statement conveyed unwittingly a warning to overseas holders of sterling that they could not rely on sterling being defended if and when it should be attacked. It was only natural, therefore, that as soon as selling pressure developed against sterling there should be a sweeping flight of foreign balances, in addition to the lengthening of leads and lags and speculative operations.

By deliberately changing its priorities to the detriment of the defence of sterling, the Government adopted a monetary policy tending to discourage sterling's role as an international currency, even before the resulting crisis gave rise to a wave of distrust. It is one thing if a Government is unable to defend the stability of its currency and quite a different thing if it has no intention of defending it at the cost of slowing down its rate of growth. With his ill-advised statement to that effect, Mr Barber deliberately divested sterling of its role of an international currency. Even if he or his successor at the Exchequer should learn his lesson from the sterling crisis of June–July 1972, it would be no easy matter to restore the necessary degree of confidence for recovering its role as an international currency.

CHAPTER EIGHTEEN

Monetary Policy and Business Cycles

ALTHOUGH in many circumstances monetary policy may aim at deliberately causing changes in price levels or exchange rates, in a large number of instances its end is to prevent such changes. Ironing out fluctuations constitutes a major objective of those in charge of monetary policy. They may direct their action against minor day-to-day movements in the money market, the foreign exchange market, or in the market for Government loans. Or they may endeavour to offset seasonal and other medium-term movements in those markets. Above all, they aim at preventing movements of prices and unwanted fluctuations in business activity over longer periods. The stabilising functions of monetary policy in the sphere of prices and exchanges were dealt with in earlier chapters. Here we propose to confine ourselves to its functions as a stabilising influence in respect of business cycles. Both the Radcliffe Report and the American Report on Money and Credit laid much stress on these functions in the post-war world.

Business cycles are regarded as the worst effects of economic freedom. Their extent is supposed to grow with the growth of quantities in our economic system – the figures of budgets, public and private debts, bank deposits, gold reserves, trade production, etc. – and with the increasing complexity of that system. Indeed, it is widely feared that unless means can be found for dealing with business cycles they may endanger the very existence of the capitalist system and the democratic way of life. It is considered one of the duties of those in charge of monetary policy to adopt measures by which to mitigate the ups and downs of business cycles, even if they are unable to prevent them altogether. Ever since the development of the modern economic system periodically recurrent booms and slumps have been causing much concern to theoretical and practical experts.

For a long time after the Second World War it was generally assumed that the 'pre-war' types of major business cycles were a matter of the past and 'post-war' cycles were much milder. There were, however, some scares and it seems to be prudent to envisage at any rate a possibility of a recurrence of 'pre-war' cycles. They varied widely in detail, but in substance they follow the same pattern.

Prolonged prosperity tends to give rise to a wave of optimism resulting in excessive expenditure, both on capital investment and on consumption. Profits expand and there is an increase of demand for labour, leading to a rising trend of wages. The resulting increase of purchasing power, accompanied by an expanding trend of bank credits, tends further to stimulate business activity until it assumes a boom-like character in many repects. The rising trend of prices encourages speculative buying of commodity stocks and of Stock Exchange securities, and big vulnerable speculative positions are created. Company promoting and the issue of new securities is stimulated by indiscriminate demand, and there is a mushroom growth of new business firms of a doubtful stability. The insistent and indiscriminate character of demand encourages an expansion of production without regard to the long-range possibility of finding markets. A large and increasing proportion of business activities comes to be financed by means of short-term credits, creating many vulnerable commitments.

Such a speculative boom obviously cannot continue for ever. For a wide variety of reasons it must come to an end sooner or later, and a sharp reaction sets in. The pendulum then swings in the opposite direction. Holders of securities and commodity stocks hasten to liquidate their holdings, thereby accentuating the slump in the commodity markets on the Stock Exchange. Many firms incur heavy losses and get into difficulties. In so far as they finance their operations with the aid of commercial credits or bank credits they may become insolvent, thereby inflicting losses on many more firms and on banks. The over-buoyant optimism that characterised the boom period gives way to an equally exaggerated pessimism. At the top of the boom cautious people rightly assume that rises in prices have been exaggerated and play for safety. During the early phases of the downward movement of the cycle it comes to be widely assumed that the slump will continue for a long time. Producers curtail their activity, traders reduce their stocks, consumers withhold their purchases in anticipation of lower prices and for fear of a decline of their incomes. They wish to preserve their liquid resources. Employment declines and the purchasing power of consumers contracts. The volume of credit becomes reduced, not only because banks want to play for safety and to curtail their commitments, but also because many creditworthy business firms are reluctant to borrow.

Both boom and slump are cumulative processes. Apart altogether from the original causes that initiated them, they tend to feed themselves as they proceed. After a while the unsound positions built up during the boom are liquidated and prices are at a more reasonable level. Nevertheless, business firms are reluctant to increase their activities. They then come to realise very gradually that it has become once more reasonably safe to increase their commitments. There is a cautious expansion of business activity, at first slow, then gradually gathering momentum, until it assumes once more a boom-like character. Another business cycle begins to take its course.

Throughout the nineteenth century business cycles recurred with a disquieting regularity. Economists disagree about the average length of the period between one slump and another, but it became a generally accepted conception that the world was bound to experience a slump at intervals of between seven and eleven years. The losses incurred through such slumps by holders of stocks and securities, business firms and their employees had come to be regarded as the inevitable price mankind had to pay for the advantages derived from a competitive free economy. This fatalism contributed to no slight extent towards the progress of Socialism favouring the adoption of State control over economic activities as an alternative to booms and slumps.

This is, of course, a greatly over-simplified picture of the business cycle. Its post-war manifestation differs from the pre-war manifestation in several important respects. Although the system of instalment buying, by which consumers increasingly anticipated their future earnings during the upswing of the cycle, existed already before the war, the spectacular post-war development of hire purchase has created a new situation. An increase of hire purchase credits is liable to accentuate booms, while a reduction is liable to aggravate recessions. An even more important change is the unrelenting pressure for higher wages which now continues even during recessions. The only difference is in respect of the slower rate at which wages are increased during recessions. This rules out the pre-war system under which automatic forces tend to restore the pre-boom situation. Moreover, under the accepted policy aiming at full employment, official action is now usually taken to reverse any recession even before it has had a chance to correct the excesses of a preceding boom.

Opinions differed widely about the causes of the business cycles. According to a large and influential school of thought they were largely if not entirely due to unwarranted credit expansion, which is responsible for the booms, leading to conditions in which recessions become inevitable. A more up-to-date explanation is that the inflationary effects of wage increases in excess of increases in productivity lead from time to time to balance-of-payments crises which induce Governments to adopt more or less drastic disinflationary measures. Once the balance-of-payments crisis is overcome, the measures are relaxed and wage inflation becomes accentuated once more. The sixties witnessed some international recessions that affected most countries regardless of their balance-of-payments position. It was due to the discouraging effect of lower profit margins resulting from excessive wage increases.

It is only natural that many experts and intelligent laymen

look towards monetary policy for relief from the curse of business cycles. Even those who do not accpet the exclusively monetary character of the business cycle are inclined to agree that measures of monetary policy could mitigate business cycles to a large degree. During the period of the automatic gold standard such measures were to a large degree automatic. Credit expansion brought about by a boom reduced the reserve ratios of Central Banks which were compelled under their statutes to take measures to maintain those ratios. This was done by an increase of the Bank Rate, leading to a contraction of credit. Such an increase very frequently constituted the danger signal which pricked the bubble of the boom. With the decline of the demand for credit the reserve ratio tended to rise, and this was followed by a decline of interest rates. Although in theory the process was automatic, in practice there always had to be someone to take decisions leading to higher or lower interest rates. Nevertheless, these decisions were largely governed by the prevailing circumstances, and more often than not the monetary authorities followed the trend rather than trying to guide it.

To the extent to which the monetary system became less and less automatic after the First World War, the responsibility of the monetary authorities for decisions taken in order to mitigate booms and slumps increased. Already during the twenties elaborate policies were pursued to that end, especially in the United States, where anti-business-cycle monetary policies were developed into a fine art following the esatblishment of the Federal Reserve System.

The post-war types of business cycles have been, up to the time of writing, so moderate by comparison with the pre-war types that, even though many quarters share the frequently recurrent feeling of uneasiness, there is a widespread belief that slumps are now a matter of the past. Yet we have no right to assume that mankind has concluded a pact with Providence outlawing cyclic crises. Each one of the recessions resulting from efforts to mitigate inflation is liable to become grossly self-aggravating and to develop into a crisis of first-rate magnitude. Indeed, the elements making for such a crisis are very much in existence all over the world; the extent of some of them is without precedent. The amounts of unsecured non-self-liquidating credits now run into hundreds of billions. Compared with their size, the Wall Street loans of 1929 and short-term credits to Central Europe in 1931 were mere trifles.

We have survived several major business failures with the amounts involved exceeding a great many times the liabilities of the Kreditanstalt in 1931, without having to witness the development of a world crisis as a result of the chain reactions they triggered off. The possibility that on the next occasion we shall not be let off so lightly is always present. The inverted pyramid of the credit structure is balanced very precariously and is liable to topple over.

The almost uninterrupted expansion accompanied by non-stop inflationary rise in prices has inevitably created many unsound positions. They might easily become evident as a result of some grave setback. Wholesale failures would produce the familiar self-aggravating effect, just as before the war, and the magnitudes involved would be a great many times larger.

Before the First World War the figure of Central Bank reserve ratios and the trend of interest rates in the open markets was regarded as the main index to guide the action of the authority. During the twenties these indices were replaced by that of the trend of the price level. It was hoped to prevent a boom by resorting to adequate measures of credit restrictions as soon as there was any indication of a rise in prices. Before very long events proved that this policy was far from ideal and failed to provide the much-hoped-for solution. As a result of the decline in the cost of production, especially in agriculture but also in industry, stable prices meant expanding profits and the development of a sweeping boom. The movement culminated in the Wall Street boom, leading to the disastrous slump of 1929, which was followed by a series of crises of unprecedented violence, and by a prolonged depression with declining prices and large-scale unemployment.

Needless to say, the boom and slump of the late twenties and early thirties was in reality a much more complex phenomenon.

What is essential is to realise that devices of monetary policy were unable to prevent the business cycle from taking its course and from assuming unusually large proportions. According to many economists, this was not because of any inherent deficiency of the measures but because they were 'too late and too little'. Monetary policy during the thirties proved to be largely helpless in face the slump and the prolonged depression. In addition to the time-honoured device of lowering interest rates and trying to expand credit facilities, other expansionary devices were adopted, such as the fiscal device of deficit financing, devaluations, etc. Eventually towards the middle thirties the slump and the depression came to an end and the business cycle showed signs of resuming its upward movement. The upswing proved to be very short-lived. It was followed by a mild trade recession in 1937.

Notwithstanding the discouraging experience of the inter-war period, expert opinion at the end of the war was practically unanimous in favouring the adoption of monetary policy measures against the recurrence of business cycles. Experts are sharply divided, however, between two schools of thought. According to the one, it should be possible to control the business cycle through the improved application of the monetary devices tried without conspicuous success in the twenties and in the thirties, supplemented by Keynesian devices, foremost amongst which are Budgetary and debt-management policies, and by policies of wage and price restraint. According to the other school of thought, the only safe way of avoiding business cycles is by means of a monetary policy aiming at the perpetuation of moderate inflation and at the maintenance of full employment by every possible means. The fact that inflation has been proceeding without major interruption ever since 1939 is quoted as evidence to prove that an expansionary monetary policy coupled with social policies aiming at maintaining a high level of steady consumption and ensuring economic growth at an accelerating rate, is capable of preventing a slump.

Those who oppose this monetary policy do so either on the ground that non-stop inflation is too high a price to pay for the elimination of the business cycle or on the ground that conditions since 1939 have been exceptional and that sooner or later the business cycle will resume its course in spite of the non-stop inflation – or possibly because of it. It must be admitted that the absence of a slump following the end of the Second World War came as a surprise to most people – not in the last place to the rulers of the Kremlin, who ever since the end of the war have been hoping for a gigantic slump that would undermine the resistance of the capitalist world.

Beyond doubt, if it were certain that a policy of non-stop 'creeping' inflation could permanently eliminate slumps, it might be well worth while to put up with the grave disadvantages resulting from that policy. The results of the post-war experience are, however, far from conclusive. Hence the insistence of the anti-inflationary school on the adoption of disinflationary monetary devices for the sake of mitigating the disadvantages of non-stop inflation. Such measures are strongly opposed by the inflationary school on the ground that they entail very grave risks. For, should they initiate a deflationary spiral, the authorities might not be able to reverse or even mitigate it.

Under the influence of the disadvantages of creeping inflation that became increasingly evident when they came to escalate in the seventies, doubts have arisen in some quarters whether to make it an aim of monetary policy to eliminate business cycles is not, after all, fundamentally wrong. While appreciating the benefits of monetary expansion and of the absence of violent slumps and of large-scale unemployment, they claim that deflationary setbacks are an essential part of the competitive economic system and that in moderation they have their advantages. For although inflation tends to stimulate the full utilisation of productive resources, they tend to be utilised in a wasteful form. We already have seen in Chapter 11 that deflationary reactions secure the elimination of inefficient units and ensure that productive capacity is employed to better advantage. It is only natural that after a prolonged inflationary experience the disadvantages of the recent trend should be felt keenly and the advantages of the trend of the more remote past should be missed. Possibly this attitude might grow stronger as and when an inflationary period continues for a long time without interruption. At the time of writing, however, elimination of business cycles remains a widely favoured end of monetary policy. In the view of many economists and of others, it should take precedence over all other ends. The monetary authorities in most countries seek to achieve this end by the 'foolproof' method of perpetuating a moderate inflationary boom rather than by the skilful application of Keynesian counter-cyclical policy.

When in 1962 there appeared to develop a threat of an old-fashioned cyclical slump, many firm opponents of inflation came round to the view that, after all, even inflation would be better than such a slump, They withdrew their support of their Government's disinflationary policy for fear that it might initiate a deflationary spiral which would get out of control. It was recalled that President Roosevelt's inflationary measures in the thirties were unable to reverse the trend, which had gone too far by then. According to the new inflationists, the counter-cyclical 'stop–go' policy must be replaced by a policy of non-stop expansion. The British Conservative Government adopted that policy in 1963 and its attitude received widespread support by British opinion under the influence of the relatively moderate increase of unemployment that developed during the winter of 1962–3. Those who still remembered the conditions during the 'thirties came to the conclusion that prevention of their recurrence must be given absolute priority among the ends of monetary policy.

With the increase of unemployment in all industrial countries during the late sixties and early seventies, the priority of the monetary policy end of stimulating business activities became firmly established. Most Governments are now more inclined to relax their disinflationary measures for the sake of reducing unemployment. The ups and downs of unemployment are the most important symptom of business cycles. The present situation differs materially from the pre-war situation not only because of the spectacular increase in the financial magnitudes involved, but also because of the appearance of the new phenomenon called 'stagflation' – the combination of intractable unemployment with even more intractable inflation. It is the outcome of the successful resistance of trade unions to monetary policy measures, to the grave detriment of their own long-term interests.

CHAPTER NINETEEN

Full Employment

THE principle that the achievement and maintenance of full employment must – or at any rate a high level of employment – must be the foremost end of monetary policy is of recent origin. It arose as a reaction to the abnormal increase of unemployment during the early thirties. The change of attitude was largely the consequence of the replacement of the automatic monetary system by managed monetary systems between the two wars. So long as monetary policy was confined to the regulation of the automatically functioning gold standard, the objective of influencing the level of employment by monetary devices had no top priority. The rule that it was the foremost task of the authorities to maintain the gold standard was considered axiomatic. When the measures needed for maintaining the gold standard caused an increase of unemployment it was assumed to be inevitable. It was one of the fundamental rules of the gold standard game to raise interest rates and restrict credit whenever the exchange was weak. In fact to a large degree this happened automatically because there was an outflow of gold as soon as the exchange depreciated to its 'gold export point' – the rate at which it became profitable to withdraw gold from the Central Bank and export it. It would not have occurred to anybody in a responsible position to argue that, rather than lose gold or prevent its loss at the cost of creating unemployment, the exchange should be allowed to depreciate. It was considered a matter of course that a decline in the volume of gold should result in a decline in the volume of currency and credit. That this was detrimental to business and employment was regarded as just an unfortunate necessity.

Once the automatic system was replaced by a managed system it followed logically that the inevitability of restricting credit for the sake of defending the international stability of the currency would be called in question. Until then it was only contested by a handful of would-be monetary reformers who were unable to make headway against the prevailing orthodox conception. Even though men such as McKenna and Keynes lent their authority to the new school of thought during the twenties, it could not make an impression until after the gold standard had to be abandoned under the force of circumstances. The extent to which the gold standard could be managed for the sake of keeping down unemployment was limited. But once monetary management became the established practice, it was open for the authorities to adopt the rule that monetary policy must primarily aim at full employment. This was not actually done in fact until 1944, when the White Paper on Employment Policy announced the acceptance by the Government 'as one of their primary aims and responsibilities, the maintenance of a high and stable level of employment after the war'. The White Paper did not actually promise full employment, and it was open for anyone to interpret the meaning of 'high level of employment'. In fact, however, the White Paper is generally considered as an official recognition that monetary policy must aim at something like full employment. The principle was reaffirmed in 1956 in the White Paper on the Economic Implications of Full Employment.

The exact degree of employment which can be described as 'full 'is largely a matter of opinion. Even the firmest supporters of the policy of full employment admit that there is always bound to be a small percentage of unemployed consisting of the unemployables and of those seasonally out of work or in transition between two jobs. Those in favour of 'high a level of employment' – as distinct from 'full employment' – are prepared to accept a certain amount of unemployment beyond that minimum, provided that it does not develop into large-scale unemployment. On the other hand, many people favour a state of affairs in which the number of unfilled vacancies far exceeds the number of those looking for employment. This latter state of affairs may be described as 'over-full employment'. It is distinctly inflationary because, human nature being what it is, it is difficult for employees to resist the temptation of taking advantage of their scarcity value. In order to be able to recruit and maintain their staffs, employers have to bid against each other for the limited supply of labour. Any new industry or expansion of existing industry can only solve its manpower problem by offering higher wages and thereby enticing the workers of other industries to come over to it. Private firms and public corporations are not in a good position to resist wage demands made under such circumstances, even if the demands are not justified by the extent of their profits. In order to be able to make a profit they have to add at least part of the wage increases to the prices of their products. The result is a rise in prices, which in turn leads to more wage demands.

In order to avoid sliding into non-stop inflation through the operation of the wages spiral, monetary policy would have to aim at a prevention of over-full employment. This is, of course, easier said than done, because the borderline between full employment and over-full employment is very indistinct. British official statistics which do not give the full picture of the employment situation showed for a long time after the war a considerable excess of registered vacancies over registered unemployed. The real extent of over-full employment must have been higher than that indicated by the figures, for a high proportion of vacancies is never registered. There was an acute shortage of labour in a great many industries in Britain throughout the post-war period, even though there was local unemployment in some districts and in some industries especially from 1969 onwards.

Yet monetary policy is not meant for correcting such a situation, which calls for non-monetary measures to correct unemployment in the districts affected, similar to British measures in the 'special areas', and measures aiming at increasing the mobility of labour. Any attempt at wiping out pockets of unemployment with the aid of general reflation would have

resulted in a very high degree of inflation. It is a mistake to
try to apply monetary measures against unemployment due to
a changing pattern of demand or other structural causes.

What was said above is not intended to make out a case
against a monetary policy aiming at full employment. Nobody
who remembers the experience of the thirties can object to the
principle of that policy. But it is necessary to realise the need for
a more elastic application of that principle in order to avoid its
inflationary effects and to obviate the bolstering up of unsound
industrial positions to the detriment of the national economy. It
must be borne in mind that a persistently adverse trade balance,
if increased through the consequences of inelasticity of labour, is
liable to cause unemployment if the gold reserve declines to
such an extent that the import of essential raw materials has to
be cut.

With the above reservations, the new monetary policy tends
to increase productive capacity. It avoids the waste of maintaining millions of idle workers as many countries did between
the wars. It attracts into productive occupation a large number
of those who had not hitherto been directly productive. Between
the wars the inadequacy of the supply of credit resulting from a
restrictive monetary policy compelled the banks to refuse loans
for purposes which were financially secure, commercially
profitable and socially useful. This they had to do in innumerable instances in spite of the existence of at least one and
a half million unemployed. Amidst large-scale unemployment,
productivity was low because of the widespread fear among
workers that if they exerted themselves they would work themselves out of employment. On the assumption that only a
limited amount of work was available, they endeavoured to
spread it out as much as possible. Hence the restrictive regulations adopted by many unions, as a result of which even those
workers who were able and willing to work harder were
compelled to limit their output.

One of the main arguments used in favour of a monetary
policy aiming at full employment was that it tended to increase
productivity by doing away with the need for restrictive

practices by trade unions, and with the workers' inclination to go slow for fear of working themselves out of employment. Since under the new policy the threat of unemployment has declined considerably, there was every reason for abandoning such practices. Unfortunately, judging by post-war experience, this was not done universally. The output per man-hour of those industries which did not have the benefit of increased mechanisation actually showed a decline instead of increasing. This was particularly true of the building industry, even though in post-war Britain there was no ground for building workers to fear that they would work themselves out of employment. 'Feather-bedding' practices often prevented automation from leading to a corresponding reduction in the cost of production in a large number of other industries. In many instances when newly-installed machinery reduced the number of hands required, the workers insisted that firms should continue none the less to employ the same number of workers. Dismissals through redundancy encountered strong resistance during a period when the workers who became superfluous through mechanisation could easily find productive employment elsewhere where they were badly needed.

A great deal could be said about the effects of 'wildcat strikes' and lack of industrial discipline on output under full employment. On balance, however, it is probably correct to claim that, notwithstanding these and other obvious disadvantages, an intelligently managed monetary policy aiming at a high level of employment is something well worth having, provided that its effect on the price level does not endanger the stability of domestic prices or the balance of payments. It is a great pity that the misuse of power by organised labour deprives mankind of the full benefit of an enlightened monetary policy. Because of such misuses the authorities often feel impelled to put the clock back and revert to pre-war credit restrictions to check inflation.

The change in the balance of power between employers and employees, and the resulting misuse of power by the latter, is all but generally blamed for the prevailing 'stagflation', in which production stagnates in spite of the stimulating effect of rising prices. The attitude of trade unions and their members prevents the adjustment of manpower to ever-changing requirements and the reduction of costs, even though this has been made possible by technological progress and the elimination of the less efficient units. In face of such a situation, monetary policy is helpless. In this sense it is correct to claim that monetary policy has lost much of its former influence on the economy.

Let us now examine some international aspects of the policy of high employment. If the same policy were applied to approximately the same extent in all major industrial countries, the resulting inflation would not affect the balance of payments. Actually, the application of the policy in practice varies, however, from country to country, largely owing to differences between monetary policies. It is inevitable, therefore, that there should be discrepancies between the extent of the rise in the price level caused by monetary expansion aiming at a high level of employment.

Hence the frequent disequilibrium affecting the balance of payments. Countries in which the policy of high employment or full employment enjoys a higher priority are liable to be outpriced both abroad and in their own domestic markets. Domestic consumption of both imported and home-produced goods increases. This results in an adverse balance of payments which is liable to affect employment unfavourably, owing to the measures the Government may feel impelled to adopt in defence of the currency. In the absence of timely measures to protect the reserve, a stage is liable to be reached at which it could no longer afford to pursue an expansionary policy. Production and consumption have to be curtailed as a result of a credit squeeze and other restrictive measures.

It is necessary to avoid the development of a new orthodoxy fully as complacent as that of the nineteenth-century econo-mists who firmly believed that if only economic factors were allowed to operate without interference, things would necessarily work out for the best. Dogmatic enthusiasts of the full-employ-ment policy, too, are inclined to believe that all that is needed is to adopt the policy of non-stop inflation for the sake of full and over-full employment, and mankind could live happily ever after. Unfortunately things are not so simple in real life. A great deal more is needed than the dogmatic application of an over-simplified formula.

There is indeed a grave danger in the new dogmatism. It came as a not unnatural reaction to the old dogmatism under which everything was naturally expected to be sacrificed for the sake of upholding the stable international value of the currency. Under the new conception, Governments are expected to be willing to sacrifice any other consideration for the sake of full employment. Beyond doubt large-scale unemployment is an evil which it should be sought to avoid and for the avoidance of which it is well worth while to sacrifice some other ends of monetary policy. It must not, however, be the only considera-tion which the monetary authorities have to bear in mind in determining the needs of their monetary policy. They have to avoid adopting courses which would eventually defeat the ends of their full-employment policy owing to the effect of domestic inflation on the balance of payments. They also have to make up their mind about the degree of inflation they are prepared to accept as a price of full employment. The policy is still in an experimental stage, and its principles will have to be established through trial and error.

The need to reconcile full-employment policy with other vital policies was clearly expressed in the American Employment Act of 1946. This declared it to be the duty of the Federal Government 'to use all practical means consistent with its needs and obligations and other essential considerations of national policy' for the purpose of creating and maintaining maximum employment in a manner calculated 'to foster and promote free competitive enterprise and the general welfare'. Under the wording of this passage the United States Govern-ment would not be under an obligation, for instance, to introduce controls for the sake of achieving or maintaining full employ-ment. Many people would not endorse this formula, which is quoted here as an example of the dilemma those responsible for major monetary policy decisions have to face. Similar dilemmas are also liable to arise in connection with the restoration or maintenance of a full convertibility of currencies, which may only be achieved or maintained in given circumstances at the cost of increased unemployment. The gold standard might have been maintained in 1931 at the cost of timely and drastic deflationary measures leading to a further increase of the existing large-scale unemployment. Governments had to decide in such situations whether convertibility or gold standard was worth the price that has to be paid for it.

In his evidence before the Congressional Committee on Monetary Policy and the Management of the Public Debt in 1952, Mr John W. Snyder, Secretary of the Treasury, said that the Declaration of Policy referred to above would have been better if it had included among the reservations the maintenance of general price stability. He remarked that if measures undertaken to promote maximum employment, production and purchasing power are prosecuted fully, they are capable of producing undesirable increases in the general price level. Yet, he declared, the prevention of sharp changes in the general price level in either direction is an essential condition of national policy and of the general welfare.

This remark shows the kind of conflicts that are liable to arise between the end of full employment and other ends of monetary policy. While the need for sacrificing other ends to a large degree for the sake of full employment is now widely realised, it would be clearly going too far to lay down an as absolute principle that for the sake of full employment all other monetary policy ends must be sacrificed in all conceivable circumstances. Situations are liable to arise in which a relatively moderate increase in unemployment, regrettable as it is, has to be considered a smaller evil than a runaway inflation or a complete depletion of the monetary reserve.

It is largely because it is now widely assumed that a high degree of employment enjoys absolute priority among the ends of monetary policy that devices such as a high Bank Rate or a credit squeeze have lost much of their former power. Trade unions are no longer afraid that their excessive wage demands, by compelling the authorities to adopt credit restrictions, might lead to large-scale unemployment. They take it for granted that as soon as any disinflationary measure really begins to hurt, it would be reversed or at any rate mitigated in order to avoid heavy unemployment at all costs. And in any case, thanks to the increased social service benefits, the fear of unemployment no longer has the same deterrent effect as it had before the war. Moreover, redundancy is often effectively resisted by strikes or threats of strikes. So long as this attitude continues to prevail, there can be no effective resistance to wage inflation resulting from the misuse of the strong bargaining power achieved by the unions thanks to the high degree of employment.

Even an increase of unemployment such as we witnessed in 1971 no longer seems to reduce the power of unions to enforce wage inflation. The extent of unemployment would have to be ruinously high before it would produce its former effect on the trend of wages and prices.

CHAPTER TWENTY

Economic Growth

SINCE time immemorial optimists had believed that secular material progress, in the form of a rising standard of living and an increase of accumulated wealth, was a natural automatic process which, after each interrruption through wars or other crises, must resume its course. Until comparatively recently Governments did not deem it necessary to intervene in order to accelerate this fulfilment of the destiny of mankind. Or they were too much preoccupied with solving their immediate problems to devote much thought or effort to policies that aimed at deliberately stimulating this secular process. Keynes's remark, quoted to boredom, 'In the long run we are all dead', certainly characterised until recently the official monetary policies of most countries most of the time. Even so, it was necessary to pay attention at times to requirements of the distant future and to strike a compromise between long-run and short-run considerations. Occasionally monetary policy was framed in such a way as to forgo temporary advantages for the sake of ultimate permanent benefits.

In more recent years Governments and their advisers became increasingly inclined to look ahead. The White Paper on the Economic Implications of Full Employment, issued in 1956, declares: 'The Government is pledged to foster conditions in which the nation can, if it so wishes, realise its full potentialities for growth.' The popularisation of growth economics has been the most significant development in post-war economic literature. To a very large degree this new branch of economics is concerned with underdeveloped countries, as the importance of speeding up their economic growth has come to be increasingly realised. At their stage of evolution inflation is an almost indispensable condition of their growth, as it breaks the deadlock caused by the inadequacy of accumulated savings and provides the means by which their natural resources can be turned to productive use.

There is also a great deal of thought given nowadays to problems of further growth in highly developed countries. Official policy is now more inclined to take into account considerations arising from the need for stimulating growth in the long run. Before the Second World War only totalitarian states were thinking in terms of five-year plans. In the middle fifties Mr Butler, in his capacity as Chancellor of the Exchequer, set up a target of doubling the British standard of living in the next twenty-five years.

Even quite recently it was widely assumed in Britain that no specific economic or monetary policies were called for in order to pursue the end of stimulating economic growth, because this end was served by the declared policy aiming at the creation and maintenance of full employment. It was taken for granted that when, as a result of that policy, all or most employable people are maintained in full employment, this necessarily serves the cause of growth. According to the Radcliffe Report, deliberate monetary measures to further growth are a novelty, and the rate of growth 'is substantially bound up with the choice of monetary measures to which governments resort for other purposes'. Thus, even in 1959 any stimulus given to growth by monetary policy was considered to be largely incidental.

This attitude has now changed considerably. The rate of growth has come to be regarded as the principal objective of Government policy, a fetish which is worshipped by politicians and economists alike. Governments are now subject to criticism if their growth targets are not sufficiently ambitious to conform to the growth hysteria of the public and of experts. Those engaged in heated argument whether the target should be, say, $3\frac{1}{2}$ per cent or 5 per cent are unpardonably unaware that the rate of growth is not determined by Ministers and their statisticians but by those actually engaged in production.

Government policy is liable to influence the trend – a deflationary policy necessarily means a lower rate of growth than an
inflationary policy – but the actual rate of growth is seldom
equal to the target figure. The discrepancy is often quite
substantial. If the workers don't put in an honest day's work
for their inflated pay, the resulting deterioration of the balance
of payments is liable to force the Government to resort to
deflationary measures which necessarily reduce the rate of
growth.

The high priority given to growth rate is not confined to
Britain. The American Committee on Money and Credit
realised the possibility of having to choose between aiming at
a higher rate of growth or pursuing other aims. It stated in its
Report: 'During the decades ahead growth should be the
predominant aim – cyclical stabilisation a subordinate [sic] yet
important aspect.'

The realisation that policies aiming at a high level of
employment and those aiming at growth are not necessarily
identical, and that a different set of measures may be required
in order to serve the cause of growth, constitutes one of the
refinements that has been discovered in post-war economics in
general and in post-war monetary policy in particular. It is
gradually being realised that while it is broadly true that a
high level of employment naturally stimulates growth and a
high level of unemployment hinders it, in given circumstances
the effect of full employment on costs and prices, and even
more on the morale of employees, is liable to be gravely
detrimental to growth.

In the past the restrictionist monetary policy inherent in the
automatic gold standard constituted a handicap to growth.
The removal of that obstacle has opened immense possibilities
for growth. It should enable mankind to derive full benefit
from the progress of technology by overcoming the inadequacy
of capital resources and of liquidity which was, under the gold
standard, detrimental to both full employment and to growth.
But whether the increase of capital resources and of liquidity
that has now become possible as a result of the adoption of less

sound banking principles and practices will necessarily produce its full beneficial effect on growth depends on the extent to which trade unions and their members practise self-restraint. Should they practise moderation, the authorities would be safe in pursuing a continuous expansionary policy making for full employment and also for balanced growth. But if excessive wage demands force the authorities to resort to a 'stop–go' policy, it is liable to check the rate of growth and even to reverse it.

Quite apart from setbacks resulting from restrictive monetary policy that is liable to be forced on the authorities by wage inflation, the rate of growth is also kept down by the frequency of strikes and other forms of industrial action and by the general decline of industrial discipline that is unfortunately liable to accompany a high level of employment.

High interest rates are detrimental both to full employment and to growth, though not necessarily to the same extent. Their direct effect is decidedly unfavourable to full employment, but this is liable to be offset by their favourable indirect effect that operates through the stimulus they give to saving and to the accumulation of capital available for investment. To the extent to which saving responds to higher interest rates – always provided that the increase in nominal rates is not unduly offset by a decline in the purchasing power of savings – they tend to facilitate investment.

Reduction of working hours, and trade union resistance to redundancy, may minimise the unfavourable effect of a disinflationary monetary policy on the volume of employment, but output suffers and growth is apt to slowed be down, if not reversed. If as a result of a credit squeeze or of hire-purchase restrictions the volume of demand for consumer goods or capital goods declines, the effect is a reduction of the amount of overtime worked rather than a reduction of the number of employed. But this solution, while in accordance with the ends of full employment, is against the interests of growth, because, apart from its obvious immediate effect on the output, it fails to change the balance of power between employers and trade unions in such a sense as to discourage excessive wage demands. It does not, therefore, facilitate the resumption of full production because it does not remove the need for credit restriction.

The handicap to growth inherent in the application of the gold standard has become replaced by another possibly even graver handicap represented by excessive demands for higher wages and shorter hours, and by the adoption of restrictive practices. But for these, the acceleration of technological progress, coupled with the more enlightened monetary policy of our days, could have ensured a much more accelerated growth during the fifties.

The end of full employment can be served, and very often is served, by short-run measures which disregard long-run requirements. Thus the creation of uneconomic industries for the sake of providing employment is contrary to the requirements of growth, because it does not make the best possible use of productive resources. Even so, that solution is preferable to general inflationary measures against local unemployment, taken in circumstances in which most districts are already subject to inflationary pressure.

In the monetary sphere a Government which takes the line of least resistance by administering an additional dose of inflation each time there is temporary or local unemployment through non-monetary causes calling for non-monetary remedies, renders a disservice to the cause of economic growth, even though it serves the cause of full employment. The resulting accentuation of the inflationary trend calls sooner or later for disinflationary measures leading to temporary but substantial setbacks in economic expansion. While unemployment caused by the disinflationary measures disappears soon after their removal, the loss of output caused by the interruption of growth has to be made good before progress could be made beyond the level already attained. Our capacity to assist backward countries in their growth is reduced each time we have to call a halt to our own growth.

Apart altogether from such setbacks, inflation itself may not necessarily serve the cause of economic growth. It is true that, if there are substantial unused resources, their utilisation can and should be stimulated by means of inflation for the sake of stimulating economic growth. On the other hand, if the economy is working near capacity – not necessarily in the entire community, but in certain industries or in certain regions – any overloading resulting from inflation tends to hinder the economic growth.

A monetary policy serving whole-heartedly the immediate ends of full employment is liable to become entirely unsuitable from the point of view of balanced economic growth. As pointed out before, it is true that situations are liable to arise in which inflation works out also to the detriment of full employment, if the resulting balance-of-payments crisis prevents a country from importing the necessary raw materials. Such a situation seldom arises, however, and it is correct to say that creeping inflation is on the whole in accordance with the requirements of full employment. But unless it is so moderate as to be barely perceptible, it is decidely unhelpful for economic growth.

On the other hand, a deliberate deflationary monetary policy, or one which tolerates the development of deflation, is obviously detrimental to the requirements of full employment and economic growth. Large-scale unemployment resulting from deflation causes a heavy setback in growth, not only through an immediate reduction of the current output but also through discouraging investment. The period of deflation during the greater part of the thirties was a period of unrelieved decline and stagnation.

We saw earlier that, as a result of the recent reduction of working hours, the effects of disinflationary measures are unfavourable to growth even though they may be favourable to full employment. In the absence of the much-criticised 'stop–go' policy, non-stop inflation would enable the trade unions to secure concession after concession in respect of reduction of hours, and to adopt restrictive practices that effectively hinder growth. Far too large a proportion of productive capacity would be applied to meet requirements of current consumption.

Yet growth depends on investment, and it is impossible to eat our cake and invest it.

Strange as it may sound, during the course of the last century and a half, periods of falling prices in Britain coincided with accelerated growth while periods of rising prices coincided with relative stagnation. In his book *Economic Development and the Price Level*, Geoffrey Maynard points out that Britain's most rapid economic growth in the whole of her history probably occurred in the first half of the nineteenth century, when prices were declining. Again during the last three decades of that century, while prices were declining, growth was at a faster rate than during the twentieth century up to the First World War, when prices were rising. During the twenties growth was faster than before the First World War, even though prices were falling.

It would of course be a mistake to conclude from the above historical evidence that a monetary policy aiming at falling prices is called for in order to accelerate growth. But the facts certainly cast doubt on the validity of the popular argument that an inflationary policy is absolutely essential in the interest of growth in advanced countries.

A more enlightened and constructive attitude of organised labour would make it possible to pursue an expansionary monetary policy uninterrupted by frequent disinflationary measures forced on the Governments by wage inflation. This would eliminate the conflict between the requirements of full employment and those of balanced growth. It would be in accordance with the self-interest of the labour movement as well as with the interests of the community.

Monetary policy aiming at growth need not and should not limit its scope to growth in the domestic economy. It is a matter of major economic, social and political interest for the advanced countries to encourage economic growth in under-developed countries. To that end Britain and other advanced countries must aim at achieving and maintaining substantial balance-of-payments surpluses, to be able to export capital to backward countries. From that point of view it is an advantage if interest rates in lending centres are not kept unduly high, as a result of domestic disinflationary measures, because backward countries can ill afford the burden of high interest rates. Moreover, if interest rates are too high, pressure in favour of aid to underdeveloped countries in the form of foreign Government loans at artificially low interest rates increases.

The extent to which Britain and other industrial countries can assist economic growth in backward countries depends almost entirely on the degree of self-restraint practised by the masses of consumers. Even if the entire incomes of the rich were confiscated and allocated to the underdeveloped countries, the extent to which it could raise the standard of living and producing capacity of many hundreds of millions of backward peoples would be quite negligible. It is not consumption by the tens of thousands or hundreds of thousands of those belonging to the higher income brackets, but consumption by the tens of millions of those in the lower income brackets, that determines what is left over for the underdeveloped countries. Monetary policy could only assist in increasing British unrequited exports of capital goods to former colonies and other underdeveloped countries by restraining current domestic mass consumption and the use of producing capacity from predominantly serving the requirements of domestic consumption. But this is not primarily a monetary problem. Since it is difficult to induce organised labour to submit to measures that would curtail its current consumption, even for the sake of economic growth at home, it appears to be bordering on the impossible to expect self-denial for the sake of economic growth abroad. Yet there is no hope for satisfactory development of backward countries unless the advanced countries are prepared to put up with monetary policies that involve widely spread sacrifices to that end. This is a matter of simple arithmetic.

Paradoxical as it may sound, a monetary policy aiming at the creation of surpluses available for backward countries may approach that end by increasing inequality of incomes, or at any rate preventing its further reduction. For, in accordance with one of the elementary principles of economics, progress towards egalitariansim tends to increase consumer demand, which again reduces the surplus available for export. In the underdeveloped countries, rapid progress towards reducing inequalities, necessary as it may seem from social or political points of view, tends to handicap economic growth. As Mr Harry G. Johnston, in his book *Money, Trade and Economic Growth*, put it, 'a poor country anxious to develop would probably be well advised not to worry too much about the distribution of income'.

The same applies, of course, also to advanced countries. Broadly speaking, egalitarianism can only be carried beyond a certain stage at the cost of sacrificing progress. One of the main reasons why until recently the United States was easily leading in respect of the rate of economic growth was the intelligent and enlightened attitude of American trade unions in accepting inequality and raising no objection to large profits, so long as their increase was accompanied by an increase of wages. And the main reason why the American economy now tends to become stagnant is that during the late fifties and the sixties the American trade unions appeared to have caught the 'English disease', by concentrating their efforts on increasing their slice of the cake, to the detriment of the size of the whole cake.

The above arguments show the possibility of conflicts between the monetary policy end of stimulating economic growth and alternative ends of monetary policy. In many situations it may be considered necessary to sacrifice the end of growth for the sake of other ends which appear to be more imperative in the short run, and which are widely looked upon as more essential even in the long run, or which have to be pursued under popular pressure regardless of the price that has to be paid in the form of sacrificing progress.

CHAPTER TWENTY-ONE

Social Objectives

The ends of monetary policy dealt with in previous chapters may themselves be means to broader ends. A monetary policy aiming at lower prices, for instance, may envisage economic prosperity or social welfare or in given circumstances even political advantages as its ultimate end. In the present chapter we are concerned with the ultimate social ends monetary policy pursues through the intermediary of its various immediate ends.

Money is intended to serve not only economic needs but also social ones. By this we mean needs arising from non-economic aspects of human relationships, and also economic needs in so far as they concern the relative position of social classes. In the origin and early evolution of money this aspect was predominant. Money was adopted largely for the purpose of satisfying requirements arising from primitive religion, political relationships, marriage, etc. It was adopted as a means for establishing and accentuating distinctions between social classes. Such deliberate monetary policy as was pursued at those early stages must have served primarily such non-commercial ends. Money was adopted largely in order to provide a standardised means by which contributions to religious ceremonies, tribute, blood money, bride price, etc., were discharged and in which wealth, the possession of which conferred on its owner social distinction and political power, was accumulated.

In a number of known instances, however, the social factor operated in the opposite direction. In many communities the State authority resisted the development of the monetary system or the replacement of a primitive money by some more advanced form of money. Rightly or wrongly, the State authority took the view that the social upheaval resulting from a departure from a natural economy or from a primitive monetary economy would entail disadvantages which would outweigh the commercial advantages of a new monetary system. This may have been the cause of the resistance of the State authority in ancient Egypt to the development of a monetary economy. We encounter many instances of resistance to the trend to replace payments in kind by payments in money in various countries in medieval Europe. In Japan too, until comparatively recently, the State authority had discouraged the replacement of rice currency by coined money in everyday use.

In all these instances the object of the official attitude was to preserve the existing social order. This aim may have been pursued for two diametrically opposite reasons. Many communities at the dawn of history must have feared that the adoption of a monetary economy might accentuate social inequality by facilitating the accumulation of wealth on the one hand and the enslavement of the poorer classes on the other. This aspect of the adoption of money was noticeable in ancient Greece, where it had led to the replacement of a patriarchal mode of life by a system of pronounced class distinctions between employers and employees. In the Ancient period and for many centuries afterwards, default on debts entailed enslavement, so that the stimulus given to the piactice of lending and borrowing by the development of a monetary system was a major factor in the extension of slavery in formerly free communities. Too much weight should not be attached to this argument, however, in view of the fact that slavery and class distinctions had existed to a very pronounced degree in ancient Egypt in spite of the absence of a monetary system.

It is much more probable that in many communities during the Ancient and Middle Ages the State authority resisted the adoption of a monetary economy and its progress because this was against the interests of the ruling classes. Generally speaking, it is probably true that on balance the abandonment of natural economy was against the interests of landowners and served those of the rising merchant classes and industrialists. This was particularly evident during the medieval period, when scarcity of metals, which gravely handicapped industry and commerce, was not unduly inconvenient to landowners, for rents and agricultural wages could usually be paid in kind.

The depreciation of the monetary unit after the discovery of the gold and silver resources of America was gravely detrimental to the princes and the landowning classes in general. They had to accept rents in depreciated currency once rents ceased to be paid in kind, because tenants were now in a position to exercise their option to pay in cash. In Japan the feudal system was endangered by the replacement of rice currency by metallic currency; hence the resistance of the ruling classes to such development.

The evolution of modern money has largely contributed towards the evolution of the present social system. It has contributed greatly to the creation of a society based on division of labour and competitive private enterprise. The primary economic objective of a better utilisation of natural resources, manpower and human inventive genius could not have achieved such advanced stages had it not been for the adoption and modernisation of money. It was inevitable that this evolution should be accompanied by social developments such as the accentuation of class differences and the relative increase in the numerical proportion of low-income classes.

During recent times more and more attention has been paid to this aspect of our monetary system. Whether this is happening through the awakening of a social conscience on the part of the higher income classes or through the growing political power of the lower income classes, the result is that Governments today can ill afford to disregard altogether the clamour for social welfare and for a levelling-down of inequalities of wealth and income. Irrespective of the political orientation of the Government, monetary policy, which formerly was placed almost entirely at the service of economic objectives, is now being placed increasingly at that of social objectives. Fortunately the two often overlap to a large degree. An increase in the volume of goods produced is a social as well as an economic objective, because it increases the means with which to relieve poverty and to raise the standard of living. Nevertheless, economic and social considerations influencing the aims of monetary policy are, in given circumstances, liable to conflict with each other. In a competitive economic system a monetary policy aiming at an extreme equalisation of all incomes serves as a disincentive and is economically disadvantageous because it discourages invention and initiative, and tends to prevent an increase of output. Besides, a more equal distribution of the national income makes for inflationary increase of consumer demand. This means that, while during periods of depression the weight of economic argument is added to that of social argument in favour of a more equal distribution of income because this makes for reflation, during periods of inflation the economic argument is strongly against it.

By raising or lowering the price level monetary policy can produce far-reaching social effects. Very often these social effects are the purely incidental and possibly unwanted results of policies aiming at higher or lower prices for economic ends. A policy of raising or lowering prices can also be pursued, however, primarily if not exclusively for the sake of the social effects of the changes involved. Any substantial changes in the price level are a highly effective method of bringing about a redistribution of wealth. It is much more effective than taxation and is liable to operate much more speedily. It is as effective a method of expropriation and it is less risky politically.

Egalitarian monetary policy can be pursued very effectively through a deliberate depreciation of currency, which process is calculated to go a long way towards wiping out the fortunes of the upper classes and reducing the economic strength of the middle classes. It does not necessarily follow that inflationary policy will produce such a social effect. Much depends on the degree and speed of inflation and the ability of the upper and middle classes to 'hedge' against currency depreciation. There is also a possibility that a large number of people may not only succeed in preserving their fortunes during an inflationary period but even manage to accumulate new fortunes through a skilful and unscrupulous exploitation of price increases.

Quite possibly wealthy classes as such do not disappear as a result of advanced inflation, but the fortunes pass into other hands. This would mean that if the inflationary policy aimed at levelling down inequalities, it would not altogether succeed in its objective. On paper there may appear to be fewer rich people. In practice this may only mean that the new rich would be more skilful in evading taxation, being unencumbered by a standard of behaviour which the *noblesse oblige* principle had imposed on former rich classes. Take-over bids, which are denounced as being a particularly objectionable source of unearned wealth, are an almost inevitable consequence of a monetary policy that generates or tolerates inflation. Nevertheless, by and large inflationary policy is likely to succeed in levelling down incomes. In particular, higher grades of salaries and professional earnings are not adjusted to rising prices to the same extent as lower grades of wages.

Inflation is a most effective way of helping the debtor classes, the relief of which may be an important social end of monetary policy. In many instances in the course of history, had it not been for currency depreciations the position of certain debtor classes, such as farmers or owner-occupiers of houses bought on mortgage, might have become intolerable. In such situations currency depreciation may be a relatively painless alternative to waves of bankruptcies that would spell widespread ruin and discontent leading to social unrest.

Conversely, a deflationary monetary policy aiming at lower prices may have for its social objective a consolidation of the position of the 'ruling classes' in their capacity of creditors. While a deflationary policy is not likely to be adopted deliberately for that purpose, a community might slide into deflation by pursuing a policy of stabilisation and exaggerating the anti-inflationary measures in order to safeguard the interests of the creditor classes.

One of the frequent objectives, declared or undeclared, of the pursuit of monetary stability is to maintain the social *status quo*. Creditor classes and recipients of fixed incomes are inclined to use their political influence for opposing any inflationary policy or any policy which, though aiming at stability, is not sufficiently anti-inflationary to safeguard against unintentional currency depreciation. Their political influence is liable to be outweighed, however, by that of organised labour which is in a position to enforce wage increases.

The development and extension of social services constitutes a most important objective of contemporary monetary policy in most modern countries. A rapid extension of the Welfare State is usually accompanied by a rising trend of prices, though this rise is not deliberate but merely incidental. On the other hand a Government determined to expand social service benefits substantially within a brief space of time is likely to be inclined to avoid committing itself to a too rigid system of monetary stability such as had existed under the gold standard. The maintenance of such a system necessarily limits the Government's freedom of action in the sphere of social services. In 1931 the National Government in Britain felt impelled actually to cut down social services for the sake of saving the gold standard which had come under fire. These cuts and other economic measures were retained and even reinforced after the suspension of the gold standard, for the sake of preventing an excessive depreciation of sterling.

Any Government is liable to be confronted with such dilemmas unless its monetary system is so fluid that the maintenance of internal or external stability of its currency has a very low priority.

Rigidly stabilised exchange parity, or determination to prevent the rise in the domestic price level, or, in the case of an elastic currency, determination to prevent an unduly heavy depreciation or to avoid the imposition of exchange control, price control, rationing, quotas and other physical controls, is apt to come into conflict with the policy aiming at an expansion of social services. Each Government has to make up its mind about the priority or the degree of priority of social services over other objectives of monetary policy. If a Government adopts the line that social services are sacrosanct and must in no circumstances be cut for the sake of a disinflationary policy, that attitude is liable to set a limit to the possible degree of deflation and is even liable to jeopardise monetary stability through inflation. The Government may feel impelled to abstain from resisting inflation too rigidly if it wishes to maintain its social services intact.

On the other hand, monetary policy may pursue the end of preventing or moderating inflation for the sake of maintaining the purchasing power of pensions and other social service benefits. It is true that it is possible to link such payments to a cost-of-living index in order to prevent a decline of their purchasing power through inflation. In practice, the adjustment of payments to a rise in prices through the operation of the cost-of-living clause is always subject to a time-lag during which the purchasing power of the beneficiaries is bound to suffer. In periods of fairly sharp and continuous price increases the time-lag is apt to be continuous because, by the time the payments are adjusted on the basis of the cost-of-living index for the previous month or quarter, prices may have risen further. For this reason, once beneficiaries of social services realise how a rise in price affects them, they may be inclined to join forces with the *rentier* classes in using their influence to induce the Government to resist inflation.

The extent to which monetary policy can pursue social objectives is not without limits. It cannot achieve distribution of more than is available for distribution, though it can increase the total volume of goods available for distribution by the pursuit of an expansionary policy. What monetary policy can do is to change the distribution of an increased volume of purchasing power. It can also convey a fictitious appearance of prosperity, during early phases of inflation, without an actual increase in the volume of goods available for distribution. It can also stimulate investment by maintaining a steadily increasing consumer demand with the aid of moderate inflation.

One of the social objectives of the monetary system is to

secure a wide freedom of choice. Even under an advanced system of rationing everything is not rationed, and in any event the rations represent only a maximum limit of the goods available. Consumers are in a position to abstain from taking up their full rations and to apply their purchasing power for the acquisition of unrationed goods instead. Under a moneyless system, like that of the Inca Empire, the consumers had no alternative to taking up their rations. Since a certain degree of freedom of choice constitutes an important social requirement in any community that is above the bare subsistence level, even in an advanced Communist society the monetary system is retained for that purpose.

Economic planning operating with the aid of financial and physical control devices may aim at reducing the dependence of production and consumption on the automatic operation of the price system. The object of economic planners is to create a system in which considerations of social utility and not those of cost of production and selling price should determine what is to be produced. Even where the social objective prevails, monetary policy remains important as a means for achieving that objective. Economic planning pursues its ends partly through monetary measures. This is so even in France where the commercial banks are nationalised. It is so in the Soviet Union, where the monetary system was repeatedly manipulated after the Second World War, in the interests of social ends as well as of economic planning.

In capitalist countries monetary policy is used for social ends to an increasing degree. There is a growing realisation of the fact that neither the increase of wealth nor the maintenance of stability are ends in themselves but merely means to the end of human happiness. Monetary policy has to serve that ultimate end, and it is not always possible to do this by serving the intermediate ends of increasing wealth or maintaining stability. Nevertheless, the means of achieving social ends are in the long run identical with the means of achieving economic ends, provided that enlightened self-interest on the part of the lower-income classes induces them to favour some compromise between social and economic ends instead of insisting on the absolute priority of the former. As we saw in the last chapter, undue pressure for higher wages is gravely detrimental to the rate of growth. Undue emphasis on social ends means that, for the sake of increasing their slice of the cake, the lower-income groups effectively prevent an increase of the whole cake which could now increase much more thanks to technological progress. They fail to realise that such an absolute increase of the cake would ensure them a larger slice than a relative increase of their share in an unchanged or slowly increasing cake.

CHAPTER TWENTY-TWO

Political Objectives

MONEY has always been an important factor both in the sphere of domestic politics and in that of international affairs. From its earliest origins monetary policy pursued political ends to a large degree. Even before money came to be used systematically as a medium of exchange, it served as a means for safeguarding, consolidating and increasing the political powers of tribal chiefs or rulers and those of the ruling classes. In present-day and recent primitive communities secret societies played a prominent role as the controlling political factor. In communities with such societies one of the main objects of the means of payment employed was to buy membership and promotion in the societies. Holding high rank in those societies meant social prestige and political power. Decisions of the tribal authority affecting the choice of the primitive means of payment or the regulation of its production and use often pursued a political end.

In external policy the possession of large supplies of some means of payment which was valued outside the community enabled the tribal authority to secure allies. This practice has often prevailed also in modern communitities. Governments with strong monetary reserves were, and still are, in a position to secure the support of other Governments. During the Ancient period certain types of money were adopted for the specific purpose of pursuing external wars. For instance, Carthage adopted coinage for that purpose before it was adopted for internal circulation.

In innumerable instances throughout history belligerent countries have abandoned the policy of monetary stability for the sake of being able to finance their wars. It is arguable, however, whether in such cases monetary depreciation can be said to have necessarily come about in pursuance of a deliberate monetary policy. In most instances the countries concerned drifted into debasement or devaluation, the extent of which was not even foreseen when it was decided to embark on a costly war. There were exceptions in which rulers are known to have been fully aware that they could only wage war if they decided to abandon monetary stability, and took deliberate decisions to that end.

An instance of monetary policy with a political objective was the well-known accumulation of gold by Germany shortly before the outbreak of the First World War. There was no pressing need for such accumulation for any economic or social purpose. It simply served the purpose of building up a reserve in anticipation of military requirements.

Money is an important instrument of political prestige. A strong and stable currency backed by a large monetary reserve confers prestige on a country. It is true that its authority is primarily economic. Countries such as Switzerland or Sweden with a strong currency enjoy a high economic prestige but their political power in the international field is limited. Nevertheless, a financially strong country is apt to carry much more weight in international politics than a financially weak and unstable country, given equal military strength. The weakening of the financial strength of a country tends to reduce its political power in the international sphere.

Britain's example after the Second World War clearly illustrates this. There have been very few instances in world history in which the relative political influence of a victorious Great Power suffered such a degree of decline as did that of Britain after 1945. To some extent this decline may be attributable to war-weariness as a result of which Britain reduced her armed strength to an undue degree. But then, this was done also by the United States – at any rate as far as conventional arms were concerned – and yet she remained one of the two leading World Powers. It was done by Britain throughout her history after each victorious war, without suffering political eclipse in consequence. And the fact that West Germany disarmed completely after 1945 did not prevent a remarkable increase of her political power and prestige in the fifties, long before her rearmament made any noteworthy progress. The main reason why after the Second World War Britain's political influence declined almost as much as if she had lost the war instead of winning it, was the decline of her economic power owing to the weakening of sterling's position. Rightly or wrongly, the Socialist Government of 1945–51 concentrated its efforts on the building up of the Welfare State in a very short time. This could not be achieved without rendering sterling vulnerable owing to the chronic balance-of-payments difficulties it entailed. The same state of affairs continued under Conservative Governments which, contrary to Tory traditions, gave freedom from want priority over freedom from fear.

As for the Labour Government of 1964–70, the story of the effect of its ill-conceived monetary policy on Britain's political power and prestige is all too familiar to call for repetition. Nor did the Tory Government that succeeded it live up to Tory traditions for sound monetary policy that would have gone some way towards restoring Britain's political influence in world affairs. The way in which Britain dishonoured both the Smithsonian Agreement and the currency agreement with the EEC by floating the pound without making any effort to resist the attack on it will long be remembered.

It is a matter of opinion whether it was worth Britain's while to sacrifice her position in the front rank of the Powers for the sake of maintaining a high level of employment and an undeservedly generous Welfare State. We are only concerned here with the bare incontrovertible fact that neither the Socialist Government nor the Conservative Government deemed it advisable to make sacrifices for the sake of maintaining Britain's political power and prestige by pursuing the right monetary policy to that end. Amidst her prolonged period of balance-of-payments difficulties, due to living right up to her means and perhaps a little beyond them, Britain was unable to resume her traditional role as a source of financial aid on a sufficient scale. On many occasions she had to be on the receiving end of financial aid. This fact alone made it difficult for her to make herself felt in the council of nations to a sufficient extent.

Even during the brief period of 1969–71 when Britain had a substantial surplus and was able to accumulate a large reserve in addition to repaying her large external short-term debts, she failed to recover her old prestige. She was reluctant to practise self-restraint in defence of the domestic value of the pound. The political importance of reducing unemployment, notwithstanding the complete absence of any co-operation whatsoever to that end on the part of the trade unions, over-shadowed the political and economic importance of possessing once more a thoroughly sound and confidence-inspiring currency. Mr Barber's announcement that the high rate of growth must take precedence over the stability of sterling was responsible for the sterling crisis of June 1972. Basic distrust generated by social-political influence on the monetary policy was responsible for the readiness with which speculators and foreign holders of sterling responded to the deterioration of the balance of payments and to troubles on the industrial front.

It seems reasonable to assume that those responsible for shaping Britain's destinies during the post-war period were fully aware that they could not have it both ways and that their decision to eat their cake in preference to keeping it was taken as a matter of deliberate policy. National greatness in the sense of political influence and prestige was sacrificed for the sake of a policy aiming at national greatness in the sense of possessing advanced social institutions and raising the standard of living. If carried too far, however, this policy might mean getting the worst of both worlds. Freedom from fear cannot be sacrificed to freedom from want with impunity in the long run. Inadequate defences entail the risk of invasion. A defeated country is liable to be exploited by its conqueror, which would mean a considerable lowering of its living standard.

On occasions, considerations of international prestige prevailed over considerations of standard of living and business prosperity. When in 1925 sterling was restored to its pre-war parity, the main object was probably the determination to safeguard Britain's reputation for financial integrity irrespective of cost. The popular slogan that the 'pound must be able to look the dollar in the face' appeared to imply, however, that considerations of political prestige were also involved.

Similarly, many of those who were in 1947 in favour of the restoration and maintenance of the convertiblity of sterling amidst difficult post-war conditions were inspired by considerations of prestige. But the possession of a freely convertible currency only makes for the economic and political prestige of a country if there is implicit confidence in its ability to maintain convertibility. Any distrust in the prospects of convertibility is liable to be damaging to its prestige and to its political power. The same is true about the stability of a currency.

In 1936 France sacrificed her security for the sake of maintaining the gold standard a little longer, by abstaining from taking military measures which could have prevented the remilitarisation of the Rhineland by Hitler. Yet timely devaluation of the franc would have mader her politically stronger and not weaker, just as the depreciation of sterling in 1931 made Britain stronger by reducing the extent to which monetary stability had to be defended at the cost of weakening national security.

Much has been said in recent years about the so-called 'dollar imperialism'. The term originally suggested that the monetary strength of the United States had been used for securing political influence. In reality dollar aid was, and to some extent still is, granted on a lavish scale too indiscriminately to uncommitted nations without any strings attached to the loans or gifts. Some of these nations considered it their birthright to receive American aid and to bite the hand that fed them.

One of the reasons why the United States persistently refused for many years to raise the dollar price of gold from its 1934 parity of $35, and why it was only raised to $38, was the belief that by raising the price of gold substantially she would have assisted the potential enemy, the Soviet Union, with its large gold production. In reality the assistance that would thus be given would be quite negligible compared with the assistance that has actually been given by the United States through handicapping herself from a financial, economic, political and military point of view by the self-imposed difficulties caused by the defence of the dollar at an overvalued level. To the extent to which the delay and the eventual inadequacy of the devaluation was inspired by the above-mentioned political consideration, it produced exactly the opposite effect to the one which had been intended.

The establishment and maintenance of the Sterling Area had pursued not only monetary and economic objectives but also political objectives. The operation of any such currency area was apt to create political as well as economic ties. It established a high degree of identity of interests between the countries of the Sterling Area. Yet Mr Heath's Government cheerfully discarded this advantage for the sake of linking up with Europe, only to jeopardise even those links as soon as their maintenance came to call for unpopular measures.

Strong countries are often in a position to compel economically or politically subordinate countries to adopt monetary policies in accordance with the interests of the 'overlords'. The countries of south-eastern Europe before the Second World War, and practically the entire continent during the years of Nazi occupation, were forced to fix their exchange rates in accordance with the requirements of the Nazi Government's policy of exploitation. Germany was able to secure a large quantity of goods of the occupied or satellite countries by fixing a high exchange value for the Reichsmark in terms of their currencies. Although the advantages thus gained were primarily economic, imperialist exploitation of that type is essentially political in character and monetary policies pursued in its service followed therefore largely political objectives.

During the late twenties French monetary policy was guided, on the candid admission of a former Governor of the Bank of

France, by considerations of foreign policy. Pressure was brought to bear on sterling in order to influence British foreign policy.

To some extent every colonial power imposes its monetary policy on its colonies, but the political character of that policy is largely a matter of degree. It has always been a popular argument in American textbooks on history that the British policy in the eighteenth century aiming at the prevention of the development of coinage in the North American colonies pursued the object of maintaining these colonies in a state of dependence on the mother country as well as exploiting them economically. It seems, however, that since the balance of payments of these undeveloped countries was bound to be strongly adverse during the phase of their rapid development – in the words of the American economist Horace White, 'they could not have both a metallic currency and an axe' – there was a trend for coins to be exported to England in any case. It is arguable that there would have been no sense in encouraging the issue and import of coins which the colonies could not in any event have retained in domestic circulation during a period when the urgent requirements of their development had necessarily taken precedence over other considerations.

It has also been suggested that the arrangement under which the British crown colonies in our time kept their monetary reserves in the form of sterling balances was inspired by political motives. Beyond doubt it strengthens the political links between the colonies and the mother country. It was justified, however, even on economic grounds, since the colonies transacted most of their foreign trade with the United Kingdom and other countries of the Sterling Area, so that is was reasonable for them to keep their monetary reserves in sterling. Moreover, Britain provided substantial financial aid to the colonies under Colonial Development and Welfare Acts instead of permitting them to spend their own sterling reserves.

Hitherto we have been dealing with the external political aspects of monetary policy. In domestic politics too monetary policy is apt to play an important and at times decisive role.

Moderate inflation may be inspired by the desire of the ruling party to secure popularity. It is always tempting for Governments to engage in costly public works schemes and to incur other expenditure liable to secure votes for them. Very often this can only be done at the cost of inflating the national currency. Such a monetary policy is condemned by the overwhelming majority of economists as inherently unsound and vicious – which strong views do not prevent a great many of the self-same economists from advocating the adoption of floating exchanges, even though that system makes it a great deal easier for irresponsible politicians to bribe the electorate by pursuing an inflationary policy.

Democracy is at its worst when opposing political parties feel impelled to outbid each other in offering bribes to the electorate at the cost of debasing the currency. The extent of political bribery during the eighteenth century – a period condemned by historians as having been notoriously corrupt – was negligible compared with the wholesale political bribery of our days, made possible by the misuse of monetary policy for political purposes.

It would be a mistake, however, to be dogmatic in condemning expansionary monetary policies inspired by political considerations as being inherently wicked in all conceivable circumstances. There are situations in which monetary expansion, undertaken primarily for political ends, is justified from a purely economic point of view. It is impossible, for instance, to repair within a brief period large-scale devastations wrought by modern wars without inflating the currency. The alternative is to spread the reconstruction over a long period of years and even decades. It goes without saying that speedy reconstruction is popular and that a Government promising to complete the task in a few years is liable to defeat the part which wants to proceed with caution and is planning to complete the task in two decades. Even those statesmen who are aware of the inflationary consequences of a speedy reconstruction, and who may take the view that the economic disadvantages of the currency depreciation it entails would outweigh the disadvantages of delayed reconstruction, would be inclined to favour speedy reconstruction for the sake of the popularity of their party. In this instance the right thing would be done for the wrong reason.

While it may be a matter of opinion whether it is worth while to sacrifice monetary stability and to put up with the disadvantages of inflation for the sake of industrialising a country within a brief period, or for the sake of completing an ambitious programme of public works, or even for the sake of establishing an advanced Welfare State in record time, there can be no two opinions about the urgency of restoring towns and villages ravaged by war only some major disaster such as an earthquake or a tidal wave. For delay in physical reconstruction would mean low output, and scarcity of goods is liable to cause a rise in prices, so that the choice rests between monetary inflation and price inflation.

The maintenance of the gold standard, or of the stable parities of an inconvertible paper currency, imposes a restraint on any political policies that would necessitate expenditure on a large scale. Indeed, according to many supporters of the gold standard and of stable parities, this is one of the greatest advantages of the system of their choice. In order to be able to proceed with costly political schemes it may become inevitable to discard the self-imposed restraint that has to be maintained so long as external monetary stability is maintained. For this reason, among others, it is broadly speaking true that conservative regimes favour a stable money. This is arguable that the more deeply it is ingrained in the minds of the public that the maintenance of such a system is a matter of vital interest and of national prestige and honour, the more the electorate is likely to support a conservative regime.

From this it would appear that it is natural for Conservatives to favour a rigidly stabilised pound and for Socialists to favour an elastic pound. Yet in 1952–3 British Conservative circles were inclined to flirt with the idea of restoring the 'floating' pound for the sake of being able to restore convertibility. It is arguable that when the pound is kept artificially stable it does not function as a barometer that would react immediately to over-spending by the Government or by the country. If sterling is allowed to fluctuate, any excessive Government expenditure or deterioration of the balance of payments would result in a depreciation which would serve as a warning signal. Those who accept this argument may hold the opinion that in pursuing a political end the monetary policy of a Conservative Government should aim at restoring the floating pound on the assumption that the advent of a Socialist Government would cause a depreciation and that fear of such depreciation might influence the attitude of the electorate.

Supporters of this view point out that in 1931, when after the suspension of the gold standard sterling became an elastic currency, the British electorate was frightened into bringing in a large Conservative majority in the hope that a Conservative Government would be in a better position to moderate the depreciation of sterling. On the other hand, those who believe that Conservative monetary policy ought to aim at rigid stability point out that had sterling been in the habit of fluctuating in August 1931, Ramsay MacDonald would not have been frightened by the prospects of its depreciation into deciding to form a National Government. The decision to allow sterling to depreciate would probably have been taken as a matter of administrative routine on an official level, possibly without even submitting it to the Cabinet. Nobody would have thought it to be out of the ordinary to witness a depreciation of sterling by 20 per cent or more. It was precisely because the importance of maintaining the gold standard and the stability of sterling around its parity of $4·86 was deeply ingrained in the minds of the British public that the threat of having to abandon the parity created such a profound impression.

There can be little doubt that, had the system of floating exchange rates been in operation during the post-war period, all British Governments, whether Socialist or Tory, would have cheerfully depreciated sterling each time it came under pressure, rather than defend it with the aid of politically unpopular measures. Each fall in the external value of sterling would have been followed by a rise in prices and wages, while a recovery in sterling would not have been followed by any corresponding fall in prices and by any cuts whatsoever in wages. Because of this asymmetry of our post-war economy, flexibility of sterling would have meant in practice its non-stop depreciation in frequent stages.

From the foregoing it is evident that even if a Government wished to use its monetary policy for furthering the ends of domestic policies, there would be room for a fundamental disagreement about the way in which this end could be achieved. In given circumstances it may be largely a matter of opinion which of two diametrically opposite courses would produce the desired result.

One of the difficulties of pursuing a political objective by means of monetary policy is that there are no absolute rules determining relations between cause and effect in this sphere. On the one hand a devaluation is liable to undermine the prestige of a Government and damage its political prospects, because it is rightly considered as a sign of weakness or an admission of having pursued mistaken policies. On the other hand measures taken to resist devaluation are almost inevitably unpopular. Following on a prolonged deflationary depression, devaluation is liable to be welcomed with relief, and the Government, in deciding to devalue, stands to gain rather than lose politically. Devaluations may be useful politically as a 'shot in the arm' providing temporary relief before general elections, especially if they are so well timed that their inevitable effect on the cost of living does not become evident until after the elections.

Monetary policy may pursue a political objective also by conferring favour on some sectional interests. Pressure in favour of bimetallism in the United States during the nineties was inspired partly by the political end of securing the support of the silver-producing States. Even though it did not achieve its purpose it was found politically necessary to retain a limited monetary role for silver.

A policy of deliberate currency depreciation may be adopted

by extreme Left regimes not only in pursuing the social objective of levelling down wealth and incomes, but also with the political objective of reducing the political power of undependable and hostile elements. Extreme Left regimes which consider it inexpedient to decree confiscation of private property without compensation can achieve the same end by more subtle devices of monetary policy. They can avoid uncompromising measures that are liable to encounter desperate resistance on the part of the owners of the confiscated property by paying them 'full' compensation in the form of Government Bonds which can subsequently be wiped out through a policy of progressive currency depreciation. On balance the effect of that policy is apt to be the same as that of nationalisation without compensation, but its form may be considered to be politically more expedient by left-wing Governments which are as yet not strong enough to pursue a frankly confiscatory policy. The same applies to former colonies which, having gained their independence, would like to gain control over industrial and commercial firms owned by foreign interests, without resorting to open expropriation.

Generally speaking, the pursuit of political objectives with the aid of monetary policy is apt to be harmful rather than otherwise, both in the sphere of international affairs and in that of domestic politics. While there is much to be said in favour of placing monetary policy at the service of social progress, its use for political ends is very often indefensible. However, we live in an imperfect world in which those in power often yield to the temptation of misusing their control over monetary policy. Anyone examining the ends of monetary policy, not as they ought to be in an ideal world, but as they are, must pay due attention to open or concealed political motives without which his picture could not be complete.

CHAPTER TWENTY-THREE

Demonetisation of Gold

ALTHOUGH changes in the monetary system have already been dealt with in a general way in Chapter 7 on 'Choice of Monetary System ', owing to the importance and topical nature of the subject of demonetising gold I propose to devote a separate chapter to that subject. For a more detailed treatment of the subject the reader is referred to my book *The Destiny of Gold* and also to *The Destiny of the Dollar*.

The idea of depriving gold of its monetary role is not new. In Ancient Greece, Sparta replaced precious metals by iron bars, and a similar system was advocated by Plato. Another attempt was made much nearer our time by John Law in eighteenth-century France. One of Voltaire's fictitious characters sought to discredit gold by producing handcuffs and other despised objects out of it, on the assumption that he could thereby reduce the desire of the people to possess gold. Between the two World Wars currency cranks of various kinds, and also two radical monetary reformers of standing, advocated the replacement of gold by managed paper currency. They predicted that in the course of time the value of that metal would be reduced to that of scrap iron.

But it was not until the late sixties that the demonetisation of gold came to be considered seriously as one of the ends of monetary policy. This time it was not advocated merely by isolated would-be reformers or by currency cranks, but by a large number of academic economists, and also by some Central Bankers and Finance Ministers, especially in the United States and Britain. While until comparatively recently academic circles were essentially orthodox and favoured a deflationist monetary policy, during the post-war decades there developed widely supported schools favouring a monetary system under which it would be even easier to inflate than it was under the Bretton Woods system. Growth-hysteria has become a respectable disease and those suffering from it have become anxious to eliminate gold from the monetary system in order to be able to devalue the national currencies as a matter of daily routine, or allow them to float, and in order to be able to expand the volume of currency with impunity.

Ministers, Government officials and Central Bankers in the two principal Anglo-Saxon countries came down in favour of a goldless monetary system, partly for the same reason as academic economists, but largely because their countries no longer possessed the amount of monetary gold required by them. Even the United States lost some three-fifths of her large gold reserve during the late fifties and the sixties, and it did not appear possible to restore an adequate reserve without submitting to a prolonged deflation. As for Britain, her gold stock declined considerably. Having realised that there was no hope for putting the clock back, the politicians and experts of the United States and Britain developed what I call a 'sour-grapes complex'. Because they were unable to regain the gold they would have liked to possess, they followed the example of Aesop's immortal fox who, being unable to reach the grapes he was after, sought to comfort himself by saying that anyhow the grapes were too sour.

The monetary role of gold was gradually reduced long before this phase was reached. Since the supply of monetary gold was unable to keep pace with growing requirements, gold coins disappeared from circulation and gold bars too came to be replaced by book entries as international reserves. The proportion of gold in monetary reserves gradually declined until it came to represent barely one-third of the monetary reserves in the free world by the early seventies. Large quantities of gold disappeared in private hoards, and the current output merely covered the industrial demand. In face of increasing pressure in favour of an accelerated rate of economic growth, politicians anxious to gain popularity sought to remove the handicap imposed on monetary expansion by inadequate gold reserves. Considerable progess was made in that direction during the sixties. The expansion of the Euro-currency market provided ample liquid resources, and so did the increase of reserves through reciprocal swap facilities and, towards the end of the decade, through the initiation of Special Drawing Rights. It was possible to expand credit without addition to the monetary gold stock. In particular, the SDRs had immense potentialities. Admittedly, the Rio de Janeiro Agreement only provided for the issue of a limited amount of SDRs and 30 per cent of it was re-payable. But it provided the formula which was subsequently used by Mr Barber for the plan to replace gold by 'paper gold'.

As SDRs constitute a means to an end, they will be discussed in detail in Chapter 42, in the section dealing with monetary policy means. What we are concerned with here is the role they played in influencing monetary policy against the maintenance of gold as the basis of money. One of the main reasons for the pressure in favour of doing away with the monetary role of gold was the growing desire to replace it by 'paper gold'. Originally SDRs were meant merely to supplement gold and foreign exchange reserves. But the declared aim of the Barber Plan was to terminate gradually the monetary role of gold alto-gether and replace it by SDRs. In order to induce Central Banks and Governments to accept SDRs in payment for export sur-pluses on a large scale, it is evidently deemed essential to elimi-nate reserve assets that were obviously preferable to SDRs. While it was conceivable that Central Banks preferred SDRs to any foreign currency, having regard to the uncertainty of the pro-spects of most currencies, it is inconceivable that any Central Bank should ever prefer SDRs to gold. The only way in which it is hoped to induce them to accept SDRs in unlimited amounts in payment for their surpluses would be the elimination of gold as an alternative means of payment.

For this reason the advocates of the use of SDRs as the principal international means of payment felt it essential to terminate the role of gold in the monetary system. They duly realised that so long as gold formed part of the reserves, any surplus country would always accept gold in unlimited amounts in payment for their surpluses, in preference to SDRs which are inconvertible and for which nobody is responsible. To ensure a favourable reception for large transfers of SDRs, it was considered essential, therefore, to do away with gold.

This of course easier said than done. The attraction of gold has been deeply ingrained in human character ever since the existence of the monetary system, and even before. Those who imagine that it could be eliminated by anti-gold progapanda must surely be unfamiliar with human nature. Yet it is only too obvious that whenever there is some trouble, whether economic or political, there is a rush to gold, not only in the East but also in countries such as France. Most people feel it is safer to hoard gold than to hold their assets in any other form. It would take more than ingenious economic arguments or political propaganda to dispose of this attitude. So long as it continues to prevail, efforts to demonetise gold are bound to fail in the long run.

The fact that the market price of gold in London is $66 at the time of writing – it is a great deal higher in India and in other Eastern markets – compared with the official American price of $38 speaks for itself. It is evident that gold is preferred to inconvertible currencies. Were the dollar to be made convertible at its present official price, or even at a higher price, the gold reserve, which is at present just under $10 billion, would disappear into private hoards and into the reserves of other countries in a very short time.

One of the main reasons why the convertibility of the dollar was suspended in 1971 was that the Pentagon insisted on retaining a substantial strategic gold reserve, which is considered necessary in case of war. The American military command is more realistic than American politicians and banks. The Pentagon is convinced that it could not depend absolutely on being able to use either foreign currencies or SDRs to meet military requirements abroad in the event of a war, and that the possession of a means of payment which is certain to be accepted unconditionally in unlimited amounts in any part of the world is essential in order to ensure the ability of the American forces to operate abroad whenever this is deemed necessary. Those responsible for American monetary policy had to take this into consideration.

It is of course conceivable that some countries might be able to demonetise gold temporarily and experimentally for relatively brief periods. During the First World War Sweden suspended the import of gold in order to check the inflation brought about by the heavy influx. But soon after the end of the war the convertibility of the Swedish krona had to be suspended because after the turn of the tide the Riksbank's gold reserve was becoming rapidly depleted. The suspension of the monetary role of gold in Sweden was due to an *embarras de richesse* and not to an inadequacy of the supply. There would be no agitation for a demonetisation of gold in the United States and Britain if as a result of a spectacular increase in its output it would be possible to cover the increased requirements for reserves. The main reason why there is such a pressure in favour of the demonetisation of gold is that its relatively limited volume is liable to handicap economic growth. But even from that point of view it is difficult to justify the policy, since other reserve currencies can be, and are in fact, used in addition to gold.

The other main reason for the aurophobia that prevails in many quarters is that the monetary use of gold implies fixed parities, and those in favour of floating exchanges are anxious to eliminate this obstacle to the adoption of their favourite system. Actually gold can fulfil the role of a reserve currency under a system of floating rates in spite of the fluctuation of its value. After all, the value of foreign currency reserves and of SDRs also fluctuates in terms of national currencies under a system of floating rates. Even though under long-established traditions the monetary use of gold is associated with stable exchanges resulting from fixed parities, there is no reason why gold should not perform the function of monetary reserve if its value were allowed to fluctuate.

A demonetisation of gold would be certain to be followed by an escalation of inflation, since the limitation of the quantity of the monetary metal constitutes nature's balancing function for the purpose of preventing an unduly rapid expansion. It was owing to the reduction of the monetary role of gold that monetary expansion came to be accelerated, and the resulting aggravation of pollution and other environmental deterioration has made many intelligent people realise that, after all, an unduly rapid economic growth is by no means an unmixed blessing. But apart altogether from its possibly disastrous environmental consequences, a demonetisation of gold might result in a runaway inflation which alone would be sufficient to bring about eventually a reaction in favour of restoring the monetary use of gold. It is not without reason that Germany and France, both countries which have experienced advanced inflation, are strongly in favour of maintaining the monetary role of gold.

It seems more than probable that aurophobia is merely a passing fashion and that sooner or later most people who are now in favour of demonetising gold will come to the conclusion that if the monetary role of gold did not exist, it ought to have been invented.

CHAPTER TWENTY-FOUR

Freedom or Restrictions?

MONETARY policy may aim at restricting the freedom of monetary operations or at eliminating restrictions on their freedom. Until comparatively recently restrictions were the rule and freedom the rare exception. Foreign exchange operations, international transfers of capital, bullion movements and even domestic banking transactions were subject to a series of restrictions. The Netherlands were one of the few exceptions from the late seventeenth century onwards. It was only during the nineteenth century that freedom became the rule and restrictions the exception, at any rate in advanced countries. There was a relapse into restrictions during the two World Wars. After the First World War freedom was restored in most countries in a relatively short time. On the other hand, after the Second World War restrictions remained in force in most countries. Although their extent came to be gradually reduced, whenever there was trouble controls were restored almost everywhere.

Between the two wars it was widely taken for granted that the return to a regime of complete freedom was a natural state of affairs. But more recently, opinion has become more divided about the basic principle of freedom versus control. Many people are highly dogmatic about it, but others are prepared to adapt their views to the changing situation.

Decisions about reinforcing or mitigating monetary controls need not necessarily be inspired by considerations of monetary policy. Exchange controls may be adopted for the sake of protecting domestic producers. Many measures regulating banking aim at safeguarding the interests of depositors, in which case they do not come within the realm of monetary policy. But in many instances, decisions about control and freedom, taken primarily for non-monetary purposes, are liable to have monetary side-effects. The basic attitude of individual countries, and within countries of political parties and individuals, varies and is apt to change. Very often Governments feel impelled to act against their basic principles under pressure of immediate necessity.

Some countries feel strongly opposed to exchange controls as a matter of tradition, but it is usually the financially strong countries that can afford to pursue a policy of freedom from controls. Thus throughout the nineteenth century and until the First World War Britain was strongly opposed to any form of controls. Thanks to her favourable balance of payments and to her large foreign investments she could afford to allow the automatic gold standard to produce its natural effects. In the domestic monetary sphere too, the rules and regulations were kept down to a minimum and most restrictions were voluntary. In the United States the adoption of exchange controls during the sixties first assumed the form of 'guidelines', many of which were subsequently replaced by statutory controls.

Many Governments feel so strongly against interfering with monetary and banking freedom that they prefer to resort to deflationary measures rather than obviate the necessity for them by resorting to controls. They even prefer to allow exchange rates or interest rates to move in an unwanted direction rather than prevent their movements by adopting controls. But this kind of bigoted dogmatism is on the decline and most Governments are now prepared to strike a compromise between their principles and the necessity dictated by the situation. They do so reluctantly, however, because they feel that controls create an artificial situation which is liable to aggravate the disequilibrium that necessitated their adoption. And since they regard controls as a temporary state of affairs, they feel that after the return to freedom the situation is liable to become even more difficult than it was before their adoption of controls.

This view is held particularly strongly in respect of statutory incomes policy. In view of the importance of that subject, it will be dealt with in a separate chapter.

There is now less dogmatism about exchange control than there was until recently. Even financially strong countries are prepared to resort to it for the sake of safeguarding themselves against an unwanted influx of foreign money. Stiff resistance against their adoption, such as was displayed by the former German Finance Minister, Professor Schiller, in 1972, is exceptional. In the predominant majority of instances exchange control is the weapon of financially weak countries and its object is to bolster up weak exchanges in preference to strengthening them with the aid of deflationary measures and devices of domestic controls. Most exchange control measures aim at preventing residents of the countries concerned transferring their capital abroad, though in many instances the balances of foreign residents are also blocked, and in some instances exchange transactions arising from trade are also restricted. This subject is dealt with in detail in Chapter 40.

Interest rates in the United States have been subject to strict regulations by the Federal Reserve authorities. Regulation Q fixes the ceiling for interest rates allowable on various types of deposits. One of the instruments of monetary policy in the United States is to change Regulation Q. The maintenance of these restrictions is not a question of dogmatism but one of practical necessity. Until September 1971 the same end was sought to be attained in Britain, not by statutory restrictions but by a voluntary cartel between clearing banks. Under its provisions, deposit rates and loan rates were fixed by a 'gentlemen's agreement'. Likewise, while in the United States and in most other countries banks were, and still are, subject to statutory reserve requirements, until September 1971 British banks observed conventional reserve requirements. But even in the absence of statutory provisions about interest rates and reserve requirements, the self-imposed rules were strictly observed by British banks.

As from September 1971 the cartel of British clearing banks

was abolished, so that in theory British banks are now entirely free to compete with and outbid each other by offering higher deposit rates or lower loan rates. This change, brought about by the Bank of England's decision, was a victory for the *laissez-faire* school. In practice, however, even in the absence of official regulations and of a cartel, the rates charged and allowed by the British and American banks have remained uniform. While changes in the rates are now brought about not by a collective decision of all banks or by official instructions but by individual decisions of each bank, they follow each other's example with the minimum of delay, so that the rates are virtually as uniform as they were under the cartel and under Regulation Q.

Simultaneously with this theoretical change in the direction of freedom there was, however, a change in Britain in the direction of control. A statutory liquidity ratio took the place of the former conventional cash ratio and liquidity ratio. The explanation of this change is that as a result of the establishment of a large number of foreign bank branches and affiliates in London, the number of banks in the UK has increased very considerably. Consequently it has become less safe to rely on voluntary discipline, especially as many overseas banks did not have the same tradition for discipline as British banks. On balance, the two measures have cancelled each other out from the point of view of control versus freedom. On the other hand, the relaxation of Regulation Q made a distinct change in favour of freedom in the United States.

The turbulent state of affairs that prevailed in the world's money markets and foreign exchange markets during the late sixties and early seventies forced some countries to abandon their previous dogmatism against controls. They adopted restrictions affecting exchanges and interest rates when they deemed this expedient, and relaxed or dropped these restrictions when they no longer considered their maintenance necessary. It would be difficult, therefore, to discern any distinct basic trend in monetary policy towards freedom or towards restrictions. While most advanced countries would prefer freedom, they are willing to make concessions in favour of restrictions for the sake of practical considerations.

There can be little doubt that, should conditions settle down to a normal state, the monetary policies of most advanced countries would pursue the end of removing restrictions as far as practicable, even at the cost of some degree of disadvantage or risk. While in totalitarian states restrictions form part of the system, in democratic countries they are only adopted under pressure of necessity and, generally speaking, their monetary policies pursue the end of maintaining or restoring freedom.

CHAPTER TWENTY-FIVE

Other Objectives

THERE is an almost infinite variety of ends that monetary policy may pursue in addition to those dealt with in the foregoing chapters. Some of the ends of monetary policy dealt with briefly in this chapter are fully as important as most of those to which separate chapters were devoted. The reason why these ends are not dealt with here so extensively is that their subject-matter has been, or will be, covered in some other chapter from some different angle. For, to a large extent, most ends of monetary policy are liable to overlap with other ends. There is also much overlapping between ends and means.

From a very early period one of the objects of monetary policy was to ensure that the quantity of money at the disposal of the community should be adequate. Long before the connection between an increase in the volume of money and the trend of prices or trade was realised, it had been known that shortage of coins had been the source of many difficulties both to the ruler and to his subjects, and had hampered the normal functioning of the economic system. In a great many instances the object of debasement was to remedy the shortage.

In modern times too, during periods of runaway inflation when the rise in prices far exceeded the increase in the volume of money, and high prices necessitated a larger volume of money, the authorities decided to speed up the operation of the printing press for the purpose of meeting the increased monetary requirements. In emergency the status of money was conferred on various objects in order to overcome the grave difficulties caused by the inadequacy of monetary circulation. The quantity of money may be increased not in order to raise prices or to lower interest rates or to create employment, but solely for the sake of having enough money in circulation to satisfy the cash requirements of the community at prevailing prices.

Reference was made in Chapter 13 to convertibility, whether in gold or in other currencies, as a means of expanding international trade. Convertibility may, however, be pursued also as an end of monetary policy for its own sake. A large section of expert opinion and public opinion in advanced countries is in favour of convertibility, not so much from the point of view of any advantages it may yield, but because it appears to symbolise economic freedom and the liberal way of life. Those who feel in such a way about it are convinced that the restoration and maintenance of the highest possible degree of convertibility should be made the foremost aim of monetary policy. In the United States this school of thought was represented for a long time by an influential group of economists favouring the restoration of the convertibility of the dollar into gold for domestic as well as international purposes, and even the resumption of the issue of gold coins. In Britain such an ambitious object has long been considered clearly unattainable, but the restoration of the highest possible degree of convertibility of sterling into dollars and other currencies is viewed with much favour in many quarters.

The maintenance of stable interest rates may be an important objective of monetary policy. Instead of using changes in interest rates as means for affecting the volume of currency and credit or the tendency of exchange rates, various monetary devices may be applied for the purpose of preventing any fluctuations of interest rates. Such fluctuations are liable to disturb trade, and there are obvious advantages in keeping interest rates stable. French monetary policy for many years before the First World War attached considerable importance to the stability of the Bank Rate. The Bank of France resorted to various devices as an alternative to changing its rediscount rate, when the situation called for such changes. In given circumstances stable interest rates may have to be achieved at the cost of fluctuating price levels or fluctuating exchanges, or through the application of various controls or other devices. Usually the object of monetary policy is to keep interest rates stable at a low level. This policy of cheap money may be an end in itself. All the anti-usury laws adopted everywhere for thousands of years pursued the end of cheap money for its own sake. There are many modern instances in which cheap money is the end of monetary policy. Since, however, cheap money is more frequently a means to other ends, we propose to deal with it in detail in a later chapter.

Influencing international capital movements is yet another possible objective of monetary policy. A capital influx may be encouraged not on account of its effect on exchange rates, gold reserves or interest rates, but in order to secure capital resources unobtainable internally. A major objective of British monetary policy has always been the attraction of short-term funds to London in order to ensure international banking activity in which the City has specialised, and to stimulate international commercial activity which is assumed to result from London's prominence as an international banking centre. Amidst the difficulties of the inter-war period the British monetary authorities often sought to attract funds to London in order to strengthen sterling or to check an inconvenient decline of the gold reserve. In such instances the influencing of international capital movements was a means to an end. On the other hand, when the object was to attract funds so as to enable the City to pursue its international financial functions, then the influencing of capital movements may be considered to have been an end of monetary policy.

The maintenance or increase of the national income is another possible end of monetary policy. It is one of the recent additions to the list of monetary objectives. Until twenty years ago regulation of the size of the national income was not considered to be part of the functions of the Government. Indeed, official national income statistics were in most countries non-existent. Today most Governments possess elaborate statistical organisations for the purpose of calculating and estimating the national income. Even though much remains to be done in this respect, the progress made since before the Second World War has been truly remarkable.

One of the reasons why national income has risen to prominence among objects of monetary policy is that under the conception that developed in recent decades, monetary trends largely depend on the size of national income. According to one school of thought, an increase in the volume of money would not in itself affect the price level were it not for its influence on the size of incomes. The idea did not make much headway during the twenties, when economic thought was largely dominated by the Quantity Theory of money, which sought to establish arithmetical relations between the volume of money and the level of prices. Nor did it carry much weight in the sixties and seventies while the 'money school' dominated the fashion of thought. During the thirties, however, increasing attention came to be paid to the connection between monetary trends and the trends of national income. But it was not until after the Second World War that monetary policy in Britain and other countries came to be guided to some extent by the desire to influence the size of national income. More often than not this is a means to some other end. Incomes policy as a means of monetary policy will be dealt with in Chapter 38. It is conceivable, however, that monetary measures may be taken mainly with the object of raising or lowering the national income or of preventing its rise or its fall.

Yet another end of monetary policy is the ironing-out of minor fluctuations as distinct from the fight against basic movements such as business cycles or inflationary and deflationary trends. Monetary policy is very often confined to reducing minor fluctuations to a minimum, whether in the money market or the foreign exchange market. It is of course difficult to draw the dividing line between minor fluctuations and major trends. The monetary authorities may seek to counteract minor fluctuations because they are anxious to prevent them from developing into major movements. On other occasions, however, it is reasonably clear that there is no such danger, and the object of neutralising minor fluctuations is to avoid such relatively minor disadvantages as they are liable to cause.

Seasonal fluctuations are among the movements which monetary policy may aim at preventing or moderating. When the Bank of England kept aloof from the foreign exchange market the dollar usually moved against sterling in the autumn as a result of seasonal demand in connection with cotton imports and other crop movements. Such restricted fluctuations did not cause much harm, as business firms were able to 'hedge' against them through forward exchange operations. Nevertheless, such seasonal movements, whether in exchange rates or interest rates, were liable to cause a certain inconvenience. Many Central Banks considered it their task to counteract them as far as possible by means of intervention in the foreign exchange market or the money market.

From 1932 till 1951 it was the policy of the Bank of England to maintain discount rates virtually unchanged. From the outbreak of the Second World War until December 1951, exchange rates were kept rigidly pegged. After the reopening of the market in 1951 sterling was allowed to fluctuate often within a narrow range seasonal influences were allowed to produce their effect, as before the war. On the other hand, the discount rate policies pursued by various Continental Central Banks often aimed, among other objectives, at preventing a temporary rise in bill rates through seasonal demand for credit during the busy seasons, such as the harvest period in predominantly agricultural countries.

Monetary policy may pursue ends of justice and equity. When a depreciation is unavoidable, steps are taken occasionally to minimise the losses incurred by certain classes and the gains unjustifiably earned by other classes. This can be done through the operation of a sliding scale on the basis of which debts are valorised according to the value of currency at the time they were incurred. There can, of course, be no more than rough justice. The same may be said about arrangements under which wages, salaries and other payments are linked to the cost-of-living index. Such devices usually pursue primarily social or economic, or even political, ends. It is conceivable, however, that in some instances they were inspired largely by considerations of abstract justice and equity, irrespective of practical consequences.

With this chapter we have completed the examination of the ends of monetary policy. We have seen that the authorities, in deciding on their monetary measures, are in a position to pursue a wide variety of objectives. Our next task is to examine the wide variety of devices with the aid of which they may try to achieve the diverse ends of their monetary policies.

Part Three

THE MEANS OF MONETARY POLICY

CHAPTER TWENTY-SIX

Alternative Means

THE foregoing chapters dealt with the ends which those responsible for decisions of monetary policy are liable to pursue. In the following chapters we propose to deal with the means which are at their disposal and by which they may try to approach these ends.

Although certain means are frequently used to serve particular ends, the same means may serve various ends and the same ends can be served by various means. Consequently the choice of the end does not necessarily predetermine the choice of the means. There must be, therefore, two distinct sets of monetary policy decisions. The authorities must first decide the aims of their monetary policy and then the ways in which these aims can be achieved. The deliberate choice of the ends of monetary policy is an essentially political decision and must always be taken at the highest level, even through the politicians ultimately responsible for the decisions may follow the advice of technical experts. The choice of means, on the other hand, is largely a technical decision and can often be taken on an official level. Nevertheless, even in this respect the political authority usually has the last word as far as major principles are concerned. For instance, it is for the Government and not the Central Bank or the Treasury officials to decide whether a rise in prices should be prevented through price controls, credit restrictions or a revaluaation of the currency, or through some other means.

To the generation that has grown up since the suspension of the gold standard in 1931 it may appear almost incredible that a quarter of a century ago many Central Banks had practically a free hand in deciding the choice of the means of their country's monetary policy, and that very often they determined even its ends. Today the only power left in the hands of Central Banks is the implementation of monetary policy decisions taken by Governments. It is only in the sphere of the technique of monetary practice that Central Banks still have a reasonably free hand. At the same time Treasuries are largely advised by Central Banks, and the latter thus retain considerable influence in the choice of means and, to a less extent, even of ends.

The curtailment of the powers of Central Banks in respect of the choice of the means of monetary policy is to some extent due to the adoption of a changed conception, under which monetary policy has come to be regarded as one of the Government's major responsiblities. To a very large extent, however, the change is due to the widening of the scope of monetary policy. Some half a century ago the range of the ends which monetary policy was to pursue, and of the means among which Central Banks had to choose was limited. Tradition largely determined the devices to be applied in given situations. The choice of devices has widened remarkably in the lifetime of our generation. Today it includes some means the application of which requires a major political decision. It is inconceivable, for instance, that the adoption or removal of exchange-control or even its substantial modification could be decided upon by technical experts alone. Such decisions are necessarily taken at a high level. They are apt to be influenced by the political philosophy of the party in office, and by the prevailing fashion in dogmatism.

In few economic spheres has there been such a remarkable change within the brief span of half a century as in that of monetary policy. We already saw in the foregoing chapters the extent to which the ends of monetary policy have become modified in our lifetime. Changes that have come about since the twenties in respect of the means of monetary policy have been if anything even more far-reaching. This is due to the coincidence of two influences One of them was the realisation through practical experience during the thirties that in given conditions traditional means of monetary policy are apt to be inadequate. The other was the influence of the teachings of Keynes, whose new monetary theories and practical monetary proposals have revolutionised the methods of monetary policy. Moreover, his victory over monetary orthodoxy has opened the way for new thinking in the post-Keynesian era.

In the domestic sphere there were until recently relatively few alternative means to choose between. While they could choose between various techniques, the only policies which the monetary authorities had at their disposal were to regulate the quantity of money by direct intervention or by changing the level of interest rates. The application of these means was based on the assumption that demand was determined by the quantity of money and that price trends must therefore be influenced by determining the quantity of money. Progressive economists and monetary experts regard this concept as out of date or at any rate over-simplified even though Friedman made a vigorous effort to revive it through his monetarist school. It is now recognised in most quarters that there are factors other than the total quantity of money which are liable to affect demand. The importance of the velocity of circulation of money has come to be realised by those responsible for decisions of monetary policy. They have also become aware the effect on changes in the volume of money that is produced through the volume of the national income and its distribution, on the volume of saving and that of capital investment.

It is no longer considered sufficient for the authorities to confine themselves to regulating the total quantity of money. It is now thought essential that they should endeavour to influence the volume of the national income – whether by influencing the volume of money or by some other means – and its distribution as between high and low income groups, as a means of determining the trend of prices. They are also expected to influence the trend of capital investment, not only its total but also allocation as between the production of capital goods and consumer goods. When the private sector of the national economy prefers to keep its funds in a liquid form, official monetary policy may have to supplement private investment by increasing public. investment. When the propensity of the public to consume is inadequate, monetary policy may have to apply devices to stimulate consumers' demand.

Monetary policy nowadays has to differentiate also between means stimulating production for the domestic market and production for exports. Indeed, the authorities may even have to adopt means to encourage exports to certain areas and discourage them to other areas.

Even within the traditional sphere of determining the quantity of money, the means employed nowadays differ materially in many respects from those employed until comparatively recently. Changes in the Bank Rate no longer play such an essential part. On the other hand, the relative importance of changing the volume of credit by means of open-market operations has increased. In some countries such as the United States, changes in the reserve requirements of commerical banks and adjustments of Treasury deposits play an important part.

In addition to determining the grand total of the volume of money, the new monetary policy tries to achieve its ends also by discriminating in favour of or against certain types of credits. There is a wide variety of devices of selective credit control. It is characteristic of the degree of encroachment of Governments on the preserves of Central Banks that even in respect of such administrative devices the decisions are now usually taken by the Treasuries.

The combination of financial controls with physical controls provided the authorities with a wide variety of new devices. The adoption and the application of such means is of course entirely a matter for the Government. It requires decisions on the highest level; and very often the adoption or removal of controls necessitates also legislation.

Fiscal means of monetary policy are employed for determining the totals of incomes and their distribution, and also for encouraging or discouraging the production or consumption of certain types of goods. The Budget has come to be regarded as a most important means of monetary policy. Although the 'monetarist school' is trying hard to put the clock back, fiscal means weapons in the armoury of monetary policy have come to stay. Likewise, Treasury operations are now amongst the weapons in its armoury. Throughout financial history monetary policy often served the end of facilitating Treasury operations. More recently, relations have become reciprocal, and as often as not the timing and terms of Treasury issues serve the ends of monetary policy.

One of the major recommendations of the Radcliffe Report and of the American Report on Money and Credit aimed at influencing the entire structure of interest rates – not only short rates but rates for various maturities – by means of open-market operations in medium- and long-term loans as well as in Treasury bills, and by means of debt management policy.

Various economic policies are adopted and followed with an eye on their effects on the monetary situation. Such policies may affect production, foreign trade, wages, etc. Indeed, generally speaking it is true to say that most decisions in the sphere of economic policy are now taken with an eye on their monetary effects.

In the international sphere too the choice of a means of monetary policy has widened considerably. Under the gold standard the Bank Rate was supposed to be the only weapon, though some Continental countries practised for many decades an elaborate *Devisen-Politik*, employing a variety of means. Even the Bank of England resorted at times to some special devices to discourage withdrawals of gold and to encourage gold imports. However, such measures were exceptional. During the thirties exchange control made its appearance, with its almost infinite variety of devices. A relatively recent development has been the adoption of international means of monetary policy by co-operation with monetary authorities of other countries or by the conclusion of international agreements and the operation of some international institution.

The choice of means of monetary policy is fully as controversial as the choice of its ends. There is the unending struggle between traditionalists and progressives. The trend is, however, towards the adjustment of traditionalist attitudes to changing requirements. 'Orthodoxy keeps catching up with me' said Keynes in 1941 on the occasion of his election to the Court of Directors of the Bank of England. The former 'heretic', whose views on monetary policy had been for many years the main target of attacks by all traditionalist critics, was made a high priest of the temple of monetary orthodoxy, not because he recanted his heresies – even though by negotiating the Bretton Woods Agreement he came down on the side of rigid exchange parities – but because they had been largely accepted by 1941 as part of the official creed.

CHAPTER TWENTY-SEVEN

The Quantity of Money

DETERMINATION of the quantity of money has always been regarded as one of the most important means of monetary policy. In the absence of official intervention to influence the the quantity of money, it is liable to be affected by a wide variety of factors, often not to the advantage of the community. The volume of money may become excessive or it may become inadequate to meet requirements. It is one of the supreme tasks of the monetary authorities to ensure that their community should have the correct quantity of money – that is, the quantity which the authorities rightly or wrongly consider to be correct in view of the ends which their monetary policy rightly or wrongly follows.

The maintenance or adjustment of the quantity of money may pursue many different ends. The most obvious end is to provide the community with the volume of money required for the smooth functioning of its economy. It is determined by the volume of business at the prevailing level of prices. Other ends, notably that of influencing the price level, may overshadow the end of meeting the community's normal monetary requirements. As we saw, however, in Chapter 25, the endeavour to satisfy the monetary requirements of the community influenced monetary policy long before the connection between the quantity of money and its value was adequately realised. Kings and Government were unaware until comparatively recently that inadequacy in the quantity of money was liable to cause a fall in prices. They assumed that the rise in prices that followed debasements of coinage was entirely due to the lowering of the metallic value of the coins and not to the increase of their quantity.

Monetary action to prevent an increase in prices by preventing an increase in the quantity of money is a comparatively modern development. It is true that it is encountered in rudimentary form in primitive communities which, in many instances, selected monetary objects in order to ensure chronic scarcity. Some communities sought to prevent an increase in the volume of money by the aid of religious taboos. For example, in certain communities monetary objects could only be collected at certain phases of the moon. In many instances surplus quantities of the monetary material were systematically eliminated through their destruction by means of religious sacrifices, or were hoarded as ornaments in places of worship or places. It has been suggested that the accumulation of coins and of monetary metals in the Temple of Jerusalem and in other ancient places of worship was a means of controlling inflation, and that the accumulated treasures were released by the priests when they considered it expedient to increase the volume of purchasing power.

The State authority was often confronted with problems arising from an excessive volume of debased coins. Generally speaking, however, until the advent of paper money with its unlimited possibilities of increasing the supply of currency, the problem of Governments was not to keep down the volume of money, but to raise it. It is true that from time to time recoinage transactions resulted in a deliberate reduction in the volume of currency. This was, however, merely an incidental result of the policy aiming at an improvement of the quality of currency by increasing its metallic content.

The discovery that changes in the quantity of money are liable to affect prices is generally attributed to Jean Bodin, who put forward his theory to that effect in 1568. In fact he was preceded by Copernicus, who in his treatise on debasement remarked in 1526 that money tends to depreciate when it becomes too abundant. It took a long time from the discovery of this truth before the monetary authorities came to adopt deliberate policies aiming at influencing the trend of prices by changing the volume of money.

During the paper-currency inflations of the modern period the Western Governments had to learn through bitter experience the effect of an increase in the volume of paper money on the level of prices – a lesson which Chinese rulers had learnt and had forgotten again many centuries earlier. They adopted policies endeavouring to limit the expansion of the note issue, though under the pressure of military requirements these limits had to be raised.

Systematic intervention to regulate the volume of currency and credit in the interest of maintaining a stable price level did not make its appearance until the nineteenth century. It has been brought to a fine art during the present century. The aim of such intervention to influence prices by regulating the quantity of money was not necessarily the maintenance of stability. During the thirties the declared policy of the United States and other countries was one of 'reflation', aiming at raising the price level, in order to correct some of the bad effects of the preceding slump, partly by deliberately increasing the volume of money. In frequent instances the authorities adopted a policy of deliberately reducing the volume of money in an effort to lower the price level, or at any rate to prevent its rise.

Another object monetary policy has often pursued by influencing the volume of money is the safeguarding of the balance of payments. If the price level in a country is too high compared with other countries, it is liable to handicap exports and stimulate imports, because foreign competitors at home and abroad are able to quote lower prices. The result is an adverse trade balance causing a weak trend of the exchange value of the currency and a decline of the gold or foreign exchange reserve. One of the ways in which this situation can be remedied is by forcing down the domestic price level by deflation, that is, by reducing the volume of money.

Yet another object that can be pursued by means of influencing the volume of money is the maintenance, increase or reduction of interest rates. Relations between the level of interest rates and the quantity of money are, of course, reciprocal. The quantity of money can be influenced by raising or lowering interest rates, because there is more inducement to borrow at low than at high rates. On the other hand, interest rates can be caused to rise by reducing the volume of money and they can be caused to fall by increasing monetary supplies in accordance with the law of supply and demand. The monetary authorities are in a position to decide at which end they should initiate their intervention. Often it is initiated simultaneously at both ends. Very often, however, the initiative is taken by the economy and official monetary policy has to choose between swimming with the tide or trying to resist it.

During periods of persistent inflation interest rates, instead of fluctuating in inverse ratio with the quantity of money, tend to move in sympathy with it. An increase in the quantity of money, by causing a rise in prices or even an anticipation of such a rise, lends to a rise in interest rates. In this respect it is necessary, however, to discriminate between nominal and real interest rates, the latter allowing for changes in the purchasing power of the monetary unit.

Determination of the quantity on money is a most important means to the end of controlling business cycles. The trend of trade responds to changes in the volume of money in three ways. An increase in the volume of money tends to stimulate business activities by providing the means for financing an expansion; by encouraging production and the purchase of goods through causing prices to rise; and by creating an atmosphere of optimism. A reduction in the volume of money tends to produce the opposite effect by curtailing the financial facilities available for business; by discouraging production and consumers' demand as a result of a falling trend in prices; and by generating an atmosphere of pessimism. Within reason, monetary expansion facilitates economic growth.

A policy of monetary expansion is one of the most effective means of achieving and maintaining full employment. By itself it is not always capable of attaining that end. An increase in the volume of credit available for producers and consumers does not necessarily mean that producers and consumers will take advantage of the increased facilities offered. In given circumstances monetary expansion has to be supplemented by other employment-creating devices. Even so, most such additional devices involve an increase in monetary requirements, so that they can only be carried out through an increase in the volume of money. Monetary expansion tends to accompany an increase of employment, whether as its cause or its affect. More money is required to finance a larger volume of employment. If the authorities prevent an increase in the volume of money to meet the increased requirements, a scarcity of money is liable to develop and to cause a fall in employment.

In medieval times the State authority often endeavoured to bring about an increase in the volume of coinage in order to facilitate revenue collection. This means of expanding the volume of money in the interest of the Treasury exist in modern times to an even higher degree. A policy of moderate monetary expansion is found useful for ensuring an increase of taxation receipts without having to resort to increasing the rates of taxation. Treasuries may also favour from time to time an increase in the volume of money in order to facilitate the issue of Government loans, or the conversion of maturing loans, or the funding of floating debt on favourable terms. As we pointed out before, this use of the device has come to be frowned upon in our time. It is used nevertheless.

The device of increasing the volume of money can be used effectively for a wide variety of social or political ends. It is possible to step up the pace of the development of the Welfare State provided that the Government is prepared to embark on monetary expansion. The same means can serve in a different way the ends of egalitarian social policy; an increase in the volume of money causes its value to depreciate, and this tends to level down wealth. In the political sphere monetary expansion is a preliminary condition of a rearmament drive on any substantial scale. Modern wars are inconceivable without monetary expansion to finance increased military requirements. In domestic policies it is possible to achieve popularity by increasing Government spending through creating real or fictitious prosperity by means of monetary expansion.

Hitherto we have been dealing with the device of determining the volume of money in a general way, with only casual references to the type of money concerned. Until the end of the seventeenth century money meant in Europe almost exclusively coins, and any monetary policy had to concern itself with determining the volume of coinage. Paper money became more or less universally adopted in Europe during the eighteenth century. Until the First World War notes circulated jointly with coins, and it was one of the most important task of monetary policy to regulate their issue. This task came to be increasingly overshadowed during the nineteenth century by the task of regulating the volume of credit. There are still even now a number of countries in which currency plays a more important part than credit. These include the comparatively backward countries with no adequately developed credit system, but also some highly advanced countries such as France, with a widespread habit of hoarding notes in preference to keeping bank accounts. On the other hand, in Britain, the United States and other countries it is the volume of deposits rather than that of notes – coins have disappeared from circulation except as token money – that matters from the point of view of monetary policy. In such countries the volume of notes is largely determined not by the authorities, but by the public, who draw on their bank balances if they need more cash and pay into their accounts any superfluous notes. Control of the volume of deposits has come to be regarded in such countries as by far the most important means at the disposal of the monetary authorities.

Changes in the volume of money must be related to changes in the requirements of the community. The same amount of money may be inadequate at a given moment and may become adequate or even excessive through changes in requirements. Such changes may be due to an increase or decrease of the population or of the territory in which the money is used. The size of requirements may be affected by changes in the scope within which money fulfils its functions. Changes in the price level are of course apt to affect monetary requirements, though not necessarily in an exact proportion to the changes, for a rise or a fall in prices is apt to affect demand for consumption and for investment.

The employment of devices resulting in an economy in the use of money, or the abandonment or modification of these devices, is apt to influence requirements materially. Above all, monetary requirements are liable to be affected by changes in the velocity of circulation of money a subject which will be discussed in Chapter 35. Such a change is apt to neutralise or exaggerate – as the case may be – the effect of changes in the quantity of money. Moreover, changes in the velocity are capable of initiating changes in prices even in the absence of changes in the quantity of money, changes which might then occur as the effect of previous changes in prices brought about by changes in the velocity of circulation. This fact alone is sufficient to invalidate the contentions of the monetarist school that prices and business trends are determined by the quantity of money.

Monetary requirements bear a close relation to the volume of goods. Any increase in the volume of goods offered for sale calls for a corresponding increase in the quantity of money if the authorities wish to maintain the same degree of relative scarcity or abundance of money, and if they want to avoid a change in the price level. In given circumstances the maintenance of the volume of money at the same level may mean the creation of scarcity or abundance as a result of changes in the requirements due to changes in the volume of goods or to any of the circumstances mentioned above. This means that the quantity of money can be changed in the absolute sense by altering its actual amount or in a relative sense by leaving its actual amount unchanged in face of changed requirements.

An increase in the volume of money is not necessarily inflationary. It may be due to increased desire to hold cash, or other liquid assets can be monetised such as they were in the USA after the Wall Street slump, and after the banking crisis of 1933. The outbreak of the second world war was followed by an increase of the cash holdings of the public in Britain owing to the possibility of a destruction of banks through air raids. Any grave uncertainty, political or economic, is liable to produce the same result. Such increase in the volume of money does not in itself mean inflation. The cash or deposits may be held not for the purpose of immediate expenditure, but as a liquid form of capital. But the possession of relatively large liquid assets increases the temption of, and opportunity for, spending, and is therefore a potential source of inflation.

CHAPTER TWENTY-EIGHT

Controlling the Monetary Circulation

In communities which have no modern banking system, or in which the public has not acquired the banking habit to a very high degree, the device of regulating the quantity of money is practised mainly by regulating the quantity of currency, that is, notes, coins or such other objects as may serve for monetary purposes. Originally the volume of currency was determined by factors largely outside the control of the State authorities. Primitive commodity-currencies were often produced or imported on private initiative. Moreover, it was usually possible to switch monetary objects from non-monetary to monetary use or vice versa. The quantity of commodity-currencies was liable to become reduced through wastage or export. In many instances, however, we encounter at an early stage intervention on the part of the State authority to determine the volume of circulating media. The production or import of monetary objects was made the monopoly of the tribal authority, or the increase of that quantity on private initiative was prevented by tribal laws or religious taboos.

The role of the State in determining the quantity of currency became particularly important with the advent of coinage, which from an early period of monetary history was a State monopoly. The minting of coins was the prerogative of kings, or of the authorities of city-states, though coins of other States were often allowed to circulate within the community. Coins were minted when the authorities considered it necessary. During later centuries, however, this monopoly became relaxed. Free coinage developed either by a cession of the right of

coinage to private mints, or at any rate by making it possible
for anyone in possession of monetary metals to have them
coined at the Mint. Under such a system there could be no
absolute official control over the quantity of new coins. Nevertheless, the State authority possessed various means with which
to influence the monetary circulation. It was in a position to
encourage or discourage the mining of monetary metals. In
many countries this was actually a State monopoly. Elsewhere
the State was in a position to forbid or stimulate the working of
privately owned metal resources. Colonial powers were able
to assist in the development of the mining resources in their
colonies. They could import the stocks of precious metals
seized in conquered territories. On the other hand, there are
also instances of official discouragement of the mining of
precious metals. This was done by some rulers in early China,
where precious metal deposits were only worked during periods
when the Government wanted to increase the quantity of
money.

Another way in which the State authority sought to influence
the quantity of coin was by preventing the export of coin and
of precious metals in general. In England such restrictions were
in force from the early Plantagenet period right to the beginning of the nineteenth century. They will be dealt with in the
chapter on exchange restrictions. According to contemporary
opinion they were largely ineffective in preventing the outflow
of monetary metals. Other legislative measures endeavoured to
ensure that the proceeds of certain exports were retained in the
form of precious metals, or that exporters to England had to
spend the proceeds on English goods.

Debasements were a very important device frequently
resorted to by kings for the purpose of preventing a decline in
the volume of money or securing its increase. Admittedly,
debasements could also pursue other objectives such as securing
a revenue for the king in the form of profit on re-coinage. In a
large proportion of instances, however, debasements were
undertaken mainly if not exclusively for the purpose of checking
the outflow of coins and their disappearance through melting

down and hoarding. Whenever there was an adverse trade balance it resulted in a drain on the monetary resources of the country. The full-weighted coins were exported in payment for goods imported. The price of the monetary metal – whether gold or silver – tended to rise above the official mint price, and no metals were brought to the Mint, so that the issue of new coins came to a standstill. In a great many instances foreign Mints offered nominally higher prices for the monetary metals, or foreign rulers 'proclaimed' a higher exchange rate for foreign coins in excess of their mint partities. There was, moreover, always a tendency for good coins to disappear in melting-pots and in hoards, leaving clipped and worn coins in circulation. Bad money tended to drive out good money.

Very often Governments resorted to the remedy of raising the mint price of the monetary metals in order to check the drain, and to attract more metals to the Mint both through import and through de-hoarding. This device was condemned by experts from the eighteenth century, largely on the ground that, taking a long view, it could not make much difference to the import and export of monetary metals, which depended on the balance of payments in the long run. In reality devaluations were helpful from the point of view of stimulating exports and discouraging imports, because of the inelasticity of domestic price levels. The lowering of the metallic value of the national currency was not followed immediately by a corresponding rise in prices. Consequently the goods of the country which had recently debased its currency were cheap for foreigners and foreign goods became relatively expensive for domestic consumers. The balance of payments tended to improve, temporarily at any rate, until domestic prices had adjusted themselves to the debased value of the currency or – what occurred much more frequently – until other countries in turn also debased their currencies. Throughout the Middle Ages and the centuries that followed there were very frequent competitive debasement races in Western Europe. Before the heavy inflow of precious metals from the newly discovered America during the sixteenth and seventeenth centuries, the main object of this currency depreciation race was to participate in the international scramble for the inadequate stock of monetary metals.

One of the main objects of the mercantilist policy, which remained dominant right to the second half of the eighteenth century, was to ensure adequate monetary supply by securing a big export surplus. Even in modern times right up to our days, Governments which would emphatically disclaim pursuing mercantilist policies seek to secure a favourable balance of payments for the sake of strengthening the gold reserves. Although since the suspension of the gold standard the quantity of currency no longer strictly depends on the size of the gold stock, a decline of the gold and foreign exchange reserve is liable to force the Government to adopt credit restrictions in order to improve the balance of payments and thus to improve its gold position.

Yet another means by which Governments endeavoured to maintain or increase the quantity of currency was by attracting foreign capital. This was done to a relatively moderate degree until the nineteenth century, when it became one of the principal means for countries with adverse trade balances to maintain or increase their monetary stock. By that time it was not so much the volume of coins that mattered as the amount of notes and the volume of deposits that could be increased under the rules of metallic standards by means of importing monetary metal out of the proceeds of foreign loans.

Governments sought on many occasions to remedy the evils of currency shortage by encouraging or confirming the use of substitute currencies whenever this was considered inevitable. The North American colonies and the West Indies, which suffered from a particularly troublesome and chronic shortage of coins, had tried to solve their problem by the monetary use of a wide variety of commodities. Usually the staple products of the country were adopted for that purpose. Although in many instances their adoption as currencies was spontaneous, the State authority usually officially recognised them sooner or later, and regulated their monetary use. Tobacco, skins and furs, cereals, pork, beef, timber, hemp, sugar, rum, cotton, etc., were made legal tender at one time or another in various North American colonies or in the West Indies. Although the use of such commodity-currencies had obvious disadvantages, it certainly relieved the scarcity of currency which would otherwise have gravely handicapped the development of these countries. In many instances the volume of these commodity-currencies increased to an embarrassing extent as a result of their monetary use, and the Governments felt compelled to intervene in order to curtail their production. This was done repeatedly and unsuccessfully in Virginia and other tobacco-growing colonies where tobacco was used as a currency.

The most effective method by which Governments came to be able to determine the volume of currency after the beginning of the eighteenth century was the issue of paper money. France, the American colonies and other countries soon discovered unlimited possibilities of increasing the volume of money with the aid of the printing press.

After some disastrous experiments in paper-money inflation, the advanced countries settled down during the relatively stable period of the nineteenth century to systems of restricted note issues. Under the established practices of metallic standards there was a self-imposed limitation on the quantity of notes to be issued. The Central Banks which in most countries were put in charge of the note issue had to maintain a certain percentage of note cover in the form of precious metals or eligible foreign exchanges. The size of these reserves set a natural if elastic limit to the extent to which it was possible to increase the volume of currency. In other countries such as Britain the banks of issue were authorised to issue notes up to a certain fixed amount – the 'fiduciary issue' – in excess of their metallic reserves. Within the limits set by these various regulations the Central Banks or the Governments were in a position to pursue their monetary policies by determining the volume of currency.

After the adoption of paper money and before the development of the modern credit system, the regulation of the volume of notes in circulation constituted one of the most important devices of monetary policy. While the regulation of the quantity of coins throughout many centuries consisted mostly of efforts to increase the volume in order to meet requirements, the regulation of the note circulation consisted mostly of efforts to keep down or reduce the volume. The temptation to over-issue was very strong ever since paper money was first invented. Apart altogether from note issues for the purpose of financing wars, there was always pressure on Governments to relax the self-imposed limitations of note issues. Until the end of the Napoleonic Wars those opposed to currency inflation were fighting a losing battle in most countries.

It was largely during the nineteenth century that a system emerged under which note issues came under automatic limitation. Whatever anybody may say against the gold standard, it must be admitted that it played an important historical role in compelling Governments to discipline themselves in respect of the use of the printing press. The solution of Budgetary problems by means of paper-money inflation was too easy, much easier than debasements in earlier centuries. There was strong temptation to take the line of least resistance. The adoption of the gold standard – or for that matter the gold exchange standard, the silver standard or the bimetallic standard, which operated in the majority of countries during the greater part of the nineteenth century – compelled Governments to exercise a certain degree of self-denial in order to maintain the metallic standard in operation. Many Governments went considerably out of their way to avoid the suspension of the convertibility of their notes, and their Central Banks pursued cautious policies to that end. Treasuries abstained as far as possible from drawing on the Central Banks in time of peace and Central Banks kept the private sector of the economy permanently relatively short of money.

This over-cautious attitude of most Central Banks during the reign of the gold standard has been subject to much criticism. Beyond doubt it handicapped economic growth during periods when the output of gold and silver was low.

It was detrimental from the point of view of social welfare. Nevertheless, viewed from the perspective of history it must be admitted that this was a useful and necessary phase in the evolution of monetary policy. Owing to the novelty of the device of paper currency and bank-credit money, it was essential that Governments and public opinion should be made to realise the need for self-restraint in the use of this device. It was necessary to educate mankind how to use paper currency and bank credit without grossly abusing it, and the gold standard was very useful from this point of view, even though its disciplining effect was only too often forgotten after the adoption of inconvertible paper currencies.

The self-imposed limitations aimed at preventing excessive issue of notes assumed various forms. Convertibility into gold and/or silver was a powerful obstacle to unlimited increase of quantity. Indeed, the original idea of paper money in Britain was that it was merely a more convenient medium of exchange than coins, and that notes issued by the Bank of England and other banks of issue must have full metallic cover. Then the 'fiduciary issue' – an amount by which the note issue was allowed to exceed the gold reserve – made its appearance. Originally very small, the fiduciary issue increased materially from the late twenties, and especially during and after the Second World War. From 1928 it became possible to raise the limit by administrative action subject to subsequent endorsement by Parliament. Increases of £50 million or more were a frequent occurrence and hardly attracted any attention. More recent legislation sought to impose some ceiling, but any self-imposed limitation has relative value only, since Governments with a majority in Parliament are always in a position to amend the legislation.

Nor was the alternative system under which there had to be a certain percentage of metallic cover any more effective except during normal and stable periods. Whenever there was pressure in favour of raising the note issue it was always possible for Governments and Parliaments to set aside or relax the provisions regarding reserve requirements.

Another method by which it was sought to limit the note issue was through the establishment of more or less independent privately owned Central Banks. Their relations with Treasuries were governed by the terms of their charter, which was granted for a definite period and confirmed by Acts of Parliament. Although there were many instances of Central Banks resisting the Government's demand for inflationary note issues, generally speaking they had been subservient to Treasuries. In any case many of them lost their legal independence after 1945 through nationalisation.

Beyond doubt technically and politically it is much easier today for Governments to inflate the note issues than it was during the nineteenth century or even during the inter-war period. The notes are no longer convertible into gold, not even in the United States, and such reserve requirements or ceilings of note issues as are in force are much more elastic. Notwithstanding this, the evil of currency inflation – within the narrow meaning of the term indicating an excess of note issue – has not increased, because in the meantime credit inflation has become the principal danger as a result of the development of the credit system in the financially advanced countries. Monetary inflation in such countries no longer assumes the form of Government borrowing from the Central Bank and putting the borrowed notes into circulation. That crude form of inflation has been replaced by a much more subtle and sophisticated form of credit inflation to be dealt with in the next chapter.

The volume of currency continues to play an important part as a means of monetary policy in countries which either do not possess a well-developed banking system or where the habit of keeping bank accounts is not widely adopted. In particular in British colonies with Currency Boards instead of Central Banks, the size of the note issue is of the utmost importance from the point of view of economic trends. The disadvantage of that system is that the authorities cannot control adequately the size of the note issue. Notes are issued against the surrender of sterling to the Currency Board. They remain in circulation until demand for sterling by importers and others absorbs them. The monetary authorities have no direct means of neutralising an excessive increase or decrease of the note issue.

If in countries with a well-developed deposit banking system the monetary authorities wish to stimulate trade by increasing the volume of money, they do so usually by causing an expansion of bank credits rather than by increasing their note issue. Conversely, if they want to discourage an inflationary rise of prices or a speculative boom, their means to that end is a curtailment of the volume of bank credits and bank credits and not a cut in the note issue.

Nevertheless, situations are apt to arise which call for intervention in the sphere of the note circulation. In a number of Continental countries the note circulation increased considerably during the Second World War and continued to increase after it. In Britain the Bank of England called in during the war all notes of a denomination higher than £5. As a drastic deflationary measure a number of Governments decreed the exchange or stamping of the notes, and blocked a large percentage of the notes surrendered, or retained it in the form of a levy or a compulsory loan. Such mopping-up operations were necessary to correct currency inflation which would otherwise have caused much difficulty. Generally speaking, however, regulation of the note issue plays a secondary part in advanced countries among the means with which monetary authorities seek to control trends. While it still represents an important proportion of the liquid resources of the community, the monetary authorities find it more convenient to concentrate on the regulation of the volume of credit on the assumption that the note issue automatically adjusts itself to changes brought about by contractions or expansions.

Even so, the importance of the amount of currency should not be underrated. It is a very useful index showing the general trend. Although the authorities do not as a rule initiate changes in the volume of money by deliberately increasing or reducing the note issue as a matter of policy, the figures of the note issue often indicate whether or not action to curtail deposits and credits is called for. They also show whether the Government's action to that end has been successful.

In countries with a highly developed deposit banking system, increases in the amount of the active note circulation are usually the effect and not the cause of an increase in prices or of an expansion of trade or of an increase in cash requirements for some other reason. Holders of sight deposits are in a position to increase their holdings of cash in accordance with the increase of their requirements. Even though the authorities are in a position to check the increase of the volume of notes, if in doing so they create an acute scarcity of notes they are liable to inflict considerable inconvenience on the community. It is a much more inconvenient form of deflation than a statutory incomes policy.

CHAPTER TWENTY-NINE

Controlling the Volume of Credit

In modern communities determination of the volume of credit plays such an important part among the means of monetary policy that many people when writing about monetary policy can think only in terms of official intervention to expand, maintain or restrict credit. Yet, although regulation of the volume of credit played some part in monetary policy in earlier centuries, until modern times the possibilities of increasing or decreasing the volume of money by means of expanding or contracting bank credits were limited. Banking consisted largely of re-lending the moneys represented by the coins left with the banks on deposit. Facilities to increase the volume of credit beyond that of the coins on deposit were limited. Indeed, since the owners of these coins were in a position to withdraw their deposits, their bankers had to retain a fairly high percentage of cash reserve in order to meet such withdrawals. There had been early instances of modern banking credit, but as a general rule all that the banker had done in earlier periods of banking history was to lend part of the coins whose owner temporarily relinquished their use.

The system under which it is possible to create large quantities of money through the operation of bank credits and deposits is a modern development. It owes its existence to two fundamental changes. One is the increased confidence of the public in the banks, as a result of which the latter need not keep more than a small fraction of their assets in the form of cash. Before banks became strong and confidence-inspiring they had to keep a large proportion of their assets in a liquid form in order to be able to meet any possible sudden withdrawals.

As and when confidence in their solvency and liquidity increased, they were able gradually to lend a larger and larger proportion of their deposits and to reduce the proportion of their liquid reserves without running undue risks. Moreover, as the banks grew bigger it became increasingly evident that insolvency of any one of them was liable to produce a run on other banks, with disastrous consequences. For this reason there was an increasing degree of co-operation between banks and also between the banks and the monetary authorities. Thanks to such co-operation it became safer to reduce the ratio of cash reserve, because banks could reasonably rely on being supported by other banks or by the authorities in case of sudden heavy withdrawals of deposits. In Britain there has been no deposit bank failure for a very long time, partly because the weak and unsound banks have long disappeared, and partly because on the rare occasions when some lesser bank finds itself in a difficult position the Bank of England enlists the aid of strong banks to acquire it or reconstruct it. The disastrous run on the American banks in the early thirties led to the adoption of a deposit insurance system in the United States. As a result of all these developments the banks are now in a position to lend or invest amounts many times larger than their own capital and reserves or their cash holdings.

The other change that has contributed to the development of the modern credit system with its capacity to expand the volume of money is the widespread adoption of the practice of keeping banking accounts. So long as the number of firms or individuals who possess banking accounts were relatively small, the power of banks to create additional money was limited. The larger part of the money they had lent was withdrawn in the form of notes which remained usually in circulation for some time before finding their way back to banks, so that they could not be re-lent to other borrowers. It was only as and when most members of the business community and a fair proportion of private individuals came to possess bank accounts that the banks acquired their present remarkable power of adding to the total volume of money.

In countries such as France where the banking habit is not so widespread, much of the proceeds of a bank loan is liable to be hoarded and the notes do not find their way back to the bank. In Britain, on the other hand, most payments are made by cheque. Even if the recipients of cash payments do not themselves possess bank accounts, the money sooner or later – usually sooner – finds its way to someone with a bank account. Before the notes issued to some recipient who has no account change hands many times, most of them are paid to someone who pays them into a bank account. They thus become once more available for relending. This is the explanation of the development of the process aptly described by Whittlesey in his *Readings in Money and Banking* as 'one of the marvels of a complex financial society'. What happens is that the amounts lent by banks return to them again and again in the form of additional deposits and become available for being lent again and again. When payments are made by cheque the money does not leave the banking system even temporarily. The fact that the proceeds of a bank loan need not necessarily return to the same bank makes no difference so long as the banking system as a whole retains them.

Moreover, in Britain and many other countries it is the practice of banks that, when they grant a loan to a customer, they simply credit his current account with its amount. The loan immediately assumes the form of an additional deposit even before it is spent.

From the foregoing it might appear that banks have un-limited power to increase the volume of credit. This would be so in the absence of any rule that a certain proportion of deposits has to be kept in a liquid form. Even though the proportion is now smaller than it was in the past, the necessity of observing the rules tends to handicap banks in expanding credit. These rules are applied in various ways in different countries. In the United States there is a statutory minimum reserve ratio in operation. It is subject to occasional changes, and its increase or reduction is a very important monetary policy device.

In Britain the ratio of eligible liquid assets to short-term sterling deposits and other short-term liabilities was fixed at $12\frac{1}{2}$ per cent and it is unlikely to be changed except on major occasions. Until September 1971 there was no official ratio, but the clearing banks had a gentlemen's agreement under which they were to keep a minimum cash ratio of 8 per cent and a minimum liquidity ratio of 28 per cent. This change was made simultaneously with the abolition of the cartel of clearing banks. Both measures aimed at stimulating an increase of bank credits by encouraging competition between banks and enabling them to expand the volume of their credits. The reduction of the liquidity ratio to $12\frac{1}{2}$ per cent has opened up the possibility of a very substantial credit expansion. Should the expansion be found extensive, the Bank would be able to call up Special Deposits on which interest is paid on the basis of the current Treasury bill rates, which is much higher than the deposit rates paid by the banks to their depositors.

The eligible liquid assets include Treasury bills, and the authorities are in a position to influence the volume of potential bank credits by increasing or reducing the amount of Treasury bills.

A decline of the total liquid assets available to the banking system, as a result of a reduction in the volume of Treasury bills, compels the banks to reduce their deposits and to that end they have to curtail credits.

Under the gold standard the bank's cash reserves were liable to fluctuations that were not initiated by the monetary authorities. An inflow of gold increased the volume of bank cash and an outflow reduced it. Central Banking under that system consisted largely of influencing gold movements and the volume of credit by means of raising and lowering the Bank Rate, thereby discouraging or encouraging the demand for credit.

Until comparatively recently direct intervention of the monetary authorities to regulate the volume of credit through determining the volume of bank cash played a relatively subordinate part. The Bank Rate was the principal instrument with the aid of which Central Banks sought to cause an expansion or contraction of credit. They increased or reduced rediscounting and other lending facilities to supplement their Bank Rate policy. Generally speaking, however, they endeavoured to achieve their end largely through the psychological effect of the Bank Rate changes. Official intervention to control the volume of credit was rather vague and indirect under that system. The authorities engaged from time to time in open-market operations, but it is only during the last thirty years or so that the system of direct and more precise control of the volume of credit has developed.

The main causes of the development of closer credit control may be summarised as follows:

(1) International monetary and economic instability followed the First World War. The degree of equilibrium that existed before 1914 was never restored for any length of time after 1918. During the twenties, when some form of gold standard operated in a large number of countries, gold reserves and foreign exchange reserves which served as the basis of the credit structure were exposed to sudden and substantial fluctuations. Under the old system this would have led to very considerable contractions and expansions of credit, causing sharp falls and rises of the price level and of employment. In the twenties, however, stability of prices and of employment came to assume a high priority. It was considered necessary, therefore, to adopt a managed form of gold standard under which the effects of the fluctuations of the metallic reserve on the volume of credit were largely offset.

(2) Simultaneously with this change and not unconnected with it, monetary science made considerable progress. A new generation of Central Bankers and Treasury officials was both able and willing to depart from the automatic 'foolproof' system practised by their predecessors. Although their progress towards the adoption of scientific monetary management was not so rapid as radical monetary reformers such as Keynes would have liked it to be, nevertheless, viewed from the perspective of history, it must now be regarded as having been revolutionary.

(3) The suspension of the gold standard in most countries during the thirties, and the further reduction of the role of gold in the monetary system after the war, removed the link between the volume of metallic reserve and that of credit. It became necessary for the monetary authorities to elaborate new practices with which to determine the volume of credit instead of leaving it to the free play of natural trends. Even in countries such as the United States the authorities find it expedient to intervene mainly in the form of open-market operations and changes in reserve requirements.

(4) From the thirties onwards, monetary policy came to pursue to an increasing degree broader economic and social ends calling for credit expansion. To that end it became necessary for the monetary authorities to take an active hand in determining the supply of credit.

(5) The spectacular increase in the amount of the public debt and in its relative importance in the economy has provided the authorities with additional inducements as well as additional opportunities for intervention. It reduced the automatic effect of Bank Rate changes on the volume of credit because, while they affect the volume of commercial bills, they do not affect that of Treasury bills which is influenced by considerations of revenue, expenditure and debt management.

One of the older devices that has been used more extensively since the Second World War is the fixing of a rediscount ceiling by which the extent to which the banks can automatically draw upon the facilities of the Central Bank is limited. This device was applied in France, where in October 1948 a rediscount ceiling was established for each commercial bank in addition to the overall maximum fixed for the banking system as a whole. Once a bank exhausted its limit it was not granted any further rediscount facilities by the Bank of France. This measure was not so severe, however, as may appear at first sight. The ceiling was fixed at something like 20 per cent above the actual figures of rediscounts at the time of its imposition. Moreover, the ceiling was repeatedly increased as and when the volume of rediscounts approached it. Above all, certain types of bills were exempted from the ceiling, and this provided a loophole through which the attempted credit restriction was circumvented. Rediscount facilities at rates above the Bank Rate (*taux d'enfer* and *taux de super-enfer*) were made available.

In Germany too a ceiling was introduced, not to rediscount facilities but to the total of acceptance credits the banks were allowed to grant. Denmark was another country which adopted a rediscount ceiling at the time of the Korean War. In 1951 Germany introduced drastic regulations limiting overall commercial bank credits and compelling commercial banks to reduce the amount of credits within three months in accordance with quotas fixed by the Government. A variant of this device was applied in some countries in the form of fixing statutory ratios between the liabilities and liquid assets of the banks or between their liabilities and their capital resources. Such ratios were altered from time to time, in order to regulate the volume of credit.

In respect of statutory reserve requirements the United States adopted an elaborate system which has played a prominent part in American monetary policy for the last thirty years. Member banks of the Federal Reserve System are required to hold on deposit with the Federal Reserve Banks a percentage of their deposits. The Federal Reserve Board is authorised to change, within prescribed limits, the percentage of these requirements. In order to restrict credit, the Federal Reserve Board raises the percentage of Reserve requirements and it takes the opposite course when it considers it expedient to expand credit.

The example of the United States was followed by South Africa, New Zealand, India and some Latin-American countries before the Second World War. Indeed, in recent years statutory authority for Central Banks to fix and change reserve requirements has become a widely adopted feature in new Central Bank legislation. Belgium, Sweden and Western Germany are among the countries that adopted the system after the war. The original idea behind the system was to safeguard the interests of depositors. Subsequently it was discovered that the power to adjust reserve requirements constitutes a very effective means of monetary policy because it was liable to influence the volume of credit. It was used extensively by a number of countries during the inflation that followed the outbreak of the Korean War. In the United States, and more recently in Germany, its use has become a matter of normal routine.

In India all banks have to maintain minimum reserves with the Central Bank. In many countries the reserves may assume the form of Government securities held on deposit with the Central Bank. In some countries the device takes the form of making it compulsory for banks to hold additional reserves against increases of their deposits. This system was adopted in Australia in 1941. Commercial banks have to maintain a certain proportion of their new assets on special account with the Commonwealth Bank. During the war almost the total of increases over 1939 had to be deposited with the Common- wealth Bank, but after the war the proportion was reduced to 45 per cent, only to be increased again to 60 after the outbreak of the Korean War. Similar measures were adopted by France, Italy, the Netherlands and some Latin-American countries.

In addition to these various measures affecting the total volume of credit, many countries employed devices limiting credits for specific purposes. We propose to deal with these devices in the next chapter.

By far the most important means for regulating the volume of credit is direct intervention to increase or reduce the amount of cash in the hands of banks, by means of official operations in Government securities. These operations are usually known under the name of open-market policy, even though they do not necessarily assume the form of buying or selling of Govern- ment securities in the open market on official account. As we shall see in the chapter dealing with Treasury operations, the management of the public debt provides Treasuries with an opportunity for increasing or reducing the volume of publicly-held Government securities by the timing of the issues and maturities. If this is not sufficient to achieve the desired end of expanding or restricting credit, it can be supplemented by open-market operations proper. Central Banks can buy or sell Government securities in order to bring about the desired change in the volume of credit. Any purchase of Government securities by the authorities from the banks places additional money in the hands of the private sector of the national economy, increases the amount of the bank's cash reserves, and enables the banks to expand credit to an amount that is a multiple of that increase. Any sale of Government securities by the authorities to the banks withdraws money from the private sector of the national economy. It reduces the amount of the banks' cash reserves and enforces a contraction of credit amounting to a multiple of the amounts involved in the sale.

Needless to say, this is a grossly over-simplified presentation of a highly involved process. Its penetrating analysis by the Radcliffe Committee and in writings by Manning Dacey and Wilfred King, among others, has provided much new detailed technical material for the student of monetary policy.

In addition to this highly powerful weapon, the United States Government is in a position to adjust the volume of bank cash with the aid of a very simple device – that of changing the volume of its deposits held in commercial banks. This device does not exist in Britain. It is true that the commercial banks are used as channels for collection and remittance of funds by the Revenue Departments, and the spending Departments keep accounts with these banks where the Bank of England has no branches. Large amounts are always in the pipeline, but they simply serve the convenience of the Departments concerned. It is not the British practice to adjust these amounts in accordance with considerations of monetary policy. On the contrary, between 1940 and 1951 the reverse of this device was applied in Britain. Under the system of Special Deposits the commercial banks were compelled to surrender to the authorities each week an amount prescribed by the Treasury. With the aid of this device the Treasury was in a position to adjust the volume of bank cash. It involved a high degree of compulsion, and it was abandoned by the Conservative Government soon after assuming office in 1951. Indeed, even the Socialist Government had intended to abandon it in due course. Nevertheless, Conservative Governments felt impelled by persistent pressure of inflation to revert to it on repeated occasions.

We have seen above that Treasuries and Central Banks possess very extensive powers for determining the volume of credit. This does not necessarily mean that they always make full use of their powers. For various reasons they may think it expedient to relinquish the initiative for determining the volume of credit systematically and confine themselves to intervening for special purposes only. For instance, the rigid pursuit of a policy of cheap money meant that, for the sake of keeping interest rates stabilised at a low level, the authorities automatically provided any amount of money that was needed in order to avoid a tightening of credit conditions. If for no matter what reason credit requirements increased in the London market during the period between the outbreak of the Second World War and November 1951, the additional financial resources were automatically provided by the authorities in order to avoid an increase of Treasury bill rates above the level at which the official policy wanted it to remain.

Another way in which the authorities can relinquish the initiative is by the issue of Government loans which are 'on tap', that is, to which the public can subscribe at any time, and the total of which is not fixed. Such issues in Britain are the Savings Certificates and Defence Bonds. It is true that if the amount subscribed mops up too much or too little of credit resources, the authorities are in a position to adjust the situation through increasing or reducing the weekly amounts of Treasury bills issued by tenders or through open-market operations, or by other means at their disposal. They can also change the 'tap' price of the marketable Government loans unloaded gradually by the Public Departments, or they can discontinue or resume their issue. From time to time the authorities relinquish the initiative for changing the volume of money by pegging the prices in the Gilt-edged market.

During the first two post-war years the Government was a regular buyer of its loans at a fixed price, in pursuing its policy of cheap money. This practice, which was discontinued by Cripps, was resumed later, though it was not pursued as rigidly as it had been under Dalton's Chancellorship. Nevertheless, whenever the banks were in a position to unload their Gilt-edged investments at an artificially maintained price, the authorities were unable to enforce their control over the volume of credit. The official support given to the Gilt-edged market provided both temptation and opportunity for expanding credit by means of realising their investments. This was realised eventually, and the Gilt-edged market was allowed to find its own level.

By pursuing the end of maintaining short-term interest rates at a fixed level, the authorities relinquished the device of adjusting the volume of money in accordance with the requirements of stability. If the brokers acting for the Government are known to be always prepared to buy Government loans at a more or less fixed price, this enables the banks to increase their cash reserves by turning their Government loans into cash. In the absence of Government intervention, if banks or other private holders want to sell Government securities they have to find private buyers who are willing to buy at a price, and the money paid for the securities merely changes hands between private holders without affecting the total amount of bank cash. If, however, the Government broker appears in the market when there are no private buyers at prices fixed by the Government, then the volume of bank cash is liable to increase whenever there is no private demand for the securities at the officially fixed price. Conversely, if banks or other private holders want to buy Government securities and are unable to find a seller willing to sell at the officially pegged price, then the authorities must provide a counterpart if they want to prevent an appreciation of their securities. The result of such operations is that some of the bank cash is mopped up.

What is important to bear in mind is that if the Government is determined to maintain Treasury bill rates or the prices of Government loans at a pegged level, the volume of bank cash is liable to change on the initiative of the banks. They can always increase their cash reserve if they want to expand credit by selling some securities to the official buyer. What is even more important, discount houses depend on being able to rediscount their Treasury bills with the Bank.

In order to be able to determine the volume of credit, the authorities have to renounce their ambition of supporting bill rates or the prices of Government loans. If these rates and prices are allowed to fluctuate freely, there is no need for the authorities to buy or sell securities unless they want to influence the volume of bank cash in order to determine the volume of credit.

It would be a mistake to imagine, however, that even in such circumstances their power to determine the volume of credit is unlimited. They are in a position to extend the maximum limit of credit facilities, but whether the actual volume of credit conforms to their policy depends not only on the willingness and ability of lenders to lend but also one the willingness of borrowers to borrow. The experience of the thirties when the United States and many other countries found that it was impossible to bring about the desired degree of monetary expansion made the monetary authorities realise the limitation of their power to regulate the volume of credit. Neither producers nor consumers are likely to avail themselves of the facilities placed at their disposal if, rightly or wrongly, they expect a decline of prices or a business depression. This was the experience early in 1972 when the relaxation of credit restraint was not followed for some time by a credit expansion. In such situations the only way in which the authorities are in a position to expand credit is through deficit financing. This method will be dealt with in Chapter 32.

Unduly sharp contraction of credit is liable to produce grave financial, economic, social and political consequences. A stage is likely to be reached at which the authorities may feel compelled to check or reverse their policy no matter how firmly they are convinced that a further contraction of credit is necessary.

CHAPTER THIRTY

Selective Credit Control

CREDIT control may be general or selective according to whether the authorities confine themselves to determining the total volume of credit or discriminate between various categories of borrowers. Until recently general credit control was all but universally in operation. One of its main disadvantages is that it tends to affect indiscriminately all sections of the national economy in so far as they depend on credit. If the monetary authorities, by reducing the volume of bank cash, compel the banking system to curtail substantially the total volume of credit, all categories of borrowers are liable to be affected irrespective of whether or not the specific conditions in their particular sphere call for any credit reductions. If the monetary authorities bring about a general expansion of credit, it is liable to stimulate not only those industries which are in need of encouragement but also those which are over-trading and should be discouraged rather than encouraged.

This defect of indiscriminate general credit control has long been realised and has often been denounced as one of the weakest spots of the 'orthodox' monetary system with which it had been associated. To some extent the disadvantages were mitigated by informal official advice given to the banks about their attitude towards particular types of loans. Such advice was usually followed to a considerable extent by most banks even in the absence of statutory powers to enforce it, There was a long way to go, however, from this informal system to the system of selective credit control which appeared after the Second World War.

During the war it was of vital importance to all belligerent countries that industrial resources should be reserved for the production of war materials and of essential civilian goods. In addition to extensive physical controls it was necessary for banks to discourage the production of superfluous goods by applying discriminatory credit controls. But the system of rationing and allocations was a more effective way of influencing production and consumption than even the most advanced system of selective credit control could possibly claim to be. After all, producers and consumers have financial resources of their own, with the aid of which they are in a position to engage in production or purchases disapproved of by the authorities even if no credits are granted to them for such purposes.

It was after the war, as and when physical controls were removed, that the need for the more extensive selective credit control became evident. In 1945, when the Bank of England was nationalised, the Treasury was given powers to issue directions to the banks through the intermediary of the Bank of England. These powers have not been used, however, by the authorities for enforcing selective credit controls. From time to time the banks were requested to discriminate in favour of or against certain categories of credits. In particular, they were requested on repeated occasions from 1951 onwards to discriminate in favour of credits for export trade, and to increase such credits in spite of the reduction of the total volume of credit due to the general policy of credit restrictions.

A type of selective credit control which was frequently resorted to even before the war in most countries was pressure on the banks to abstain from granting credits for speculative purposes. In Britain in 1945, immediately after the end of the war in Europe, the banks were requested to abstain from granting large credits for financing speculative buying, and also for the satisfaction of personal needs and for financing holdings of securities or of commodity stocks. When Sir Stafford Cripps became Chancellor of the Exchequer in 1947 he caused the Bank of England to request the banks to discourage loans for the purchase of real property and not to expand credit for financing instalment buying of consumer goods. When pressures on sterling developed in 1949 the banks were requested to curtail credits in general but to make exceptions in favour of those producing goods for export to 'hard currency' markets or producers of goods which would otherwise have to be imported from 'hard currency' countries.

Britain is particularly well placed for the application of such selective controls owing to the fact that most of her banking activities are concentrated in the hands of a very small number of big banks with very well-established traditions of cooperation with the Bank of England. In addition Britain possesses a well-established institution for the purpose of enforcing effective credit control. The Capital Issues Committee was created some years before the war for the purpose of controlling public issues on the London market. Under the chairmanship of Lord Kennet it suceeded in creating one of the few watertight controls in existence. After the war its sphere was extended from public issues to bank loans in excess of £50,000. The banks had to submit any such loans for approval to the Capital Issues Committee, which was thus in a position to exercise a very advanced form of selective credit control, even though loans of smaller amounts remained outside its scope.

Selective credit control was applied in a high degree in the United States after the war. In particular, selling on the instalment system is subject there to far-reaching discriminatory control. The percentage of initial payments is fixed for each trade and also for real property deals. By changing that percentage the Government is in a position to influence the volume of transactions. The length of the period over which deferred payments can be allowed is also subject to statutory regulations. Similar measures were adopted in a less advanced form in Britain as a result of the sterling crisis in the fifties and sixties. They were relaxed after the crises had passed.

Such control serves primarily a monetary end in that it tends to moderate inflationary buying pressure. It has been an idea of long standing to seek to control business trends by encouraging or discouraging instalment buying. During periods when the purchasing power in consumers' hands is already excessive it is considered inexpedient to encourage them to use their future earnings in advanced for immediate purchases. On the other hand, during periods when trade is handicapped by deficiency of consumers' purchasing power it can be usefully supplemented by facilitating the spending in advance of future earnings with the aid of deferred payments arrangements. Regulation of the terms of the instalment system therefore constitutes a highly serviceable means of monetary policy. The same end can be achieved not only by prescribing the terms on which industrial and commercial firms may sell on the instalment system, but also by inducing the banks to limit or expand the amount of credits made available for that purpose. The difficulty about this latter method is that it is not easy for banks to ascertain the extent to which loans granted to merchants or manufacturers are used for financing instalment buying. And even if some form of watertignt control could be devised, there would be nothing to prevent borrowers from diverting their other resources to the financing of instalment business, thanks to bank loans for other purposes which would release those resources. Moreover, hire purchase finance companies, by offering very high deposit rates, are in a position to attract funds which enable them to dispense with bank credits.

France introduced in 1947 a rule under which commercial banks were to discriminate against borrowers who were assumed to be able to raise the necessary funds by alternative ways – through increased sales efforts, through liquidating excessive stocks, through using the owners' personal financial resources, or by making public issues. This system proved to be largely ineffective, as there were many ways in which the rule could be circumvented.

In Australia, New Zealand and Canada bank loans for the purpose of capital expenditure were on various occasions officially discouraged in order to compel potential borrowers to raise the necessary funds in the capital market.

Selective credit control need not necessarily assume the form of a ban on unwanted types of operations or a discrimination in favour of types enjoying priority. In Belgium the National

Bank applies differential rediscount rates according to the type of the transaction financed by the Bills presented for rediscount. Its rules of eligiblity for rediscount take into account a list of priorities. During periods of adverse balance of payments the rediscount rates for bills financing exports are reduced. When there is an export surplus this practice can be reserved.

As a general rule selective credit controls are not established in detail by legislation. They are usually adopted in broad outline and are adjusted by means of informal agreements between the authorities and the banks. In countries where commercial banks are nationalised, selective credit control is of course on an official basis. In France, for instance, the official economic planning body's decisions affect the relative credit control exercised by the nationalised banks. In some other countries too, the Central Banks have statutory authority to determine the purposes for which loans can be granted. They have no power, however, to discriminate in favour of or against individual borrowers. Such countries include Australia, New Zealand, India, the Philippines and some Latin-American countries.

Selective credit control constitutes a means of monetary policy in so far as it affects the total volume of money. The distribution of credit resources within the various categories is a matter of credit policy rather than monetary policy, unless the steps taken aim at influencing the monetary situation. In most instances of post-war selective credit control the aim was to reduce or keep down the grand total by means of discriminating against what were considered inessential or less essential types of credit.

Discrimination affecting credits for financing capital investment also constitutes a useful means of monetary policy. Thanks to Keynes, the important role played by the extent of capital investment in the monetary situation is now generally realised, and the need for regulating the volume of capital investment as a means for influencing monetary trends has become a normal part of monetary policy. The immedediate effect of diverting financial and physical resources towards the erection of factories is that less is produced for immediate consumption. The prices of consumer goods tend to increase or their decline is checked or slowed down. Cuts in capital investments tend to produce the opposite effect. Capital investment is of course largely financed out of capital resources rather than bank credits. The Capital Issues Committee in Britain excercised a highly effective selective control over the raising of long-term funds by means of public issues or private placings. But capital expenditure can be financed also out of the capital and undistributed profits of the firms concerned or by means of public issues, or borrowing on mortgage from non-banking sources. Selective credit control in this sphere cannot claim to be comprehensive so long as it is confined to banking loans. While public issues are subject to control, smaller loans by insurance companies, building societies, trust funds, etc., and private placings, are outside the scope of monetary policy in most countries.

Yet another direction in which selective credit control constitutes a means of monetary policy is in its effect on the balance of payments. A persistent import or export surplus is liable to affect the monetary position and it calls for official intervention. One way in which the foreign exchange can be strengthened is by discriminating in favour of export industries in the allocation of credit or in rediscounting facilities. We saw above that this is done in several countries. Selective control of credit in relation to international commercial and financial transactions was applied on various occasions under the Exchange Control regulations. More will be said about this in Chapter 40.

It is essential to realise the limitations of the influence of a selective credit control as a monetary device. in so far as it consists of diverting credit expansion into specific spheres. It is necessary to bear in mind that the purchasing power represented by the additional credits granted for specific purposes does not vanish into thin air once the money is spent for those purposes. Recipients of the money are in a position to spend it once more. Even though part of it is taken away in taxation or disappears through genuine saving or through repayment of debts, or through the acquisition of newly-issued Government loans, part of it is bound to be spent again and again. Each time it is spent it tends to produce the same effect on the monetary situation as it did when it was spent the first time. This is what is called the 'multiplier effect', the total of which is probably several times the effect of the original transaction. After the first transaction the authorities have no longer any control over the purpose for which the additional purchasing power is used.

It is because of this limitation of the effect of selective credit controls, rather on the strength of all-too-familiar doctrinaire arguments against selective control, that indiscriminate quantitative credit controls cannot be dispensed with. If the authorities are anxious to avoid inflation they cannot give banks a free hand to lend to industries which need encouragement unless at the same time the grand total of credit is subject to limitation. They may find that the purchasing power originating from credits granted for specific approved purposes may work its way round into demand of an entirely unwanted character. Nothing short of quantitative restrictions could safeguard against such demand. For this reason it is a mistake to imagine that general restrictions are an old-fashioned device which is liable to be superseded completely by more scientific methods of selective restriction. The two methods should complement each other.

Selective credit control can play an important part in a policy aiming at an insulation of loans to the Government from loans to the private sector of the national economy. Owing to the large size of the public debt, most Governments are reluctant to raise interest rates in order to discourage over-trading or a rising trend of prices. Dear money is a costly device from the taxpayer's point of view. Nevertheless, in recent years the British Government among others came to adopt the view that an increase in the burden of public debt through a policy of dear money is not an excessive price to pay for resisting inflation. This view can be endorsed if high interest rates are really able to prevent a rise in prices and if there is no other less costly way towards achieving that end. Thanks to devices of insulation it is possible to some extent to safeguard the public debt against having to bear the full burden of an increase of interest rates. About this more will be said in Chapter 33.

One form of selective credit control is applied to Euro-currency deposits. While the Bank of England does not interfere with Euro-currencies, many Central Banks adopt measures to regulate their volume, More will be said about this in Chapter 41.

Another form of selective measures relates to foreign deposits. Countries with revaluation-prone currencies seek to discourage an unwanted influx by fixing a special reserve ratio for foreign deposits or compelling banks to deposit a certain percentage of such deposits with the Central Bank.

CHAPTER THIRTY-ONE

Influencing Interest Rates

FROM the dawn of history the State authority has been concerned with the level of interest rates. The policy of cheap money was not invented by Keynes; it is almost as old as the monetary system itself. Throughout the ages tribal laws, religious laws and more advanced legislation have tried to set a limit to interest rates. There were such attempts in the Code of Hammurabi and in other ancient codes of law. The ancient Jews went so far as to forbid altogether the charging of interest on loans. The same principle is also found in the Koran and many strict Mohammedans observe it to this day, though many others find ways to circumvent it. The medieval Church came out strongly against the charging of interest which was considered usury.

The enforcement of cheap money by means of anti-usury laws was never very effective. Its circumvention was the rule and its observance the exception. In Babylonia the statutory rate was a modest 20 per cent, but according to Woolley it was usual to charge 25 per cent on loans in silver and $33\frac{1}{3}$ per cent on loans in grain. In backward countries even in our day interest is quoted per month or even per day, because the figure of the annual rate would be too staggering. Writers on money from Aristotle onwards condemned usury. St Thomas Aquinas laid down the maxim that 'money breeds no money' in support of his arguments against usury. Notwithstanding the severity of penalties, interest rates were charged and they were most of the time above the legal maximum, under the influence of the almost perpetually pressing demand for loans.

The State authority took it on itself from time to time to fight high money rates by means other than those of the largely ineffective anti-usury laws. For example, in the Roman Empire Antoninus Pius and Alexander Severus reduced interest rates by lending public money on mortgage.

Although economic considerations must have influenced the efforts to lower interest rates, these were inspired first and foremost by social and political considerations. Measures against high interest rates may be considered to fall within our definition of monetary policy even if their object is not to expand currency or stimulate trade, but to allay the misery and discontent of the debtor classes.

It was only quite recently that intervention to influence interest rates has become a means of monetary policy in the more restricted sense of the term. Modern Central Banking did not develop until the nineteenth century. With it developed the Bank Rate policy which was for over a hundred years – and according to some economists still is – by far the most important weapon at the disposal of State authorities in the monetary sphere. It is a curious fact worth remembering that the first move towards adopting that weapon in Britain was the repeal of the anti-usury laws that had fixed maximum limits of interest rates.

Beyond doubt the Bank Rate has played a most important part over a long period in the economic life of all modern countries. It largely determined the whole structure of interest rates, especially those on short-term loans. Monetary policy in the popular sense of the term is concerned mainly with short-term interest rates such as discount rates, rates on day-to-day loans, on bank advances, deposits, etc. There are approximate and fluctuating differentials between these rates and the rate at which Central Banks are prepared to rediscount bills discounted by banks or, in the case of the Bank of England, by discount houses. These differentials, however, differ considerably according to whether a country is rich or poor in financial resources. In countries which possess well-established money markets the interest rates quoted in the open market are mostly below the Bank Rate, even though rates charged on bank loans are above it. In financially poor countries – and even in some more advanced countries where industries depend on short-term credit for much of their working capital, through lack of adequate capital resources – the Bank Rate is not the maximum but the minimum rate for all types of interest rates. Since the Central Bank is only prepared to satisfy a fraction of the total credit requirements, the bulk of it has to be satisfied at rates higher than those charged by the Central Bank. However this may be, what matters from the point of view of the use of the Bank Rate as a means of monetary policy is that the level of interest rates in general can be moved up or down by means of changing the Bank Rate.

The conception underlying a Bank Rate policy is that high interest rates tend to discourage borrowing while low interest rates tend to encourage it. Consequently, by raising or lowering the Bank Rate the authorities are in a position to cause an increase or a decrease in the quantity of money. A higher Bank Rate tends to induce would-be borrowers to abstain from borrowing and debtors to repay their outstanding loans. It also tends to induce lenders to be more cautious in granting further loans, and even to call in existing loans, because of the possibility of a further rise of interest rates and of commercial difficulties arising from high interest rates. With the aid of high interest rates the authorities can discourage new enterprise or the expansion of existing enterprise, because high interest rates increase both cost and risk attached to business activities. The mere gesture of an increase of the Bank Rate tends to produce a psychological effect which at times is quite out of proportion to its actual material effect.

Another way in which the authorities can make themselves felt with the aid of the Bank Rate is through its effect on holders of stocks of commodities or manufacturers. A high Bank Rate raises the interest charges on loans with the aid of which such stocks are carried. For this reason their holders may become more inclined to sell at a lower price rather than carry the stocks and pay high interest rates over a prolonged period.

This, together with the decline of spending by producers and consumers, tends to cause a fall in prices.

Conversely, a reduction of the Bank Rate, by bringing about an all-round reduction of interest rates, tends to encourage firms and individuals to borrow; it tends to stimulate new ventures and the accumulation of stocks of raw materials or finished products. Consequently it tends to increase business activity and to raise prices. This effect of the Bank Rate is not so dependable, however, as its effect in the opposite sense. The powers of the authorities to bring about an expansion of business activities through low interest rates are not nearly as effective as their powers to reduce business activity by means of high interest rates. Even the latter powers cannot be depended upon absolutely. The Bank Rate may have to be raised to a very high level before it breaks a boom. And in a runaway inflation, such as the German inflation of 1923, even a 90 per cent Bank Rate is useless. Situations are apt to arise in which the Bank Rate, in order that it should produce the desired effect, has to be raised to a crisis level, with disastrous consequences.

Even under less extreme conditions of inflation in the sixties and seventies, Bank Rates became largely ineffective owing to the sharp rise in the price level.

Hitherto we have only been dealing with the effects of the intervention of the authorities in the sphere of interest rates on the internal economy. Its international effects are, however, equally important. The authorities may raise the Bank Rate not only for the purpose of restricting credit but also for the purpose of attracting money from abroad. In an international monetary centre such as London the use of the Bank Rate for that purpose is apt to be very effective in normal conditions. Higher interest rates tend to induce overseas banks and others to transfer their money to London in order to take advantage of the higher yield. British banks with liquid funds abroad may decide to repatriate their money At the same time foreign debtors may hasten to repay their short-term debts in preference to renewing them at such high interest rates. This was what happened in August 1914 when the Bank Rate was raised to 10 per cent at the outbreak of the war and there was a wholesale repayment of credits by foreign debtors. A lowering of the Bank Rate tends of course to produce the opposite effect.

By means of influencing the international flow of funds with the aid of Bank Rate changes the authorities were in a position under the gold standard to influence international gold movements. By raising the Bank Rate they created a demand for sterling, which appreciated in the foreign exchange market to the point at which it became profitable to ship gold to London. Conversely, a reduction of the Bank Rate tended to cause an outflow of funds and the resulting selling pressure on sterling tended to depreciate its exchange value to a level at which it became profitable to withdraw gold from the Bank of England and sell it abroad. By means of raising or lowering the Bank Rate the authorities were thus in a position to raise or lower their gold reserve. This in turn expanded or curtailed the volume of money, for during the days of the automatic gold standard the amount of currency and credit was determined by the size of the gold reserve.

It was not until the managed gold standard was adopted during the twenties that it became possible for the authorities to secure an increase or a reduction in the volume of money to some extent independently of the size of their gold reserve. During the thirties the quantity of money ceased to depend on the size of the gold reserve, even though Exchange Equalisation Account operations did, in Britain, influence the volume of bank credits. Even in countries such as the United States where in theory the credit structure continued to be based on gold, in practice it is possible to alter the volume of credit independently of the amount of the gold reserve through enacting changes in the reserve requirements which the banks have to observe. In the United Kingdom the credit structure was detached from its gold basis in the twenties when the authorities were empowered to increase or reduce the 'fiduciary issue'. When there was an unwanted outflow of gold and the Bank of England did not wish to raise the Bank Rate it advised the Government to raise the fiduciary issue, so that the same amount of gold could serve as a basis for a larger amount of money.

As a result of these changes the Bank Rate weapon ceased to be absolutely essential for the purpose of regulating the size of the monetary reserve for the sake of preparing the way for an expansion or a contraction of credit. It may well be asked whether the change was for the better. It is true that excessive dependence of the level of interest rates and of the volume of credit on the caprices of the gold output and on international gold movements was a weak spot of the monetary system. But on the basis of post-war experience it is arguable that dependance on the caprices of nature and on international gold movements was a smaller evil than being at the mercy of politicians who seek to gain popularity by pursuing policies of cheap money for the sake of winning an election.

One of the reasons why the Bank Rate is apt to be ineffective for international purposes is that forward exchange rates tend to adapt themselves to changes in interest parities brought about by Bank Rate changes. But owing to the multiplicity of interest parities resulting from the existence of a number of parallel money markets, swap margins cannot be equal to all interest parities, so that the difference of the effect of Bank Rate changes on the different sets of interest rates creates ample scope for movements of funds through interest arbitrage. We shall return to this subject in Chapter 39.

One of the purposes for which Bank Rate changes are used is to influence the trade balance. A high Bank Rate, by causing a decline of domestic consumption and of prices, tends to stimulate exports and to discourage imports. As a result of its effect on the trade balance it tends to bring about in due course an inflow of gold in addition to the inflow caused by its effect on the movements of funds referred to above. Conversely, a reduction of the Bank Rate, by causing domestic consumption to expand and prices to rise, tends to discourage exports and encourage imports, leading to an outflow of gold. It takes some time, however, before these effects are produced, and they are only produced as and when the Bank Rate changes affect the price level in the desired sense.

Many economists regard the Bank Rate as the ideal weapon with the aid of which to mitigate booms and slumps. They firmly believe that booms and slumps could be eliminated altogether if only the authorities resorted to the necessary Bank Rate changes in good time and to a sufficient degree. Even those who deny that the Bank Rate is in a position to control the business cycle readily admit that it is an effective weapon against unsound speculative fever and over-trading. On the other hand, there is a growing feeling that the Bank Rate is ineffective against inflation. The orthodox view is that this is because that weapon is not used in good time and to a sufficient extent. But the Radcliffe Committee took the line that the inadequacy of the Bank Rate weapon is due to its inability to influence rates of medium- and long-term loans to a sufficient extent.

The authorities had no unlimited power to determine the level of interest rates during the period of the automatic gold standard. Their hand was very often forced by influences which they were unable to control. If the discount market got it into its head that there was a likelihood of an increase of the Bank Rate, the market rate of discount was apt to rise to the level of the Bank Rate and the Central Bank was forced to raise the Bank Rate. During the period of prolonged cheap money due to lack of demand for credit, the market rates of interest were apt to lose touch with the Bank Rate, which then became entirely ineffective. Under the new system of managed inconvertible currencies the authorities are much more influential in determining interest rates than they had ever been under the gold standard. Whether as a result they are also influential in determining the trend of prices is another question.

Thanks to their new techniques, the authorities are in a position to change the volume of credit without having to change the level of interest rates. They can 'peg' interest rates through open-market operations. The Government can keep interest rates at an artificially low level by bringing about a credit expansion that satisfies all the demand for credit at the prevailing low interest rates. As already stated above, this was actually done in Britain throughout the Second World War, right up to 1951. In order to maintain Treasury bill rates at the level chosen by the monetary authorities, the authorities were prepared to buy at the official rate unlimited amounts of Treasury bills offered for sale. In doing so, however, the authorities expanded the volume of money, thereby providing the technical means without which the progress of post-war inflation would have been handicapped.

While technically the authorities certainly possess devices with the aid of which they can maintain interest rates at a desired level, in practice they have to balance the advantages derived from this policy with the disadvantages of inflation. A stage may be reached – as indeed it was reached both in Britain and in the United States – at which the authorities arrive at the conclusion that it is not worth their while to maintain cheap money at such a high cost.

Hitherto we have been dealing with monetary policy as it concerns short-term rates of interest. The authorities have also to intervene, however, to influence long-term rates of interest. This form of intervention is very old because Treasuries always tried to manipulate the markets with the object of bringing down or keeping down interest rates at which they could borrow. It is only recently, however, that efforts to lower or keep down long-term interest rates have come to be regarded as forming part of the Government's monetary policy as distinct from debt-management policy.

Intervention to check unsound Stock Exchange booms has come to be considered to form part of the duties of the monetary authorities. The Bank Rate was used on many occasions for that purpose, not only because its increase is a gesture of warning against undue optimism but also because it raises the interest charges on loans with which speculative purchases of the securities are financed. During periods of boom, however, a slight increase in interest charges is in itself not sufficient to deter most speculators from carrying their speculative positions with the aid of borrowed money. A 6 per cent interest rate costs only ½ per cent per month, and even its increase to 1 per cent per month would add very slightly to the cost and risk of a promising speculative operation in stocks or in commodities. Speculation on the Stock Exchange or in commodity markets can be discouraged not so much through an increase of interest rates as by a curtailment of the amount of money available for that purpose.

What is true about the limitation of the influence of interest rates on Stock Exchange speculation and on speculation in commodities is also true, though to a less extent, concerning loans for industrial and commercial purposes. If, rightly or wrongly, the trade takes the view that demand is likely to be good and that prices will continue to rise, then a slight increase in interest charges is not likely to discourage business activity financed with borrowed money. In particular, firms with a quick turnover can afford to disregard higher interest rates. If they have reason to assume that the transactions financed with bank loans liquidate themselves in three months, then an increase of interest charges by 2 per cent per annum will only reduce their profit by ½ per cent. In their case, as in the case of Stock Exchange loans, dear money is apt to be ineffective unless it is supplemented by credit restrictions. It would be unwise to assume that high interest rates necessarily reduce the volume of credit to the desired extent. So long as there is a rising tendency of prices and the business outlook appears to be favourable, the large majority of borrowers will be willing to pay the higher interest rates. Indeed, in a sellers' market it is usually possible to add the interest charges to the prices of the goods, so that dear money, instead of bringing down prices, may even contribute to some slight extent to their increase. In the case of building costs, this increase is apt to be substantial.

Another consideration which has to be borne in mind is that in a period of very high taxation such as has existed in Britain since the Second World War, and especially in the sixties and early seventies, the deterrent effect of high interest rates is lessened by the fact that interest charges are allowable as expenses for the purposes of taxation. Those firms which are unable to add the higher interest charges to the prices of their goods may be comforted by the thought that a very large part of the additional cost will be borne by the Treasury.

A doctrine which has developed under the influence of our post-war experience is the so-called 'availability doctrine', according to which the thing that matters is not the cost of credit and capital but their availability. In given circumstances high interest rates do not automatically reduce either the supply of financial resources or the demand for them. High Bank Rate has to be supplemented by credit restrictions.

While the lessons of the thirties have shown that cheap money is not all-powerful in bringing about a trade recovery and a rise in prices, the lessons of the fifties have proved the limitations of dear money in correcting excessive business expansion and consumption and in reversing the rising trend in prices. Nevertheless, it would be a mistake to underestimate the importance of the Bank Rate among the means of monetary policy. The realisation of its limitations should not be regarded as an argument against its use, but merely against its exclusive and isolated use and against excessive reliance on it. Employed in conjunction with other devices, the increase or reduction of interest rates can be very helpful and even indispensable for the achievement of the aims of monetary policy.

Above all, Bank Rate policy proved to be helpless in face of trade union pressure for higher wages. While it was reasonably effective in checking or moderating demand inflation, it was largely helpless to resist cost inflation owing to the change in the balance of power between employers and employees. It is true that, whenever high interest rates reduced profit margins and gave rise to pessimism about the business outlook, employers' resistance to wage demands stiffened and wage inflation tended to slow down even if it did not come to a halt. But in order to be wholly effective in checking cost inflation, the Bank Rate would have to be raised to a level at which it would produce wholesale bankruptcies and large-scale unemployment. The memories of the experience of the thirties effectively prevent this generation of statesmen and administrators from going as far. Perhaps some years hence, when those memories have faded more into oblivion and when creeping inflation will threaten to develop into galloping inflation, a new generation of statesmen and economists might revert to the ruthless use of the Bank Rate weapon.

The development of an international market in foreign currency deposits – especially in Euro-dollars – has considerably weakened the power of the monetary authorities to influence interest rates. The interest rates quoted on Euro-dollar deposits, for instance, are determined to a large extent by factors operating independently of domestic interest rates in the United States or in Britain. The monetary authorities have yet to learn, through experience, how to reassert their full control in face of the operation of a market in which interest rates are determined by outside influences. The monetary policy problem arising from the development of Euro-currency markets will be examined in Chapter 41.

CHAPTER THIRTY-TWO

Fiscal Policy

THE deliberate and systematic use of the Budget in the service of monetary policy is of recent origin. In the old days the means employed in order to achieve the ends of monetary policy were essentially monetary. It hardly occurred to anyone of influence to advocate any radical departure from this traditional practice until Keynes came to advocate the use of fiscal and other non-monetary means. The deliberate use of the Budget for the purposes of monetary policy was an essential part of the Keynesian revolution. In the sixties and early seventies the monetarist counter-revolution led by Milton Friedman sought to put the clock back, and its propaganda succeeded in some instances in influencing Governments to some extent. But, broadly speaking, deliberately created Budgetary surpluses and deficits continued to play a very vital part in determining monetary supply–demand relationships.

Until the thirties Budgetary weapons of monetary policy were almost entirely unknown. Yet from the earliest period of the evolution of State authority, public finance has played an overwhelmingly important part in the economies of most communities. Indeed, at a primitive stage payments made to and by the tribal authority constituted the bulk of monetary turnover. Trading between tribesmen was based mostly on natural economy. A standardised means of payment arose very frequently from the need to pay tribute and fines to the tribal authority, which in turn rewarded those who served it by payment in the same standardised objects.

During a more advanced period taxation and expenditure decisions had very often a strong incidental bearing on monetary policy without actually serving as its instrument. Rulers were frequently confronted by the dilemma whether to raise taxation or spend less, or alternatively to cover their financial requirements out of profits on the debasement of the coinage. In some instances at any rate, princes and their advisers preferred to refrain from embarking on a war rather than debase the currency. In other instances Parliament granted supplies on the condition that the king did not tamper with currency. During a more recent period Napoleon insisted on pursuing a highly orthodox fiscal policy to avoid currency inflation, as a reaction from the disastrous monetary experience of France during the Revolution.

The nineteenth century provided many instances, in Latin America and elsewhere, of Budgetary deficits leading to currency depreciation. Most countries with inflated currencies appeared to make no conscious effort to try to safeguard the currency by means of sound Budgetary policies. The currency depreciations were attributed mostly to the adverse balance of payments, and borrowing abroad was regarded as the obvious remedy. Those responsible for the monetary policies of the countries concerned were – or pretended to be – entirely oblivious of the connection between Budgetary deficit and adverse trade balance.

It was not until the inter-war period that the close connection between a sound Budget and sound currency came to be widely realised. The financial reconstruction schemes elaborated under the auspices of the League of Nations insisted on balanced Budgets as a means of ensuring the success of monetary stabilisations. The principle was rather vague, however. It was not until the thirties, largely under the influence of Keynes, that Budgetary manipulations came to be widely adopted as a means of monetary policy – presumably because in the then prevailing conditions the use of the Budgetary weapon for monetary purposes meant unbalancing the Budgets instead of balancing them. One of the reasons why it was so easy for Keynes to find converts among statesmen from Roosevelt downwards was that the new policy, far from involving sacrifices, meant taking the line of least resistance. It became convenient, therefore, for

Governments to believe in the connection between the Budget and the monetary situation.

The nineteenth-century idea of a sound Budgetary policy was that its aim must be simply to keep down expenditure, cover it with the aid of taxation, and, if possible, produce a revenue surplus for the gradual reduction of the public debt. When in the reconstruction schemes of the twenties balanced Budgets were insisted upon, this was done primarily with the object of inspiring confidence in the stability of currencies that had become discredited by advanced inflation. The same spirit inspired the draconian measures adopted in Britain during the crisis of 1931. The newly-formed National Government endeavoured to restore confidence in sterling by drastic cuts in expenditure and heavy additional taxation. The material effect of these measures was bound to be a sharp contraction in the volume of money, which was bound to accentuate the prevailing economic depression. Indeed, unemployment rose to new record figures during the months that followed the adoption of Budgetary measures. Nevertheless, it was rightly considered preferable at that time to restore the morale of the country by inspiring confidence in sterling rather than to adopt measures to stimulate trade by means of a monetary expansion which would have accentuated the prevailing distrust in sterling.

The strength of the case for supplementing conventional measures of monetary policy by Budgetary measure came to be realised during the thirties, partly as a result of evidence showing that the conventional measures were largely ineffective in the prevailing conditions. One country after another tried in vain to bring about a trade revival with the aid of the time-honoured device of 'cheap money'. It was found that low interest rates signally failed to induce producers and consumers to borrow and spend. The need for direct Government intervention to stimulate trade by means of public expenditure came to be realised in many countries.

The idea was not altogether new. It was advocated from various quarters during the early post-war period and throughout the twenties. The suggestion that the Government could and should spend its way back to prosperity came to be associated with Lloyd George, whose election programme in 1929, endorsed by Keynes, advocated large-scale public works as a means for overcoming the perennial trade depression. Long before his manifesto appeared, however, the idea was strongly pressed on him without effect when he was Prime Minister. Harold Nicolson's biography of George V contains the text of a letter written by the King's private secretary. Lord Stamfordham, in 1921, urging Lloyd George to embark on public works to relieve unemployment. In 1923 in the United States one of the conclusions arrived at at the President's Conference on Unemployment was that public works should be curtailed in booms and expanded in depressions. The recommendation was forgotten, however, during the years of prosperity in the late twenties.

President Roosevelt was the first to apply the new policy on an extensive scale. One of the basic principles of the New Deal policy was large-scale Government expenditure, not only on public works but also to subsidise farmers and various classes of consumers in order to expend their purchasing power. This was done in the United States on an unprecedented scale between 1933 and the outbreak of the Second World War. These measures constituted measures of monetary policy because, in addition to creating employment directly, they were meant to bring about monetary expansion. Apart from creating additional demand as and when the Governments was spending in excess of its revenue, the amounts thus spent were re-spent again and again by their recipients, so that the additional demand created by unbalancing the Budget was in the long run a multiple of the actual amount involved.

Unfortunately it is easier to introduce subsidies than to discontinue them after they have ceased to be necessary for reflationary purposes. Long after the basic trend turned inflationary in the United States, the subsidies continued, adding to the inflationary pressure.

Keynes provided theoretical foundations for the new policy by putting forward his theory on the relation between saving and investment. The substance of this theory is that, if the amount of saving by the public is in excess of the amount spent on capital expenditure, the demand for goods tends to fall short of supply. This means trade depression and unemployment. The remedy advocated is to increase capital investment through larger public expenditure on capital investment. According to his theory, the existence of large-scale unemployment does not necessarily generate automatically influences tending to restore a high level of employment. In the absence of government intervention, unemployment is liable to continue indefinitely.

The execution of the new policy meant a deliberate unbalancing of the Budget. This was in direct contradiction to the traditional fiscal policy under which a Budgetary deficit is something which must be fought at all cost and tolerated only as a matter of unavoidable necessity. This conception was not discarded altogether. Most of those favouring the new policy did not advocate a non-stop rise in the public debt through a perennial Budgetary deficit. The idea was that, taken one year with another, Budgetary surpluses and deficits should offset each other. Budgetary policy should aim at deficits during years of depression and surpluses during years of boom.

During the thirties the Swedish Government announced that it had abandoned the idea of balancing the Budget in each financial year and that it would aim henceforth at balancing it over the entire period of a business cycle. This principle was later adopted by Congressional Committees in the United States and also by the British White Paper on Employment Policy issued by the Coalition Government in 1944. This document rejected the idea of 'a rigid policy of balancing the Budget each year regardless of the state of trade'. The Chancellor of the Exchequer was to take into account the requirements of trade and employment in framing his annual Budget. At the same time the White Paper emphasised that the Government did not contemplate any departure from the principle that the Budget must be balanced over a longer period. Dealing with practical details, the White Paper suggested that capital expenditure by the Government, which in the past had generally followed the same trend as private capital expenditure – it was reduced during depressions and increased during booms – should in the future be adjusted so as to correct excessive tendencies in private capital expenditure instead of accentuating them. It should be increased when private investment is declining and should be reduced when private investment is excessive. Another suggestion was that the Government and the local authorities as large purchasers of certain types of consumer goods should vary the volume of their orders according to the general state of trade. Finally, it was suggested that the rates of contribution to the proposed National Insurance scheme should be adjusted so as to be high during periods of boom and low during periods of depression, even though the expenditure under such a scheme on unemployment benefits is apt to be high during periods of depression and low during periods of boom.

The new monetary policy bears the marks of the one-sided influence of the prolonged depression of the inter-war period. Although its advocates sometimes paid lip-service to the use of their devices also as a means to resist booms and inflations, they primarily envisaged its use as a means to expand purchasing power and stimulate trade during a depression. With the advent of the Second World War the problem to be faced was, however, one of moderating the inevitable inflation that accompanied it. There could be no question of applying Budgetary methods to counteract the inflationary trends. Owing to the heavy cost of a modern war, all belligerent countries, and even many neutral countries, had to unbalance their Budgets to an unprecedented degree. It was assumed, however, that at the end of the war history would repeat itself and that the world would experience once more a post-war slump similar to that of the early twenties. The White Paper on Employment Policy envisaged a two-way monetary policy in which the Budgetary weapon was to play a prominent part both as a defence against booms and as a cure for depressions, but most people expected it to be applied primarily against a post-war slump.

After the war the first Socialist Chancellor of the Exchequer, Dr Dalton, declared it to be the Government's policy that the Budget should be balanced not in each financial year, but over a period of years. The ease with which expenditure that was not unavoidable was authorised – Dr Dalton candidly admitted that he authorised it on one occasion 'with a song in his heart' – formed part and parcel of the Government's policy. For two years the Budget had produced large surpluses, thanks to high taxation. The vicious spiral of inflation was proceeding, however, not through Budgetary deficits, but through overfull employment and the rapid extension of social services. Sir Stafford Cripps, who succeeded Dr Dalton as Chancellor in 1947, hoped to break this vicious spiral by mopping up surplus purchasing power with the aid of an excess of revenue over expenditure. His policy was largely ineffective, however, because in spite of Budgetary disinflation, inflation was kept going by means of credit expansion and an increase of consumers' purchasing power through rising wages and social service benefits. This situation became further aggravated during Mr Gaitskell's Chancellorship through a rise in world commodity prices. In any event, in the early fifties it would not have been practicable to use the Budgetary device for disinflationary purposes, because the growing cost of rearmament became a major factor in the shaping of Budgets. Whatever purchasing power was mopped up with the aid of Budgetary surpluses was promptly released as a result of the increase in the volume of credit brought about by regular intervention to support Treasury bills and Gilt-edged securities.

By the middle fifties the device of running the post-war version of the business cycles with the aid of Budgetary surpluses and deficits had virtually faded into oblivion. The Conservative Chancellors of the Exchequer inherited from their Socialist predecessors a formula in extenuation of a perennial Budgetary deficit – that of differentiating between 'above the line' and 'below the line' Budget, the first representing current items and the second capital items. So long as the Budget balanced above the line it did not matter if it had a deficit below the line. This piece of plausible sophistry was eagerly accepted by Governments and Parliaments, and Press comments frequently refer to a Budgetary surplus even though the deficit below the line is

year after year in excess of the surplus above the line. Yet from
the point of view of its monetary effects it is a fact that it is
an overall deficit that counts. It was not until 1963 that his
obvious fact came to be realised and admitted.

Since the application of Budgetary devices in monetary policy
is of recent origin, its full implications and details have not yet
been worked out. According to an over-simplified view, the
monetary situation can be governed simply by producing a
Budgetary surplus or deficit of the required size. In reality it
makes a considerable difference whether a surplus is achieved
through an increase of taxation or through a reduction of expenditure, and whether a deficit is created through an increase
of expenditure or through a reduction of taxation. It stands to
reason that during a period of trade depression an increase of
purchasing power through tax reductions is not likely to produce the desired results because most producers and consumers
are not inclined to employ their additional purchasing power.
The right way of unbalancing the Budget in such circumstances
is through an increase of public expenditure.

Conversely, during a period of boom or inflation it would be
a mistaken policy to create a Budgetary surplus by means of
high taxation. Owing to the rising trend of prices a large proportion of taxpayers, whether individuals or firms, are in a position to pass on the burden of higher taxes by securing higher
and yet higher wages or prices. The correct Budgetary method
of resisting inflation in such circumstances is to create a Budgetary surplus by means of reducing expenditure. This was not
done in Britain either under Socialist Governments or under
Conservative Governments to a sufficient extent.

Not until 1968–9 was a large Budgetary surplus achieved, and
even then it was achieved with the aid of excessive taxation and
not by means of cutting expenditure. The purpose of this exercise was to eliminate the perennial balance-of-payments deficit,
which is an essentially monetary policy end. The Budgetary
surplus, which continued during the following three years, did
in fact largely contribute towards the achievement of a huge
balance-of-payments surplus, but there is no means of knowing

to what extent this result was due to the revenue surplus and to what extent to the devaluation of 1967.

Owing to the non-stop increase of expenditure, the revenue surplus failed to check inflation which continued to escalate. This experience was used by the monetarists as an argument against fiscal monetary policy. Yet the fact that inflation continued unabated between 1969 and 1972 provides an equally effective argument against the monetarist school, considering that during most of that period interest rates were abnormally high and credit squeezes were applied from time to time. They were just as ineffective in checking inflation as the Budgetary surplus. The inability of the revenue surplus to produce its normal effect on demand was due to the fact that, given the balance of power between employers and employees, the latter were able to maintain and increase their purchasing power in spite of the high taxes imposed on them. Had the revenue surplus been brought about by a reduction of public spending, it would have been much more effective in influencing the balance of payments much sooner and in slowing down inflation.

A policy of using the Budget for monetary purposes must discriminate also according to the nature of the changes in revenue or expenditure. The monetary effect of an increase or reduction of revenue or expenditure varies according to the type of revenue or expenditure increased or reduced. It would be a mistake to try to fight inflation with the aid of high taxation alone. But it is both practicable and in given circumstances advantageous to use certain types of taxation for discouraging certain types of spending. The use of purchase tax for the discouragement of spending on luxuries may be prompted by economic and social motives; at the same time it is an anti-inflationary device because, by discouraging spending on consumer and durable goods, it tends to moderate wage demands. The taxation of company profits and the prohibitive rate of surtax and death duties in Britain pursues a similar combined purpose. There is, of course, another side to it. A case can be made against almost any tax on the ground that in given circumstances it tends to cause a rise in prices. What is even more important is that unduly high taxation by acting as a disincentive, tends to be detrimental to productivity and tends, therefore, to accentuate a rising trend of prices through keeping down the rise in the volume of goods.

In respect of expenditure we pointed out earlier that it can serve primarily as a stimulus to production if it assumes the form of public works or primarily as a stimulus to consumption if it increases the purchasing power of large classes of consumers. The difference is not so marked, however, as some Keynesians would like us to believe. For the multiplier effect and the accelerator effect of the additional purchasing power will not be confined to the original purpose of the expenditure. Money spent on public works is liable to be re-spent by its recipients on consumer goods, while purchasing power created in order to stimulate consumer demand may lead to an increase of capital expenditure.

The use of the Budget for the purposes of monetary policy has its disadvantages and limitations. Those who believe that it could or should replace conventional methods of monetary policy take an unduly one-sided and unrealistic view. For one thing, both changes in taxation and changes in expenditure are clumsy and cumbersome devices. The Budget cannot be revised at frequent intervals. The legislative machinery that has to be set into motion is complicated and slow. As a general rule there can only be one Budget each year, and even in exceptional circumstances there are never more than two Budgets. Yet the monetary situation is liable to change suddenly and its changes are liable to call for urgent measures. It would be unwise to await the next Budget to counteract monetary trends which could easily be handled during their early stages, but which might get out of control if allowed to proceed for months. One partial solution is the granting of powers to the Executive to change certain taxes by administrative action, subject to subsequent approval by Parliament. This saves the time spent on preliminary Parliamentary approval. Even so, it usually takes further months before these measures produce their full effect on the monetary situation. On the revenue side, frequent changes of taxation have considerable disadvantages. On the expenditure side the volume of public works cannot always be easily adapted to the changing requirements of monetary policy. Certain kinds of public works have to go on in boom and slump alike. They cannot be arrested as soon as this appears necessary from the monetary point of view without incurring grave capital losses. Nor can they be initiated or resumed at a moment's notice. Roads cannot be neglected altogether during booms in order to be able to spend more on them during slumps.

The Plowden Report struck a blow in 1962 against the use of public capital expenditure for the purposes of monetary policy. It protested against such 'stop–go' methods and suggested by implication that the entire burden of a disinflationary policy should be borne by the private sector of the economy. This formula is a godsend to inflationist demagogy aiming at discrediting 'stop–go' and substituting non-stop inflation for it.

The Budgetary weapon is particularly useful for situations in which cost inflation and demand inflation are not running concurrently. Certain tax cuts can mitigate costs without unduly increasing demand, while certain tax increases can curtail demand without unduly increasing costs. But if excessive wage increases cause both cost inflation and demand inflation to increase, remedy lies outside the fiscal sphere.

It has been suggested that domestic requirements of monetary policy should be met by the use of the fiscal device, while the Bank Rate should be reserved for its international requirements. Such a discrimination appears to be impracticable, however. One of the reasons for the unpopularity among many economists of the Budgetary devices of monetary policy is that their use has reinforced the supremacy of Treasuries over Central Banks. Ever since the First World War the influence of Treasuries has been gaining ground. The development of the use of Budgetary devices in monetary policy further increased the relative importance of Treasuries, not only as the authorities determining the ends and means of monetary policy, but also as the executing hands of monetary policy decisions. Everybody has to realise that it is impossible to put the clock back, and that the supremacy of

Treasuries in the planning and execution of monetary policy is firmly established. This was due not only to the realisation of the potentialities of the Budgetary device, but also to the increased importance of the part played in the monetary situation by the management of the greatly increased public debts. About this more will be said in the next chapter.

CHAPTER THIRTY-THREE

Debt-Management Policy

THE monetary trend is liable to be influenced by Treasury operations to a considerable degree. We saw in Chapter 29 that the volume of money tends to expand or contract according to the amount of Government securities bought by the authorities from the private sector of the national economy or sold to them by that sector. We saw that, when the Government sells securities to the banks, the cash reserve of the latter becomes reduced correspondingly, while the sale of securities by the banks to the authorities increases the amount of bank cash. If the securities are sold to non-banking buyers their purchasing power is reduced, and inasmuch as payment is made out of the bank deposits the amount of bank cash is also reduced. Conversely, if non-banking sellers cash their maturing Government securities or re-sell them to the Government, their purchasing power increases and their additional bank deposits tend to increase bank cash.

Actually the effect of Treasury operations on the volume of money depends on the category of securities held by banks that is affected by them. If the banks' holdings of long-term loans or bonds increases, it means a corresponding reduction of their liquid assets – unless the bonds mature in the very near future – so that their capacity to lend to their customers becomes reduced. But if it is their holdings of Treasury bills that increase, it enables them to increase their lendings. We saw earlier that the Bank of England is prepared to rediscount Treasury bills at any time without limit, so that holdings of Treasury bills can be monetised whenever necessary.

The amount of Treasury bill issue, which thus largely

determines the volume of bank credit, depends partly on the Treasury's debt-management, partly on the Budgetary position, partly on the Treasury's ability and willingness to bear the extra cost of medium- and long-term issues, and partly on the public's willingness to acquire Government securities.

The management of the public debt is very important in modern conditions, owing to its almost uninterrupted rise in most countries. Although borrowing by the State authority is a very ancient practice, its relative importance from the point of view of the monetary situation remained small so long as the loans were provided by a few wealthy bankers and the totals involved were moderate even allowing for the difference in conditions. In Britain it was not until the end of the seventeenth century that a public debt in the modern sense began to develop. Until then the public debt was considered to be the king's personal debt, and any king who died without having redeemed his loans was criticised for his improvidence. It was during the eighteenth century that the public debt came to be regarded as something permanent and its obligations came to be held widely by the public. Its amount remained relatively small until the Napoleonic Wars, and even during the greater part of the nineteenth century it was not sufficiently large for Treasury operations to play systematically a decisive part in the monetary sphere.

The sharp increase in the public debt during the two World Wars has brought about a far-reaching change in the monetary system. In Britain, Government stocks, bonds and bills now represent a very large proportion of the assets held by the private sector of the national economy. Capital movements between the Treasury and the private sector are liable to be substantial and tend to affect the volume of money considerably. The same is true of many other countries also. Mr Snyder, Secretary of the United States Treasury in the Truman administration, in his evidence before the Joint Congressional Committee on Monetary, Credit and Fiscal Policies, remarked in 1949 that the public debt is now interwoven with the financial structure of the entire economy. The importance of its management from the point of view of monetary policy is due not only to the increase of its size, but also to the broadening of its ownership. In Britain there are millions of holders of Savings Certificates, and their attitude, like that of holders of other Government securities, can react on the monetary situation.

The Treasury's role in influencing the monetary situation through its attitude towards the public debt is manifold. In the first place, it is the Treasury's duty to pursue policies aiming at maintaining public confidence in Government loans. This is of course in accordance with the Treasury's own interests from the point of view of being able to borrow easily and at relatively low rates and to convert or renew maturing debts on relatively favourable terms. At the same time, it is of the utmost importance also from the point of view of monetary stability that the Treasury should do its utmost to uphold confidence in Government loans. For large-scale non-renewal of maturing loans or withdrawal of loans subject to termination at the holders' option is liable to produce strong inflationary effects.

During periods when it is inevitable that there should be a Budgetary deficit, and it is not part of the official monetary policy to use the deficit for pursuing monetary expansion, it is the Treasury's task to ensure that the purchasing power created by excess of Government expenditure over revenue is mopped up through loan operations. It is important that there should not be too long a time-lag between the creation of additional purchasing power through deficits and its mopping-up through loans. We saw in an earlier chapter that when additional purchasing power is created, its repeated use is apt to multiply its effect. It is important therefore that Treasuries should mop up the additional purchasing power before it has exercised its multiplier effect too many times.

As we saw above, it is not a matter of indifference from the point of view of the monetary situation in what form the Treasury issues its loans to cover deficits. If they assume the form of short-term Treasury bills they do not directly mop up consumers' purchasing power. Indirectly they expand the basis of credit and enable banks to increase their deposit liabilities by eightfold the amount involved. Marketable long-term securities are much better from the point of view of mopping up purchasing power, but not nearly so good as non-marketable securities such as Savings Bonds or Savings Certificates. The latter are the ideal medium through which purchasing-power inflation can be neutralised, provided that confidence in the stability of sterling is maintained. Any wave of distrust, or expectation of higher prices for consumer goods, is liable to induce holders to cash their Savings Certificates, thereby recovering the purchasing power they had temporarily relinquished in favour of the Government. While the sale of marketable bonds and stocks by one investor to another does not effect the volume of purchasing power, if it causes a slump in the price of Government loans the Treasury may feel impelled to intervene in order to safeguard the Government credit by buying up the bonds offered by private holders. In doing so it increases the purchasing power of the private sector of the national economy.

The extent to which a change in the attitude of the public may affect the monetary situation was illustrated by a letter by Mr William McC. Martin, Jr (later Chairman of the Federal Reserve Board), when he was Acting Secretary of the United States Treasury, to the Chairman of the Committee on Banking and Currency of the Senate on 4 May 1949. He pointed out that should 5 or 6 per cent of the realisable Government securities be converted into cash, the increase in bank deposits and notes would be enough to reduce the gold reserve below the legal minimum.

The Treasury is in a position to influence the monetary trend by means of a deliberate policy in the sphere of its debt management. The importance of this factor was realised in the United States much earlier than in Britain. In 1952 the Joint Congressional Committee on the Economic Report published in two volumes a report on monetary policy and the management of the public debt which contains a wealth of information bearing on the subject. Until the appearance of the Radcliffe

Report in 1959 there was no corresponding official publication in Britain. Both the Macmillan Report and the White Paper on Employment Policy ignored the subject. According to the American report, there is evidence that from the early days United States Treasury officials were thinking about Treasury finance in relation to the money market as a whole. In 1793, in a Report to Congress on loans, Alexander Hamilton said that one reason for the timing of Government purchases of Government bonds was that 'during the winter in this country there is always a scarcity of money in the towns'. In 1857 Secretary Cobb supplied additional funds to the market by purchasing Government bonds from the public. This was done on frequent subsequent occasions and the Treasury's powers were used equally frequently also in the opposite direction.

With the emergence of the Federal Reserve System the Open Market Committee of the Federal Reserve Board developed the policy of systematic intervention to regulate the volume of credit by means of buying or selling Government securities. This policy has already been dealt with earlier. Between the wars the Bank of England developed a somewhat similar policy. By buying or selling Treasury bills it expanded or reduced the volume of bank credit.

In Britain the amount of Treasury bills allotted to the British banks through the weekly tenders, compared with the amount of their holdings maturing during the same week, largely influences the volume of credit. Before the war the Treasury was able to regulate bank cash fairly accurately by determining the amounts offered at Friday's tenders. But since the war a large and varying proportion is taken up by foreign banks, and to a less extent by non-banking holders, which complicates matters.

Both in Britain and in the United States open-market operations played an important part in monetary policy after the Second World War. Treasury bill rates were maintained artificially stable at a low level by means of buying unlimited amounts of bills which were offered and which would have raised the bill rates in the absence of official intervention. In

Britain this policy was pursued much more rigidly than in the United States. The Treasury bill rates were maintained rigidly pegged at $\frac{1}{2}$ per cent from 1945 until the advent of the Conservative Government in October 1951. Intervention in the market for long-term loans was also much less subtle in Britain while it lasted. Up to 1947 the British Treasury was engaged in systematically bolstering up the market in Government loans in pursuance of Dr Dalton's policy of cheap money. With the advent of Sir Stafford Cripps to the Exchequer this policy was abandoned and Government loans were allowed, from time to time, to find their own level. On repeated occasions the Treasury issued 'tap loans', leaving it to the market to determine the volume of Government issues.

In the United States the policy of supporting Government loans by official purchases through the intermediary of the Federal Reserve Banks was continued right up to 1951. It was not, however, as one-sided a policy as the one pursued in Britain on various occasions. American official intervention in the Government loan market operated both ways. When in the latter part of 1946 and early 1947 an upward trend developed in the bond market, the Treasury felt impelled to intervene to counteract this trend in the interests of long-term stability of bond prices. To that end, large amounts of bonds were unloaded. When in October 1947 weakness developed in the bond market, the Treasury intervened by buying up large amounts of bonds. Although the primary object of these operations was to maintain the stability of Government bond prices, its secondary object was to maintain stability of long-term interest rates. From this point of view the American policy differed fundamentally from the British policy, which aimed at lowering long-term interest rates rather than maintaining them stable. In face of the irresistible upward trend of interest rates in the sixties, Britain too had to abandon the hopeless resistance.

After the outbreak of the Korean War American intervention to prevent a fall in bond prices resulted in a heavy expansion of credit. Evidently the requirements of stability of bond prices came into conflict with the requirements of monetary stability. Eventually the latter consideration prevailed and the United States Treasury decided in 1951 to abandon the rigid support of the bond market, though it continued to afford it intermittent support at a lower level.

A great deal depends not only on the amount of the national debt, but also on its holders. It is not a matter of indifference from the point of view of the monetary situation whether the Government loan is taken up entirely by banks or is subscribed by the general investing public. The more widely it is held by the public, the larger is the extent to which it tends to immobilise purchasing power which would otherwise be in the hands of producers and consumers. If the securities bought by the public are paid for out of bank deposits, then the operation kills two birds with one stone. In addition to its direct effect on the consumers' purchasing power, it also reduces the amount of bank cash and therefore leads to a reduction in the volume of credit. But even if a loan is taken up by the banks, it immobilises their liquid resources and reduces their lending capacity. During the Second World War it was inevitable that Government loans should be financed largely by the banks. After the war it was possible to tranfer very gradually a large proportion of the public debt from the banks to private investors. Both in Britain and in the United States the official policy after the war aimed at placing the largest possible amount of the public debt with the general public.

Treasury operations as devices of monetary policy are not without their disadvantages. The Treasury's interests as a large debtor and borrower may conflict with the requirements of monetary policy. We saw above that when confronted with such a dilemma the British Treasury in 1947 and the United States Treasury in 1951 sacrificed considerations of debt management for the sake of those of monetary policy by allowing long-term interest rates to rise in order to avoid additional inflation. On other occasions, however, it was considerations of monetary policy which were sacrificed. Since the thirties the Treasuries of the world have discovered that as debtors and borrowers they are in the unique position of being able to determine the interest rates they pay. There is a strong temptation to use and abuse this power. Fortunately this temptation has been tempered by the extension of the Treasury's functions, which now cover not only the management of public finances but also the supreme direction of economic policy. Before the war Treasuries would have been inclined to make the utmost use of their power to lower the interest rates on their debts, since in those days their principal if not their only function was to safeguard the taxpayers' interest and to that end it was their duty to secure loans on the cheapest possible terms. Today Treasuries are responsible for the economic stability and prosperity of their countries. They have to think twice before embarking on a policy which, while it assists them in keeping down the cost of public debt, increases their difficulty in performing their broader economic functions satisfactorily. This dual role of the Treasury is admittedly not without grave disadvantages. At the same time it has the advantage of compelling the Treasury to view its role from a broader standpoint, and it tends to prevent it from the misuse of its powers to determine interest rates.

Attempts have been made in various countries to reconcile the narrower interests of Treasury as borrower and debtor with its broader interests as the authority in charge of the national economy. There are various devices with the aid of which it is practicable to maintain Treasury borrowing rates at a relatively low level without having to overstimulate the private sector of the national economy by making money too cheap and too easy. It is possible for the monetary authorities to insulate to some extent interest rates on Government loans from those on private issues.

Support of the market in Government loans is one of these devices. On the face of it it might seem that if the Treasury supports its own issues while it allows private securities to find their own level, the yield of the former tends to be relatively lower than that of the latter. In practice, however, an abnormally low yield on Government issues tends to divert funds towards investment in private securities, and this tends to reduce the discrepancy between their respective yields. More-over, systematic support of the market in Government securities on a large scale produces an inflationary effect on the level of prices of private securities owing to the increase in the volume of funds available for investment.

A more effective method of insulation is the control of the market of new issues. With the aid of such control the Govern-ment is able to keep down the volume of private issues whenever the Treasury intends to appear in the market with a new issue or with a conversion operation. Under the system of control the Treasury can ensure for itself a high degree of priority over the financial resources of the country. There is no need for it to compete against the private issues by offering costlier terms. In Britain this device came to be applied also to credit trans-actions in excess of £50,000, which required authorisation by the Capital Issues Committee.

For some time, until September 1971, competition of private demand for funds was also hampered by the device of fixing a ceiling for credits which each bank was authorised to grant to private customers. Although the main object of this restriction was to resist inflation, the fact that overdrafts to nationalised industries did not come under the credit limits speaks for itself. Since from 1968 the Budgetary deficit was replaced by a surplus this restriction on lending to the private sector no longer served the purpose of facilitating Treasury borrowing, even though local authorities continued to compete for the liquid funds available.

Another device was the adoption of legislation under which banks were under obligation to invest a certain proportion of their assets in Government securities. Although the main object of this system was to restrict credit expansion and to reinforce the security of deposits, it went some way towards insulating the public sector and shielding it from the effects of credit squeezes. The system is in operation in various forms in the United States, Belgium, France, Italy, the Netherlands and Sweden, among other countries. No such reserve requirements were in operation in Britain. British banks are, however, always willing to co-operate with the authorities to ensure the success of Government issues, all the more so since they hold large amounts of Government securities, so that it would be to their disadvantage if the failure of a Treasury issue caused a fall in the Gilt-edged market. Moreover, since short-dated Government securities are eligible, this provides an incentive for banks to hold them.

In most countries certain funds must be held in trustee securities. In view of the large amount of such funds, legislation preventing their investment in many types of private securities secured a considerable demand for Government securities. In Britain the Government relinquished this advantage by amending the list of trustee securities in 1961, admitting a number of private securities.

With the aid of these and other devices, Governments are in a position to restrict credit to the private sector of the national economy in pursuance of a disinflationary policy, without having to put up with an increase of the interest rates on their own loans corresponding to that of the interest rates on private loans and credits. The discrepancy cannot, however, be increased unduly. In this, as in many other respects, the extent to which monetary policy can create and maintain artificial situations in defiance of economic trends has its limits.

Among the fiscal devices of monetary policy, that of Treasury operations is distinctly more elastic and adaptable than that of Budget operations. This in spite of the fact that Treasury operations, too, have to be guided at times by considerations other than monetary policy. There can be no doubt that fiscal devices have come to stay. Even though it has become once more fashionable to advocate a reduction of the Treasury's role to the traditional function of collecting taxes, authorising expenditure and managing the public debt, it seems to be most unlikely that the clock will ever be put back. It would be impossible to revert to the system under which the sole object of Treasury operations was to cover Budgetary deficits by means of borrowing and to renew maturing debt or convert

Government loans at the lowest possible interest rates. That aspect of the Treasury's duties must of course remain prominent, in view of the importance of keeping down the burden of the greatly increased public debt. From time to time the Treasury's narrower interests are bound to be overshadowed, however, by major considerations of monetary policy which are or can be affected by the terms on which Treasury operations are arranged.

For example, even when the proportion of the floating debt is not uncomfortably high, the Treasury may decide to fund some of it in pursuit of objectives of monetary policy. Although debt funding must mean an increase in the burden of the interest service, prevailing circumstances may justify the sacrifice if as a result the monetary situation is adjusted in accordance with the requirements of monetary policy. On more than one occasion since the War interest rates on Savings Certificates were raised, not because the Treasury found it difficult to secure the necessary funds through other channels, but because from the point of view of monetary policy it was considered expedient to mop up some of the purchasing power of the lower income groups. Many similar examples could be quoted to illustrate the extent to which Treasury operations are now based on broader principles than they were in the past.

A characteristic instance of Treasury operations inspired by considerations of monetary policy was provided by the funding of a large amount of Treasury bills in Britain at the end of 1951. The object of this operation was to reduce the liquidity ratio of the banks – that is, the proportion of their liquid assets to their total assets – thereby discouraging excessive expansion of credit. During the middle fifties this method of resisting inflation came to be strongly advocated both by banks and by financial writers. While Keynes suggested de-funding as an effective means of reflation, these experts suggested funding as an effective means of disinflation. As it concerns the degree of liquidity of the economy, we propose to deal with it in the next chapter.

CHAPTER THIRTY-FOUR

Influencing Liquidity

IN the last chapter we examined the ways in which Treasury operations of financing a Budgetary deficit or of funding or de-funding the public debt are liable to affect the quantity of money. Reference was made to the new device of influencing the entire structure of interest rates instead of concentrating on short-term rates, by applying the policy of funding and de-funding to the whole range of maturities. In view of the relative novelty and recently discovered importance of this means of monetary policy – in the past, intervention in the market for medium- or long-term loans served the purpose of debt management and not that of monetary policy – it is necessary to examine it in greater detail.

Distinction must be made between the two aspects of the new device: its bearing on the cost of borrowing by the private sector and on the availability of money, actual or potential. Both aspects are important. Intervention for the purpose of influencing relative interest rates for various maturities amounts to a form of selective credit control – the diversion of private funds from short-term to long-term employment and vice versa. Intervention for the purpose of changing the degree of liquidity of the economy amounts to encouragement or discouragement of spending by firms and individuals by making it easier or more difficult for them to monetise their investments.

Progress has certainly been made, and is still being made, in the sphere of monetary policy, from simple to more sophisticated devices. During earlier periods monetary policy operated through changing the volume of coins, and later of notes. More recently the authorities aimed at changing the size of bank cash which determined the limits of deposits and credits. Even more recently they aimed at influencing the banks' total liquid resources. And now they are interested in the extent to which the private sector itself is capable of bringing about an increase or reduction of the cash basis of credit. Modern monetary policy aims at increasing or reducing the amounts of assets of various degrees of graded liquidity with the object of facilitating or discouraging their monetisation through conversion into bank balances.

As a general rule the shorter the average maturity of the public debt, the easier it is for banks, firms or individuals to force the authorities to increase the volume of Treasury bills by simply cashing in their maturing bonds instead of renewing them under the Government's funding offers. It is true that the remedy is ultimately in the Treasury's hands, as debt de-funded through non-renewal can always be funded again – at a price, by offering to holders higher interest rates on longer maturities. But the Treasury may not want to pay that price in the form of a further increase of interest charges on the public debt.

It is because of the Treasury's unwillingness to disregard the cost of funding that the authorities view with concern the increased degree of liquidity of the public debt since the war. It limits their influence during periods when their monetary policy aims at resisting inflation. This concern was expressed by official witnesses in their evidence before the Radcliffe Committee. The Governor of the Bank of England spoke about the great difficulty caused by the extent of 'liquidity or near-liquidity in the sense of bonds maturing just ahead of you all the time'. In the evidence it was stated that between 1931 and 1957 the proportion of the debt maturing within five years increased from 8 to 24 per cent of the total, that of debt maturing between five and fifteen years from 7 to 25 per cent. In the United States between 1946 and 1960 the average maturity of the public debt declined by more than half.

While in the last chapter we were concerned with the excessive volume of actual Treasury bills, here we are concerned with the potential increase in that volume as a result of non-renewals of short- and medium-term loans which are maturing all the time. It is not only the actual amount of cash that determines the willingness of its holders to spend it, invest it or lend it. If banks and business firms, and even private investors, hold a large proportion of their assets in the form of bonds which they expect to be able to cash at par within a relatively short time, or which they are in a position to sell at a relatively small loss, they are more inclined to use their actual liquid assets for the purpose of spending, investing or lending than they would be if they held loans of longer maturities whose realisation at market prices might involve a heavier capital loss.

It has always been the basic debt-management policy of all Treasuries to lengthen the maturity of the public debt in so far as it is possible to do so without having to pay unduly high additional interest charges on longer maturities. This end was pursued, not for any purpose of monetary policy, but solely in order to be safeguarded against the risk of having to meet maturities at an awkward moment and in order to have a better chance to choose the right moment for conversions. The idea of managing the debt in accordance with the requirements of a counter-cyclical monetary policy was a Keynesian innovation. The basic principle of the new policy is that the average maturity of the public debt should be lengthened during booms and shortened during recessions. This may involve sacrifices to the taxpayer, because during inflationary periods the demand for longer maturities declines, so that investors have to be attracted by offering them higher yields – unless they are attracted by other methods such as the issue of bonds carrying an 'index clause' (under which the amount of interest and repayment increases in proportion to the increase of the cost-of-living index or some other index), or of Premium Bonds, as suggested by Manning Dacey. But there are overwhelmingly strong arguments against bonds with an index clause, and only a fraction of the investors are attracted by Premium Bonds. In view of this, counter-cyclical debt management might mean that the debt is always funded when, owing to inflation, this must be done on terms unfavourable to the Treasury, while it is always de-funded when deflationary conditions would make funding advantageous. The tax-payer would get easily the worst of both worlds. It is very much a matter of opinion whether, and to what extent, the advantages derived from this policy would outweigh its costs.

Until comparatively recently it was widely assumed that Bank Rate changes were liable to affect all maturities. In reality the degree of fluidity of capital movements between various types of Government loans varies very much according to circumstances. It is usually higher during inflation than during deflation, though even during inflationary periods wide discrepancies are liable to develop. Hence the need for intervention if the authorities want to influence the structure of interest rates or the liquidity of the private sector of the economy. It may not be sufficient to confine this to the sphere of debt management. In given situations, debt management policy has to be supplemented by active open-market operations extending over a wide range of maturities.

The task arising from the new official interest in the liquidity of the community is twofold. First, there is the need for finding a once-for-all solution to the problem of excessive liquidity inherited from the war. This was to a large degree the result of the method of financing the war by means of short- and medium-term loans instead of irredeemables as in the First World War. In addition, in Britain and other countries the nationalisation of very substantial sectors of the economy resulted in the conversion of very large amounts of equity stock and debenture stock into Government loans. Even though these loans are long-term, they are more easily marketable in large amounts than the stocks they had replaced. Nor have holders any sentimental attachment to them as a great many had to, say, railway stocks, which had been held by the same families for generations. There is more inclination and opportunity for monetising the nationalisation stocks, even though their holders may have to take a substantial loss.

The liquidity of the community declined in Britain and in

other countries during the late fifties and in the sixties, though it is still much above its pre-war level. Opinion is divided as to whether further reductions would be expedient. Whether or not the authorities are able and willing to deal with the problem of excessive liquidity, they can make the best of the situation by making use of the new device for regulating the degree of liquidity. To that end they have to depart from their previous policy of confining their two-way operations to bills.

In Britain the issue in 1962 of two loans, one long-term and one short-term, through the operation of the 'tap' system (under which the loans are available to buyers at prices fixed from time to time by the Treasury), seems to indicate that the new policy is meant to be pursued systematically. The American attitude was until recently that open-market operations should be confined to Treasury bills. The Federal Reserve Board's Open Market Operation Committee laid down the 'bills only' doctrine in 1953, with the reservation that official operations in Government bonds are justified in case of 'disorderly conditions' in the bond market. By this was meant a state of affairs in which a fall in bond prices, so far from being self-corrective, accentuates the selling pressure and tends to be self-aggravating. But from February 1961 the range of maturities in which open-market operations were carried out was widened considerably.

Even before this change in American policy, the Radcliffe Report put forward the proposal that monetary policy should be concerned with the entire structure of interest rates: not only with their level but also with the differentials between them. While the Committee seeks to minimise the importance of influencing short-term interest rates by means of conventional devices or open-market operations, it is inclined to overstate the importance of the device of its choice which it presents as the centre of monetary policy. This attitude was critised, among others, by Dacey, who, while in favour of funding, deems it superfluous for the authorities to seek to influence liquidity by extending the maturity range of their open-market operations. He takes the view that, by influencing the quantity of money, the authorities can also influence demand for medium- and long-term loans. Actually, changes in the grand total do not affect demand for any particular maturities, and interest differentials detrimental to the community are liable to arise.

According to one theory, in the absence of official intervention realisation of securities does not affect the aggregate demand by firms and individuals, for each seller has to find a buyer. In reality, transactions between non-banking buyers and sellers are liable to affect demand, according to whether sellers intend to make active use of their increased liquid resources and according to whether buyers who immobilise their resources would have made active use of them if it had not been for their purchase of bonds. The result of the change in ownership may well be an increase or decrease in the velocity of circulation of money. And if the buyers intend to cash their holdings of short-term bonds on maturity, they force the Treasury to increase the Treasury bill issue, which leads to credit expansion if the additional bills find their way to the banks.

The transfer of Treasury bills from banks to non-banking holders may be regarded as a form of short-term funding, because their holders renounce the use of their purchasing power so long as they hold the bills. It is true that the banks' cash resources are increased to a corresponding extent. But under the modern practice in Britain it is the total of liquid reserves that matters, so that the conversion of Treasury bills into cash does not make much difference.

In the United States the practice of acquiring Treasury bills by non-banking investors has increased considerably since the war, but in Britain it is confined to large institutional investors. It has been suggested that a reduction in the amount of Treasury bill units would popularise them among non-banking holders and would therefore assist the authorities in keeping tighter control over bank credits.

The new device of influencing the structure of interest rates is important from the point of view of enabling the authorities to maintain high short interest rates for the sake of defending the exchange, while reducing long rates for the sake of stimulating investment. While low interest rates on all maturities are calculated to encourage a domestic business revival, long maturities are less important from the point of view of international movements of funds than short maturities. For most foreign funds are employed in short loans, so that a reduction of short rates is liable to cause heavier withdrawals of such balances than a reduction of medium or long rates. This means that intervention to lower long rates may stimulate the domestic economy without leading to an outflow of funds to an extent comparable to the outflow resulting from a reduction of short interest rates.

In this respect, however, the situation is liable to change. From time to time arbitrageurs become actively interested not only in short bonds but even in longer maturities. For instance, there was heavy foreign buying of French *rentes* during various periods in the thirties. Nevertheless, situations frequently arise in which the monetary authorities, by operating on the interest structure, are able to eat their cake and keep it – to encourage domestic capital investments by lowering long yields, and yet to retain foreign balances by maintaining high short yields. This was done in the United States in 1961 when the Federal Reserve authorities, in order to defend the dollar, kept bill rates around 2 per cent while buying bonds to cause an increase in the amount of resources. Apart altogether from such situations, intervention operating on the whole structure of interest rates may be advantageous in order to overcome frictional discrepancies due to market imperfections and institutional rigidities.

According to the new conception, the extension of the range of open-market operations, together with the enlistment of debt management in the service of monetary policy, has the advantage of providing better channels for the spreading of the effect of monetary action on the economy. From this point of view the increase of the public debt and its wider distribution since the war is considered to have greatly facilitated the task of monetary authorities who are now able to reach sections of the economy which were in the past largely immune from their influence. By adjusting interest-rate differentials between the various sectors of the market for Government loans, the authorities are in a position to increase or reduce liquidities. It has been contended with little exaggeration that if a public debt did not exist it would have to be invented for the sake of providing a very serviceable means of monetary policy. 'A widely held public debt may increase the effectiveness of monetary policy', the American Report on Money and Credit remarked, 'by providing a better network for its swift transmission throughout the economy.'

The basis of the new policy is the assumption that spending is affected not only by the amount of the money the potential spenders, lenders or investors actually possess, but also by the amounts they are in a position to raise through the realisation of their assets. By deliberately causing a depreciation of medium- and long-term loans, or at any rate by preventing their appreciation, the authorities can discourage their monetisation, because many holders become reluctant to take a capital loss. But this is a double-edged weapon. If investors arrive at the conclusion that the policy of lowering the prices of their bonds is likely to proceed further, they might decide to cut their losses and sell out even if they had not originally intended to do so. Conversely, when the authorities are engaged in lowering the yield of their bonds by open-market purchases, investors and speculators are liable to operate in the same sense, on the assumption that the official tactics would continue. Possibly the authorities may like this reinforcement of their action, but this need not necessarily be the case.

The encouraging effect of a reduction in the average maturities of the public debt is liable to influence not only those firms which depend on borrowed money but even those which finance themselves with the aid of their undistributed profits. They will be inclined to use up their cash reserves on the assumption that it would be easy to monetise their liquid investment if this should prove to be necessary.

A reduction of average maturities of investments may affect the attitude of banks. In possession of bonds with a shorter average maturity they are inclined to lend more, on the assumption that they would find it easy to monetise their short investment in case of need. A lengthening of the average maturity of their investments, on the other hand, might induce them to keep sown this lending so as to avoid having to realise investments at a loss. Non-banking investors too are inclined to immobilise their liquid resources if they are able if necessary to monetise their short bonds at a small loss or even without a loss. It is an accepted rule that the velocity of circulation of money is apt to rise and fall with the increase or decrease of liquidity. Short maturities are looked upon as money-substitutes or near-money, and in their possession holders of money are more inclined to spend or lend.

The new technique can be used for influencing the total of market resources, by releasing or mopping up additional money, but it can also be used without affecting the grand total, if the authorities mop up the resources released through buying other maturities. Such two-way open market operations leave total resources unchanged – unless they affect the volume of Treasury bills, in which case under the British system the volume of credit is affected to a higher degree.

One advantage of broadening the sphere of open-market operations is that this may reduce the extent to which monetary policy must cause fluctuation of short interest rates. If the whole burden of a counter-cyclical policy rests on bill rates, they are bound to be subject to wider changes than they would be if the official operations are spread more widely over medium and long maturities as well as bills.

The authorities may resort to their new tactics also for the sake of influencing Stock Exchange trends in general. But here again theirs is a double-edged weapon. In the long run a reduction of yields on bonds is apt to divert capital into equities. In the short run, however, investors and speculators may want to cash in on the rise in the Gilt-edged market by switching from equities into bonds.

The new policy need not be confined to Government bonds. In Britain the market for new issues was controlled by the Capital Issues Committee, so that it was possible for the authorities to exert influence over the maturities of private issues or of foreign Government issues, for the sake of reinforcing their debt-management policy, and open-market operations.

One of the criticisms directed against the new policy in the form in which it is advocated by the Radcliffe Report is that, while devoting much attention to Treasury tactics aiming at influencing the supply of assets of various degrees of liquidity, it devotes too little attention to the problems of influencing demand for them. The conventional devices affecting the volume of money, underrated by the Radcliffe Committee, have surely a considerable and often decisive influence on the demand for Government loans. Admittedly, changes in the velocity of circulation are liable to influence demand. But, as Dacey pointed out, the Committee had no use for the concept of velocity. Yet, if it is disregarded, the logical conclusion would be that the Treasury is quite capable of influencing the aggregate demand for Government loans simply by using its control over the quantity of money. Even so, there would remain the problem of controlling the interest differentials between various maturities, and this calls for sophisticated debt management and for elaborate open-market operations in the Gilt-edged market.

Beyond doubt, the new device has wide possibilities, though it may take some time before its theory and technique are fully developed through trial and error. Its scope will increase as and when the banks adopt the practice of thinking in terms of average maturities or graded maturities rather than drawing a more or less rigid line between liquid and non-liquid assets. Indeed, it is conceivable that a few years hence the banks will reckon their liquidity on some formula based on the ratio between the average maturity of their assets and of their liabilities.

CHAPTER THIRTY-FIVE

Influencing the Velocity of Circulation

THE ends of monetary policy may be pursued by influencing the volume of money in relation to the volume of goods in several different ways. A contraction or expansion of the volume of currency and credit may caused either directly or by means of changing interest rates. As we shall see in a later chapter, the same end may be achieved through a change in the relative volume of money as a result of increasing or reducing the volume of goods available for sale. Another alternative is to change the effect of a given amount in money by influencing its velocity of circulation. By making money circulate faster or slower, the authorities are in a position to produce effects similar to those of an expansion or reduction of its quantity.

There is no need for us to enter into the highly involved controversy about the meaning of the velocity of circulation of money. For our purposes it means the average number of times money changes hands during a given period through payments for goods and services. Its turnover through purely financial transactions or through gambling does not count from our point of view. If we allowed for the use of money when it changes hands for purposes other than payments for goods and services, the Principalty of Monaco could claim that the velocity of circulation of her currency is many times larger than that of any other country. Since, however, the speed with which money passes from hand to hand in the Casino of Monte Carlo does not in the least affect the price level, it may be disregarded from a monetary point of view. The same is true about the velocity of circulation of money changing hands in connection with Stock Exchange transactions. While the amount of bank balances used for that purpose is a factor, since it is not available for commercial transactions, the speed with which these balances circulate between investors, speculators, brokers and jobbers does not affect the price level. What matters from the point of view of a monetary policy is the velocity of circulation of money in connection with commercial transactions, that is, in its use in payment for goods and services.

In itself the quantity of money would be unable to affect the price level if its velocity of circulation were nil, as is the case with permanently hoarded money. It is through changing hands that money affects prices, and the more often it changes hands the more it is liable to affect prices. This fact was realised at a very early stage in the development of monetary theory. Writers in the seventeenth century had already a vague idea that money is only effective if it is circulated and that its effectiveness increases with its velocity of circulation. Cantillon was the first to point out clearly in the middle of the eighteenth century that an increase of the velocity of circulation produces the same effect as an increase in the quantity of money, and that a decline in the velocity of circulation is liable to counteract an increase in its quantity. He expressed the view that if an excessive supply of money raises prices too much, the prince or the legislator should try to delay the circulation of money in order to avoid an undue increase in the cost of living.

To put it briefly, money is effective as a factor affecting the price level only in so far as it is used in purchases of goods and services, and the degree of its effectiveness depends on the frequency with which it is used. The authorities may be in a position to increase or reduce the quantity of money in pursuing some end of monetary policy, but their efforts are liable to be frustrated if an increase in the quantity of money is followed by a corresponding slowing down of the velocity of its circulation or if a reduction in the quantity of money is accompanied by a corresponding increase in its velocity of circulation. While the quantity of money depends on the authorities, its velocity depends first and foremost on the willingness of consumers and producers to spend. An increase in the quantity of money merely provides the means to enable producers and consumers to spend more. If the additional money is not available, they cannot spend more, unless they increase the velocity of circulation of the existing quantity. But if additional money is made available, they may or may not make use of the additional facilities. If they do not spend more it means that, although the volume of money is laiger, the average number of times it changes hands becomes smaller, and the situation is apt to remain the same as it was before when the quantity of money was increased.

Conversely, an increase in the velocity of the circulation means that producers and consumers spend more even in the absence of an expansion in the volume of money. Holders of currency and of bank deposits may decide to spend more freely because they anticipate higher prices, or for various other reasons. Their additional spending has the same effect as any additional spending resulting from an increase in the quantity of money. As we tried to explain in an earlier chapter, if an amount is spent the purchasing power it represents does not disappear but becomes available for the recipients to use again and again. Each time the money is spent it adds to the volume of demand. In the absence of goods, the additional demand tends to cause an increase of prices, irrespective of whether it originated through an increase in the quantity of money or through the faster circulation of the existing quantity. If the spirit moves the owners of the money to spend more freely so that the money changes hands more frequently, this increase in the velocity of its circulation may even offset some degree of curtailment in its quantity. The 'multiplier effect' of an increase in spending is apt to be several times its original effect.

In reality, what often happens is that when the quantity of money changes, its velocity of circulation also tends to change in the same sense. A rising trend in prices caused by an increase of the quantity of money stimulates buying, and the larger quantity of money is liable to change hands more frequently. Conversely, when the quantity of money is reduced, the resulting declining trend of prices tend to discourage buying, so that the velocity of circulation tends to slow down. In the absence of official intervention, changes in the velocity of circulation thus tend to accentuate an upward or downward movement.

Changes in the velocity of circulation affect not only the trend of prices but also the trend of business activity. The resulting increase or decline in consumer demand and capital investment causes an increase or decline in production and turnover, and an increase or decline in profits. A trade boom may be brought about not only as a result of an increase in the volume of money but also as a result of a more frequent use of the existing volume of money. This may occur, for instance, through an anticipation of a rising trend of prices or through a wave of optimism about business prospects.

The fact that the authorities have not the same power to determine the velocity of circulation as they have to determine the quantity of money came to be fully realised during the thirties. The United States and many other countries embarked on a policy aiming at stimulating trade and causing a rise in prices by means of pumping money into circulation. It was found, however, that the response of the economies of the countries concerned to the increase in the quantity of money was very disappointing. Simultaneously with the increase in the quantity of money, its velocity of circulation declined, because consumers and producers were not inclined to increase their spending on consumer goods and capital goods respectively. Indeed, since producers and consumers were reluctant to borrow, the monetary authorities were unable to bring about the desired degree of expansion of credit through increasing the cash reserves of banks. The only way in which they were able to add to the monetary supply of the private sector of the national economy was by unbalancing their Budgets through additional public expenditure. Even this device had a limited effect on the economy because the velocity of circulation of the additional money thus created was inclined to be sluggish. Many recipients did not re-spend the money they received, so that the 'multiplier' effect of the purchasing power created by the Government was relatively small. Moreover, since business circles viewed with distrust such Government interference with the economy, they were inclined to curtail their activities.

Yet it is well to bear in mind that it is only through the multiplier effect that an increase in the volume of money can produce its full effect on the price level. An increase in the quantity of currency and credit by, say, 10 per cent is not liable to cause an increase of the price level by anything like 10 per cent unless the additional money is spent several times. Admittedly, in a sensitive market, such as are most commodity exchanges, an increase of the demand by 10 per cent tends to produce an instantaneous effect. On the other hand, retail merchants do not mark up their prices by 10 per cent merely because on a given day or during a given week or month their turnover has increased by 10 per cent. Nor do manufacturers or wholesale merchants necessarily quote higher prices to retailers as soon as the latter increase their orders by 10 per cent. The stocks of goods held by the trade would easily absorb a once-for-all additional demand of such magnitude without any effect on prices. It is only when, as a result of the repeated re-spending of the additional money, the increase in the demand has become sufficiently persistent that merchants and manufacturers in many lines of goods may feel justified in taking advantage of it by raising their prices. It is necessary to realise this in order to appreciate the importance of the velocity of circulation among the factors affecting the price level.

The experience of the thirties gave rise to a wave of defeatism about the helplessness of monetary policy, as a reaction to the realisation of the falsity of the earlier belief according to which there are practically no limits to the powers of monetary policy in influencing the trend of prices and the course of economic activities. The defeatism was largely due to the realisation of the extent to which a decline of the velocity of circulation of money is liable to nullify the effects of monetary policy devices aiming at the increase of its quantity.

Again during the fifties and sixties a wave of defeatism developed as a result of the failure of official efforts to check inflation in spite of restraining the expansion of credit. What happened was that the velocity of circulation of deposits increased considerably. For instance, the expansion of instalment financing meant that large amounts were lent to hire-purchase finance companies, as a result of which the ownership of formerly idle deposits passed into the hands of holders who made active use of them. Even though the increase in the total volume of bank deposits did not keep pace with the expansion of business or with the rise in prices, the conversion of dormant deposits into active deposits made up the difference. This was one of the reasons why in the late fifties and in the sixties the effect of the restrictive monetary policy on the price level was as disappointing as that of the expansionary monetary policy had been in the thirties.

Having regard to the evidence of the helplessness of monetary devices to revive trade in the thirties or to check inflation in the sixties, the revival of the dogmatic belief in the unlimited power of monetary devices was indeed strange. It is difficult to understand the enthusiasm with which the monetarists propagated their discredited dogma, and even more difficult to understand its widespread acceptance. Although the monetarists did pay lip-service to their realisation of the effect of changes in the velocity of circulation, their emphasis was so one-sidedly on the effect of changes in the quantity of money that the general impression conveyed by their theory was distinctly one-sided and misleading. The monetarists are largely responsible for the widespread disappointment, leading to a feeling of defeatism, according to which we are helpless in face of irresistible trends. In reality, monetary policy is by no means as helpless in the sphere of the velocity of circulation as it appeared to be in the thirties and in recent years. There are various means by which the authorities are able to accelerate or slow down the velocity of circulation as an alternative to changing the quantity of money or as a means of ensuring the effectiveness of changes in the quantity of money. The following are the means which monetary policy can use for speeding up the turnover of money:

(1) *Increase of Government Expenditure.* Provided that it is not offset by an increase of revenue, this has the immediate effect of

increasing the quantity of money. At the same time it also tends to increase its velocity of circulation through the operation of the multiplier. It stands to reason that any additional large-scale expenditure, whether initiated by private interest or by the Government, is apt to put new life into the economy and to stir up a certain amount of activity resulting in an increase in the velocity of circulation. If private interest are not prepared to respond to an increase of their resources available for expenditure, then it is up to the Government to initiate the process. If the Government increases the volume of money through money-market operations, that in itself need not give rise to any additional spending. On the other hand, if the Government increases the volume of money by embarking on additional capital expenditure or by adding to the consumers' purchasing power, without taking away the new surplus by an increase of taxation, it is liable to increase also the velocity of circulation. The fact that in the thirties the American economy was slow in responding to 'New Deal' expenditure was largely due to the special circumstances referred to above.

(2) *Reducing Taxation.* Any reduction of direct taxes, provided that it is not accompanied by a corresponding reduction in public expenditure, tends to increase the purchasing power of the private sector of the economy. The chances are that at least part of the increase will be spent and re-spent again and again, thereby causing an increase in the velocity of circulation. A reduction of indirect taxation is apt to produce a similar effect, because lower prices are apt to tempt consumers to spend. For instance, a reduction of tobacco duty is liable to be followed by an increase of spending on tobacco. If some of the burden of taxation is shifted from those who are liable to spend to those who are liable to save, the result is an increase in the velocity of circulation.

One of the gravest mistakes of the monetarist school is that it presents the adoption of its teachings as a preferable alternative to adopting fiscal devices of monetary policy. In reality, the application of monetary devices may have to be reversed in face of irresistible demand for money unless they are supplemented by fiscal devices which affect the velocity of circulation, or by some other devices which reduce monetary requirements.

(3) *Repayment of Public Debt.* If the Government repays a maturing debt held largely by the public, the chances are that at least some of the recipients will spend the proceeds. In addition to the increase in the volume of money, its velocity is also likely to increase. No such dual effect is produced if the debt is held by banks, insurance companies, etc., though it is possible that the money thus released may be lent to people who in turn will spend it and would produce a multiplier effect.

(4) *Lowering of Interest Rates.* This tends to increase not only the quantity of money but also its velocity of circulation because it provides an inducement to borrow more and therefore to spend more freely. The private sector need not necessarily respond to this inducement, however, any more than it need respond to an increase in the volume of credit.

(5) *Moral Pressure and Propaganda.* In addition to increasing their own spending, Governments can accelerate the circulation of money by encouraging the spending of others. Moral persuasion, such as official declarations to the effect that now is the time to embark on capital investments or to purchase consumer goods, may or may not meet with the expected response, but it is reasonable to assume that the public is more inclined to spend if it is officially encouraged to do so. The organisation of festivities and various other devices are at the Government's disposal to reinforce its appeal by creating an atmosphere of optimism.

(6) *Removal or Relaxation of Restrictions on Instalment Buying.* If a minimum percentage of initial deposits in hire-purchase contracts has been fixed by the Government, its reduction or elimination tends to encourage consumers to engage in such purchases. A similar effect is produced by an increase of the maximum period officially fixed for the repayment of instalment debts, or by the removal of that restriction.

(7) *The Provision of 'Inducement Goods'.* In a country which has experienced a period of scarcity of goods, it is easy for the authorities to stimulate buying activity through arranging for the

reappearance of various kinds of goods which had been un-obtainable for some time past. The reappearance of such goods is liable to induce consumers to spend more freely. Inducement goods are used in backward countries to tempt the population to take up industrial employment in order to be able to spend more. In such situations the effect of the increase in the velocity of circulation on prices is liable to be offset in the long run by an increase in the volume of goods.

(8) *Increased Frequency of Payments.* This is one of the means, suggested by Cantillon more than two centuries ago, by which to provide trade with more money without an increase in the quantity of money. He argued that if rents were made payable more frequently the effect would be the same as that of an in-crease in the quantity of money, because the change in the practice would reduce monetary requirements, at the same time as increasing the velocity of circulation. Smaller amounts would change hands more frequently. The same result could be obtained if wages and salaries were to be paid at more frequent intervals. It is doubtful whether such an increase in the velocity of circulation would materially affect the demand.

(9) *Stepping up the Settlement of Accounts.* Delays or the absence of delays in the settlement of liablities by the public sector, by business firms or by private individuals make a consider-able difference to the velocity of circulation. Business firms could increase the velocity of circulation by settling their accounts promptly and by inducing their customers to act like-wise.

The following are the means at the disposal of the mone-tary authorities for reducing the velocity of circulation of money:

(1) *Moral Pressure and Propaganda to Discourage Spending.* In the same way as some members of the public are influenced in favour of spending when encouraged by official statements, economy campaigns are liable to meet with some response. The way the British public responded to exhortations of this kind in 1931 is an outstanding example. The National Savings Move-

ment also provides a useful instrument, though it works mainly through its effect on the quantity of money.

(2) *Reduction of Facilities for Spending*. This can be done by means of rationing or by allowing the supplies of goods to become exhausted. As a result the public will have less opportunity for making purchases. If the amount thus saved is invested in Government loans, it reduces the quantity of money. If it is accumulated in cash or bank balances it reduces the velocity of circulation.

(3) *Fiscal Devices*. An increase in the total amount of taxation unaccompanied by an increase of public expenditure would reduce the volume of money and would not directly affect the velocity of its circulation. It is possible, however, for the Government to leave the total substantially unchanged and shift the burden of taxation from classes which are likely to save to classes which are likely to spend. In doing so, the quantity of money would remain unchanged but the velocity of circulation would decline. A Budget surplus would indirectly lower the velocity of circulation in so far as it would cause a decline of prices and would tend to discourage spending. The multiplier effect would operate also in this direction. A reduction in the purchasing power of a single firm or individual could initiate a whole chain of reductions and their cumulative effect is liable to be a multiple of the amount with which the total purchasing power was originally reduced through higher taxation.

(4) *Government Borrowing*. This would not only reduce the volume of money but would also reduce its velocity of circulation, in the same way as repayment of some of the public debt would increase the velocity of circulation of the increased volume of money.

(5) *Raising Interest Rates*. At the same time as tending to lower the quantity of money, higher interest rates tend to lower its velocity of circulation by discouraging borrowing and spending.

(6) *Adoption or Reinforcement of Restrictions on Instalment Buying*. The imposition of a minimum percentage of initial deposits in hire-purchase contracts, or the increase of that percentage,

tends to discourage spending. A similar effect is produced by the fixing of a maximum period for the repayment of instalment debts, or by a reduction of such a period if previously fixed by the Government.

(7) *Reduced Frequency of Payments.* The suggestion of increasing the velocity of circulation of money through increasing the frequency of payments can be applied also in reverse direction. The authorities may make their payments at less frequent intervals and may try to induce others to act likewise in order to lower the velocity of circulation of money.

(8) *Delays in Meeting Liabilities.* We saw above that a stepping-up of the settlement of accounts and other liabilities tends to step up the velocity of circulation. In a similar way, the slowing-down of the settlement of liabilities tends to slow down the velocity of circulation.

There are other more far-fetched suggestions for devices to alter the velocity of circulation. During the early part of the nineteenth century Jeremy Bentham advocated interest-bearing money as a means of slowing down the velocity of circulation. A hundred years later Silvio Gesell advocated the opposite device, namely, the issue of notes which have to be stamped every week by their holders. His idea was that, in order to avoid the cost of affixing stamps on the notes, holders would hasten to spend their money and the velocity of circulation would thus increase.

Conceivably, the increase of the denomination of notes tends to slow down their velocity of circulation, and the reduction of their denomination tends to produce the opposite effect. Adam Smith observed that small money circulates faster than big money. The British Government's decision during the Second World War to withdraw Bank of England notes in excess of £5 may well have caused an unintentional increase in the velocity of circulation because, apart from other reasons, notes of small denomination do not lend themselves to hoarding to the same extent as notes of larger denomination.

Another factor observed by early writers on the subject was the difference in the velocity of circulation according to whether the money is held by wealthy people or by poor people. The former tend to hold larger cash balances, while the latter may feel impelled to spend their money as soon as they receive it. For this reason, among others, an egalitarian redistribution of wealth would tend to accelerate the velocity of circulation.

CHAPTER THIRTY-SIX

Determining the Quality of Money

HITHERTO we have been dealing with those means of monetary policy which are related directly or indirectly to the quantity of money. Monetary policy is concerned, however, also with the quality of money. In a narrower sense the quality of money means its intrinsic value, that is, its value for non-monetary purposes. In a broader sense the term covers also the buying capacity of money – which is a thing different from its purchasing power, as we propose to show below – and also the degree of the security of credit through which money originates under the modern system.

The money authorities are concerned with the quality of money either because it affects its quantity or because they accept the view that its purchasing power depends on its intrinsic value or its buying capacity. It stands to reason that if a high standard is set for the quality of the monetary object, whether it is sea-shells, or cattle, or coins, or credit through the granting of which deposits are created, it is bound to limit the quantity. If those in charge of monetary policy are anxious to avoid inflation, they can do so either by fixing direct limits to the quantity of money or by setting a high standard for its quality. At the same time, those who regard money as a commodity may feel that any deterioration of its intrinsic value must necessarily entail a corresponding decline of its purchasing power, apart altogether from the inflationary effect of an increase in its quantity.

We saw in earlier chapters that from an early phase in monetary history the State authority took it on itself to protect the money of its community against depreciation through private debasements. In many instances before the adoption of metallic currency the choice of the monetary object or the confirmation of its monetary use by the State authority aimed at making its debasement difficult. Coinage was introduced for that very purpose. Nevertheless, in innumerable instances the State authority itself debased its coinage for its own benefit or for the real or imaginary benefit of the community. From an early stage debasement was regarded as a State monopoly, even though private debasements had been the rule rather than the exception. On the other hand, from time to time the official monetary policy aimed at raising the quality of currency operations of re-coinage and other measures to eliminate clipped or counterfeit coins from circulation.

A policy of debasement stood to benefit the Treasuries largely because of the prolonged time-lag between the debasement and the rise in prices that followed it. It is often suggested by economic historians that debasement was a futile method from the point of view of the monarch who practised it, because, having depreciated his currency, he had to accept taxation in terms of that depreciated currency. In reality, however, some time had to pass before prices responded to the lowering of the quality of the coinage through debasement. For one thing, the general public was slow to notice a reduction in their metallic content. Moreover, as we pointed out before, prices, wages and other payments were very inelastic during the medieval period. This meant that the possession of a larger number of coins of the same denomination secured through debasement conferred on the monarch a lasting if not permanent advantage. He was in a position to finance wars or extravagant Court expenditure by increasing the number of coins minted out of the same quantity of metal. Had the price level responded spontaneously, his gain would have disappeared in a very short time.

In this respect the position was substantially the same as it is under modern inflation. The increase in the volume of money assists in the financing of a war largely because there is a time-lag between monetary expansion and its effect on the price level. The moment prices have caught up with the degree of monetary inflation or debasement, the advantage brought by the time-lag ceases, and the State authority can only secure further advantages by further doses of debasement or inflation. It is true that the State stands to benefit by the entire additional purchasing power created through debasement or inflation incurred in connection with a Budgetary deficit, while the adverse effects of higher prices are spread between the public and private sectors of the national economy. Even so, in the long run the State stands to pay dearly for its short-lived gains.

The effect of debasement on prices would have been even slower if it had not been accompanied by an increase of the quantity of currency. Prices were rising not only because the public came to realise gradually that the intrinsic value of the coins was lower, but also because the increase of its circulation created additional purchasing power during the transition period between the increase in the quantity of coins and the full adjustment of the price level to this increase.

All but the most irresponsible princes and their advisers were most reluctant to resort to debasement. It usually encountered strong opposition and caused much discontent. In England the Rolls of Parliament record complaints against debasements, and some kings were compelled to give an undertaking to abstain from tampering with the coinage. On the other hand, historians have the highest praise for kings who pursued the opposite policy by restoring the coinage to its original quality. These operations were not nearly as popular, however, in contemporary opinion as they are with the historian. They entailed grave inconveniences since they were bound to produce deflation. Producers and traders were at times almost as loud in complaining against the restoration of coinage as they had been against its debasement. When in A.D. 274 Aurelian attempted to restore the integrity of the debased Roman coinage, he was faced by a dangerous insurrection, the suppression of which cost the lives of 7,000 soldiers. In a more recent characteristic instance in 1650, Stuyvesant tried to improve the quality of the wampum shell currency in New

Amsterdam, but the deflation his measures entailed threatened to produce financial disaster, so that less than four months after issuing the ordinance he had to reverse it, and loose and imperfect bead-strings had to be accepted once more as legal tender.

The operation of Gresham's Law by which bad money tends to drive out good money has set a limit to many attempts at improving the quality of coinage. In many instances in monetary history coins of high quality regularly disappeared through hoarding or export, in defiance of the official monetary policy. Coins of low quality remained the main circulating medium. Nevertheless, strong and sound Governments aimed at maintaining the high quality of their coinage. Roman gold coins in ancient time, Byzantine coins during the Middle Ages, and sovereigns in more recent times acquired a world-wide reputation for their high quality.

Paper currency has, of course, no intrinsic value. Until recently it was widely held that its quality depended on its convertibility into gold or silver or, if it was inconvertible, on the prospects of its convertibility. The latter element was present even while the notes were actually convertible, because the size of the metallic reserves affected the prospects of being able to maintain their convertibility. Any action leading to an increase of the metallic reserve unaccompanied by an increase in the quantity of money tended to improve the quality of the notes. The proportion of the metallic reserve to the note circulation was regarded as the measurement of that quality. Once the convertibility of notes was suspended, their quality was deemed to be determined entirely by the prospects of a resumption of their convertibility.

Although in some countries there is an agitation for a restoration of convertibility into gold coins, in Britain and most other countries such a change has long been considered out of the question. On the other hand, the quality of money may be considered to depend partly on the degree of its convertibility or prospects of convertibility into other currencies and partly on its buying capacity. This latter term should not be confused with purchasing power, which depends on the level of prices. The buying capacity of a money has nothing to do with the price level, but with the diversity and range of goods and services on which the money can be spent. Towards the end of the Second World War the purchasing power of money was reasonably well maintained with the aid of price controls and rationing. Its buying capacity declined, however, very considerably, because most commercial stocks were exhausted and the range of goods and services which could be bought was very limited. The position was the same in many countries.

It was one of the tasks of monetary policy in the early postwar period to raise the buying capacity of money, through the increase in the range of goods on which it could be spent, by means of production or import. This end was gradually achieved, so that while the purchasing power of money continued to decline almost incessantly, its buying capacity increased materially during the early post-war years. The improvement of its quality did not prevent the depreciation of its purchasing power, though it seems reasonable to assume that had it not been for the increase of its buying capacity the fall in its purchasing power would have been even more pronounced. There would have been much less incentive to work or to sell goods in return for payment in a money which could hardly buy anything beyond one's meagre rations.

The quality of credit is yet another sphere in which monetary policy can function. It is regulated primarily by the banks themselves, who lay down certain rules mainly to safeguard their own interests by making sure that the credits are well secured and reasonably liquid. In pursuing sound banking principles they improve the quality of credit and of the money it creates, at the same time as limiting its quantity. The authorities may take a hand by giving the banks guidance when this is considered necessary. Long before the advent of scientific monetary management the banking community was in the habit of expecting some degree of guidance in this sphere from the Central Bank, which was considered to be in a better position than individual banks to judge the general trend. In any case, Central Banks had their own set of rules about bills which were eligible for rediscount, and these rules largely determined the requirements of all banks in this respect.

A high quality of credit money can be assured by insisting that bills and bank advances should be self-liquidating. Bills are seldom eligible for rediscount by the Central Bank unless they mature within three months. The quality of money created through bills or advances repayable in three months – during which period the goods whose production they finance may reasonably be expected to be sold – is obviously higher than that of money created in connection with unproductive Government expenditure or even with productive long-term capital expenditure. There is, of course, no noticeable difference between notes or bank deposits created through self-liquidating credits and those created through an increase of Budgetary expenditure. Nevertheless, even in the absence of an actual physical difference such as existed between full-valued and debased coins, there is bound to be some sort of intangible difference in favour of money produced through self-liquidating transactions financing the production of easily marketable goods. Any money created through long-term investment or unproductive Government expenditure remains in circulation and continues to give rise to additional demand each time it changes hands. On the other hand, money arising through self-liquidating short-term transactions is withdrawn when the credit is repaid and is reissued again in connection with some new productive self-liquidating transaction.

It is, or should be, the aim of monetary policy to ensure that any money created through unproductive or long-term transactions should be withdrawn at the earliest possible moment as a result of saving by the community. This end can be achieved through inducing the public to acquire newly-issued Government loans or other long-term securities. In doing so they relinquish for some time at any rate the use of the purchasing power they possess. The ideal state of affairs is when all capital investment and Budgetary deficits are financed out of savings immediately as and when they arise. In such circumstances most money in circulation would originate through self-liquidating transactions. Money originating through capital expenditure or Budgetary deficit should only be allowed to remain in circulation if monetary policy aims at an increase of prices or of business activity. It is important that in conditions of full employment the inflationary trend should not be accentuated by allowing such money to produce its full multiplier effect.

Discriminatory credit policy aiming at discouraging credits to branches of industry in which there is evidence of over-trading also contributes towards maintaining the high quality of credit money, in addition to preventing an undue increase in its quantity. It prevents the development of situations in which credits originally meant to be self-liquidating become frozen.

The quality of money was at its highest when it possessed full intrinsic value or at any rate when it was freely convertible into money with full intrinsic value. It tended to decline as and when the monetary role of gold diminished and the possibility of inflating it increased accordingly. There would be a further deterioration of the quality of money if the monetary role of gold should come to be eliminated altogether – which is the declared intention of the Governments of the United States and Britain.

The depreciation of money in the late sixties and early seventies was due in part to the spectacular increase of its quantity resulting from the expansion of the Euro-dollar market and of similar markets. But the deterioration of the quality of money caused by the non-self-liquidating and unsecured character of these and other credits has also contributed to the process of depreciation.

CHAPTER THIRTY-SEVEN

Price Controls

MEASURES affecting the quantity, price, quality or velocity of money aim at influencing business trends, but also at influencing the price level by affecting one of the factors that normally determine the trend of prices. They aim at affecting the volume of demand for goods and services. In resorting to these measures, monetary policy does not aim at resisting the operation of economic laws. On the contrary, it seeks to employ normal economic tendencies for its purpose. We now propose to examine in this chapter devices of monetary policy which aim at defying economic laws by preventing or hampering their natural operation. It is the object of price controls to prevent normal economic factors from producing their natural effect on the price level, or at any rate to moderate this effect. In this chapter we are no longer concerned with devices influencing the quantity of currency and credit in relation to the volume of goods and services. What we examine is the steps that the Government can take in order to achieve their desired ends without resorting to such devices.

Price controls are a very ancient means of monetary policy. They were already employed in the Hittite Empire during the fourteenth century B.C. An elaborate code fixed the price of domestic animals, agricultural products and other objects, and the wages of artisans, agricultural labourers, etc. An even more elaborate system of price fixing was adopted in the Roman Empire by Diocletian in the fourth century A.D. Throughout the Middle Ages highly elaborate systems of price controls were in force in many communities, especially in the practically closed economies of the cities with an advanced system of guilds. It was only comparatively recently that price fixing was virtually abandoned by most Governments. The nineteenth century was the century of the free play of economic forces. During and after the two World Wars, especially the Second World War, however, mankind reverted once more to price controls on an extensive scale.

The usual object of price controls is to achieve 'inflation without tears' by suppressing its natural effect on prices. This is considered necessary in given circumstances for several reasons. We saw in the previous chapter that inflation, like debasement, is liable to benefit the State to a particularly high degree during the time-lag between the issue of additional money and the completion of the rise in prices it tends to produce. It is obviously to the interest of the authorities, there-fore, to seek to prolong the transitional period by delaying or preventing prices from adapting themselves to the increased volume of money. Apart from this, it is to the interest of the whole community that the pace of currency depreciation should be mitigated and slowed down. Of course, the community's interests would be better served if the Government, instead of suppressing the effects of inflation, refrained from inflating. But if inflation is unavoidable – for instance in the interests of national defence – there is much to be said for suppressing its effects on prices as far as possible during a critical period.

Price controls pursue also social and political ends when they are largely confined to necessities and their object is to ensure adequate supplies for the poor. 'Rationing by purse' may be sound economics, but in given circumstances it may be anti-social, and it is apt to be unsound politics. Even from a purely economic point of view it is advantageous in given circumstances to keep down the prices of the essential com-ponents of the cost of living so as to avoid large-scale demands for wage increases as a result of a rise in the cost of living, provided that such an artificial state of affairs is maintained for a limited period only.

Even the most extensive system of price controls is unable to cover the whole range of goods and services available for sale.

Usually it begins with a relatively small number of necessities in short supply, spreading gradually over a wider and wider range of goods and services. A discrepancy develops between the trend of the controlled and uncontrolled sections of the price level and tends to widen considerably. If, as is often the case, price controls are accompanied by rationing, the public is unable to take full advantage of the artificially low prices by buying as much as it would like and could afford. Since the percentage of its inflated purchasing power that is used in the acquisition of rationed necessities thus declines, more will be available for the acquisition of uncontrolled goods and services.

The necessities are protected from the full effect of inflationary buying pressure, but that pressure exists nevertheless and becomes diverted towards the uncontrolled section of the price level. This means that while rises in the controlled section are kept lower than would be justified by the prevailing degree of inflation, rises in the uncontrolled section will tend to be more than proportionate to that degree. However, since a large part of the uncontrolled goods and services do not affect the cost of living of the wage-earners, their rise does not tend to accelerate the progress of inflation by leading to wage demands. A monetary policy which results in an unduly low price level in the controlled section of the economy and an unduly high price level in the uncontrolled section may be far from ideal, but it serves its purpose of delaying inflation. Provided that the artificial situation created is not unduly exaggerated or prolonged, its results are apt to be beneficial on balance in given circumstances.

Legislation enacting price controls must contain penalty provisions in order to be effective. Since, however, the system runs counter to economic laws and to human nature, even drastic penalties very often fail to discourage a large section of the public from breaking the law. In Britain the public is essentially law-abiding. Even so, the operation of price controls and rationing was accompanied by the development of black markets, if only on a relatively small scale. In other countries the policy of price controls was largely defeated by the extent of the black markets. In countries such as France or Italy the evasion of the law was the rule and its observance the exception. Only a fraction of the requirements and necessities could be covered on the basis of the controlled prices, so that for all practical purposes the price level in the black markets had to be regarded as the effective price level. Even in Soviet Russia and other Communist countries there have been black markets in spite of the threat of the death penalty, which was unable to ensure watertight price controls. This was realised after a while, and an officially tolerated free market in many goods was allowed to develop.

Penalty clauses in themselves are unable to ensure effective price controls. They have to be supplemented by other measures such as Government trading, or trading under licence, or subsidies. One of the reasons why rationing and price control of many necessities was incomparably more effective in Britain than in other countries was that the major part of the supplies had to be imported, and it is comparatively easy to control imports. The Government secured the necessary supplies from overseas by means of bulk buying, often on long-term contracts. In order to secure the supplies produced within the country, the Government had to adopt a system of subsidies. The farmers received the full price for their products in accordance with prevailing conditions. The consumers were charged considerably less and the difference was paid by the taxpayer in the form of subsidies. Likewise, the Government re-sold the imported food at a loss at the taxpayer's expense. During the fifties this system was replaced by one under which farmers received subsidies to compensate them for the superiority of their cost to those of producers abroad.

The failure of a policy of price controls through wholesale evasion has grave disadvantages from an economic, social and political point of view. It was largely responsible for the series of successive currency devaluations which France and Italy had to make after the Second World War. It was also largely responsible for the strength of the Communist Party in France and Italy. The inability of the lower income groups to meet their requirements for necessities otherwise than through purchases in the black market must have been largely responsible for the atmosphere of discontent in which subversive activities were thriving.

On the other hand, the success of price controls also entails grave disadvantages, because it tempts Governments to make excessive use of them in spite of the gross distortion of the economy it produces. This point is best illustrated by the effects of rent control. Rents are one of the few categories of prices the control of which can be enforced effectively not only in Britain but even in countries where price controls are generally ineffective. Because of the ease with which landlords can be compelled to continue to let their premises at uneconomical rents, a situation has developed in which these rents are no longer sufficient to meet the cost of essential repairs. Consequently rent-controlled property is allowed to deteriorate, and in many instances it becomes uninhabitable after prolonged rent control.

Moreover, artificially low rents tend to stimulate excessive demand for housing accommodation. Even the most effective housing drive which diverts an unduly large proportion of the nation's resources from other essential requirements is unable to keep pace with this demand. Rent control artificially stimulates the demand for something which cannot be supplied in sufficient quantity to meet the increased demand. The same thing is of course true about the price control of meat and other foodstuffs in short supply. But they at least can be rationed so as to ensure equal distribution on the basis of the artificially low prices. Since, however, rationing of housing accommodation is impracticable – except under dictatorship – the result of rent control is that those in possession enjoy the full advantages of low rents while those who are unfortunate enough to have to look for accommodation are either unable to meet requirements or have to pay exorbitant prices.

Since it is difficult if not impossible to ration and price-control certain necessities such as fresh vegetables or fruit, the cost of living of the lower income groups cannot be safe-guarded altogether against the effects of inflation with the aid of price controls. Since the artificially low prices and rationing of many necessities reduces the amount that can be spent on them, all but the poorest classes are liable to have a surplus purchasing power which they may employ on the purchase of luxuries. This means that in practice the taxpayer's money that is spent on subsidising price-controlled necessities, subsidises in reality also the purchase of luxuries.

On the other hand, it is argued that it is right that in the Welfare State necessities should be made available to all, if not free of charge, at any rate at very low prices. To that end a perpetuation of subsidised food and other necessities is favoured by many people even at the cost of economic disadvantages such as the perpetuation of high taxation. There are many other arguments for and against price controls, but it is outside our scope to deal with them.

Most economists admit that there is a great deal to be said for price controls during an emergency such as a war or even in conditions such as a rearmament drive, provided that the artificial situation that they create is not unduly exaggerated. Against its obvious advantages it is necessary to offset the disadvantages of the disequilibrium it creates. It tends to be cumulative in character. The longer price controls are applied, the more artificial the situation tends to become. This does not necessarily mean that they must be condemned unconditionally as a means of monetary policy. What it means is that those applying them should be fully aware of their long-range disadvantages, instead of working under the delusion that State authority is omnipotent and is in a position to defy permanently the law of supply and demand.

Price controls are apt to stimulate artificially the demand for goods the supplies of which cannot keep pace with the demand. Consumption in any given country may be raised by price controls beyond the level which that country can afford. The result is an adverse balance of payments which may eventually compel the Government to apply measures by which to reduce the volume of purchasing power or to devalue.

Government trading is another device by which Governments may seek to prevent or moderate a rise in prices. Its primary aim is usually outside the realm of monetary policy. The Government may embark on buying up supplies in order to secure scarce stocks or to ensure their fair distribution. It is a highly controversial point whether bulk buying by Governments makes for higher or lower prices. Long-term contracts with producing countries may have a steadying effect on the prices of imported food and raw materials and may play therefore some part in a policy of stabilising the price level.

A reduction of customs duties is a much less artificial way of enforcing price reductions. It was resorted to by West Germany in the late fifties; and by France and Spain in 1963.

Yet another means by which the Government may try to intervene in order to influence the price level is legislation against monopolies and restrictive practices. One of the main arguments in support of such legislation is that it is likely to result in lower prices within the range of goods to which it applies. On the other hand, it must be admitted that monopolies and restrictive practices have a steadying influence on the price level, while unfettered competition is apt to cause instability. If, rightly or wrongly, a Government adopts price controls, their enforcement is greatly simplified by the existence of monopolies or of practices such as resale price maintenance, under which the trade associations ensure the maintenance of officially approved prices.

Monetary policy possesses devices not only for preventing a rise in prices or bringing about their reduction, but also for pursuing the opposite end. In given situations the authorities may aim at preventing falls in prices or at enforcing their rise by devices of price control. The fixing of maximum prices in general may serve the purpose of raising prices because in given circumstances maximum prices are apt to become minimum prices. By raising maximum prices the authorities may ensure favourable prices for producers.

Price controls are in some instances supplemented by controls of wages. They too can operate in both ways. The Government may fix or influence a wage ceiling in an attempt at slowing down inflation, or it may fix minimum wages. The former is an instrument of monetary policy, the latter an instrument of social policy, though it does produce also a monetary effect. The attempt to prevent or mitigate the rise of wages came to be looked upon in the sixties as one of the most important means of monetary policy. It will be discussed in detail in Chapter 38.

CHAPTER THIRTY-EIGHT

Incomes Policy

ALTHOUGH the influence of changes in the volume of incomes
on the value of money is no new discovery, it was not until the
middle fifties that monetary authorities came to take a really
active interest in it. Until then they accepted, consciously or
otherwise, the conventional formula of the quantity theory of
money, under which prices were determined by the quantity of
money and, to a less extent, by its velocity of circulation and by
the volume of goods. Yet already, during the First World War,
the German economist Robert Liefmann had put forward an
alternative theory claiming that an increase in the quantity of
money is only inflationary as and when it results in an increase
of incomes. There can be little doubt that consumer demand
largely depends on the total of tens of millions of consumers'
current incomes, even though their willingness to spend their
incomes, to accumulate or draw on their capital, and to incur
or repay debts must also be taken into consideration. Spending
by business firms too is affected by their current profits, even
though in their case the relative importance of accumulating or
drawing on capital resources and of borrowing is much higher.

The reason why during the fifties the monetary authorities
in Britain and elsewhere came to take an increasingly active
interest in the trend of incomes was not a belated acceptance of
the long-neglected Liefmann theory – which faded into oblivion
during the inter-war period – but their realisation that the
policies based on the quantity theory had failed to produce the
desired results. They found that, although credit squeezes
tended to curtail the volume of money, wages continued to
advance as a result of the change in the balance of power in

favour of the trade unions since the war. It became possible to enforce wage increases even during recessions, although the extent of such increases was admittedly smaller than those enforced during booms. With mild exaggeration it has been forecast that the British Shipbuilding Workers' Unions will enforce a wage increase the day before the last British shipyard is closed down for lack of orders.

Many quarters have reluctantly come to the conclusion that, in order to be able to check inflation with the aid of the devices based on the quantity theory, the credit squeeze would have to be so drastic as to reduce demand very considerably and to make it thereby entirely unprofitable for employers to continue production after having conceded further 'unearned' wage increases. It would not be possible to bring this about without creating unemployment on a very large scale, which was contrary to the official policy aiming at full employment. The American Report on Money and Credit reached the conclusion that the cost of checking inflationary booms by means of restrictive monetary policies could be so high in terms of unemployment or lower growth that alternative means should be sought to be applied.

The authorities of various countries did in fact try on many occasions such alternative ways by which to check an excessive rise in incomes. In Britain Sir Stafford Cripps tried in the forties to persuade employers and employees to accept a voluntary restraint on dividends and wages. Subsequent Chancellors of the Exchequer and Prime Ministers, too, frequently resorted to exhortations to that end. Broadly speaking, until the late fifties these exhortations met with some measures of response on the part of employers but with virtually none on the part of employees. And from about 1959 onwards the former, too, discarded such self-restraint as they had practised in earlier years until the advent of the Labour Government.

Throughout the post-war period wage demands were limited only by the maximum increase organised labour expected to be able to secure without having to resort to major strikes. Employers, on their part, after displays of more or less token resistance, cheerfully conceded any wage demands which they expected to be able to pass on to the consumer. Fears of not being able to raise their prices to a sufficient extent, or of encountering consumer resistance, or of competition, were the only considerations that imposed some slight restraint on them in conceding increases. Owing to the escalating increase of employees' incomes, there was never any noteworthy consumer resistance, and business firms felt reasonably safe in assuming that their competitors too would add, as a matter of course, any wage increase to their prices.

In face of this attitude, exhortations by the authorities that wage increases must not exceed the increase in productivity met with scant response until the middle sixties. There was an acute scarcity of labour in most industries most of the time, and labour knew how to exploit its scarcity value. Employers, in their effort to attract labour, conceded increases even in addition to rates agreed in national wage agreements. They also conceded very costly 'fringe benefits'. As such benefits have greatly improved working conditions, they constituted a welcome manifestation of progress. Unfortunately there was no sign of any willingness on the part of most employees to show their appreciation by contributing towards the achievement of higher productivity. Like the higher wages, these benefits too were largely 'unearned'.

The fact that wage increases continued unabated during the period of stable cost of living in 1958–9 disposes of the trade unionists' argument that they merely endeavoured to maintain the level of real wages in face of the decline in the purchasing power of money. The annual rounds of wage increases effectively prevented manufacturers from passing on to the consumer declines in costs resulting from mass production, automation, falls in prices of raw materials, etc. They saw no point in temporarily reducing the widely advertised prices of their goods, since the next wage increase would compel them to raise their prices to their previous figures or even above them.

There was until the late fifties a fair degree of self-imposed restraint on dividends, not so much in public-spirited response

to official appeal as on account of the policy of most managements to become largely self-financing by retaining a large
proportion of their profits. This practice, a result of the
managerial revolution, kept down Stock Exchange values for a
long time, thereby keeping down capital gains, because Stock
Exchange prices are largely determined by actual yields and
prospects of yields rather than by the intrinsic value of undistributed profits. It was not until the increase of reserves led to
bonus issues or take-over bids that substantial rises developed
in equities. Such transactions became increasingly frequent
from the late fifties, and their mere anticipation caused Stock
Exchange prices to soar. This, together with the growing
anticipation of a non-stop expansion of profits, resulted in
substantial capital gains which contributed towards increasing
consumer demand, especially for luxuries.

It would be a mistake, however, to believe that the addition
of, say, £100 million to dividends or to capital gains has the
same inflationary effect as the addition of the same amount to
total wage payments. In so far as the beneficiaries of dividends
and capital gains belong to higher income brackets, the
inflationary effect of their higher incomes or capital gains tends
to remain relatively moderate, for the following reasons:

(1) A larger proportion is taken away in taxation of corporations and of shareholders, especially in countries where
capital gains are also subject to taxation.

(2) A larger proportion of taxed profits is saved.

(3) A larger proportion of what is not saved is spent on goods
whose prices do not affect the cost of production or the cost of
living.

If the recipient of an increased dividend or the beneficiary of
a capital gain bids up the prices of French post-impressionist
paintings or of English eighteenth-century silver, it does not
put up either the cost of living or the cost of production. If, on
the other hand, he buys a Rolls-Royce or builds a new house,
his transaction does tend to affect both cost of living and cost
of production. The additional demand for labour tends to
cause an increase in the total wage payments, through addi-

tional employment, or through additional overtime paid at higher rates, or through additional wage increases enforced as a result of the increase in the demand for labour.

The conclusion from the above argument is that increases of profits, dividends and capital gains – or, for that matter, of professional earnings or salaries in the higher brackets – are only inflationary if, and to the extent to which, they become eventually translated into an increase of wage payments or of other incomes of the lower brackets. This does not mean that, in so far as the additional higher earnings or capital gains are spent on goods which do not affect the cost of living or the cost of production, the surplus consumer purchasing power vanishes into thin air. Its fate depends on the way the sellers of such goods in turn use the proceeds. They may save it or they may use it to repay debts, or they may spend it on goods which do not affect the cost of living or the cost of production. But to the extent to which they spend it on other kinds of goods or services they do accentuate inflation, because they lead to higher demands for consumer goods and to larger payments of wages. So the originally non-inflationary increases of higher incomes or of capital gains may gradually become inflationary through their multiplier effect, even though much of the additional purchasing power completely disappears in the process through taxation, saving, debt repayment or non-inflationary purchases. Even to the extent to which the effect becomes inflationary, it is produced more slowly.

On the other hand, increased wages are immediately inflationary in two different ways: they directly increase the cost of production and they directly increase consumer demand for goods whose prices increases tend in turn to affect cost of production and cost of living – a combination of 'cost-push' and 'demand-pull' inflation. The stipulation that wage increases must be granted unconditionally 'with no strings attached' means that they are not accompanied by any increase in output, so that their effect on cost of production is a matter of simple arithmetic. If shorter working hours are conceded without any corresponding cuts in basic wages, the inflationary effect is even more pronounced, because more overtime is worked at higher pay rates. Additional overtime working – provided that it does not result from a reduction of working hours – does result in an increase in output. In spite of this, it is inflationary because of the higher overtime rates of pay. Moreover, because employees are anxious to increase their overtime earnings, they tend to slow down, in order to secure more overtime pay. For these reasons, even if there is no cut in working hours at basic pay rates, increased working of overtime adds more to wage payments than to output and tends to increase both cost inflation and demand inflation.

From the above it appears that it is mistaken to regard, for the purposes of monetary policy, higher profits and higher wages as if their inflationary effects were identical. The difference between their effects has been largely ignored in the course of the controversies over the need for wage restraint. Yet it weakens the economic case in favour of restraining profits to the same extent as wages, in pursuing a disinflationary policy of income restraint.

The main inflationary effect of higher profits lies in the psychological stimulus given to wage demands – about which more will be said below – and in their effect in stimulating production. Higher profits also enable and encourage employers to concede higher wages, and they are able to increase their manpower by outbidding other employers in order to attract labour. In other countries trade union leaders realise, and are able to satisfy the rank and file, that high profits are in accordance with the interests of employees. This is the attitude of most American trade unionists. As Galbraith implied in a famous passage in his book *The Affluent Society*, the British labour movement is almost alone in continuing to cling to outdated emotional egalitarianism.

Higher profits tend to accentuate inflation also through the pipeline effect of increasing output described in Chapter 10. Owing to the time-lag between the input (the amount spent in order to increase production) and the appearance of the output on the market, the additional demand for capital goods and consumer goods resulting from the increase of input exerts its pressure making for higher prices long before the additional output begins to exert pressure in the opposite sense. This means that monetary policy has to run in order to stand still – it has to make disinflationary efforts if it aims at neutralising the 'pipeline effect' of increasing production on prices during the transitional period.

In view of the above argument about the difference in the degree to which additional wages and profits generate inflation, there is everything to be said, from a purely economic point of view, for differentiating between them for the purpose of monetary policy. While expanding profits tend to stimulate both current employment and economic growth – always provided that they are kept within bounds by competition unfettered by monopolies, restrictive practices or unduly high tariff walls – wage increases that are in excess of the expansion of the output simply increase the cost of production and the cost of living, to the detriment of consumers, of employers and, ultimately, of employees themselves. They compel the authorities from time to time to resort to disinflationary measures that hamper the expansion of production and lead to the curtailment of overtime, to short-time working and to unemployment. Trade unions had only themselves to blame for the increase of unemployment in Britain during the late sixties and in 1970–1. Had it not been for their excessive wage demands, and for their restrictive practices that prevented a corresponding increase in productivity, there would have been no need for the Government to adopt disinflationary measures.

Such is the extent of the influence of wages on the price level that, according to Professor J. R. Hicks, the monetary system has become elastic and can accommodate itself to changes in wages. 'Instead of being on the Gold Standard, we are on a Labour Standard.' Perhaps the term 'Wages Standard' would be even more appropriate. Under that system, he remarked in an article in the *Economic Journal* in 1956, the value of money is a mere by-product of the process of wage-fixing. Amidst post-war conditions, if there is not enough money to meet the increased requirements resulting from higher wages, an increase in the velocity of circulation that is liable to accompany demand inflation tends to meet the deficiency. So it is substantially correct to say that under the Wages Standard the monetary circulation adapts itself to the higher level of wages, just as under the gold standard it adapted itself to the volume of gold. So much for Professor Friedman's monetarist school.

It has become a widespread habit, not only on the part of spokesmen of the labour movement but on the part of all shades of expansionists, to condemn the measures adopted to check or slow down inflation. They hardly ever mention that such measures are necessitated almost entirely by excessive wage demands which are, therefore, indirectly responsible for the setbacks brought about by the resulting disinflationary measures. It is true that there are irresponsible inflationists who press the Governments to disregard rising prices and to proceed with expansion even if it does accentuate the inflationary wage spiral. But the more sober view is that monetary policy should give a high priority to the aim of checking or moderating inflation, preferably with the aid of devices that would not cause unemployment or check expansion.

The adoption of a wage policy is by far the most important device to that end. It has to pursue a twofold objective:

(1) To determine labour's fair share in the benefit resulting from the increase of productivity, by fixing a limit to wage increases in any given year, either in terms of an actual percentage or in relation to the rise in the output.

(2) To ascertain the relative remuneration of various categories of labour and thereby to bring the present 'leapfrogging' of wage claims to an end.

A century of Communist–Socialist propaganda has succeeded in popularising the ideology based on the Marxian assumption that all goods and services are the products of labour and that anybody not directly engaged in the production of goods obtains an 'unearned' share in the proceeds. Once this ideology is accepted, it appears to follow from it logically that labour is entitled to the full benefit resulting from technological progress or from other methods of increasing productivity.

Conclusions of a totally different character would be reached if the argument were based on different ideological premises. Spokesmen of middle-class interests could argue to their own satisfaction that, so far from exploiting physical labourers, the middle classes are themselves exploited as a result of excessive wages. They might claim that, were it not for the savings and brains of the middle classes, physical labourers would be doomed to a very low standard of living, considering that all the equipment that has increased the output was the result of middle-class inventions and was produced with the aid of the savings which middle classes had accumulated and had been prepared to risk.

This picture is of course a fantastically absurd distortion, but no more so than is the Marxian ideology. Yet the masses of workers swear by that ideology even if they are not consciously Marxists and are in fact entirely unfamiliar with the writings of Karl Marx. Unless they can be made to realise that there is another side to the argument, it would be impossible to come to some reasonable and mutually acceptable formula that would lay down some reasonable principles – subject to variation from case to case and from time to time – on the basis of which each side would receive a fair share. In the absence of such compromise a large section of expert opinion is inclined to support the monetarist policy aiming at the prevention of inflation solely with the aid of credit squeeze.

If only it were possible to make the trade unions realise that the alternative to a sensible wage policy is either non-stop inflation or disinflationary measures that would inevitably check progress towards a higher standard of living, possibly they might show more willingness to accept some compromise in their relative slice of the cake, in order not to obstruct the increase of the whole cake. Failing such compromise, a large section of expert opinion is likely to come to the conclusion favouring a monetary policy which aims at a prolonged interruption of economic growth, and even at bringing about a temporary setback, for the sake of bringing trade unions to a more resonable frame of mind towards the adoption of an incomes policy. For it is assumed that, once a sensible incomes policy is adopted, progress could be resumed at a sufficiently increased rate to compensate, and more than compensate, for such a setback.

An understanding about the approximate share of employees must be accompanied by an understanding between the various trade unions about their relative share in that total. In the absence of an agreement on wage differentials between skilled labour and unskilled labour as well as between the various occupations, it would be impossible to prevent 'leap-frogging' of wage claims. Any major wage concession to one category would continue to trigger off other wage claims and each category would continue to seek to improve its relative position at the expense of the masses of consumers.

One of the essential conditions of successful monetary policy is to prevent inflation resulting from 'leap-frogging' wage increases by groups in a strong bargaining position, followed by wage increases that have to be granted sooner or later to groups in weaker bargaining positions for the sake of preventing a depletion of their manpower below the level at which their essential if unprofitable services could be maintained.

The familiar answer to any attempt at pleading for a better spirit in labour relations is that the 'working classes' cannot by expected to make 'unilateral sacrifices' while employers derive full benefit from the 'free-for-all' system. The answer to the contention that any wage restraint must be accompanied by a restraint on profits and dividends is that, in order to be logical, any falls in profits and cuts in dividends must be accompanied by corresponding cuts in wages. The acceptance of the principle that wage-earners are entitled to increases when profits and dividends rise but must remain immune from effects of unfavourable business conditions would create new privileged classes. Yet, in defiance of logic, and even though, as we sought to prove above, higher profits and dividends are not nearly as inflationary as higher wages, it is widely considered advisable to make concessions by meeting to some extent the egalitarian point of view for the sake of allaying discontent. Although from a purely economic point of view an incomes policy which is confined to wages and to lower-bracket salaries would be more effective, it would in practice encounter strong resistance, and it is, therefore, strongly argued that it should also cover corporation profits and dividends.

While it would be practicable to restrain dividends, this would discourage the provision of risk capital and would reduce the incentive for managements to take reasonable risks for the sake of being able to pay higher dividends. The result would be a strong discouragement of experiments with new devices and inventions whose marketability is as yet unproven. Investors would not deem it worth their while to depart from the conservative type of shares which pay a reliable 6 per cent year after year.

When it comes to trying to restrict profits, it is not only inexpedient but even impracticable. Profits are a residual item which are liable to fluctuate. Their upper limit can only be fixed by means of imposing some form of confiscatory tax on amounts in excess of that limit – such as the Excess Profits Tax in Britain during the Second World War – but this would only encourage wasteful production, since there would be no advantage in keeping down costs once the limit is approached. Those who argue in favour of restricting dividends and profits overlook the fact that they are liable to decline from time to time, and that profits might give way to losses, while wages are virtually a 'one-way street'.

What matters from the point of view of a successful monetary policy is that an agreement about incomes policy should not be achieved at the cost of accepting a degree of egalitarianism that would greatly discourage individual initiative and would thereby tend to reduce or keep down the production of goods and services. Inflation resulting from a decline or inadequate increase in the output would get the worst of both worlds. It would combine the disadvantages of an inflation with those of a depression. If an expansion of the output is accompanied by inflation, it creates at any rate an atmosphere of prosperity which, artificial as it may be to some extent, contributes to the welfare and happiness of the majority at the expense of those with fixed incomes. But rising prices brought about by contracting or inadequately increasing the output, accompanied by continuous rises in nominal wages, would mean a decline of employment concurrently with rising cost of living.

When trade unions in Britain express suspicion that incomes policy simply means wage restraint they are not far from the truth. But since it is the unending succession of unilateral wage concessions and other concessions to employees that is primarily responsible for the erosion of the currency, it does not seem unreasonable to expect the wage-earners to make a long-overdue contribution towards progress by agreeing to some measure of restraint and to a co-ordination of their claims. Any further wage increases should be conditional on increases in productivity.

The adoption of an incomes policy must not mean depriving employees of their share in the benefits of progress. Since the maintenance of progress depends on an expansion of consumer demand, it is absolutely essential, in order to avoid a repetition of the crises of the thirties, to distribute enough purchasing power among the lower income groups to enable them to buy the increased volume of goods and services produced.

CHAPTER THIRTY-NINE

Foreign Exchange Policy

MOST authors dealing with the subject of monetary policy consider foreign exchange policy as a thing apart. Yet the policies aiming at influencing the domestic monetary situation and those aiming at influencing the foreign exchange situation are closely interrelated. Measures affecting the volume, purchasing power, velocity of circulation or quality of money are liable to react on exchange rates. Conversely, any noteworthy and sustained rise or fall in the exchange rates is liable to react on the internal monetary situation. Indeed, the internal and international aspects of money are two inseparable aspects of the same thing. As a general rule, anything that concerns the one is bound to concern the other, Internal price levels and exchange values are apt to be influenced by the same factors and also to influence each other reciprocally. Monetary policy may use foreign exchanges as means to pursue its ends in respect of the internal monetary situation. It may also use various monetary or non-monetary devices to influence the foreign exchange situation.

Beyond doubt, exchange rates constitute the most obvious and the most sensitive barometer indicating the value of money. The metaphor, however, is not altogether correct. No barometer has ever yet been known to have influenced the weather in the least; on the other hand, movements on exchanges are liable to react sharply on the internal monetary situation. This fact has long been realised. Indeed, from time to time it has been grossly exaggerated by Governments guilty of the mismanagement of their currencies. It was convenient to put the blame for the deterioration of the internal monetary situation on exchange depreciation over which they claimed to have no control. The great debasement of Henry VIII in 1551, one of the most flagrant instances of currency juggling in British history, provided an early instance of that attitude. Those responsible for it were at pains to put the blame on speculators, even though the depreciation of the exchange merely expressed the debasement of the coinage. Again in Britain during the Napoleonic Wars the official view that the increase of the Bank of England's inconvertible note issue was not the cause of the depreciation of sterling in terms of gold – which was claimed to be the consequence of the adverse balance and speculation – was upheld in face of the more enlightened views put forward by Ricardo and the Bullion Committee.

However, one-sided as the view is that the internal value of money depends on its exchange rate, it contains a sufficient degree of truth to make it evident that monetary policy, concerned with maintaining the internal stability of money, cannot afford to ignore exchange rates, and that any action taken in respect of foreign exchanges has very strong bearing on the internal monetary situation.

The authorities can influence the foreign exchange position to a great extent by means of devices applied to the internal monetary position. In addition, there are general devices of economic policy which can be used for influencing foreign exchanges directly in the desired sense. The authorities have a powerful weapon in their ability to influence international capital movements. We saw in earlier chapters how short-term capital movements respond to changes of interest rates, The same factor affects also long-term capital movements – to a lesser extent – in that it influences the extent of lending and of borrowing abroad.

Monetary policy is able to influence the level of long-term interest rates. The Government, by influencing the yield of its own long-term loans through open-market operations and other devices, also influences the rate of interest at which foreign borrowers can cover their requirements in the loan market. It can encourage or discourage domestic borrowers to cover their capital requirements abroad. In addition, it can impose official or unofficial embargoes on the issue of foreign loans in the domestic market as an alternative to discouraging them by means of raising the interest rates on its own loans. An unofficial embargo on foreign loans was more or less in operation in Britain during the greater part of the inter-war period, as a means of safeguarding sterling against adverse pressure through over-lending. It was replaced by an official embargo at the outbreak of the Second World War, and right up to the time of writing the issue or private placing of securities for the benefit of foreign borrowers requires special permission.

A more sophisticated device is to impose reserve requirements on long-term or short-term funds raised abroad in general and in the Euro-currency market or in the Euro-issue market in particular. Since the middle sixties, borrowing and lending in these markets has overshadowed in importance operations in conventional markets. Encouragement or discouragement of such operations influences considerably not only domestic money markets and capital markets but also foreign exchange markets.

Yet another way in which the authorities can safeguard the exchange value of sterling against the effects of excessive lending abroad is through insisting that the proceeds must be spent within the lending country. This principle was adopted to an increasing degree during the inter-war period by Britain, as a sharp contrast to her liberal attitude before the First World War. Even the United States resorted to it in connection with the operations of the official Import-Export Bank. In the case of Marshall Aid and U.S. military aid, and of subsequent financial aids, the rule was that a large part of the dollars received must be spent in the United States, though a certain proportion was made expendable in the receiving country and on 'off-shore purchases' in third countries.

Customs tariffs and embargoes on imports are frequently adopted not for the purpose of protecting domestic industries against foreign competition, but for the sake of protecting the national exchange against pressure through an adverse trade balance, An outstanding instance of customs tariffs adopted for that purpose was that of the McKenna Duties. They were adopted during the First World War not in order to protect the British motor industry and the other industries concerned against American and other foreign competition, but in order to safeguard sterling against excessive selling pressure. Most of the discriminatory quantitative import restrictions adopted during and after the Second World War pursued a similar aim.

Hitherto we have been dealing with indirect official intervention to safeguard exchanges. The authorities have, however, a wide variety of means of influencing exchange rates also by means of direct intervention in the foreign exchange market. The object of such intervention is to keep the rate stable, or at any rate steady; or to moderate a depreciation or appreciation of the exchange; or to cause a depreciation or appreciation, according to the ends monetary policy pursues.

The maintenance of an absolutely stable exchange rate is know as 'pegging'. It was applied extensively during both World Wars. During the First World War free dealings in the foreign exchange market were maintained, but the New York agents of the British authorities had instructions to buy all sterling offered in New York at the official rate of $4.76. Likewise, the French franc was pegged for years in relation to both sterling and the dollar. During the Second World War the maintenance of fixed exchange rates was achieved not by official intervention in the foreign exchange market, but by means of instituting an official monopoly of exchange dealings at fixed official rates.

When in 1951 dealings were resumed in the foreign exchange market of London, the authorities fixed the upper and lower limits of exchange rates at which they were prepared to buy or sell dollars in order to prevent the sterling–dollar rate from rising or falling beyond those limits. Some scope was allowed for fluctuations within a narrow range, so that the policy was not of pegging but one of maintaining sterling steady around its official parity of $2.80. The same system of 'support points' was adopted by most Governments that adhered to the International Monetary Fund.

From time to time during the thirties various exchange rates were maintained reasonably steady over prolonged periods by means of systematic official intervention whenever there was a tendency for the rates to depart from the rate or from the approximate level at which the authorities wanted to hold them. But the aims of the official monetary policy are often more ambitious than the mere maintenance of the exchanges at a given level. The authorities often deem it necessary for a variety of reasons to intervene in order to bring about an appreciation or a depreciation of the exchange. Instances of the latter course can be found during the period of competitive currency depreciations in the thirties, More often than not, the authorities did not actually intervene by operations causing their currency to depreciate. They merely abstained from supporting it against an adverse trend. This meant that while they intervened to buy up any excess of supplies of foreign exchanges, they did not intervene to make up for any deficiency of supplies but allowed the rate to find its own level at which private supply and demand balanced. Over a period this meant that they drained the market of a large proportion of the foreign exchanges, so that it was unable ot meet the demand unless and until the exchange depreciated. By such means it was possible to build up a foreign exchange reserve and to bring the exchange rate to a level at which the task of supporting it became easier.

Throughout monetary history the authorities of various countries frequently intervened to prevent an unwanted depreciation by methods much more active than those practised for the purpose of holding the rate at a fixed figure. Many instances can be quoted of attempts at 'squeezing' those speculators who gambled for a depreciation of the exchanges concerned. We saw in Chapter 12 that the accumulation or defence of the gold reserve is one of the major ends of monetary policy, for the sake of which the authorities are at times prepared to put up with the disadvantages of fluctuations of exchange rates. Such fluctuations provide them with opportunities for profitable intervention.

In the nineties there was a successful squeeze of 'bears'

speculating against Russian rouble notes. The Finance Minister, Count Witte, achieved this aim by suddenly forbidding the export of rouble notes from Russia. Speculators in Berlin who had sold roubles for future delivery were unable to deliver the roubles they had sold. As a result of their efforts to buy. the rate went to a high premium. The speculators were taught a sharp and costly lesson, and for some time they kept away from the rouble. Thirty years later M. Poincaré carried out a somewhat similar 'bear squeeze' against speculators in francs in 1924. As by then speculation was no longer in notes but in exchanges, the prohibition of supplying speculators with notes was replaced by a restriction on franc credits to be granted to them. This, together with active intervention with the aid of credits raised in London and New York, brought about a sharp appreciation of the franc and gravely penalised speculators. Since French finances remained shaky, speculative attacks against the franc were resumed from time to time. In 1926 Poincaré intervened once more successfully and secured stabilisation for the franc for a period of ten years. During the late thirties, however, the franc came under fire again and many attempts at official intervention failed to produce a lasting effect. There are many instances of such 'bear squeezes' during the sixties, carried out with the aid of the IMF and groups of Central Banks.

It is evident that the authorities stand a better chance of effective intervention if they have scope for manoeuvring with the exchange. The scope of any manoeuvring is bound to be very limited if the rate has to be kept within a very narrow range. If the speculators know that sterling will not appreciate in any circumstances above $2.42, then their risk in speculating against it even when it is quoted at the low limit of $2.38 appears to be negligible. Many of them consider it well worth taking on the chance of making a large profit in case the authorities should be unable to prevent a substantial depreciation. On the other hand, if the upper limit of sterling exchange is not fixed, then speculators are not in a position to calculate the extent of their risk, which may well be considered by many people so heavy as to offset their chances to make a profit. This is one of the arguments in favour of a flexible sterling. But there are many much weightier considerations against it.

From an early period various Governments recognised the advantages of active intervention aimed at bringing about an appreciation of the exchange. This was done repeatedly and extensively in the sixteenth century by Gresham, who operated on behalf of his Tudor masters in the Antwerp market. In a Memorandum attributed to him, written some four hundred years ago, he advocated the establishment of what would be called in modern language an Exchange Stabilisation Fund. The only reason why his advice was not followed was that the Government could not spare the funds required for the purpose. Even in the absence of regular resources he managed, however, to raise substantially the valuse of sterling on more than one occasion, or at any rate to safeguard it against depreciation. In my *History of Foreign Exchange* I quote a number of similar early instances of official intervention.

During the eighteenth and nineteenth centuries the policy of active intervention had fallen into disuse. Official foreign exchange policy in more recent times largely followed the principle Gresham stated in paragraph 8 (1) of the Memorandum attributed to him: 'The waye to rayse the exchaunge for England: By making money scante in Lumbard strete.'

Throughout the nineteenth century and right up to the early thirties of the present century, the British monetary authorities largely confined themselves to influencing exchange rates by means of raising and lowering interest rates. They abstained from active intervention in the foreign exchange markets. Under the gold standard, exchange rates were allowed to take care of themselves. They fluctuated freely between gold import points and gold export points.

For a long time the Bank of England did not even have a foreign exchange department of its own. It was not until the early thirties that it came to assume an active role in the foreign exchange market, acting on behalf of the Treasury. After some costly initial mistakes the Exchange Equalisation Account became a formidable factor, and its interventions were on balance highly successful. By the middle thirties it became so efficient that speculators left sterling severely alone, and the turnover in foreign exchanges was confined largely to genuine commercial and arbitrage operations. The authorities intervened from time to time in order to prevent or mitigate the effect of seasonal or other temporary demand for dollars. Some big requirements such as those of large tobacco-importing companies were satisfied directly in circumvention of the market in order to obviate the psychological effect of the evidence of a sudden heavy demand for dollars. Towards the end of the thirties, however, it became necessary once more to intervene actively in the market.

Other Central Banks adopted a policy of active intervention long before the Bank of England. During the nineteenth and early twentieth centuries it was part of the functions of the Austro-Hungarian Bank to relieve the market of seasonal surpluses of exchanges and to supply the market between export seasons, This. together with resistance to speculative fluctuations, has long been regarded as forming part of the normal functions of monetary policy.

During the First World War the monetary authorities of a number of countries embarked on a much more ambitious task. They attempted to defend the national currency against depreciation in defiance of the fundamental adverse trend caused by internal inflation and the strongly unfavourable trade balance. Although prices in Britain were rising much faster than in the United States, the official policy maintained right up to 1919 the sterling–dollar rate at a discount of about 2 per cent of the pre-war parity of 4.86. This was possible so long as imports were handicapped by war-time lack of shipping space. Immediately after the war, however, lower prices in the United States resulted in heavy imports, and when the sterling-dollar rate was unpegged it immediately depreciated sharply. France and Italy had a similar experience.

In the Second World War exchange stability was achieved by exchange control which, together with import control, continued during the post-war period. For this reason it was possible to maintain the exchange rate at its war-time figure up to 1949 when the Government felt impelled to devalue sterling. This experience shows that attempts at maintaining exchange at an artificial level are liable to fail in the long run even if they are supported by a system of controls which tends to isolate, to a high degree, the economy of the country concerned from world economy.

Hitherto we have been dealing with intervention in the form of operating in spot exchanges, There have been, however, many instances of intervention in the form of official forward exchange operations. In 1931, for instance, sterling was defended by means of official selling of forward dollars. In 1927-8 the Bank of France diverted an unwanted influx of funds by means of swap operations.

In 1957 and on other occasions the Exchange Equalisation Account intervened in support of forward sterling. The technique of this and similar interventions by other monetary authorities is described and analysed in detail in my *Dyamic Theory of Forward Exchange* which gives an account of the wide variety of methods applied. In particular, during 1961–2 this device came to be adopted very widely in order to support the dollar. For years the Bundesbank tried to regulate the flow of foreign funds to and from Western Germany by selling dollars to German banks for limited periods on more favourable terms than those obtainable in the market. The development of the Euro-dollar market made official intervention in the forward exchange market even more essential.

Intervention in forward exchanges assumed very considerable importance between 1964 and 1967. The Labour Government applied the device originally for the limited purpose of gaining time for adoption the measures required for supporting sterling against the heavy attacks to which it became subject as a result of the wave of distrust generated by the balance-of-payments deficit and Socialist policies. Having realised, however, that it was possible to support sterling by selling forward dollars the Government did not possess, it grossly misused the device by abstaining from adopting sufficiently strong measures to deal with the disequilibrium. In November 1967 the short position of the Exchange Equalisation Account reached such gigantic proportions that the Government felt impelled to devalue. Losses on the excercise amounted to hundreds of millions of pounds.

In given circumstances official intervention in forward exchanges serves a useful and constructive purpose. But it is too tempting to abuse the device. The subject is dealt with in detail in my *Dynamic Theory of Forward Exchange*.

CHAPTER FORTY

Exchange Restrictions

EXCHANGE restrictions have a direct bearing on the international monetary situation because their main object is usually to prevent a depreciation of the exchanges, which would take place in their absence. Consequently, exchange restrictions have a bearing also on the internal monetary situation of the country adopting them. For, as we pointed out in the last chapter, the internal value of money is liable to be influenced considerably by exchange movements. Admittedly, exchange restrictions are used occasionally for the purpose of protecting domestic producers or influencing the trend of foreign trade for its own sake rather than for the sake of producing a monetary effect. In the majority of instances, however, their object is mainly monetary.

In their origins exchange restrictions mostly assumed the form of bans on international movements of coins and precious metals. The first known instance is the prohibition of the import of coins in Sparta. The death penalty was imposed on those in possession of hoards of foreign coins. This was partly because the possession of such hoards, consisting as they did mostly of the coins of Athens or some other hostile State, was taken as evidence of treason. The main motive, however, was probably the desire to safeguard the local currency of iron bars against being discredited through the use of a more valuable and more convenient currency. Another instance of early attempts at exchange restriction was the efforts of various Roman Emperors during the period of decline to check the drain on precious metals due to the adverse balance of trade with the East.

The first legislative evidence of exchange restrictions in England is contained in the Statute of Stepney in 1299 which imposed a ban on the export of coins. Subsequent statutes confirmed this and extended it to cover the export of bullion. This restriction remained more or less in force, as far as the export of sovereigns was concerned, right up to 1819. It was the manifestation of the bullionist conception which dominated economic thought during the late Middle Ages and the beginning of the modern period.

It is easy to criticise the short-sightedness of the policy of trying to prevent the export of coin and bullion by means of embargoes and by compelling exporters to surrender to the authorities the proceeds of their exports. Admittedly, these devices caused a great deal of inconvenience and were not easily enforceable. The alternative device to restrictions was, however, competitive debasement, which was obviously the worse of the two evils. The dilemma which confronted various Governments during the fourteenth and fifteenth centuries was substantially the same as the one that confronts many present-day Governments, namely, whether to allow their exchanges to depreciate or to bolster them up with the aid of exchange restrictions. Both solutions were resorted to during that period. Exchange restrictions were considered preferable and were almost constantly in force. They had, however, to be supplemented by debasements from time to time, largely because they could not be enforced to a sufficient extent to safeguard the supply of coins and precious metals.

The Statute of Westminster in 1343 was inspired by bullionist policy. It laid down the rule that merchants exporting wool must surrender two marks of silver for each sack of wool exported. Similar measures were passed on many subsequent occasions. During the same period attempts were also made to apply the bilateralist principle of balancing trade with individual countries through the Statute of Employment under which foreign merchants selling goods in England were compelled to spend the proceeds on the purchase of English goods within a limited period.

In addition to restrictions on bullion movements and on the disposal of the proceeds of exports, restrictions on transfers of money abroad by means of bills of exchange also made their appearance at an early stage. Bills of exchange as a means for settling claims arising from foreign trade were first adopted in Italy during the thirteenth century, and became increasingly popular in England largely through the activities of Italian merchants and bankers established in London. Nor were they confined to direct payments for foreign trade transactions. They became a favourite method of transferring balances whenever this was more profitable than bullion shipments or whenever bullion shipments were forbidden. It took some time before the rulers and their advisers realised that from the point of view of their supplies of coins it makes little difference in the long run whether the proceeds of imports into their countries are remitted through the physical transfer of precious metals, in coin or bullion, or through transactions in bills of exchange. In a number of Statutes – for instance in a Statute of Richard II in 1390 – shipment of coin and bullion was forbidden, but transfers through bills of exchange were lawful. As a result it became the regular practice of Italian merchants to secure the remittance of the proceeds of their exports to Britain by means of triangular exchange operations through the Low Countries. They employed sterling bills for the settlement of their purchases in the Low Countries, and the latter used these sterling bills in payment for wool, and later for cloth, imported from England. Consequently, England lost the bullion proceeds of these wool and cloth exports as effectively as if she had allowed the Italians to repatriate their balances in the form of bullion.

It took some time to realise this fact. When it was eventually realised, Statutes were enacted forbidding transactions in bills of exchange except under special licence. The preamble of the Statute passed under Richard III in 1483 accused the Italians of transferring money by exchange 'to the king's great damage and to the impoverishment of his subjects'. It was repealed two years later by Henry VII, under whose efficient administration the country's monetary position became sufficiently strong to make such extreme measures of restriction superfluous. It had to be resorted to again, however, under the less prudent administration of Henry VIII. In 1531 merchants were forbidden once more to engage in exchange transactions without special licence. During the rest of the Tudor regime the granting of such licences was made from time to time the responsibility of the Royal Exchanger. Among others Sir Thomas More filled that important post for some time. From time to time the control was relaxed after a while. Exchange restrictions had similar ups and downs also in other countries. Progress towards freedom did not begin until the eighteenth century, and our century witnessed a relapse into controls during and after the two World Wars and also during the crises of the thirties.

Throughout the sixteenth century lively controversy was raging around the question whether or not to prohibit exchange transactions. Gresham himself was against it because he felt confident that he was able to safeguard the exchanges by means of intervention instead of restrictions. We saw in the last chapter that his confidence in this respect was well founded on achievement. Nevertheless, he himself resorted to exchange restrictions on occasions, compelling English merchants to surrender to him part of the proceeds of their sales of cloth in Antwerp.

Disposal of the bullion owned by the subjects was considered a royal prerogative, which was exercised by Charles I in 1940 when he seized the bullion deposits of merchants in the Tower. Under Charles II there were indications of a more liberal tendency. The re-export of foreign coins and bullion was permitted. It was not until the early part of the nineteenth century, however, that freedom of gold movements was fully established. During the period of economic liberalism the art of exchange restrictions came to be forgotten altogether, so that when it became necessary to revert to them during the two World Wars all the rules had to be learnt from the beginning. In any case, in the meantime the entire monetary system had undergone considerable changes.

Such was the reluctance to depart from liberal principles that for a long time during the First World War it remained legally possible to export gold. The Bank of England's notes remained convertible. It was not by legislative measures but by refusal of shipping space and facilities under the War Risk Insurance scheme that a *de facto* embargo on gold exports was gradually adopted. Not until after the end of the war was the export of gold made illegal. All the time the foreign exchange market remained free of restriction and was controlled by means of intervention. In other countries, on the other hand, exchange restrictions were put in operation during the war and the export of precious metals was prohibited. Most of these restrictions were removed after the stabilisation of the currencies during the twenties.

During the monetary crises that followed the suspension of the gold standard in 1931 Britain retained the freedom of exchanges and bullion movements, preferring to allow sterling to depreciate rather than to hold it stable by means of restrictions. Germany, on the other hand, having had an overdose of currency depreciation after the First World War, considered restrictions the lesser evil. A number of countries in Central Europe and elsewhere followed the German example, while others got the best or worst of both worlds by adopting exchange restrictions at the same time as devaluing their currencies.

During and after the Second World War exchange control was applied everywhere. It became the rule – especially as far as transfers by residents were concerned, but they applied to a large extent also to non-residents – and freedom of exchange transactions was the exception. Only countries in a very strong financial situation, such as the United States, Switzerland and West Germany, could afford to do without restrictions, and even they had to revert to it in the sixties and seventies.

Let us now examine briefly the various types of exchange restrictions that came to be adopted by most countries after 1931, and more especially during and after the Second World War. They can be divided, broadly speaking, into two categories according to whether they aim at restricting capital movements or current trade transactions. An unofficial embargo on long-term investments abroad was in force in Britain for many years before 1939. At the outbreak of the war it was reinforced by an official ban on the transfer of capital outside the Sterling Area. The British authorities went even further by ordering the surrender of existing holdings of foreign currencies and foreign investments. During the First World War they sought to achieve the same end without applying compulsion, by imposing a special tax on the yield of securities which the Treasury wanted to acquire for its own requirements. By the beginning of the Second World War liberal traditions had weakened sufficiently for the Government to adopt, after some hesitation, direct official restrictions in this sphere as in the sphere of bullion exports. Most belligerent countries and many neutral countries acted likewise.

Free dealings in exchanges were suspended in Britain at the outbreak of the war. But it was not until June 1940, by which time the dollar assets were depleted, that more or less water-tight exchange controls came to be adopted. Their enforcement was made easier by Britain's insular position which obviated the need for controlling long land frontiers. In Germany, war-time controls had already been achieved before the war by the application of draconian measures which in time of peace are only possible in a totalitarian country.

The operation of exchange restrictions in various countries provided an opportunity for the adoption of a wide variety of monetary devices. In 1931, the system of 'exchange clearing' was inaugurated between Hungary and Switzerland. It was subsequently adopted by a large number of countries. In substance it is a sophisticated version of the Statutes of Employment that operated in England many centuries earlier. The basic principle was that the proceeds of exports had to be spent in the importing country. The system lent itself to an almost infinite variety of methods that came to be known as 'Schachtian devices', even though the ex-President of the Reichsbank did not invent all of them. Substantially they were based on the principle that in a troubled world the debtor is in a strong position to insist that creditors should go out of their way to enable him to pay his debt. The system was grossly abused by Germany before and during the war. Having bought large quantities of goods from her various satellite countries in Central and south-east Europe, they were compelled to buy from Germany unnecessary goods – such as mouth-organs and aspirins – or goods at high prices, in order to receive payment at all. Nevertheless, the system has the advantage of making creditor nations realise that they must import in order to be able to export.

We said earlier in this chapter that one of the main objects of exchange restrictions was to prevent transfers of capital. In Britain and other countries war-time restrictions were imposed not in order to prevent foreigners from withdrawing their capital, but in order to prevent their own nationals from sending their capital abroad. In Germany, on the other hand, the object of restrictions adopted in 1931 was to prevent the withdrawal of national as well as foreign capital. Subsequently similar restrictions were also imposed in Britain, though sterling was not blocked as a rule in the strict sense of the term. For one thing, it was always possible to transfer capital within the Sterling Area. Foreign holders of sterling were also in a position to switch their investment subject to certain limitations. Above all, foreign owners of sterling were permitted to sell their sterling to residents of their own country or of the group of countries to which their country belonged from the point of view of British exchange regulations. Various types of sterling accounts developed with varying degrees of transferability. Accordingly, in foreign exchange markets abroad they were quoted at varying rates.

This system, described as 'multiple currency practice', was brought to a fine art in Germany before the war. The various types of Reichsmarks held by foreign owners were allowed to be used for certain strictly defined purposes. Some of them were available to travellers in Germany; others could be spent on certain types of German goods. If the German Government was keen on stimulating the export of some goods, permission was granted for these goods to be paid for in certain types of blocked Reichsmarks. Owing to their limited use these Reichsmarks were quoted at a substantial discount abroad as a result of which foreign importers were able to secure the goods in question – the so-called 'additional exports' – at a low price.

Another system of multiple exchange rates was the one practised in the Argentine. Before the war exporters were compelled to surrender their foreign exchange to the Government at a rather unfavourable rate, while importers had to bid against each other at auctions to obtain the foreign exchange they needed. This practice secured considerable profit to the Argentine Government. After the war the system pursued was that of differential exchange rates according to the types of imports and exports. If the Argentine Government wanted to stimulate the import of certain goods, the necessary foreign exchange was allotted to importers at a favourable rate, otherwise they had to pay much less favourable rates. Conversely, if the Argentine Government wanted to encourage certain exports the exporters received more favourable rates when surrendering their foreign exchanges. It would be easy to multiply the instances of the more or less involved currency practices arising from exchange restrictions. The above instances should suffice, however, to give the reader an idea of the nature of these practices and the range they cover.

In most instances the original object of exchange restrictions is to keep down the demand for foreign currencies within the limit of the supply and to ensure that the supply available is used for approved purposes. In the course of their application, however, the purpose of exchange restrictions usually tends to broaden. From a technical device they are apt to develop into a major instrument of economic policy. There are strong arguments against their application. Behind the shelter of exchange restrictions the domestic price level is apt to lose touch with the world level to some extent. The wider the discrepancy, the more stringent are the measures needed to bolster up the artificial position.

The belief in the possibility of isolating the national economy from world economy with the aid of exchange restrictions tends to encourage the adoption of costly inflationary economic and social policies, such as a country under a liberal monetary regime could not risk in face of international competition. Beyond doubt, those policies are apt to secure considerable advantages under the shielding cloak of restrictions, but only at the cost of making the situation increasingly artificial and dependent for its existence on the efficiency of isolation. Whether the result is worth the cost is largely a matter of opinion and is one of degree.

In democratic countries, it was found to be impossible for any one country to isolate effectively the national economy from world trends with the aid of exchange control. In spite of the efficiently enforced elaborate exchange control that was retained in Britain after the Second World War, the trade recession in the United States during 1947 reacted sharply on her monetary position. So in a different way did the boom provoked by the Korean War, stock-piling, and the rearmament drive in 1950–1. Above all, it became evident in 1949 – when sterling had to be devalued as a result of persistent speculative pressure – and to a lesser extent on other occasions, that exchange restrictions were an inadequate safeguard in face of a speculative campaign against its currency. It is true that under a regime of exchange controls it is impossible to undertake speculative operations in the pre-war sense of the term. British banks were not permitted to grant credits to foreign banks, so that the extent to which foreign speculators were in a position to 'go short' in sterling – that is, to sell for future delivery sterling they do not possess – was limited. There were, however, other ways in which sterling became undermined through a persistent speculative campaign. Foreign debtors in sterling deferred payment as long as possible if they anticipated a devaluation, in order to be able to repay their debts in cheaper sterling. Importers of British goods were inclined to defer their orders for fear that their competitors might be able to cover their requirements a little later with the aid of cheaper sterling and would be able therefore to sell their British goods at lower prices.

Whether or not these anticipations prove to be correct, so long as they prevail they are apt to cause a heavy drain on the gold reserve. No exchange restrictions are able to safeguard the currency against such a drain. Nor is there any way of ascertaining the potential limits of the adverse pressure. Unless the gold reserve is well above immediate requirements, it might decline below danger level before the drain comes to an end.

Notwithstanding their shortcomings and disadvantages, exchange restrictions are in given circumstances the lesser evil. Inconvenient as they are, the community may have to put up with them in the interests of safeguarding the national economy from the shocks of heavy international capital movements and exaggerated speculative attacks. Nor is it possible to minimise their inconvenience by relaxing their severity. According to a popular conception, the ideal solution would be to confine restrictions to capital transfers while allowing complete freedom for payments arising from current commercial transactions in the broader sense of the term. Unfortunately, freedom of commercial transactions rules out the possibility of effective control over capital transfers. Exchange restrictions are indivisible. Any substantial degree of liberalisation can only be achieved at the cost of a decline in the efficiency of their enforcement. To some extent it is practicable to confine restrictions to transfers by residents in the country concerned, though even in this respect experience has been far from satisfactory.

Towards the end of the fifties exchange control in Britain and in other Western European countries was greatly relaxed as far as foreign residents were concerned. There was later some degree of liberalisation also for capital transfers by residents. But when a currency came under attack, exchange control was reinforced again and again. Even in the United States the dollar scares of the sixties compelled the Administration to introduce 'guidelines' some of which later assumed statutory character. France removed her exchange controls at the beginning of 1968, but was impelled by the troubles of May 1968 to restore them.

What is essential is that Governments adopting and maintaining exchange control should not work under the misconception that it provides the solution of their difficulties and that they can effectively isolate their economies from the world economy. Only totalitarian States such as the Soviet Union can make exchange control more or less watertight. In any case, under the shield of exchange controls fundamental disequilibrium remains in existence, which would have had to be dealt with in the absence of exchange control.

CHAPTER FORTY-ONE

Euro-Dollar Policy

FREQUENT reference has been made throughout this book to the Euro-dollar market and to Euro-currency markets (markets in foreign currency deposits) in general. But owing to the outstanding importance of Euro-dollars and their impact on foreign exchanges, local money markets, capital markets, and the gold market, it is necessary to deal with the subject in greater detail. Since Euro-dollars are of outstanding importance among Euro-currencies, we propose to concentrate primarily on the attitude of the monetary authorities towards the Euro-dollar market.

That market developed in London spontaneously, without any deliberate effort on the part of the Bank of England to create it. But it was the restrictions imposed on foreign credits in terms of sterling in 1957 which brought about its initial expansion. While isolated Euro-dollar transactions can be traced back to the early fifties, it was from 1957 that they became sufficiently systematic to be considered a market. The Bank of England's attitude towards it was one of benevolent neutrality. It did not actively encourage its development, but it abstained from discouraging it, having realised that its development would go a long way towards maintaining London's importance as a banking centre in spite of the restrictions on sterling credits. This benevolent neutrality continued to be applied when the market came to assume considerable dimensions, and when it led to the development of London Dollar Certificates of Deposits. But the Bank deemed it necessary to keep a watchful eye on Euro-currencies and required the banks to report their Euro-currency commitments in their returns.

While limits were imposed on the covered and uncovered foreign exchange commitments of UK banks, no such limits were applied to the lending and borrowing of Euro-dollar deposits by them, even though the Bank did indicate its disapproval if it appeared from their returns that they were overtrading. Thanks to the liberal attitude of the authorities, the London market in Euro-dollars has retained its supremacy and has been largely responsible for the establishment of a large number of American and other foreign bank branches and affiliates for the sake of having direct access to that market.

Thus the British official policy towards the Euro-dollar market was largely negative: the authorities abstained from interfering with it even though they followed its development closely. The authorities of other countries followed a much more active policy. During the early phases of its development countries which were short of capital encouraged their banks and non-banking firms to borrow in the London Euro-dollar market or in the smaller Euro-dollar markets that arose in other financial centres. But since Euro-dollar transactions came to assume increasing importance, Central Banks came to realise that in the absence of official intervention the increasing possibility of borrowing Euro-dollars weakened their control over the volume of credits and over interest rates in their domestic money markets. For a long time this was not realised adequately, and a number of Central Banks actually encouraged the expansion of the Euro-dollar market by lending dollars on a large scale for the sake of the higher yield they could obtain, or by encouraging private transactions in dollars through the provision of swap facilities on favourable terms.

In due course some of the Central Banks came to realise that the expansion of the Euro-dollar market greatly weakened their control over their monetary systems. As a result of the ability of banks to borrow in the Euro-dollar market, the monetary authorities found it more difficult to apply a credit squeeze when they deemed it necessary to do so. Local interest rates came to be influenced by Euro-dollar rates. Even though forward margins affected the differentials when the borrowers deemed it necessary to cover the exchange risk on Euro-dollar deposits switched into their national currencies, very often the dollars borrowed were re-lent in dollars, so that the cost of covering did not arise. Euro-dollar borrowing also assisted borrowers to finance excessive amounts of imports, as well as providing facilities for financing gold hoarding and speculative transactions in foreign currencies.

A number of Governments deemed it necessary to resort to various forms of exchange control in order to regulate the flow of Euro-dollars. In some instances a ban was placed on the switching of the proceeds into local currencies or on the re-lending of the deposits to non-banking customers. In Germany, banks were not permitted to use the swap facilities provided by the Bundesbank for lending dollars in the Euro-dollar market. In Japan, banks were not permitted to pay high interest rates on borrowed Euro-dollars. A limit was placed on the excess of the rates above the prevailing standard rates for first-class borrowers, but this restriction was often circumvented by the payment of some form of supplement to the lending banks.

The most frequently used form of restriction was the imposition of reserve requirements on Euro-dollars borrowed abroad. This measure was applied by the Federal Reserve authorities when they found in 1968–9 that their credit restraint was largely frustrated by the gigantic influx of funds borrowed by London branches of American banks in the Euro-dollar market. The initial effect of this restriction was negative, because the American banks increased their borrowing in order to cover their reserve requirements. It was only when interest rates in New York became competitive with Euro-dollar rates that American banks ceased to borrow and gradually repaid most of their borrowed Euro-dollar deposits.

The West German and Swiss authorities found it difficult to resist the unwanted influx of foreign moneys which continued to flow in even though local interest rates were very low. Even the imposition of negative interest rates failed to check the influx of hot money, because it was employed in the Euro-mark market or in the Euro-franc market where it could earn interest.

Although both Germany and Switzerland were strongly opposed to every form of exchange control, they felt impelled to resort to them for the sake of checking the influx.

While large-scale borrowing of Euro-dollars by American banks influenced interest rates in New York from time to time, it also came to influence interest rates in London and in other markets. Very often local interest rates were affected considerably by the extent to which American banks borrowed or repaid Euro-dollar deposits. The way in which Euro-dollars came to influence local monetary conditions was through arbitrage on a large scale. Euro-dollars were used for switching into sterling and lending the proceeds to local authorities or employing the proceeds in some other parallel money market. All this tended to affect the rates in the local market, even though swap rates tended to mitigate the effect of such operations when it was deemed necessary to cover the exchange risk.

The level of Euro-dollar rates came to play a decisive role in the free market in gold. It was the spectacular increase of Euro-dollar rates in 1969 that forced hoarders and speculators to take their profits or cut their losses rather than carry their positions at such a high cost. The decline of Euro-dollar rates in 1970-1, on the other hand, encouraged private demand for gold and contributed to a large degree towards the sharp increase of its free market price. This experience, and even more the important part played by borrowed Euro-dollars in the speculative purchases of revaluation-prone currencies in 1969-72 or speculative sales of borrowed dollars, made it evident that the monetary authorities could not afford to remain indifferent towards trends in the Euro-dollar market.

Another characteristic experience was that of the German authorities in 1972 when their effort to check inflation was largely frustrated by German borrowing of Euro-currencies in Luxembourg and elsewhere. To discourage this, heavy reserve requirements were imposed on Euro-dollar borrowings. Other Governments followed the same policy.

Since the Euro-currency markets are essentially international markets, the need for the application of international policies to regulate their trends came to be realised. The Bank for International Settlements was particularly well placed for applying such policies, because of the statistical information it was able to collect about the amounts of Euro-currency transactions. In the late sixties it initiated a policy of active intervention, partly on its own account and partly with the aid of deposits it held on behalf of the Central Banks represented on it. These operations were not on a sufficiently large scale to influence fundamental trends; their aim was confined mainly to ironing out fluctuations. At the same time, both the BIS and the IMF sought to discourage Central Banks from lending their dollar reserves in the Euro-dollar market, having regard to the spectacular increase in the volume of Euro-dollars in the late sixties and early seventies.

The escalation of the expansion of the Euro-dollar market was at first attributed to the large-scale American borrowing. But it was found that in spite of the repayment of these Euro-dollars the turnover continued to increase. The need for a co-ordinated effort to influence the trend of the market became therefore increasingly obvious.

One of the important developments in the early seventies was the emergence of a Euro-dollar market in New York and in other American financial centres. Originally this market was largely confined to dealing with Nassau during American business hours while London was closed. But gradually the extent of operations in non-resident dollar deposits increased and the turnover assumed considerable importance.

CHAPTER FORTY-TWO

Special Drawing Rights

In many instances it is impossible to separate the means of monetary policy from its ends. The device of Special Drawing Rights is one of these instances. Their use constitutes an end – the establishment of a system by which balance-of-payments deficits of some countries are automatically offset by balance-of-payments surpluses of other countries. In the absence of some such device it is necessary for deficit countries to endeavour to improve their balance of payments in order to eliminate their deficits and to settle indebtedness arising from past deficits, or at any rate to obtain financial assistance from abroad in order to meet the deficit temporarily. It is necessary for surplus countries to allow their balance of payments to deteriorate or to accept payment in the form of claims on deficit countries. The object of SDRs is to relieve deficit countries of the need for making an effort to balance their accounts either by exertions to improve their balance of payments or by raising loans. This at any rate is expected to be the position if the Barber Plan – which at the time of writing is not yet in force – should come to be adopted.

At the same time as being an end of monetary policy – the elimination of balance-of-payments discipline – the system of SDRs is also meant to constitute a means. It is intended to be a new device with the aid of which deficit countries are able to pay for their import surpluses, a new means of payment which surplus countries are willing to accept in payment for their export surpluses. This means of payment is to be created by the IMF and need not be earned by the recipients either by mining precious metals or by exporting in excess of imports, and it need not be secured by incurring an additional external liability. This at any rate is the formula of the Barber Plan which intends to eliminate the credit element from the limited SDR system established under the Rio de Janeiro Agreement.

In the form in which it was proposed by Mr Barber at the annual meeting of the IMF in September 1971, the device constitutes a revolutionary innovation. It means the conjuring of international reserves, so to speak, out of thin air, their creation by the stroke of a pen. The General Drawing Rights of the IMF constitute an external liability which the recipients will have to repay sooner or later. The Special Drawing Rights, even in their original form, create purchasing power which can be allocated to Governments participating in the scheme without any *quid pro quo*. The recipients may keep them in their portfolios as part of their monetary reserves – though 30 per cent of the amount allocated is subject to repayment – or they may use them for acquiring foreign currencies or for the repayment of liabilities incurred in foreign currencies. The revised formula under the Barber Plan eliminates the credit element from the device, which will become a free gift, without any obligation of repayment.

Under the scheme it will become the duty of all participating Governments to accept SDRs if called upon by the IMF to do so, in return for foreign currencies in their reserves. This means that surplus countries or countries holding large foreign currency reserves can be compelled to convert part of their foreign currency holdings into holdings of SDRs. To the extent of the allocations of SDRs by the IMF deficit countries will be relieved of any necessity for them to make an effort to reduce their domestic consumption or to increase their production for the sake of restoring the equilibrium of their balance of payments. The same end will be achieved without exertions by making use of the SDRs obtained from the IMF as a free gift, as a kind of manna falling from Heaven.

In substance, the formula will amount to making it obligatory for surplus countries to accept these fictitious means of payment in settlement of their claims arising from export surpluses. It will also enable recipients of SDRs to export capital or to repay external liability without having to acquire foreign currencies to that end in an honest way, either with the aid of export surpluses or even with the aid of borrowing, or with the aid of regaining possession of capital formerly lent abroad or repatriating moneys previously exported.

On the face of it, this device might appear to be a miraculous ideal solution of the balance-of-payments problem. It obviates the necessity of trying to solve it by the adoption of floating exchanges, which, according to their advocates, automatically restore equilibrium by allowing exchange rates to float to the level at which imports and exports (in the broadest sense of the term) would offset each other. As we saw in Chapter 14, there are many flaws which prevent that system from operating satisfactorily in practice. In any case, even if it could possibly achieve its end of maintaining or restoring equilibrium of international accounts, that end would be achieved at the cost of having to put up with the disturbing effects of unstable exchanges that might develop into currency chaos and economic wars. The SDR system claims to be able to achieve the end of automatically balancing international accounts without the disadvantage of disturbing the stability of exchanges, with all its consequences. Indeed, it claims that its application prevents unwanted depreciations and appreciations.

Unfortunately, the system is too good to be true. It is not given to mankind to achieve advantages without making efforts or sacrifices or taking risks. In any case, it is open to argument whether it would be to the interests of mankind that the SDRs system – or for that matter the system of floating exchanges – should operate flawlessly and should provide an automatic solution of the balance-of-payments problem. For if it obviated the necessity to make efforts to eliminate an import surplus or to become sufficiently credit-worthy to settle the deficit by borrowing or importing capital, it would eliminate the balance-of-payments discipline. It would amount to the application of the permissive society to the economic and financial sphere.

In an ideal world there would be no need for balance-of-payments discipline. Every nation, and within the nations every individual, would make every effort to maintain and increase productivity and to practise sufficient self-restraint to be able to pay for the goods and services required. Unfortunately ours is far from being an ideal world. There are admittedly some nations and individuals that enjoy working for the sake of working and consider it a matter of national honour or personal self-respect to remain solvent to uphold their dignity and the respect of other nations, or individuals. But there are, alas, other nations or individuals that only work and practise self-restraint to the extent to which they are forced to do so by balance-of-payments discipline, or, in the case of individuals, the need for remaining solvent – by the knowledge that failure to do so might deprive them of the means enabling them to buy the goods and services they need and are unable to produce themselves.

Owing to the debasement of national character in our permissive society, the extent to which balance-of-payments discipline is needed to ensure productivity and self-restraint has increased and is still tending to increase. Nations which formerly set an example as the spearheads of progress have now come to behave as if they took it for granted that the world owed them a living, and a good living at that, irrespective of whether or not they deserved that living. Having been a model nation for centuries, the British people has come increasingly under the influence of the 'English disease', and this disease seems to be spreading over the United States and many other nations. Indeed, no nation seems to be completely immune from it, even if the extent to which it has been caught varies, from nation to nation.

The elimination of the balance-of-payments discipline would greatly contribute towards the increasing debasement of character all over the world. It is difficult enough to induce workers to put in an honest day for their pay even in existing conditions amidst which idleness and lack of self-restraint is liable to carry its own penalty sooner or later in the form of a decline in the standard of living. It would become a great deal more difficult to expect peoples and nations to earn their living once it becomes evident that there is no need for making any exertion or for practising any self-restraint to ensure that the means for paying for purchases are available. It would be as if everybody obtained unlimited overdraft facilities from their banks with no questions asked – one of the provisions of the Barber Plan is that the IMF must not try to ascertain for what purpose the beneficiary Government wants to use the SDRs – and with no obligation to repay the overdrafts. It would be a kind of Welfare State-cum-Social Credit system of international proportions, with the same demoralising effect, only on a much vaster scale.

Possibly a time might come when we shall all have sufficiently strong characters to resist the temptation to abstain from abusing such a system. As things are at present, the temptation to abuse it would be irresistible. Why should we work if we could have a good time without working? It is true that every country could not have a deficit at the same time, and one country's deficit would be bound to be the surplus of another country, or of several other countries. But should balance-of-payments discipline no longer force any of us to aim at surpluses and avoid deficits, it would inevitably lead to an extreme all-round demoralisation and to an all-round decline of efforts to achieve progress. That is to say, this would be the result of the operation of the SDR system if it could operate flawlessly.

Fortunately for the welfare of mankind in the long run, the system carries within it its own destruction. Because it is bound to be abused by Governments unable or unwilling to resist pressure in favour of achieving cheap popularity through getting something for nothing to an increasing extent, SDRs are bound to be allotted on a gigantic scale. It will be difficult for them to refuse costly demands by their electorates, since everybody will have assumed that it will be a matter of 'ask and ye shall be given'.

So long as the quantity of SDRs is limited, as it is at the time of writing, they are freely acceptable and all Central Banks and

Treasuries are willing to hold them. But the increase of their amount to tens of billions, and even hundreds of billions, is bound to make Treasuries and Central Banks of surplus countries think twice. It will make them increasingly conscious of the fact that SDRs are inconvertible, unsecured and non-self-liquidating, with an intrinsic value equal to the price paid by paper-mills for old ledgers sold to them for re-pulping purposes.

Admittedly, participants in the scheme are under obligation to exchange SDRs against currencies if instructed by the IMF to do so – so long as they remain participants. The moment any country should decide to contract out rather than increase further its holding of 'paper gold', the IMF would have to repay its holding of SDRs in excess of its original allocations by forcing other participants to increase their holdings. A stage might be reached – indeed, it is bound to be reached sooner or later – at which surplus countries would either do their utmost to cease to have any surplus by becoming deficit countries, or would contract out of the scheme rather than accept more book entries in payment for their export surpluses. Whenever a country contracts out, its holdings would have to be taken over by other countries, and it would become even less attractive to hold SDRs. To avoid other countries' unwanted SDRs being dumped on them, more and more countries would contract out.

The only reason why SDRs are acceptable is the assumption that they could be passed on to other countries. The more countries were to contract out, the less acceptable SDRs would become. Withdrawals from the scheme would tend to become self-aggravating. It seems highly probable that in due course the scheme would reduce itself to absurdity.

CHAPTER FORTY-THREE

Physical Controls

THE use of physical controls as a means of monetary policy is one of the most highly controversial sections of a highly controversial subject. They are ignored in most pre-war books on monetary policy. In so far as post-war literature deals with them they are almost invariably treated as an expedient for which there may be an explanation and possibly even an excuse in time of war, but which is something entirely abnormal and reprehensible in time of peace. Yet physical controls had been in use as a normal device of monetary policy from very early times. In particular, physical control of foreign trade to safeguard or increase the monetary stocks of precious metals had been a generally adopted practice for many centuries. It was only during the liberal nineteenth century that these means of monetary policy, together with exchange control and other controls, fell into disuse in most countries. Those brought up amidst the liberal traditions of a more stable period strongly resented the revival of physical controls in the thirties of this century. They are understandably inclined to condemn the use of physical controls as an unmitigated evil in all conceivable circumstances except in time of war.

Beyond doubt there is a strong case against the perpetuation of physical controls as means of peace-time monetary policy. In given circumstances, however, there are valid arguments in their favour. In any case, owing to their widespread use it is necessary to examine them. In the unsettled conditions of the post-war world some degree of physical controls was retained for some time. Their use as a means of monetary policy has been greatly mitigated in advanced countries during the fifties and sixties, but it is likely to be resumed whenever conditions become more difficult.

For our present purpose physical controls mean direct Government intervention to determine the volume and nature of production, distribution, consumption and foreign trade. All such controls may be used as very effective means of monetary policy. They had already been so used extensively before the Second World War, owing to the realisation that in the then prevailing conditions it was inexpedient to rely entirely on the automatic working of economic tendencies or even on conventional means of monetary policy.

Government intervention to determine production may serve non-monetary economic purposes. It may aim at raising the standard of living or the taxable capacity of the community. It may want to add to the military strength of the nation by increasing its economic strength. It may constitute a means of monetary policy if Government intervention to raise the volume of production by non-monetary means aims at keeping down or lowering the price level, or at improving the exchange position by increasing the exportable surplus and by replacing imports by home production. These aims may be pursued through conscription or direction of manpower. Such intervention need not be confined, however, to an effort to raise the total output. It may aim at influencing the output of some specific categories of goods, and diverting manpower from the production of goods which are not considered essential from the point of view of the monetary policy that is pursued.

Productive capacity may be diverted from certain lines to other lines not only for reasons of monetary policy but also from considerations of social utility, or from a variety of economic considerations. Such measures may serve the purposes of rearmament. Controls of production constitute means of monetary policy only if they aim at influencing the price level or the balance of payments. Under the mercantilist system Governments planned the production of their countries with the object of improving the balance of payments and thereby securing an inflow of monetary metals. This object is very much in the mind of Governments in modern times also, though it does not occupy quite such a central position in their policies as it did during the days of mercantilism. Britain's post-war policy aimed at reserving much of the country's productive power for industries which were in a position to export, especially to the dollar area, or which produced goods that would obviate the need for imports, especially from the dollar area. Discrimination in the allocation of raw materials in favour of dollar-earning or dollar-saving industries clearly indicated the predominantly monetary character of the motive behind these physical controls.

Selective control of production may aim at keeping down or lowering the price level either from the point of view of the domestic monetary situation or for the sake of improving the balance of payments. To that end, production is diverted from luxuries to necessities in order to keep down the prices of the latter by increasing their supply. This is essential from the point of view of keeping down the cost of living and the cost of production. Standardisation is yet another method of official intervention aiming at keeping down or reducing prices. One of the main purposes of the Utility scheme operated in Britain during the Second World War and right up to 1952 was to lower the cost of production by means of mass production. This served the dual purpose of keeping down prices for the domestic consumer and increasing the competitive capacity of British producers in foreign markets. When it was found that in a buyers' market the quality of utility goods no longer satisfied Britain's overseas customers, the scheme was abandoned.

Government intervention need not necessarily aim at keeping down prices. In special circumstances it may aim at keeping up or raising prices of staple exports. It is true that the main object of 'valorisation' schemes is to safeguard the interests of the substantial section of the population directly or indirectly dependent on the production of these goods. This is a non-monetary aim. But the adverse effect of unduly low export prices on the balance of payments and on the monetary situation also plays an important part in the adoption of such devices. In some instances the stocks of staple products bought by the

Government were kept in buffer-pools to be released as and when market conditions became more favourable. Some of these supplies were eventually destroyed in the interest of maintaining high prices. This was done in the Brazilian coffee valorisation scheme during the inter-war period. Alternatively, the Government intervened to limit the production of the commodities concerned. Thanks to higher prices for the staple exports, the terms of trade changed in a favourable sense.

Physical controls may play a very important part in the sphere of distribution. Although rationing is usually regarded as a means of social policy ensuring equal shares for all, it is at the same time a most important means of monetary policy. Combined with price controls, it is aimed at suppressing the full effect of inflation on the price level. It has come to be regarded as an indispensable device in time of war, and also during difficult periods in times of peace. At the beginning of the Second World War the Governments of belligerent countries had to choose between two alternative economic policies. They could have prevented an increase of purchasing power through the application of highly drastic taxation. Or they could ensure by means of rationing that in spite of the expansion of purchasing power everybody should receive a fair share of the limited supplies of essential goods. Although they went a long way towards adopting the first alternative, they could not have carried it to its logical conclusion without hampering the war effort by depriving producers of the incentive of the profit motive. For this reason, instead of embarking on a 100 per cent disinflationary policy of taxation, they tolerated a certain degree of inflation as an incentive, and adopted rationing for the sake of ensuring equal distribution of necessities.

When it is considered inevitable to inflate in the interest of national defence, there are two ways in which the excess of purchasing power can be dealt with, in so far as it cannot be mopped up by means of borrowing. If prices are allowed to rise in accordance with the increased purchasing power, supply and demand become balanced at a higher price level. This has the disadvantage of accelerating the pace of inflation, for in the circumstances higher prices inevitably increase the Budgetary deficit and thus lead to the creation of additional purchasing power. They also lead to wage demands. The alternative is to control prices at a relatively low level, dealt with in Chapter 37. In the absence of physical controls the application of this device would result in a rapid depletion of the supplies which on the basis of the artificially low prices are necessarily inadequate to meet the inflated demand. For this reason it is essential that price controls should be accompanied by rationing whenever practicable. The combination of price control and rationing prevents the consumers from spending too much of their inflated purchasing power on essential goods. And if the production of luxuries is restricted by physical controls, a situation may arise in which the public has to save willy-nilly a large part of its surplus purchasing power in the absence of opportunities to spend it. The nation is thus forced to save part of its earnings and the Government is able to employ a substantial proportion of the nation's financial resources and productive capacity for the economic requirements of the war effort, or of rearmament.

However necessary physical controls may be in pursuit of war-time monetary policy, their use in time of peace gives rise to much temptation to over-spend, because of the possibility of suppressing the normal effects of inflation. The idea that it is possible to have 'inflation without tears' may go a long way towards encouraging the pursuit of a policy of non-stop inflation in time of peace. Though it may be intended to be moderate, such inflation is liable to gather momentum as it proceeds. The application of physical controls to suppress the visible effects of inflation on prices and on supplies is apt to create a vicious spiral. The continuation of inflation tends to make controlled prices increasingly artificial and to add to the cost of the subsidies with the aid of which these prices are kept down. Larger subsidies, in turn, mean a larger inflationary Budget deficit.

Finally, physical controls in the service of monetary policy include controls over foreign trade. Historically speaking, these were the first physical controls to serve monetary ends. The medieval kings in England and on the Continent adopted a series of measures of direct control to ensure that imports did not exceed exports. In modern times physical controls of imports for monetary purposes include general bans on imports and the imposition of bans on imports from 'hard currency' countries. They also include the imposition of import quotas, fixing quantitative limits to certain imports from certain countries. Such quotas were greatly reduced during the late fifties and early sixties in the countries of Western Europe. But in the late sixties and early seventies physical controls were beginning once more to rear their ugly heads.

Government intervention to check imports may serve many non-monetary ends such as the protection of domestic industries in order to ensure full employment. Its essentially monetary character is particularly prominent when import restrictions are adopted in order to safeguard the balance of payments and avoid the necessity for the devaluation of an over-valued currency. Although the same effect can be achieved also by means of exchange control, very often both devices are employed at the same time in order to make the system watertight. On other occasions it is not practicable or expedient to resort to exchange restrictions, and the Government depends entirely on quantitative import restrictions for the defence of its exchange.

Physical controls are often presented as an alternative to financial controls. In given circumstances, however, they complete each other. Even those who disapprove of controls for the sake of controls must at times yield to some extent to practical necessity. Controls should not, however, be used for their own sake, only when their use is made necessary by conditions in which their absence would make it difficult or costly to achieve the legitimate ends of monetary policy solely with the aid of financial devices.

CHAPTER FORTY-FOUR

Other Economic Devices

MONETARY policy decisions, in addition to serving immediate monetary ends, often serve broader economic ends. Conversely, measures in the sphere of economic policy often serve the purposes of monetary policy. The reciprocity of relations between monetary policy and economic policy may best be characterised by the saying, well known in golfing circles, that he who plays golf for the sake of keeping fit is wise, but he who endeavours to keep fit for the sake of playing good golf is even wiser. Monetary policy is pursued in the interests of a healthy economy, but efforts are often made to improve economic conditions for the sake of achieving sound monetary conditions.

This does not mean that all action of economic policy which tends to affect the monetary situation should be considered to come within the sphere of monetary policy. Very often the monetary effect of such action is secondary, incidental or purely unintentional. It is only if economic action is taken at least partly for the sake of producing a monetary effect that it constitutes a device of monetary policy.

The introductory paragraph of this chapter may convey the impression that economic action taken for the sake of monetary effect is always necessarily in the right direction. Unfortunately this is by no means so. As we pointed out in an earlier chapter, a bad monetary policy is none the less a monetary policy for being bad.

The monetary situation can be influenced to a considerable extent through economic devices affecting production. Monetary inflation can be reversed either through monetary deflation or through an increase in the volume of goods to offset the excessive volume of purchasing power. A successful production drive is an effective disinflationary device, provided that it is not accompanied by an increase in the wages bill equal in amount to, or larger than, the increase of the output. It is true that increasing production is usually preceded by rising prices because it is achieved through more capital investment, higher employment and higher wages. In so far, however, as productivity is increased through a better utilisation of equipment and labour and through harder work, it is definitely a very effective disinflationary device. An increase of productivity tends to produce a disinflationary effect not only by increasing the volume of goods available, but also by reducing the cost of production per unit. Any Government action taken in order to increase productivity for the sake of lowering prices or preventing their rise constitutes a monetary policy device. We saw in Chapter 43 that there is ample scope for such action in the sphere of physical controls. But the Government can intervene to increase the output without necessarily resorting to physical controls.

Another economic device serving monetary ends in the sphere of production is the encouragement of certain branches of production – if necessary at the expense of other branches – to increase the supply of necessities in order to keep down the cost of living. The same volume of output tends to produce a different effect on the monetary situation according to the extent to which it represents necessities. This subject was touched upon in the chapter dealing with the physical control of production. In this chapter we are concerned with diversion of productive efforts in the desired directions through other devices. If an unduly large proportion of productive capacity is used for the production of luxuries, the volume of output of necessities tends to be inadequate in comparison with the increase in the purchasing power of consumers. The inadequacy of the output of necessities tends to accentuate the rising trend of prices. The remedy is, of course, a diversion of productive capacity from luxuries to necessities as a means of counteracting or moderating the rise in prices. In our affluent society, however, yesterday's luxuries tend to become today's necessities. The range of goods which is within the reach of the lower income groups has widened and is still widening.

Another alternative is a wages policy, the direct effect of which on the monetary situation was discussed in detail in Chapter 38. Under it wages in various trades, instead of being determined by the relative scarcity of labour in the trades concerned and by the level of prices that buyers of the goods concerned are prepared to pay, would be determined by the aims of economic policy to encourage the production of certain goods and to discourage the production of others. In the absence of a wages policy producers of luxuries who can afford to pay high wages are able to divert much-needed manpower from the production of necessities. With the aid of a national wages policy it would have been possible during the period of high employment to secure the manpower needed for a substantial increase of the coal output without having to outbid less essential trades competing for the manpower. This would have materially improved the monetary situation in Britain, both through the increase in the production of necessities and the regulation of the wages spiral. It might have been possible to prevent the motor industry from attracting rather more than its fair share of manpower with the aid of excessive wages. It might have been possible to liquidate redundant sections of the textile industry by fixing wages lower in comparison with those fixed in other industries which, with the aid of increased manpower attracted by higher wages, could have more effectively served the export drive and would have contributed towards the strengthening of sterling. Even when in 1952 large-scale unemployment developed in the textile industry, it was very difficult to induce textile workers to switch over to other industries rather than remain unemployed in the hope of securing re-employment in the textile industry.

The above example shows the importance of mobility of labour as an economic factor of monetary policy. Mobility of labour can be increased by devices other than a national wages policy. One of the objects of the housing drive is precisely to increase the mobility of labour so as to make it possible to to re-employ, to the best advantage to the national economy, workers who become unemployed and who cannot find employment in their own districts. Owing to the shortage of housing accommodation, the degree of mobility of workmen, especially those with families, is very low. Consequently, local pockets of unemployment can exist for a long time in some districts even though other districts are able to offer employment and attractive wages. Thus the housing drive may also be regarded as serving partly monetary purposes, since its success in increasing the mobility of labour would lead to a disinflationary increase in production in general and to an increase in the production of exportable goods in particular.

Easing of the housing shortage as a means for the internal and external strengthening of sterling could be achieved not only through a housing drive aiming at satisfying the demand for accommodation, but also through a reduction of that demand by means of an increase of rents. It is largely owing to the artificially low level of rents resulting from rent control and the subsidising of council houses that the supply of housing accommodation is never able to catch up with the demand. The artificial character of controlled or subsidised rents became accentuated through the sharp rise in practically every other item in the cost of living and in uncontrolled rents.

The system that operated in this sphere in Britain and in many other countries created an absurd situation, in that the State authority artificially stimulated demand for something which it was unable to supply in adequate quantities and which it was unable to ration to secure equitable distribution of the limited supply. A partial de-control of rents and the increase of the level of controlled rents, by reducing the inflated demand for housing accommodation, went some way towards solving the problem of housing shortage and thereby increasing the mobility of labour. On the other hand, the beneficial effect of this on the monetary situation was offset to a large degree by the rise in the cost of living caused by higher rents, leading to more wage demands. Moreover, the policy had distinct disadvantages from a social and political point of view. Even so, the balance of advantages is decidedly on the side of an upward adjustment of rents. In Britain progress in that direction was far from adequate. There are still millions of houses under rent control or with subsidised rents.

An economic device which has a very close bearing on monetary policy is the Government's attitude towards the adoption of the system under which wages and salaries are adjusted to changes in the cost-of-living index. The Government can encourage the increasing adoption of that system by applying it in the Civil Service or by adopting legislation ensuring its application by private employers. This latter device is in operation in Australia, where there is provision to that effect in the Constitution. Minimum wages are not fixed by collective bargaining, but are adjusted each quarter by the Federal Arbitration Court on the basis of the cost-of-living index. Beyond doubt this system is calculated to accelerate the pace of inflation by cutting down the time-lag between a rise in the cost of living and the rise in the cost of production through higher wages. Governments and Parliaments in some countries are inclined to adopt or encourage this system, or at any rate abstain from resisting its adoption, out of sheer necessity, for social or political considerations. Nevertheless, it is arguable that it tends to mitigate the effect of inflation on the wage-earning classes and to avert troublesome industrial disputes which would produce inflationary effects through reducing the output. It is one way of reducing some of the evil social effects of inflation at the cost of accentuating the speed of its progress. Its adoption implies taking the line of least resistance as an alternative to adopting a firmer anti-inflationary policy which would obviate the need for the adoption of the index-number standard.

In the sphere of foreign trade too, economic devices can be applied as instruments of monetary policy. From this point of view it is necessary to discriminate between conditions of full employment and those of large-scale unemployment. A country which is producing to the limit of its capacity cannot increase its exports or reduce its imports without affecting the volume of goods available to satisfy domestic demand. In such countries an adverse trade balance is an anti-inflationary device because by increasing the supply of goods available it tends to prevent or mitigate the rise in trend of prices due to excessive purchasing power. Conversely, in such circumstances the success of an export drive necessarily reduces the already inadequate supplies of goods available to satisfy domestic demand. It therefore tends to accentuate the rising trend of prices.

It is only in exceptional circumstances that Governments may resort to a deliberate increase of the adverse trade balance for the sake of counteracting an inflationary trend. This was done in some countries of Western Europe immediately after the Second World War. The devastation caused during the hostilities materially reduced their productive capacity, a large part of which had to be employed for reconstruction purposes. In order to satisfy the urgent requirements of consumers and thus to mitigate the bidding-up of prices of the inadequate supplies of goods, the Governments of these countries endeavoured during the first few post-war years to import as much as possible and to refrain as far as possible from exporting essential goods. Trade negotiations during the early post-war period were totally different from the usual trade negotiations in which the parties are trying to persuade each other to admit the largest possible quantity of each other's goods. In 1945–7 the Governments of countries which had suffered much physical devastation were at pains to persuade each other and more favourably placed Governments to export more to their respective countries without insisting on importing more unless they were prepared to accept luxuries.

When, however, there is unemployment, an export surplus is an unqualified blessing. It strengthens the monetary situation by increasing the gold reserve. It does not affect domestic supplies because there is ample productive capacity to meet both domestic requirements and export requirements. As a decline in the gold reserve is liable to lead to a depreciation of the national currency, export drives and import restrictions amidst conditions of unemployment constitute devices in defence of monetary stability. There is an almost unlimited range of economic actions tending to affect the trade balance, thereby constituting acts of monetary policy.

In situations in which the authorities deem it necessary to discourage the influx of foreign funds without resorting to exchange restrictions they can apply restrictions on interest rates paid by banks on foreign deposits. They may even ban interest on foreign deposits altogether and may make it compulsory for banks to charge a negative interest rate. This was done by Switzerland and by Germany during the late fifties and the early sixties.

In the sphere of production, diametrically opposite policies may serve monetary ends. In given circumstances a Government may find it expedient to create a scarcity of goods in order to force consumers to save part of their inflated purchasing power. On the other hand, if a Government finds that this policy acts as a disincentive and tends to discourage production it may reverse the policy by encouraging the production of 'incentive goods' which might make workers work overtime. In either case the monetary situation is liable to be affected.

In theory, a scheme to compensate employees who become redundant as a result of technological progress or other methods of increasing productivity serves the purpose of resisting inflation, because it is supposed to lessen trade union resistance to the adoption of labour-saving methods. But any such scheme is bound to increase the bargaining power of the trade unions, because it reduces the extent of fear of unemployment. The adoption of redundancy schemes might well prove to be inflationary on balance, unless it is made conditional upon concessions by the trade unions, such as the mitigation of their restrictive practices or the adoption of disciplinary measures against unofficial strikes.

In my *Economic Consequences of Automation*, published in 1956, I advocated the adoption of redundancy schemes providing for compensation of those who lose their jobs as a result of technological progress. But on the basis of the experience of recent years I have arrived reluctantly at the conclusion that the remedy I had proposed proved to be largely ineffective. It failed to diminish resistance to redundancy. And yet there can be no progress unless labour-saving inventions are permitted to save labour.

In many of the instances dealt with in this chapter, economic devices are employed partly and even largely for non-monetary purposes. Nevertheless, they may be regarded as coming within a broad definition of monetary policy devices if their adoption serves to an appreciable extent the purpose of influencing the monetary situation, either directly or at any rate indirectly.

Part Four

CONCLUSION

CHAPTER FORTY-FIVE

International Monetary Policies

THOSE responsible for the shaping of monetary policy must have realised many centuries ago that their power to determine monetary trends in their respective countries was limited by the exercise of a similar power by the monetary authorities of other countries, or by the influence of monetary trends abroad that developed in the absence of intervention by those authorities, or through the ineffectiveness of their intervention. Clashes between the monetary policies of various countries became only too evident during the periods of frequent debasements when the advantages gained by the debasement of one currency were wiped out by the debasement of other currencies. Bullionist policies under which the export of coins or precious metals was prohibited failed to produce the desired result partly because other countries adopted similar bans. The world-wide character of price trends, in face of which monetary policies of particular countries were largely helpless, has been traced by economic historians to the period of ancient Greece, In several instances, prices in the countries of the Mediterranean civilisation during the Ancient period appeared to move largely in sympathy even though there is no reason to suppose that the monetary policies of these countries were uniform. The same is true in many instances about movements of world prices in subsequent periods.

It was not until the nineteenth century that the international character of some major factors affecting the monetary situation in individual countries came to be adequately realised. Economists and administrators became increasingly aware that their respective policies were largely helpless in face of major international trends, caused by such factors as changes in the world output of precious metals or decisions of other countries to change their monetary standards. Attempts were made from time to time to influence these international trends by means of international agreements on subjects such as the demonetization of silver. Generally speaking, however, the conception prevailed that the automatic working of the gold standard was trusted to produce the desired results in the long run.

It was considered to be part of the sovereign rights of any independent State to determine its monetary system and its monetary policies. The extent of international co-operation in the monetary sphere remained negligible until the First World War There were, it is true, some monetary unions such as the Latin Monetary Union or the Scandinavian Monetary Union, the member countries of which adopted identical mint parities. The practical results of such unions were, however, modest. There was no co-ordination of their monetary policies, and in spite of the identity of their mint parities there were often substantial discrepancies between their exchange rates. The franc was on a 'limping standard' and the Spanish peseta – also a currency of the Latin Monetary Union – was inconvertible. The lira, too, had its ups and downs.

During the First World War close co-operation was established between the Western Allies. Britain and the United States provided a means for supporting the exchange rates of France and Italy, and the United States provided the means for maintaining sterling at a fixed rate in relation to the dollar. Soon after the termination of hostilities the system of monetary co-operation was brought to an end.

The currency chaos that developed during the early twenties made the world realise the need for international action to bring some order and co-ordination in the sphere of monetary policy.

Under the gold standard up to the First World War, the need for subordinating the monetary policy of any country to the requirements of the monetary policies of other countries was not very obvious. When, towards the middle twenties, one country after another endeavoured to stabilise its currency it became evident, however, that co-operation was of vital importance in order to make the gold standard work. The monetary authorities of the leading countries realised that, owing to the rise in prices since 1914, the volume of monetary gold was not adequate. For this reason, in order to prevent a world-wide deflation through a scramble for the world's limited gold supplies, a number of countries which had stabilised their currencies with the aid of the League of Nations were persuaded to adopt the gold exchange standard instead of the full gold standard. Their note cover was allowed to include currencies convertible into gold, primarily dollars and sterling, in addition to gold. As a result the same gold stock served as a reserve for two currencies.

Some degree of uniformity was established by the League Finance Committee between the monetary systems and policies of countries which it had assisted. Close co-operation was established between a large number of Central Banks. The movement culminated in the establishment of the Bank for International Settlements at Basle, which institution had for its purpose the pursuit of a systematic co-ordination of monetary policies. Before it had a chance to produce any tangible results, however, the economic crisis that followed the Wall Street slump of 1929, accentuated by the suspension of the gold standard in Britain two years later, brought the movement abruptly to a halt.

Even though the BIS continued to function and provided an opportunity for monthly meetings of Central Banks Governors at Basle until the outbreak of the war, owing to its inability to give effective assistance its influence on monetary policy was negligible. Moreover, it came under a cloud of suspicion when, after the Nazi occupation of Prague, it surrendered the Czechoslovak National Bank's gold deposit to the Reichsbank. It became the subject of strong criticism, and it was not for many years later that it came to be vindicated by the realisation that it had acted in accordance with the legal position, and by its strict neutral attitude during the war.

The period between 1931 and 1936 was characterised by a wave of unfettered monetary nationalism. Each country pursued monetary policies which appeared to be in accordance with their immediate interests, without regard to the effect on other countries. The history of competitive debasements of earlier centuries repeated itself. There was a competitive currency depreciation race between several countries, each one of which aimed at 'exporting unemployment' to other countries by depreciating their exchanges in order to undersell their rivals. The benefit derived by Britain through a depreciation of sterling in 1931 was largely cancelled out by the depreciation of the dollar two years later. An attempt to bring some order into the currency chaos at the World Economic Conference of 1933 failed completely, because the participating Governments were utterly incapable of seeing each other's point of view. The United States in particular, under Roosevelt, adopted an aggressively nationalist policy, while France stubbornly refused to consider an adjustment of the parity of the franc.

By that time the Sterling Area had come into existence. It provided an example of close co-ordination of monetary policies within a group of countries whose interest were substantially identical. There was also a much looser association called the 'gold bloc', consisting of a number of Western European countries which endeavoured to maintain the gold standard and to avoid devaluation. The United States under President Roosevelt was in favour of bold and unconventional experimenting with currency. Finally, a large number of economically weaker countries – foremost amongst them Germany – adopted policies of monetary isolation with the aid of exchange control and exchange clearing. There appeared to be no common ground between them. Each country or group of countries endeavoured to work out its salvation in its own way in total disregard of the vital interests of the rest of the world.

During the years that followed the failure of the World Economic Conference the need for a co-ordination of national monetary policies came to be gradually realised. The disadvantages of unrestricted national sovereignty in the monetary sphere became increasingly evident. Looking back upon that troubled period, it must now appear absurd that statesmen of standing should have imagined they could serve the fundamental interest of their respective countries by refusing to compromise in matters of monetary policy. It should have been evident to them that any action affecting the monetary situation in any one country was liable to affect other countries.

In particular, it was realised that the determination of the exchange rates could not be a matter of indifference to other countries. The need for the regulation and co-ordination of conflicting rights and interest in other sphere of international relations has long been recognised. There have been many international agreements to co-ordinate matters such as air-traffic regulations, or radio wave-lengths, or water rights, in the interests of all concerned. Under any of these agreements the participating Governments relinquish part of their sovereignty. They renounce their right to operate on any wave-length they choose because they realise that if the other Governments were to excercise their freedom to do so the inevitable result would be chaotic conditions in the ether. The same is true about monetary policies.

The realisation of this truth resulted in the conclusion of the Tripartite Agreement in 1936 between the United States, Great Britain and France. Subsequently, several other countries adhered to it. The Governments concerned agreed not to engage in competitive currency depreciation and to consult each other before bringing about substantial changes in the exchange value of their currencies. A more elaborate version of this principle eventually became the basic rule of the Bretton Woods Agreement on which the world's post-war monetary system came to be founded.

During the Second World War, as during the First World War, there was a high degree of monetary co-operation between the allies. As the war appeared to be drawing near its end, efforts were initiated to establish the post-war rules under which monetary policies should be co-ordinated. During 1943-4 two rival plans were under consideration. They were the British Keynes

Plan and the American White Plan. Under the former an International Monetary Union was to be established with powers to create a new money of its own for the settlement of international balances. Its rules were devised in such a way as to provide inducement to creditor countries to reduce their export surpluses and accept an import surplus.

The White Plan, too, provided for the creation of an international institution, but it was to have no power to create money. Its resources would consist of funds to be contributed towards capital by member countries. Nor did this institution provide any inducement for creditor countries to be 'good creditors'. Although the majority of countries would have preferred the Keynes Plan it was inevitable, in view of the overwhelming financial strength of the United States, that the White Plan should in substance be accepted.

The Bretton Woods Agreement, concluded in 1944, opened a new chapter in the history of international monetary relations. It stipulated that member countries should not in future change the gold value of their currencies, without the consent of the International Monetary Fund, beyond the extent of 10 per cent on either side of their original parities. The Fund would grant its consent if in its opinion the proposed change was necessary in order to correct come 'fundamental disequilibrium'. In given circumstances the Fund is granted the right to advise member countries regarding their domestic monetary policies. It does not have the power, however, to compel Governments to take the necessary steps for dealing either with a persistently adverse balance of payments or with a persistently favourable balance of payments. The Bretton Woods rules provide also for the removal of exchange restrictions. Most member countries complied with this rule to a large degree, even though there were many relapses, with or without the consent of the IMF.

Regulated adjustment of exchange parities or of actual exchange rates became a recognised form of international monetary co-operation. The object was to ensure that if and when an adjustment of exchange rates became inevitable, it should be carried out in an orderly fashion and in such a way as to avoid competitive currency depreciations. If the price level in a country was too high and for economic, social or political reasons its lowering through deflation was impracticable, the disequilibrium in relation to price levels of other countries had to be corrected sooner or later through devaluation. What mattered from the point of view of other countries was that devaluation should merely aim at correcting the existing disequilibrium instead of creating a new disequilibrium in the opposite sense through an exaggerated reduction of the exchange value of the currency concerned.

If devaluation is excessive, the price level in terms of other currencies becomes unduly reduced, and this may force other countries either to deflate or to devalue. It was to avoid this that the countries participating in the Tripartite Agreement, and subsequently those who accepted the Bretton Woods system, adopted the rule not to change their exchange parities to any substantial degree without consultation with the other participating countries or, after 1946, the International Monetary Fund. The revaluation of the D.mark by 5 per cent in 1961 provided a striking instance of upward parity adjustment for the sake of international co-operation, even though its effect on the foreign exchange market was disappointing, because it gave rise to fears of further adjustments of parities. This experience repeated itself in the late sixties and early seventies.

The difficulty is to ascertain the correct exchange rates representing equilibrium. Unfortunately this is not a matter of simple arithmetic. It does not entirely depend on the ratio between the price levels of the countries concerned, nor even on the ratio between indices based on exported and imported goods. Moreover, occasionally it is necessary and justified to devalue a currency to a greater degree than appears to be called for on the basis of the arithmetical relation between price levels. This was the case with sterling in 1949. To restore confidence in sterling it was deliberately undervalued with the full consent and approval of the United States Government and the International Monetary Fund. It is humanly impossible to calculate the correct level, and there is apt to be a tendency to err on the safe side. What matters is that the countries concerned should endeavour to do so in a spirit of understanding towards each other's difficulties, and that they should avoid competitive currency depreciations which would be against the interests of all.

International co-operation may assume the form of a reciprocal undertaking not to operate in the exchanges or money markets of a country without first consulting its authorities. This form of co-operation had already reached an advanced stage before the establishment of the Bank for International Settlements. One of the rules of the co-operation between Central Banks that developed during the twenties was that the participating Central Banks agreed to transact business exclusively with each other and to close their accounts with other banks. This did not necessarily mean that they abandoned their right to carry out transactions which did not meet with the approval of the Central Bank of the country concerned. For instance, during the late twenties the Bank of France decided to repatriate in gold a large part of its sterling balances in spite of the disapproval of this policy by the Bank of England. In the sixties it converted its dollar holdings into gold in spite of the disapproval of the Federal Reserve authorities. It meant, however, that all operations in the foreign exchange market and money market and all bullion shipments went through official channels, which were thus in a better position to mitigate the effects of such transactions through timing and co-ordination. This rule was abandoned in the late fifties as far as Euro-currencies were concerned. A great many Central Banks adopted the practice of lending Euro-dollars and other Euro-currency deposits to foreign commercial banks or merchant banks.

Another means by which Governments would be able to help each other in the maintenance of the stability of their exchanges was through co-operation in the enforcement of exchange restrictions. This form of co-operation has not reached a very advanced stage. Most Governments show themselves utterly indifferent to the infringement of the laws of other countries as far as exchange restrictions are concerned. Black markets in

the currencies of countries with exchange restrictions are tolerated, and so is the misuse of various special accounts in restricted currencies. For instance, no effort was made by the
United States authorities to stop leaks in the British exchange
control that arose through the misuse of various types of sterling
of limited convertibility for indirect purchases of Sterling Area
commodities for export to the United States. That practice was
only terminated as a result of the abolition of such species of
sterling.

The only effective way in which a large and increasing number
of Governments have come to co-operate in maintaining each
other's exchange restrictions has come about not for monetary
but for fiscal reasons, in the form of bilateral agreements against
double taxation and tax evasion. Under these agreements the
contracting parties undertake to communicate to each other
the incomes earned by each of its nationals in each other's country. Since 1946 there has been in existence such an agreement
between Great Britain and the United States. The United States
Government communicates to the British Government the
American incomes of residents in the United Kingdom, and the
British Government communicates to the United States Government the British incomes of residents in the United States. The
main aim of this arrangement is not to prevent the evasion of
the British exchange control but to prevent tax evasion and
double taxation. Nevertheless, its effect is to make the evasion of
exchange control more difficult. The number of similar agreements in operation is increasing steadily.

Above all, there is scope for international assistance to maintain exchange rates in the sphere of co-ordinating domestic
monetary policies. If the price level in one country is too high
and the resulting adverse balance of payments threatens to
undermine the stability of the exchange, this disequilibrium can
be put right either through deflation in the country concerned
or through inflation in other countries. Up to now there has
been very little co-operation of this kind. Admittedly, it would
involve considerable sacrifices on the part of countries which
are to adapt their monetary policies to the requirements of some

other country. In his book, *The Dollar*, Harrod draws attention to an early instance of such co-operation. In 1927 the Federal Reserve authorities eased credit conditions in the United States mainly for the sake of assisting Britain and other countries. More recently, the Bank of England and the Deutsche Bundesbank are believed to have lowered the Bank Rate mainly in order to relieve pressure on the dollar in the early sixties. In 1962 Britain repaid the favour, received thirty-five years earlier, by lowering the Bank Rate partly for the sake of obviating the necessity for the Federal Reserve authorities to raise their Bank Rate.

Yet another means of monetary policy in the international sphere was the mitigation of a scarcity of gold. If scarcity was due to maldistribution, then the country or countries which possess an unduly large proportion of the world's stock of gold could contribute towards the solution by lending freely to other countries, or by lowering their tariff walls, thereby reducing their gold surplus. This attitude was adopted by Britain throughout the nineteenth century. In spite of a persistently favourable balance of payments, Britain never kept an unduly large gold reserve because she was willing to import the goods of her debtors and to re-lend her surpluses in the form of long-term loans and investments or short-term credits. When after the First World War the United States became the principal surplus country, she did not pursue the same course to a sufficient extent. As a result she accumulated and retained an excessive proportion of the world's monetary supplies, and most other countries were left with gold reserves that were inadequate for their requirements. After the Second World War the United States came to pursue a more liberal policy of lending – indeed, too liberal from the point of view of maintaining an adequate gold reserve.

Various devices were adopted during the twenties as a result of the co-operation of the Central Banks to economise in the use of gold in order to mitigate this scarcity. The most effective, if unintentional, help came, however, through the unilateral action of the United States in raising its official buying price of gold to $35 an ounce in 1934.

Owing to the rise in prices that has taken place since then, the monetary stocks of gold have become even less adequate than they were before 1934. To remedy this situation the United States Government has been urged from various sides to raise once more the dollar price of gold substantially as part of an all-round increase of the price of gold in terms of all currencies. Such a measure was expressly provided for in the Bretton Woods scheme. In spite of this the United States only raised the price of gold, with the utmost reluctance, to $38 in 1972. Meanwhile, much of the American gold holding found its way back to Western Europe.

The 'gold rush' of 1960 gave rise to an arrangement between Central Banks to co-operate in order to prevent the London market price of gold from rising to an abnormal premium. The dollar scare and sterling scare of 1961 led to the Basle Agreement, under which Central Banks provided mutual and reciprocal support to each other's exchanges. Most important of all, a number of Central Banks agreed to retain a larger part of their dollar reserves instead of converting them into gold.

The end of maintaining a stable price level is difficult to attain unless the domestic policies adopted for its sake are supplemented by international action. Unless there is virtually complete economic isolation such as exists in Communist countries all the time and in capitalist countries in times of war, the internal economy of any country is exposed to international trends to a very large extent. If there is a rising trend in world prices, no single country can isolate itself from it unless it raises the exchange value of its currency. If the world trend is downwards, the only way in which a country can maintain the stability of its domestic prices is through a devaluation of its currency. For the sake of avoiding changes in parities while maintaining the stability of the domestic price level, it is essential that a large number of countries should co-operate in reducing to a minimum the fluctuations of world prices. Progress in that direction has been negligible. It has been confined to international agreements aiming at the stabilisation of a few important commodities. In order to be effective the policy would have to cover a large number of commodities, and attempts at price-fixing would have to be supplemented by the creation of international buffer-pools which would remove from the markets any large surpluses and would cover deficiencies. Although such schemes have been under discussion, they belong to the realm of the distant future.

During the thirties it was imperative to reverse the prevailing deflationary trend. To that end the co-ordination of national monetary policies would have been very helpful. Instead each country endeavoured to work out its salvation independently of the others and very often at their expense. There were no co-ordinated efforts to reverse the downward trend of world prices. After the Second World War the world trend became distinctly inflationary. Again there was no co-ordinated international policy to check this unwanted trend. Even though various international organisations did their utmost to exhort the Governments to put their respective houses in order and stop their inflationary domestic policies, or at any rate to keep in step regarding the degree of their internal inflations due to excessive increases of wages, they had no power to compel sovereign States to comply with their wishes.

Exhortation appears to be still the most frequently employed means in the sphere of international monetary policy. The International Monetary Fund and the economic organisations of the United Nations and of the European Common Market miss few opportunities to urge the member Governments to implement their various undertakings under the Bretton Woods Agreement and other agreements, and to behave in accordance with the requirements of international economic co-operation. Actually, many Governments abandoned multiple exchange practices, relaxed exchange controls, and restored a high degree of convertibility of their currencies, in addition to removing or relaxing quotas and other import restrictions. But there has been no co-ordination of basic monetary policies.

The truth is that so long as countries retain their political sovereignty, their Governments, Parliaments and public opinion will want to exercise it in the sphere of monetary policy in accordance with what they rightly or wrongly regard as the national interest. It is only if and when some form of World Government should ever be created that the adoption of international means of monetary policy in pursuance of international ends would become a practical possibility to any considerable extent. It is just conceivable, however, that within more limited spheres such as the Common Market, far-reaching co-ordination of monetary policies might be achieved eventually.

In 1952–4 the Governments of the Sterling Area countries succeeded in co-ordinating their internal and external monetary policies to a considerable degree in order to stop the drain on the gold reserve. It was agreed to initiate disinflationary measures and to adopt drastic import restrictions. A plan for the eventual restoration of sterling convertibility was elaborated with the approval of all Sterling Area Governments. These decisions constituted a remarkable progress compared with the earlier state of affairs in which the monetary policies of these Governments were largely independent of each other, especially in the domestic monetary sphere. On the other hand, there was inadequate co-ordination, during the late fifties and the sixties, of their policies of resisting inflation.

Another instance of progress towards international monetary policy within a limited geographical sphere was the operation of the European Payments Union. A clearing system was established but it did not operate for very long. On the other hand, the establishment of the European Common Market led to a more ambitious scheme of European monetary integration. The first step towards it was a narrowing of the spread of the support points of exchange rates between the six countries of the EEC on 24 April 1972. Britain joined the arrangement on 1 May, but a few weeks later she abandoned it and allowed sterling to float.

The exchange control measures adopted by Britain simultaneously with the adoption of floating rates brought the Sterling Area virtually to an end. The restrictions on capital exports and other restrictions came to be applied to all countries of the Sterling Area with the exception of the Irish Republic. This meant the termination of the most effective international monetary co-operation system that has ever existed, after having been in existence for forty years.

On the other hand, six months earlier the Smithsonian Agreement of 1971 provided an outstanding instance of international co-operation in the form of a realignment of parities which was negotiated within a few days. At the same time it was agreed to broaden the band between support points. While it took years to negotiate the Bretton Woods system, the Smithsonian system that was to replace it was agreed upon over a weekend. It was all the more unfortunate that the EEC deemed it wise to depart from it four months later, and that the floating pound came to jeopardise it six months later. It opened up the possibility of a currency war between rival blocs and of a relapse into currency chaos, even if up to the time of writing the British move produced no such disastrous effects.

The goal of international monetary co-operation is to persuade surplus countries to cover automatically the deficit of deficit countries, either by accepting the latters' currencies in payment for their surplus and holding them until a change in the balance of payments leads to an automatic settlement, or by accepting some form of international means of payment placed at the disposal of the deficit countries by some international institution. The effort made by Keynes to persuade the United States to agree to some such scheme met with no response. But when the United States became a deficit country, she eagerly seized upon the formula provided by the Barber Plan – which was basically the same as the Keynes Plan had been – for the issue of SDRs.

Extensive international monetary co-operation is by no means an unmixed blessing. There is the risk that excessive mutual assistance – especially if it comes to be granted automatically as it is intended to under the Barber Plan – produces a demoralising effect on deficit countries. The willingness of surplus countries to accept a formula under which deficit countries have no incentive to correct the deficit encourages the latter to pursue unsound policies, as they can do so with impunity. In an effort to increase international liquidity, expert opinion is inclined to overlook the fact that artificial international liquidity is no substitute for the correction of fundamental disequilibrium. An overdose of foreign assistance undermines the balance-of-payments discipline. It has become unfashionable to pay attention to this aspect of the problem.

CHAPTER FORTY-SIX

Monetary Theory and Monetary Policy

ALTHOUGH this book is not directly concerned with the theoretical aspects of money, it contains frequent reference to various monetary theories on which monetary policies are based. We now propose to examine very briefly the relationship between monetary theory and monetary policy. It is widely believed among laymen and even among students of economics that economic theory is expected to provide an infallible or at any rate reasonably dependable guide for the use of statesmen and administrators in the shaping of their economic policies. According to this conception, if only the Governments could be prevailed upon to accept the correct monetary theory – *i.e.* the theory that is considered to be correct by the policy advisers concerned – on which to base their monetary policies, they could not go wrong.

Unfortunately things are not so simple in real life. No economic theory can be claimed to provide the full practical solution, because the chances that it covers all possible economic situations are extremely remote. Any single economic theory which would try to allow for all possible situations would be so involved that it would be unintelligible to all but a few select academic economists. And the chances are that even then some unknown factors would be overlooked. Most theories in the past resorted to over-simplification by limiting the range of factors to be allowed for.

During the nineteenth century and the early part of this century the so-called static economic theory predominated, under which the rules were based on the assumption that the overwhelming majority of factors would remain 'neutral'. By such means it was possible to establish rules how certain factors are liable to affect the economic situation provided that other things remain unchanged. This method found application in the monetary sphere in the form of the quantity theory of money. The practical conclusions inferred from it hold good only on the assumption that factors other than the quantity of money remain the same.

The building-up of such hypotheses is undoubtedly of great value provided that those who create them and those who study them constantly bear it in mind that they are broad general propositions which only operate within the limits set by the hypothesis itself, and that in a practical situation the results indicated by the theory are liable to be modified. So long as this is borne in mind, monetary theories can be of great use to those in charge of managing the monetary system. If on the other hand they are interpreted in a dogmatic spirit, it is liable to lead to entirely wrong conclusions and to do much more harm than good.

In post-war years attempts were made to develop a so-called dynamic economic theory which aims at allowing for the effects of some factors which had been assumed to be 'neutral' for the purposes of static economic theory. In the monetary sphere too, dynamic theory had been gaining ground. It is undoubtedly nearer to practical requirements than the static theory. Even so, a really comprehensive watertight dynamic monetary theory which allows for every possible factor has not yet been elaborated, and it is doubtful if it ever will be. Some essential factor is almost bound to be overlooked, partly because new factors are liable to arise or existing factors are apt to increase or decline in importance, and partly because human behaviour cannot be reduced to terms of mathematical accuracy.

In the past, most administrators and politicians responsible for monetary policy were not familiar with monetary theory, and therefore had every reason for distrusting it. Indeed, even now, high Treasury officials and Central Bankers are essentially practical men with neither time nor inclination to acquire too profound a theoretical knowledge. While Treasuries usually have economic advisers, until recently those in a position to take or influence monetary policy decisions were practical administrators with relatively little theoretical background. As for the politicians on whom ultimate responsibility for major monetary policy decisions rests, they are usually devoid of theoretical knowledge. It is only in recent times that a generation of Treasury and Central Bank officials has arisen which has due respect for economic theory and has mastered its basic principles.

Generally speaking, it is true that theoretical monetary economists have had relatively little share in shaping monetary policy. There were, of course, exceptions. In Britain, Goschen, one of the leading theoretical experts on foreign exchange and the author of a standard work on its theory, became Chancellor of the Exchequer. An instance of monetary policy being guided by a theoretical economist was the regime of Keynes at the Treasury from 1940 to 1946. In his capacity of adviser he influenced to a considerable degree the monetary policies of three Chancellors of the Exchequer. Likewise, President Roosevelt's 'Brains Trust' played a decisive role in shaping the monetary policy of the United States for some time after 1933. During and after the First World War the Swedish school of economists played a prominent part in shaping the monetary policies of their country. Helfferich, in his capacity of Finance Minister of the German Reich during the First World War, had ample opportunity to put his monetary theories into practice. It was the irony of fate that, even though he was one of the leading advocates of 'hard money', he was fated to pursue an inflationary policy that prepared the way for the great collapse of the mark in 1923.

It does not necessarily mean, however, that once a monetary economist is given an opportunity to determine monetary policy either as a Finance Minister or as head of a Central Bank or as a 'power behind the throne', he would always necessarily aim at putting his favourite monetary theory into operation. The moment he assumes a responsible post he gains access to a wealth of information which is liable to modify his views. Confronted with the responsibility for taking practical decisions that are liable to affect the lives of many millions of people within his country and even beyond its borders, he might be inclined to reconsider his views in the light of practical considerations which he had hitherto disregarded. During the Second World War a large number of academic economists became temporary officials for the duration. Most of them left the Civil Service with their attitude more or less modified under the influence of their practical experience. This did not necessarily mean that they came to the conclusion that their pre-war theories were wrong. What happened was that they realised the limitations of those theories as a practical guide to monetary policy. Or they may have realised that it is often politically impracticable to follow a monetary policy which would be an ideal solution from a purely economic point of view.

Notwithstanding this, in the course of monetary history monetary theory and monetary policy were proceeding on parallel courses to a remarkable degree. For centuries the mercantilist school dominated both literature on monetary theory and monetary policy. The development of credit theories coincided with the emergence of paper currency and bank credit in the modern sense. The liberal school of economists reigned supreme in monetary theory during the nineteenth and the early part of the twentieth century, which was on the whole an era of economic and monetary liberalism. So long as the gold standard reigned almost unchallenged as the theoretically ideal monetary system, the monetary policies of the most advanced countries aimed at its maintenance. Theories and policies of managed money were almost entirely unknown; they appeared simultaneously during the inter-war period.

The facts should not be regarded as necessarily indicating the unilateral influence of monetary theory over monetary policy. The relations between the two have always been largely reciprocal. Monetary economists could not always claim credit for having guided statesmen and administrators in the shaping of monetary policy. Very often they themselves were guided by practical developments decided upon largely under the stress of practical expediency. On many occasions the role of economists was confined to elaborating theoretical foundations for policies which had been adopted largely independently of their influence.

A characteristic instance of the passive role economists were liable to play was provided by the experience of the so-called 'gold scare' in 1937. During the first half of that year Stock Exchanges, foreign exchange markets, commodity markets and trade in general came under the depressing influence of a growing belief that it was the intention of the United States Administration either to lower its official buying price for gold or to suspend or limit the free import of gold. Many thousands of theoretically illiterate bankers, brokers, speculators and businessmen arrived at the conclusion, without any guidance by theoretical economists, that the United States authorities were contemplating some such action for the sake of preventing a boom. Thereupon theoretical economists set out to provide somewhat belatedly – after the gold scare had already been in progress for months – a theoretical foundation for this assumption by producing figures and arguments in support of their contention that on the basis of the American price of $35 an ounce the world's monetary stock of gold was in excess of requirements. When it became evident that the United States authorities did not intend to change their buying price for gold or to interfere with the free influx of gold, all the theoretical reasoning in favour of such action subsided almost overnight.

An instance to show that practical monetary policy often precedes in chronological order the theoretical foundations on which it is based is provided by the policy of fighting deflation by means of public works. Keynes advocated this policy before the General Election of 1929, when in his much-quoted pamphlet *Can Lloyd George do it ?* he came out whole-heartedly in support of Lloyd George's electioneering programme of employment-creating public works. It was not until 1936, however, that Keynes elaborated the theoretical foundation for that policy in his *General Theory*. One of the principles laid down in that book was that equilibrium was possible under large-scale unemployment. He endeavoured to disprove the classical theory according to which full employment was the only conceivable state of equilibrium and any unemployment constituted temporary disequilibrium which was liable to become adjusted through the automatic working of natural economic trends. Under the classical concept any form of Government intervention to create employment was rejected as being more, harmful than good. Under the principle laid down by Keynes, on the other hand, economic factors operating automatically cannot be depended upon for restoring full employment. Once this theoretical rule is accepted, the next step is to infer from it the logical conclusion that, since full employment is not necessarily reached through the automatic working of economic tendencies, it is for the Government to intervene and create additional employment with the aid of monetary and other devices. On the basis of Keynes's theory this conclusion is unanswerable. It is worth noting, however, that he reached his conclusion in 1929 and it was not until seven years later that he elaborated the premises from which it follows. In his biography of Keynes, Harrod draws attention to this interesting point.

However, it would be idle to deny that, consciously or otherwise, politicians and administrators in charge of monetary policies are liable to come under the influence of the prevailing monetary theories. Whether or not this is a good thing depends not only on whether the theory is right or wrong, but also on the way it is applied. It is necessary to bear in mind that the same theory may serve as a basis for several different policies.

Moreover, changes in the economic situation and the other relevant circumstances are apt to affect the suitability of a monetary theory as a basis for monetary policy. There can be little doubt that nineteenth-century economic liberalism, on which the policy of maintaining the automatic gold standard was based, was in accordance with Britain's requirements between the end of the Napoleonic Wars and the beginning of the First World War. Unfortunately that classical theory continued to dominate British monetary policy long after the conditions which had justified it ceased to exist. Hence the grave mistakes made during the twenties. The theory which had once been a suitable guide for the monetary policy ceased to be suitable amidst changed circumstances.

Another instance of bad theory being responsible for bad policy occurred after the Second World War. There is every reason to believe that the mistaken popular definition of inflation was largely responsible for the inflationary policies adopted in Britain and in many other countries. Under the definition accepted in substance by most monetary theorists and by many practical men, inflation was the state of affairs in which 'too much money was chasing too few goods'. From this principle politicians wishing to take the line of least resistance inferred that, provided that the rise in prices was not due to a previous increase in the volume of money, there was no inflation. This meant that if the price level rose as a result of excessive increase of wages or of incomes in general, or of some other reason unconnected with Government policy, and if the rise in prices resulted in pressure for an increase in the volume of currency and credit to meet increased requirements, the Government concerned did not consider it its duty to resist the trend for the volume of currency and credit to adjust itself subsequently to the higher level of prices. If only Ministers, officials, economists and the general public realised that the upward movement of the vicious spiral in which prices, cost of living, wages, cost of production, etc., are chasing each other constitutes inflation irrespective of whether the rise in prices preceded or succeeded the increase in the volume of money, there might have been more determined resistance to the expansion in the volume of money following on previous increases of prices.

One of the instances in which correct policy emerged from good theory is the acceptance by policy-makers of the differentiation between cost inflation and demand inflation, calling for different measures. Another instance is that the realisation of the essentially dynamic influence of forward exchange induced the monetary authorities in the early sixties to overcome their reluctance to intervene in the forward exchange market.

Even a correct monetary theory is liable to be misused when it is applied as a basis of monetary policy. It is a fatal mistake to imagine that merely because a theory is good it necessarily provides a complete guide to practical action. Monetary theory is only meant to apply to a hypothetical situation. It is bound to over-simplify conditions and its conclusions are always subject to the provision of 'other things being equal'. In practice other things are hardly ever equal. Those in charge of monetary policy have to allow for these 'other things' instead of merely making reservations about them, as theoretical economists often do, in order to safeguard themselves against being blamed if forecasts based on their theories should prove to be incorrect. The trouble is that even though they and their theoretical advisers pay lip-service to the reservation, they are liable to become hypnotised by the broad principle of the theory and are inclined to apply it as if it were a hard-and-fast rule. Therein lies the danger of static theory.

Having said all this, it is necessary to emphasise that monetary theory is indispensable as a background for monetary policy. It is, of course, conceivable that a Government may stumble on the right solution in spite of the absence of any theoretical background. The chances are, however, much more in favour of finding the right solution if they are aware of the broad theoretical implications, always provided that the theories are applied with care and discrimination.

CHAPTER FORTY-SEVEN

Limitations of Monetary Policy

THE monetarist school is not alone in taking it for granted that Governments and Central Banks have unlimited power in determining monetary trends and, through them, economic trends. It is a widely held belief that the authorities are able to regulate the economy by applying the right devices of monetary policy to the right degree, in the same way as one is able to regulate the temperature of a bath by turning on and off the hot-water tap and the cold-water tap. It is a matter of opinion whether it would be an unmixed blessing if this belief were correct, and the monetary authorities had unlimited power. After all, Finance Ministers and Central Bank Governors, and their expert advisors, are far from being omniscient and infallible. They are known to have made innumerable mistakes in exercising their powers to devise and execute monetary policies, and the greater is their power the graver their mistakes are liable to be. So it is perhaps as well that monetary policy has its limitations, especially if the decisions rest with men who are dogmatic, incompetent or just unlucky in their hunches or in the choice of their economic advisers.

Most practical men concerned with monetary policy are more or less aware of the limitations of their policies in bringing about the results aimed at. On the other hand, many economists who advise them officially or unofficially are inclined to think that if only the Treasuries and Central Banks accepted their advice, the nation concerned and the world at large could live happily ever after. They are oblivious of the limits of the extent to which the monetary system or the economy is liable to respond to the measures that might be adopted or are adopted on their advice. Not only do they consider themselves infallible, but they are convinced that what they consider the right measures are bound to produce a full effect.

The adherents of the monetarist school are among the worst offenders in this respect. They are firmly convinced that by simply regulating the quantity of money, Governments would be able to produce the desired effect on the trend of prices and of business activity. As already pointed out before, they are unaware that the same changes in the quantity of money are not likely to produce the same effects. The effect of the changes is liable to be modified by the elasticities of the various factors involved, due largely to the response of producers, merchants, bankers and consumers to the changes.

When the quantity of money is increased, it does not necessarily mean that the demand increases to anything like the same proportion, if at all. As we saw earlier, it is possible that the velocity of circulation of money declines, because the increase in its quantity inspires distrust among producers, consumers and intermediaries. On the other hand, it is equally possible that the effect of the increase in the quantity of money becomes self-aggravating, so that in addition to its quantity its velocity also increases. In that case the effect is liable to be much more than what those in charge of monetary policy were bargaining for. Human psychology is a most important element and it is liable to influence the effect of material changes in either direction. It is absolutely incalculable.

Moreover, even the actual increase in the quantity of money by means of the measure adopted to that end is not a matter of simple arithmetic. The fact that the Central Bank makes it possible for banks to expand credit does not necessarily mean that they will in fact expand credit, or at any rate it does not necessarily mean that they will expand it to the extent intended by the authorities. Even if the credit is available, it does not necessarily mean that the banks' customers will take advantage of the relaxation of the former limitations. They might prefer, for a variety of reasons, to abstain from increasing the amount of their borrowing even if the money is made available to them at lower interest rates. For instance, the prolonged reflationary policy of cheap money during the thirties was slow in producing its effect, because banks' customers were pessimistic about the prospects and did not dare to increase their production or their inventories of materials. The uncertainty of the outlook discouraged consumers from increasing their purchases. It took quite a number of years before they overcame their reluctance and before the volume of money was expanded in accordance with the official policy and the additional credit that was available came to be used for increasing business activity and consumption.

In such a situation it is not always advisable to try to force the pace. Roosevelt's 'new deal' did produce plenty of additional money through public spending on a large scale and through other reflationary measures, but amidst the then prevailing conditions his policies inspired distrust in the business world and many producers and merchants abstained from making full use of the increased credit facilities available to them. It took some time before they and the consumers came to recover from the effects of their disastrous experience of a few years earlier. Likewise, bankers took some time to overcome sufficiently the memories of the series of crises to be keen on expanding credit.

The monetarist school is right in casting doubt on the effectiveness of fiscal policy, owing to the time-lag between the Government's decision to adopt an expansionary policy through budgetary deficits and the actual effect on the quantity of money. But the effect of changing the quantity of money through changes in interest rates or reserve ratios or open-market operations is also far from being the exact science which the monetarist school claims it to be. In fact, changes in certain taxes, such as the purchase tax for instance, are more likely to affect the volume of consumer demand immediately than changes in the volume of money.

The fact that money is available at a lower interest rate need not necessarily induce producers and businessmen to borrow more. They might be discouraged from doing so if they fear a decline in prices or in demand. Likewise, an increase in interest rates is not certain to discourage demand, for credit for borrowers might expect to be able to pass on to the consumer the extra cost of higher interest charges.

A policy of high interest rates is likely to lose much of its effect as and when the public becomes inflation-conscious and gets into the habit of thinking in terms of real interest rates instead of money interest rates. An interest charge of 8 per cent, or a profit of 8 per cent, only represents 2 per cent if the price of goods rises by 6 per cent. In respect of the cost of production it is not the change in the general price level that matters but the change in the prices of the goods directly concerned. And even in that respect the potential borrower must take into consideration not only the likely increase of the prices at which he expects to be able to sell his goods, but also the likely increase of the cost of production. If wages and other elements in the cost of production tend to rise faster than prices, then the fact that real interest rates based on the general price level or even on the prices of the goods concerned are reduced to 2 per cent does not induce manufacturers to increase their producing capacity. Even a negative real rate of interest is in such situations unable to induce them to take advantage of the credit facilities available to them.

Production of capital goods with long delivery dates is particularly difficult to influence by monetary policy devices during periods of wage inflation when the cost of production is liable to increase considerably before the contract can be completed. This accounted largely for the depressed state of the shipbuilding industry in the late sixties and early seventies. Unsatisfactory labour relations are also liable to frustrate the effects of monetary policy. The likelihood of strikes and of other industrial action is apt to discourage business firms even if on the face of it the production and purchase of goods promises to be profitable.

Above all, the frequency of unofficial strikes is a strong deterrent. Employers are able to some extent to anticipate official strikes by allowing their inventories of raw materials, fuel and semi-products to run down, so that they need not lose much interest during a prolonged strike. But if wildcat strikes erupt unexpectedly, the deliveries of stocks will continue to arrive during strikes and, in addition to loss of interest, the firms are liable to be confronted with problems of storage. They are in a position to some extent to take into account the possibility of official strike when wage agreements with the trade unions expire, so that they arrange delivery dates accordingly. But unofficial lightning strikes in their plants or in other plants or industries on which they depend upset their calculations and expose them to the payment of penalties for late deliveries.

Such possibilities are entirely independent of the effects of monetary policy. During periods when unofficial strikes are particularly frequent, Central Banks and Governments are entirely powerless in inducing industry to expand by making money plentiful and cheap. The deterioration of industrial relations in recent years in Britain and in other industrial countries has gone a long way towards making monetary policy ineffective. The only form of monetary policy that is liable to affect the business trend is the policy of statutory pay restraint. Even that policy is not foolproof, for it does not provide absolute safeguards against unofficial strikes. But, as I tried to prove in Chapter 38, it is more effective than any other kind of monetary policy.

CHAPTER FORTY-EIGHT

The Future of Monetary Policy

THE present generation has seen revolutionary changes in the sphere of monetary policy. In our lifetime monetary policy has become much broader and more diversified in its aim and much more scientific in its methods. Its techniques have become much more sophisticated. Its management is no longer a task that part-time amateurs following time-honoured rules could reasonably be expected to perform. Today those in charge of the management of monetary policy are required to know incomparably more about it than their predecessors did. Admittedly, their superior knowledge does not safeguard their communities against mistakes which are made in spite of the adoption of scientific methods – and indeed often because of it. There can be no doubt, however, that the authorities today are much better equipped for carrying out their increasingly difficult task. They can rely on the services of first-rate experts who are fully familiar with the theoretical background and have at their disposal a wealth of relevant factual and statistical information which did not exist until recent years.

Monetary theory itself has made remarkable progress in the past forty years after its century of relative stagnation during the period between Ricardo and Keynes. The progress of monetary theory opened up wide possibilities for monetary policy to pursue its new ends with the aid of new means.

The ends of monetary policy, like those of economic policy in general, have undergone a far-reaching change in recent years. The accent is now on social rather than economic ends. Politicians aim at achieving the highest degree of welfare for the largest possible numbers, if necessary even at the cost of sacrificing stability. Indeed, when the economic requirements of higher productivity come into conflict with the social requirements of egalitarianism, the chances are that more often than not the latter is allowed to prevail. In the choice and application of the means, too, efficiency is often sacrificed. Rather than apply too unpleasant effective remedies, ineffective remedies are applied.

The question is, are these trends which are now affecting the choice of the ends and means of monetary policy likely to continue? There can be little doubt that the priority of social ends over economic ends will be maintained, and more than maintained, under a democratic regime and under the changed balance of power which points increasingly towards a virtual dictatorship by trade unions. In this respect, as in so many other respects, it seems to be impossible to put the clock back. Which is to some extent all to the good. Never again will public opinion in democratic countries look upon a slump brought about by mistaken monetary policy as an act of God. The public is not likely to tolerate policies which prefer to create perennial large-scale unemployment and business depressions rather than abandon the stubborn defence of parities at an obviously indefensible level. It seems more than probable that monetary policy will tend to conform willy-nilly to the popular view as to how to secure the highest degree of immediate advantages for the largest numbers.

In earlier editions of this book I expressed my hope that in the future Governments and Parliaments would not always necessarily pursue escalating inflationary policies in order to satisfy popular clamour for 'bread and circuses' – or, in modern terms, for increasing social service benefits and colour TV sets. I expressed the hope that in the course of time a more enlightened spirit might prevail over the present orgy of unenlightened short-sighted self-interest. On the basis of the experience of the last decade or so, I have reluctantly come to a less optimistic conclusion. It now seems to me probable that even if some honest and courageous democratically elected Government should adopt an anti-inflationary monetary policy, it might be prevented from carrying it out by the undemocratic and anti-democratic attitude of trade unions, which consider themselves increasingly above the law.

The large unions will exploit the strength derived from the sheer weight of their numbers to the full, and the smaller unions will exploit their considerable nuisance value, for ensuring wage increases far in excess of the increase in productivity. Yet even to the extent to which wage increases are claimed to be justified by previous increases in the cost of living, the rise in prices of goods and services is itself largely the consequence of their previous unearned wage increases and those of their fellow-unions.

The only hope for a change in this attitude – if it can be called a hope – is that sooner or later some major crisis might bring the working classes to their senses. Judging by their utter indifference towards the public interest in face of the crises of recent years, it would have to be a crisis of catastrophic dimensions to make them realise that a stage is bound to be reached beyond which they cannot possibly benefit by inflicting ruin on the community. Runaway inflation or mass unemployment might induce them to respond to a disinflationary policy instead of trying to contract out of the effects of inflation or stagflation.

The elimination of the balance-of-payments discipline through a demonetisation of gold, and an over-generous allocation of SDRs, will make it even more difficult for Governments to try to make the unions see sense. Why should the unions moderate their demands if the effect of wage inflation on the balance of payments is automatically remedied by the use of SDRs to meet the deficit? The first step towards a return to reason would be to make the advocates of ingenious devices realise that nothing but hard and honest work can produce the desired effect, and that they render a grave disservice to the community by misleading it into believing that smart conjurers' tricks in monetary policy are a substitute for hard and honest work.

Bibliography

T HE most valuable sources for material on monetary policy are the publications of the Bank of England, the Federal Reserve Board, the Federal Reserve Bank of New York and other Central Banks, and the annual reports of the International Monetary Fund and the Bank for International Settlements.

AHEARN, D. S., *Federal Reserve Policy Reappraised*, New York, 1963.

ANGELL, JAMES W., *The Behaviour of Money*, New York, 1936.

ARDAKAR, B. P., *The Theory of Monetary Policy*, London, 1935.

ASCHEIM, J., *Techniques of Monetary Control*, Baltimore, 1961.

ASHTON, T. S., and SAYERS, R. S. (eds.), *Papers in English Monetary History*, London, 1953.

BAGEHOT, WALTER, *Lombard Street*, new ed., London, 1931.

BAREAU, PAUL, *The Sterling Area*, 2nd ed., London, 1950.

BELL, J. W., and SPAHR, W. E. (eds.), *A Proper Monetary and Banking System for the United States*, New York, 1960.

BLOOMFIELD, A. I., *Capital Imports and the American Balance of Payments*, Chicago, 1950.

BRESCIANI-TURRONI, C., *The Economics of Inflation* (translated from Italian), London, 1937.

BRITTAN, S., *The Price of Economic Freedom*, London, 1970.

BROWN, W. A., *England and the New Gold Standard*, London, 1929.

BURNS, A. R., *Money and Monetary Policy in Early Times*, London, 1927.

Prosperity Without Inflation, New York, 1957.

CANNAN, EDWIN, *Money: Its Connexion with Rising and Falling Prices*, 8th ed., London, 1935.

CANTILLON, RICHARD, *Essai sur la nature du commerce en général* (translated and edited by Henry Higgs), London, 1931.

CASSEL, GUSTAV, *Money and Foreign Exchange after 1914*, London, 1922.

The Downfall of the Gold Standard, Oxford, 1936.

CHALMERS, E., *International Interest Rate War*, London, 1972.

CHALMERS, R., *A History of Currency in the British Colonies*, London, 1893.

CHANDLER, LESTER V., *The Economics of Money and Banking*, New York, 1948.

CLARKE, W. M., *The City in World Economy*, London, 1965.

CLEGG, H. A., *How to Run an Incomes Policy*, London, 1971.

COFFEY, P., and PRESLEY, J. R., *European Monetary Integration*, London, 1971.

COHEN, B. J., *The Future of Sterling*, London, 1971.

Commission on Money and Credit, Report of, New York, 1961.

Committee on the Working of the Monetary System, Report of, London, 1959.

  Minutes of Evidence, London, 1960.

  Memoranda of Evidence, London, 1960.

CONAN, A. R., *The Sterling Area*, London, 1952.

CRAIG, SIR JOHN, *The Mint: A History of the London Mint from A.D. 287 to 1948*, Cambridge, 1953.

CROWTHER, SIR GEOFFREY, *An Outline of Money*, rev. ed., London, 1959.

CURRIE, LAUCHLIN, *The Supply and Control of Money in the United States*, Cambridge, Mass., 1934.

DACEY, W. MANNING, *The British Banking Mechanism*, London, 1951.

DILLARD, DUDLEY, *The Economics of J. M. Keynes*, London, 1950.

DURBIN, E. F. M., *The Problem of Credit Policy*, London, 1935.

EINZIG, PAUL, *International Gold Movements*, London, 1929.

  Exchange Control, London, 1934.

  Monetary Reform in Theory and Practice, London, 1936.

  Primitive Money, in its Ethnological, Historical, and Economic Aspects, 2nd enlarged ed., London, 1966.

  Inflation, London, 1952.

  The Economic Consequence of Automation, London, 1956.

  The Control of the Purse, London, 1959.

  In the Centre of Things, London, 1960.

  The History of Foreign Exchange, London, 1962.

  A Dynamic Theory of Forward Exchange, 3rd ed., London, 1967.

  Foreign Exchange Crises, London, 1968.

  Leads and Lags, London, 1968.

  The Euro-Bond Market, 2nd ed., London, 1969.

  A Textbook on Foreign Exchange, 2nd ed., London, 1969.

  The Euro-Dollar System, 4th ed., London, 1970.

  The Case against Floating Exchanges, London, 1970.

  The Case against Joining the Common Market, London, 1971.

  Parallel Money Markets, 2 vols., London, 1971–2.

  The Destiny of the Dollar, London, 1972.

  The Destiny of Gold, London, 1972.

ELLIS, HOWARD S., *German Monetary Theory*, Cambridge, Mass., 1934.

(ed.) *A Survey of Contemporary Economics*, Philadelphia, 1949.

FEAVEARYEAR, A. E., *The Pound Sterling: A History of English Money*, Oxford, 1931.

FEDERAL RESERVE BOARD, *The Federal Funds Market*, Washington, 1959.

FFORDE, J. S., *The Federal Reserve System, 1915–1949*, Oxford, 1954.

FISHER, IRVING, *The Purchasing Power of Money*, rev. ed., New York, 1920.

Stabilizing the Dollar, New York, 1920.

FRIEDMAN, MILTON, *Essays in Positive Economics*, Chicago, 1953.

A Theoretical Framework for Monetary Analysis, New York, 1971.

GALBRAITH, J. K., *A Theory of Price Control*, Cambridge, Mass., 1952.

GAYER, ARTHUR D., *Monetary Policy and Economic Stabilization*, 2nd ed., London, 1937.

GOLDENWEISER, E. A., *Monetary Management*, New York, 1949.

GOSCHEN, GEORGE J., *The Theory of Foreign Exchanges*, 2nd ed., London, 1863.

GRANT, A. T. K., *The Machinery of Finance and the Management of Sterling*, London, 1967.

GREGORY, T. E., *Foreign Exchange Before, During, and After the War*, Oxford, 1921.

The Gold Standard and its Future, 3rd ed., London, 1934.

GREIDANUS, TJARDUS, *The Value of Money*, London, 1932.

GURLEY, J. G., and SHAW, E. S., *Money in a Theory of Finance*, Washington, 1960.

HABERLER, GOTTFRIED VON, *Prosperity and Depression*, Geneva, 1939.

HAINES, W. W., *Money, Prices and Policy*, New York, 1961.

HALL, N. F., *The Exchange Equalization Account*, London, 1935.

HALM, GEORGE N., *International Monetary Co-operation*, Chapel Hill, N.C., 1945.

HAMILTON, EARL J., *Money, Prices, and Wages in Valencia, Aragon, and Navarre, 1351–1500*, Cambridge, Mass., 1936.

HANSEN, ALVIN H., and CLEMENCE, R. V. (eds.), *Readings in Business Cycles*, London, 1953.

HANSEN, BENT, *A Study in the Theory of Inflation*, London, 1951.

HARRIS, S. E., *Monetary Problems of the British Empire*, New York, 1931.

John Maynard Keynes, New York, 1955.

(ed.) *The New Economics: Keynes' Influence on Theory and Public Policy*, New York, 1947.

The Dollar in Crisis, New York, 1961.

HARROD, R. F., *International Economics*, London, 1933.
  The Life of John Maynard Keynes, London, 1951.
  The Dollar, London, 1953.
HAWTREY, R. G., *Currency and Credit*, 4th ed., London, 1950.
  Capital and Employment, 2nd ed., London, 1952.
HAYEK, F. A. VON, *Monetary Theory and the Trade Cycle*, London, 1933.
  Prices and Production, 2nd ed., London, 1935.
  Monetary Nationalism and International Stability, London, 1937.
HEILPERIN, M. A., *International Monetary Economics*, London, 1939.
HELFFERICH, KARL, *Money* (translated from German), London, 1927.
HICKS, J. R., *A Contribution to the Theory of Trade Cycle*, Oxford, 1950.
H.M. STATIONERY OFFICE, *Report of the Committee on Finance and Industry*, London, 1931.
HIRSCH, F., *Money International*, London, 1967.
HOLMANS, A. E., *United States Fiscal Policy*, London, 1961.
HOMER, SIDNEY, *A History of Interest Rates*, New Brunswick, N.J., 1963.
INSTITUTE OF BANKERS, *Monetary and Banking Policies*, London, 1955.
JOHNSON, BRIAN, *The Politics of Money*, London, 1970.
JOHNSON, H. G., *Money, Trade and Economic Growth*, London, 1962.
KEYNES, J. M., *Indian Currency and Finance*, London, 1913.
  A Tract on Monetary Reform, London, 1923.
  A Treatise on Money, London, 1930.
  The General Theory of Employment, Interest, and Money, London, 1936.
  How to Pay for the War, London, 1940.
KINDLEBERGER, C. P., *The Dollar Shortage*, New York, 1950.
  International Economics, New York, 1953.
KNAPP, G. F., *The State Theory of Money* (translated from German), London, 1924.
KNIGHT, F. H., *The Ethics of Competition and Other Essays*, London, 1935.
KURIHARA, KENNETH K., *Monetary Theory and Public Policy*, London, 1951.
LAVINGTON, F., *The English Capital Market*, London, 1921.
LEAGUE OF NATIONS, *Report of the Gold Delegation of the Finance Committee*, Geneva, 1930 and 1932.
LIPFERT, H., *Internationale Finanz-Märkte*, Frankfurt, 1964.
LUTZ, F. A., and MINTS, LLOYD W. (eds.), *Readings in Monetary Theory*, London, 1952.

MACDOUGALL, SIR DONALD, *The World Dollar Problem*, London, 1957.

MCKENNA, REGINALD, *Post-War Banking Policy*, London, 1928.

MACRAE, NORMAN, *The London Capital Market*, London, 1957.

MARSHALL, ALFRED, *Money, Credit, and Commerce*, London, 1923.

MAYNARD, GEOFFREY, *Economic Development and the Price Level*, London, 1962.

MILLIKAN, MAX F. (ed.), *Income Stabilization for a Developing Democracy*, New Haven, 1953.

MINTS, LLOYD W., *Monetary Policy for a Competitive Society*, New York, 1950.

MISES, L. VON, *The Theory of Money and Credit*, new ed., London, 1953.

MOULTON, H. G., *Can Inflation be Controlled ?*, London, 1958.

MYRDAL, GUNNAR, *The Political Element in the Development of Economic Theory* (translated from Swedish), London, 1953.

NATIONAL INDUSTRIAL CONFERENCE BOARD, *Gold and World Monetary Problems*, New York, 1966.

NEVIN, E., *The Mechanism of Cheap Money*, Cardiff, 1955.

NIEBYL, KARL H., *Studies in the Classical Theories of Money*, New York, 1946.

NOGARO, BERTRAND, *A Short Treatise on Money and Monetary Systems* (translated from French), London, 1949.

ORGANIZATION FOR EUROPEAN ECONOMIC CO-OPERATION, *The Problem of Rising Prices*, Paris, 1961.

PAISH, F. W., *Studies in an Inflationary Economy*, London, 1962.

PIGOU, A. C., *The Veil of Money*, London, 1949.

QUIGGIN, A. HINGSTON, *A Survey of Primitive Money*, London, 1949.

RIST, CHARLES, *History of Monetary and Credit Theory from John Law to the Present Day*, New York, 1940.

ROBBINS, LIONEL, *The Great Depression*, London, 1934.

ROBERTS, B. C., *National Wages Policy in War and Peace*, London, 1958.

ROBERTSON, SIR DENNIS H., *Banking Policy and the Price Level*, London, 1932.

Essays in Monetary Theory, London, 1940.

Money, rev. ed., London, 1948.

Utility and All That and Other Essays, London, 1952.

Britain in the World Economy, London, 1954.

ROBERTSON, D. J., and HUNTER, L. C. (eds.), *The British Balance of Payments*, Edinburgh, 1966.

ROBEY, R. (ed.), *The Monetary Problem: Final Report of the Royal Commission to Inquire into the Relative Values of the Precious Metals, Presented to Parliament 1888*, New York, 1936.

ROBINSON, JOAN, *The Rate of Interest and Other Essays*, London, 1952.

ROLFE, S. E., *Gold and World Power*, London, 1966.

ROOVER, RAYMONDDE, *Gresham on Foreign Exchange*, Cambridge, Mass., 1949.

ROYAL INSTITUTE OF INTERNATIONAL AFFAIRS, *The International Gold Problem*, Oxford, 1931.
Monetary Policy and the Depression, Oxford, 1933.
The Future of Monetary Policy, Oxford, 1935.

RUEFF, J., *Combats pour l'ordre financier*, Paris, 1972.

SAYERS, R. S., *Bank of England Operations, 1890–1914*, Oxford, 1936.

SCAMMELL, W. A., *International Monetary Policy*, 2nd ed., London, 1961.

SCHMÖLDERS, GÜNTER, *Geldpolitik*, Tübingen and Zürich, 1962.

SCHNEIDER, E., *Money, Income and Employment*, London, 1962.

SELDON, A. (ed.), *Not Unanimous: A Rival Verdict to Radcliffe's on Money*, London, 1960.

SHAW, EDWARD S., *Money Income and Monetary Policy*, Chicago, 1950.

SHAW, W. A., *The History of Currency, 1252 to 1894*, London, undated.

SOHMEN, E., *Flexible Exchange Rates*, Chicago, 1961.

SPEARMAN, DIANA, *The Sterling Area*, London, 1953.

STIGLER, G. J., and BOULDING, K. E. (eds.), *Readings in Price Theory*, London, 1953.

STRANGE, SUSAN, *Sterling and British Policy*, Oxford, 1971.

SURANYI-UNGER, THEO, *Comparative Economic Systems*, New York, 1952.

SWANN, NANCY LEE, *Food and Money in Ancient China*, Princeton, 1950.

TEW, BRIAN, *International Monetary Co-operation, 1945–1960*, London, 1960.

THOMAS, BRINLEY, *Monetary Policy and Crisis: A Study of Swedish Experience*, London, 1936.

ULMAN, L., and FLANAGAN, R. J., *Wage Restraint: Incomes Policies in Western Europe*, Los Angeles, 1971.

U.S. GOVERNMENT PRINTING OFFICE, *Monetary Policy and the Management of the Public Debt*, Washington, 1952.

WAIGHT, L., *The History and Mechanism of the Exchange Equalization Account*, Cambridge, 1939.

WALKER, JOHN R., *Bank Credit as Money*, New York, 1937.

WARREN, G. F., and PEARSON, F. A., *Gold and Prices*, New York, 1935.

WASSERMAN, M. J., HULTMAN, C. W., and ZSOLDOS, L. *International Finance: Theory, Practice, Institutions*, New York, 1963.

WHITTLESEY, CHARLES R., *Principles and Practice of Money and Banking*, New York, 1948.

(ed.) *Readings in Money and Banking*, New York, 1952.

WICKSELL, KNUT, *Interest and Prices*, London, 1936.

WILLIAMS, JOHN H., *Post-War Monetary Problems and Other Essays*, Oxford, 1949.

WITHERS, HARTLEY, *The Meaning of Money*, 6th ed., London, 1937.

WOLFE, MARTIN, *The French Franc Between the Wars, 1919–1939*, New York, 1951.

YANG, LIEN-SHENG, *Money and Credit in China*, Cambridge, Mass., 1952.

YEAGER, LELAND B., *International Monetary Relations*, New York, 1966.

Index